AS Core Studies
and Research Methods

PSYCHOLOGY

AS Core Studies
and Research Methods

PSYCHOLOGY

OCR

Philip Banyard and
Cara Flanagan

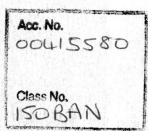
Published in 2008 by Psychology Press
27 Church Road, Hove, East Sussex, BN3 2FA
www.psypress.com

*Psychology Press is part of the Taylor & Francis Group,
an Informa business*

Copyright © 2008 by Psychology Press

British Library Cataloguing in Publication Data
A catalogue record for this book is available from the British Library

ISBN: 978–1–84169–728–4

Cover design by Richard Massing
Typeset and project managed by
GreenGate Publishing Services, Tonbridge, Kent
www.ggate.co.uk

Printed and bound in Slovenia

Contents

Introduction

Chapter 1
Psychological investigations

Chapter 2
Cognitive psychology

Chapter 3
Developmental psychology

Chapter 4
Biological psychology

Chapter 5
Social psychology

Chapter 6
Individual differences

Acknowledgements

The authors would like to acknowledge the contribution of the following to the development of this book; Patrick Hylton, Mark Griffiths, Alex Haslam, Beth Black, James Stiller, Mark Holah, Kathy Bach and Mike Cardwell. We would also like to thank Psychology Press for their confidence in this project and their relentless good nature in dealing with us, especially Lucy Kennedy, Tara Stebnicky, Mandy Collison and Veronica Lyons. Thanks also to the team at GreenGate (Dave Mackin in particular) for the design of the text and their willingness to accommodate the demands of the authors.

Phil Banyard would like to acknowledge the encouragement and support he received from the teachers and examiners of the OCR specification. Their contributions and enthusiasm were the major drivers in the development of the course. He would also like to acknowledge the patience of his co-author, the hope that swirls around the City Ground, Nottingham, and the unforgettable piano playing of Mrs. Mills.

The authors

Phil Banyard

Phil Banyard is Senior Lecturer in Psychology at Nottingham Trent University. He has been involved in GCSE and A Level psychology for more years than he can count and has marked more exam papers than he has brain cells left. He wrote the original OCR specification and was Chief Examiner for 14 years. It is a testament to medical science that he still teaches, writes texts and ties his own shoes. His continued support of Nottingham Forest shows extreme loyalty or lack of imagination depending on your point of view.

Cara Flanagan

Cara Flanagan is an experienced teacher and senior A level examiner. She has written a wide range of articles and textbooks for A level psychology students, and regularly speaks at student conferences and teacher INSET courses. She has recently gone to her first ever football match and hopes to be able to converse on the subject with her like-minded colleagues soon.

Illustration Credits

Introduction

Chapter 1

Chapter 2

Chapter 3

Page 71 (left): © Bobby Yip/Reuters/Corbis. Page 71 (right): © Christophe Calais/In Visu/Corbis. Page 73 (top): © Bettmann/CORBIS. Page 73 (bottom): From DeVries, R. (1969) Constancy of generic identity in the years three to six. *Monographs of the Society for Child Development*, 34 (Serial No. 127). Reproduced with permission of Rheta DeVries. Page 75 (left): Reproduced with kind permission of Professor Peter Bryant. Page 75 (right): Reproduced with kind permission of Judith Samuel. Page 80: © "20031015" – Noah Kalina. Reproduced with permission. Page 81 (bottom): © Bettmann/Corbis. Page 83 (left): © Images.com/Corbis. Page 83 (right): Reproduced with kind permission of Professor Albert Bandura. Page 85 (left): © Bettmann/Corbis. Page 85 (right): Reproduced with kind permission of Professor Albert Bandura. Page 86: Reproduced with kind permission of Professor Albert Bandura. Page 88 (left): © Benjamin Lowy/Corbis. Page 88 (right): © Tom & Dee Ann McCarthy/Corbis. Page 91: © IAN HODGSON/Reuters/Corbis. Page 92 (top): © Peter Aprahamian/Corbis. Page 93: © Bettmann/Corbis. Page 93: Extract from *Another Time* by W. H. Auden. Copyright © 1940 W. H. Auden, renewed by The Estate of W. H. Auden. Extract used by permission of Faber & Faber Ltd. Page 94 and page 95: Redrawn from Freud (1909) Analysis of a phobia in a five-year-old boy. In J. Strachey (Ed. and trans.) *The standard edition of the complete psychological works: Two case histories* (vol. x), pages 5–147. London: The Hogarth Press. Page 96 (right): © Bettmann/Corbis. Page 98 (top): Reproduced with the kind permission of www.philsophersguild.com. Page 98 (bottom): © Corbis. Page 100: © Grant Smith/Corbis. Page 101 (top): © Blue Lantern Studio/Corbis. Page 102: © Morgan McCauley/Corbis. Page 103 (left): AFP/Getty Images. Page 103 (top-middle): © Swim Ink 2, LLC/Corbis. Page 103 (bottom-middle): © 2005 Getty Images.

Chapter 4

Page 110 (bottom-left): © Visuals Unlimited/Corbis. Page 110 (top-left): From Damasio H, Grabowski T.J., Frank R.J., Galaburda A.M., Damasio A.R., The Return of Phineas Gage: Clues About the Brain from the Skull of a Famous Patient, *Science*, 264, 1102–1105 (20th May 1994). Copyright © AAAS. Reproduced with permission. Page 110 (top-right): © Providence Holy Cross Medical Center. Reproduced with permission. Page 112 (top): © Mediscan/Corbis. Page 114: Reproduced with kind permission of Dr Eleanor Maguire. Page 116 (top-middle): From Eleanor A. Maguire, David G. Gadian, Ingrid S. Johnsrude, Catriona D. Good, John Ashburner, Richard S.J. Frackowiak and Christopher D. Frith (2000). Navigation-related structural changes in the hippocampi of taxi drivers. *Proceedings of the National Academy of Science*, 97, 4398–4403. Reproduced with permission. Page 118 (left): Reproduced with kind permission of Professor Jennifer Eberhardt. Page 118 (middle): Reproduced with kind permission of Professor Adrian Raine. Page 118 (top-right): Living Art Enterprises, LLC/Science Photo Library. Page 118 (bottom-right): © Brooks Kraft/Corbis. Page 122 (right): © Nathaniel Welch/Corbis. Page 123 (right): © Bettmann/Corbis. Page 124 (top): Time & Life Pictures/Getty Images. Page 124 (bottom): © Bettmann/Corbis. Page 125 (top-right): © Lester Lefkowitz/Corbis. Page 125 (bottom-right): BSIP, LAURENT/LAE.HOP AMER/Science Photo Library. Page 128: © Reuters/Corbis. Page 132: Martin M. Rotker/Science Photo Library. Page 134: SCIENCE PHOTO LIBRARY. Page 137: Adapted from Sperry, R.W. (1968) Hemispheric deconnection and unity in conscious awareness. *American Psychologist*, 23, 723–33. Copyright © American Psychological Association. Reproduced with permission. Page 138 (top-left): Living Art Enterprises, LLC/Science Photo Library. Page 138 (middle): © JOE GIZA/Reuters/Corbis. Page 140 (left): © Corbis. Page 140 (right): © DreamWorks Animation/ZUMA/Corbis. Page 143 (top): Courtesy of www.adbusters.org. Page 143 (bottom): © Karen Norberg 2006. Reproduced with permission.

Chapter 5

Page 150: © ELIANA APONTE/Reuters/Corbis. Page 151 (top): © Reuters/Corbis. Page 151 (bottom): © Hulton-Deutsch Collection/Corbis. Page 152 (top): © epa/Corbis. Page 152 (bottom): Photograph by Ronald L. Haeberle. Page 153: Photo of Stanley Milgram by Eric Kroll. Reproduced with permission from Alexandra Milgram. Page 154 (left) and page 155 (bottom): From the film *Obedience* © 1968 by Stanley Milgram. Copyright © renewed 1991 by Alexandra Milgram and distributed by Penn State Media Sales. Permission granted by Alexandra Milgram. Page 154 (right): Milgram advert from *Obedience to Authority*. Copyright © 1974 Pinter & Martin: New York. Reproduced with permission. Page 158: Getty Images. Page 160: © Sigfrid Eggers/Van Parys Media/Corbis. Page 161: © Bettmann/Corbis. Page 162: © Mohammed Saber /epa/Corbis. Page 163 (top and bottom): Reproduced with permission of P.G. Zimbardo Inc. Page 165: Reproduced with kind permission of Professor Reicher and Professor Haslam. Page 166 (top and bottom): Based on data from Stephen Reicher, S.D. & Haslam, S.A. (2006). Rethinking the psychology of tyranny: The BBC prison study. *British Journal of Social Psychology*, 45, 1–40. Page 168 (top): © Exclusive to THE WASHINGTON POST/epa/Corbis. Page 168 (bottom): Getty Images. Page 171 (bottom): © Alberto Ruggieri/Illustration Works/Corbis. Page 172: Time & Life Pictures/Getty Images. Page 173 (top): © The Gallery Collection/Corbis. Page 173 (bottom): © Eldad Rafaeli/Corbis. Page 174 (top): © Bernd Obermann/Corbis. Page 174 (bottom): From I.M. Piliavin, J. Rodin & J.A. Piliavin (1969). Good samaritanism: an underground phenomenon? *Journal of Personality and Social Psychology*, 13, 289–299. © 1969 The American Psychological Association. Reproduced with permission. Page 175 (top): Reproduced with kind permission of Professors Jane and Irving Piliavin. Page 178 (top): © MERCURY PRESS/CORBIS SYGMA. Page 183 (left): Reproduced with permission of P.G. Zimbardo Inc. Page 183 (right): Courtesy of Columbia University Archives.

Chapter 6

Page 191 (top): © Eleanor Bentall/Corbis. Page 191 (bottom): © Richard Hutchings/Corbis. Page 192 (top): © Blue Lantern Studio/Corbis. Page 192 (bottom): © Jeff Vanuga/Corbis. Page 193: © Christie's Images/Corbis. Page 195: © Don Hammond/Design Pics/Corbis. Page 196: © Images.com/Corbis. Page 198: © CinemaPhoto/Corbis. Page 200: Getty Images. Page 202: © Reuters/Corbis. Page 203: © Bettmann/Corbis. Page 204 (top): © John Springer Collection/Corbis. Page 204 (bottom): From article by Thigpen and Cleckley, page 136. Thigpen, C.H. and Cleckley, H. (1954) A case of multiple personality. *Journal of Abnormal and Social Psychology*, 49, 135-151. Copyright © American Psychological Association. Reproduced with permission. Page 208: Copyright © Michael Deas. Reproduced with permission. Page 212: © ALEX GRIMM/Reuters/Corbis. Page 213 (left): © Leo Mason/Corbis. Page 213 (right): © Steve Allen/Brand X/Corbis. Page 215: Reproduced with kind permission of Professor Mark Griffiths. Page 218 (left): From Townsend, J. (1993). Policies to halve smoking deaths. *Addiction*, 88, 43–52. Reproduced with permission from Blackwell Publishing. Page 218 (right): © Colin McPherson/Corbis. Page 220: © H. Armstrong Roberts/Corbis. Page 221: © CORBIS. Page 222 (left): © Bettmann/Corbis. Page 222 (right): © Archivo Iconografico, S.A./Corbis. Page 223: © Hervé Hughes/Hemis/Corbis.

Welcome to Psychology

What is psychology?

I know we pretend to be interested in everybody and everything but when it comes down to it, the most interesting thing in life is ME. This is partly a selfish thing because we clearly care more about what happens to ourselves than what happens to anyone else (oh don't pretend it's anything else), but it is also a logical thing. Let's face it, I am the person that I know most about. For everyone else I have to guess what is going on and rely on them to tell me about it.

When you think about yourself then you are confronted by some BIG QUESTIONS. These questions are so big that they are bigger than anything you can possibly imagine and then some. They are so big that it is not possible to get a full answer. Not now, nor in the future. We can only ponder and speculate on these things. The biggest question is 'Who am I?' and following on from this are three questions that form the core of any psychology course:

- Why do I think like this?
- Why do I feel like this?
- Why do I behave like this?

Thinking, feeling and doing

It is helpful to break down our experience of the world into these different spheres of thinking, feeling and doing. As a first thought you'd probably think that they are all connected and our feelings match up with our thoughts and the things we do are driven by these thoughts and feelings. Nothing could be further from the truth and that is one of the first puzzles of psychology and one of the things that makes people so interesting.

Take one of the author's (Phil's) response to global warming for example. He THINKS that global warming is real and that we should all try to reduce our carbon footprint. On the other hand although he FEELS sad when he sees films of penguins falling off an ice floe, the depth of his feeling does not match his belief that the world will suffer big consequences if we don't act soon. In fact he FEELS sadder when Nottingham Forest lose than when he watches films about the environment. And what does he DO about it? Well he doesn't consume that much but he still goes on holiday abroad when he can, he keeps his house warm and he has never been to a bottle bank (unless you include Threshers that is). This is not a unique state of affairs and it highlights how our feelings do not necessarily match with our thoughts or our behaviour.

Psychology doesn't have the answers to why we think, feel and behave in the ways that we do, but it does give us some evidence that helps us understand these processes a little better. In the introduction to Chapter 1 we develop this idea a bit further and look at how we can measure what we think, what we feel and what we do.

What is psychology about?

Psychology is mainly interested in individuals. What makes them tick, how they make decisions and how they interact. This distinguishes it from sociology which is mainly interested in groups of people and how they develop and react. At this time, psychology is very popular in Western countries because we are looking for individual solutions to personal problems and it seems as if psychology might provide some of the answers. Psychology is about how we make sense of the world and how we behave in it. It's about how we see, hear and touch, how we think, remember and concentrate, how we develop and maintain our identities and how we interact with others.

If you watch daytime television you might well think that psychology is mainly about relationships, body language and the lives of celebrities, but you would be wrong. If you study the subject at college or university, however, then you will probably not deal with any of these issues. What happens on the daytime television sofa is that self-appointed experts tell you things you probably already know. Listen closely, they won't tell you anything new, they are just filling time with harmless nonsense. We think that the psychology you will study on your course is much more interesting.

Defining psychology

In 1890 the US psychologist William James defined psychology as *'the science of mental life.'* Today it is commonly defined as *'the science of mind and behaviour.'* The key word for us is 'science' because it emphasises that the study of psychology is one that looks at evidence rather than opinion, and is prepared to put that evidence up for public scrutiny.

A common expectation of psychology is that it is about therapy and long conversations with bearded strangers about your mother. Nothing could be further from the truth.

Activity

Talk the talk

Any subject has its own language. If you take your car to the garage then the mechanic will use words that you have never heard before in explaining why your expensive motor is actually a heap of junk. And if you go to buy a computer, then the talk of Ram Rom Rum and Rim leaves you baffled and confused. To start with you might find some of the language of psychology quite confusing but don't be put off. Learn the terms and the ideas will become much more clear. Try and use a new psychological word every day. Start with 'cognitive'. Use that word in a sentence with your friends/mum/cat in the next hour.

Other words to try:

Defence mechanism
Validity
Delusion
Placebo

You are already a psychologist

It's true. You already use psychology in your daily life. If you didn't, you would find life very difficult indeed. For example, when you walk down a shopping street how often do you physically bump into someone? Very rarely I would guess. The trick in not bumping into someone is to estimate how fast they are travelling and what direction they are going in. That way you can compute whether your paths are likely to collide. This is quite clever but it is also something a fairly basic computer can do. What is more remarkable is that you can read the intentions of the other person and guess which way they are going to go. We all change direction several times as we dodge down a busy street but we are able to judge where the other people are going to go and therefore avoid bumping into them. In effect you have to read their minds to see where they are planning to go. You are a mind reader.

Not only are you a mind reader, you are also an emotion reader. You are a pretty good judge of a person's emotional state and you are able to judge when someone is angry or happy or sad. This is a very handy skill and can get you out of some tricky situations. We are not perfect at this skill but by and large we get these judgements right more often than we get them wrong.

So in summary, you already use psychology to judge speed and distance in the world, you also use it to read people's minds and you can also read their emotions. These are all very remarkable skills and they are only the start of the many amazing things that you can do and which you commonly take for granted. In this text we want to build on the psychology you already know and use and show you some of the other things we know about how people tick.

To walk down a street without bumping into people you have to be a mind reader.

Key studies in psychology

Some subjects are based mainly around theories. Psychology is not one of these. The core of psychology is made up of evidence gained from research studies. Psychology is a patchwork of scientific studies that, at their best, give us some new insights into what it means to be a human being. These studies give us our next level of questions as we try and get some insights into the BIG QUESTIONS mentioned on the left. For example in this text we will be looking at the following questions:

- If you split someone's brain in half will they become two people?
- Can you teach language to a chimpanzee?
- How easy is it to tell the difference between the sane and the insane?
- Do London taxi drivers have bigger brains than the average?
- If someone asked you to kill another human being would you do it?
- Does watching violence make children more likely to be violent?
- Can you become addicted to gambling?
- Can two personalities exist in the same body?
- How reliable is eyewitness testimony?

You've got to admit that there are some pretty good questions here. And each one of these questions is at the heart of one of the core studies in this text. It would be untrue to say that the studies give clear answers to the questions but they give us some clues and many of them will make you think differently about yourself and other people.

All the studies can be seen as a story, and this is probably a good way to study them. They all have a back-story, the things that happened before this story commences. This back-story is often the reason for the study being carried out. For example the study by **Milgram** was an attempt to explore the behaviour that was observed during the Second World War. The studies also have some afters to them (a sequel of you like) where the ideas have been developed after the original study. With the Milgram study, for example, it is still referred to even though it is nearly 50 years since it was carried out. We put each of the core studies in context by showing the ideas that stimulated the study and some of the work that has been carried out since.

How do they know that?

One of the very big advantages of looking at a small number of key studies in psychology is that you get a feel for how psychology is carried out. And if you get a feel for how psychologists get their evidence then you can make up your own mind about quite how good that evidence is. A question to ask anyone who is telling you some FACTS is 'how do you know that?' We explore this idea a bit further in the section on **Being Sceptical in Psychology** but for now just think about this one; when a health professional says we should eat five fruit and vegetables a day to protect our health, how could they know that?

The more we know about how evidence is collected and how people come up with their conclusions then the less we are going to be taken in by dodgy science and dodgy newscasts.

Wonder and scepticism

We think the best way to approach psychology is with a twin sense of WONDER and SCEPTICISM. The sense of wonder is necessary because the more you think about human behaviour the more wonderful it becomes. For example, how did you manage to learn language without ever having a lesson? And how are some people able to create fantastic pieces of music or original art that can inspire a generation? On the other hand we need to keep a sceptical eye on the information that is fed to us. What is their evidence? And how did they get it? In the USA it is estimated that around 5 million people believe that they have been abducted by aliens. Despite the number of people reporting this experience it still seems very unlikely to the authors that this has in fact happened to anyone. Later in the text (page 40) we suggest how you can be sceptical of the information you are presented with.

We hope that this text helps you develop your sense of wonder about people and how they think, feel and behave while at the same time developing a healthy scepticism about the conclusions that are sometimes drawn from the flimsiest of evidence.

Final thought

In this text we have tried to follow the suggestion of the great twentieth century scientist Albert Einstein who is credited with saying, *'Everything should be made as simple as possible, but not simpler.'*

How to use this book

Chapter 1 is different to the other chapters because it is concerned with the overarching topic of how psychologists find out about behaviour (PSYCHOLOGICAL INVESTIGATIONS).

The other five chapters in this book are each concerned with an area of study in psychology and each looks at THREE CORE STUDIES related to that area of study.

Each of these core study chapters follows the same plan:

- Page 1 is a **table of contents**.
- The first double-page spread is an **introduction** to the area of psychology (cognitive, developmental etc).

Each core study is presented following the same format:

- **Starters**: Background material.
- **Core study**: A detailed description of the core study covering an abstract, the aims, method and results of the study plus conclusions or a discussion. There are also questions to answer, activities and biographical notes.
- **Evaluation**: Some themes to consider plus ideas for a debate in class.
- **Afters**: research that came afterwards plus links to other studies.
- **Questions for you**: multiple choice questions and exam-style questions to assess your knowledge and understanding.
- **Key issue**: Covers various 'themes' identified in the specification such as reductionism, nature–nurture, self-report methods (see page XIV).

Each chapter ends with **diagrammatic summaries** of the three core studies plus some ideas for **further reading** and other things.

Finally there is a set of **exam-style questions** with **student answers** and **examiner comments**.

The chapters are presented in the order they appear in the specification but there is no law that says you have to study them in this order. We have endeavoured to write the book so it can be read in any order. You can do all cognitive core studies first or just one cognitive core study and then a social one. We have tried to make each core study 'standalone' though inevitably this is not exactly possible. There are some concepts that occur all over the place, such as ethics or ecological validity or experiments. You may need to skip around to other sections of the book – it won't be a bad thing to read some of the key issues several times, in the context of different core studies.

Subjects or participants?

In most of the core studies in this book the people in the studies were called 'subjects'. We have changed this in most cases to the more modern 'participants'.

During the 1990s there was a move to use the term 'participant' instead of 'subject' in order to reflect the recognition that participants are not passive but are actively involved. They search for cues about how to behave and this may mean that they behave as researchers expect rather than as they would in everyday life. The use of the term 'participants' acknowledges this participant reactivity.

The term 'subjects' also reflected a power relationship in research studies. Typically the researcher holds the power in the research setting because he/she knows what the experiment is about and knows the procedures to be followed. This often leaves the 'subject' powerless. It is to be hoped that the change of the term from 'subject' to 'participant' is more than just a cosmetic one and that, in more recent studies, the participant isn't quite as powerless. It may not be a good idea to rewrite the old studies and start calling the subjects 'participants', because they weren't. They were treated as passive respondents to the experimental situations set up by psychologists and they were rarely dealt with as colleagues. However, we have generally adopted the term 'participants' in this book to encourage its use and the meanings that go with it.

A 'subject' is someone who obeys their superior. In psychological research the term 'subject' was commonly used refer to people in a study other than the researcher, which reflects the power relationship between researcher and subject. More recently the term 'participants' has become more common.

What is a core study?

The OCR AS specification is based around 15 psychological studies. The studies have been selected either because they are classic studies in psychology or because they illustrate important issues in psychology.

What is a 'psychological study'? When psychologists (and other scientists) conduct research they write a report, published in a magazine or 'journal'. One report might contain details of several investigations or just one investigation. Each core study is one of these reports (also called an article). Journal articles are usually divided up as follows:

Abstract
A summary of the study.

Introduction/Aim
What a researcher intends to investigate. This often includes a review of previous research – theories and studies – which leads up to the aims for this particular study. The researcher(s) may state their research prediction(s) and/or a hypothesis/es.

Method
A detailed description of what the researcher(s) did, a bit like writing the recipe for making a cake. The main point is to give enough detail for someone else to replicate (repeat) the study. Replication is important to be able to check the results – if someone repeated the same procedure, they should get the same results and this shows that the results weren't just a fluke.

Writing the procedure includes describing the participants (the sample), testing the environment, the procedures used to collect data, and any instructions given to participants before (the brief) and afterwards (the debrief).

Results
This section contains what the researcher(s) found, often called statistical data, which includes descriptive statistics (tables, averages and graphs) and inferential statistics (the use of statistical tests to determine how significant the results are).

Conclusions
The researcher(s) attempt to indicate what the results mean, for example making generalisations about people based on how the participants behaved in the study and with reference to other research studies.

Discussion
Finally, researchers discuss the results of the study. They might propose one or more explanations of the behaviours that they observed. The researchers might also consider the implications of the results and make suggestions for future research.

Read the originals
We have provided fairly detailed accounts of each core study but it is a good idea to look at the original articles. In many cases these can be found on the web and we have given the links at the end of each chapter (in the further reading section). If the original report is not on the web then you can give the full reference for the study to your local library and they will obtain photocopies through the British Interlibrary loan service for a small fee.

Core study 1, the study by Loftus and Palmer. This is the first page of the original article.

JOURNAL OF VERBAL LEARNING AND VERBAL BEHAVIOR 13, 585–589 (1974)

Reconstruction of Automobile Destruction: An Example of the Interaction Between Language and Memory[1]

ELIZABETH F. LOFTUS AND JOHN C. PALMER

University of Washington

Two experiments are reported in which subjects viewed films of automobile accidents and then answered questions about events occurring in the films. The question, "About how fast were the cars going when they smashed into each other?" elicited higher estimates of speed than questions which used the verbs *collided, bumped, contacted,* or *hit* in place of *smashed.* On a retest one week later, those subjects who received the verb *smashed* were more likely to say "yes" to the question, "Did you see any broken glass?", even though broken glass was not present in the film. These results are consistent with the view that the questions asked subsequent to an event can cause a reconstruction in one's memory of that event.

How accurately do we remember the details of a complex event, like a traffic accident, that has happened in our presence? More specifically, how well do we do when asked to estimate some numerical quantity such as how long the accident took, how fast the cars were traveling, or how much time elapsed between the sounding of a horn and the moment of collision?

It is well documented that most people are markedly inaccurate in reporting such numerical details as time, speed, and distance (Bird, 1927; Whipple, 1909). For example, most people have difficulty estimating the duration of an event, with some research indicating that the tendency is to overestimate the duration of events which are complex (Block, 1974; Marshall, 1969; Ornstein, 1969). The judgment of speed is especially difficult, and practically every automobile accident results in huge variations from one witness to another

[1] This research was supported by the Urban Mass Transportation Administration, Department of Transportation, Grant No. WA-11-0004. Thanks go to Geoffrey Loftus, Edward E. Smith, and Stephen Woods for many important and helpful comments. Reprint requests should be sent to Elizabeth F. Loftus, Department of Psychology, University of Washington, Seattle, Washington 98195.

as to how fast a vehicle was actually traveling (Gardner, 1933). In one test administered to Air Force personnel who knew in advance that they would be questioned about the speed of a moving automobile, estimates ranged from 10 to 50 mph. The car they watched was actually going only 12 mph (Marshall, 1969, p. 23).

Given the inaccuracies in estimates of speed, it seems likely that there are variables which are potentially powerful in terms of influencing these estimates. The present research was conducted to investigate one such variable, namely, the phrasing of the question used to elicit the speed judgment. Some questions are clearly more suggestive than others. This fact of life has resulted in the legal concept of a leading question and in legal rules indicating when leading questions are allowed (*Supreme Court Reporter*, 1973). A leading question is simply one that, either by its form or content, suggests to the witness what answer is desired or leads him to the desired answer.

In the present study, subjects were shown films of traffic accidents and then they answered questions about the accident. The subjects were interrogated about the speed of

Introduction

The AS examination

First of all, you can read the specification – you can download it from the OCR website (http://www.ocr.org.uk).
There are two exams, which are outlined below.

Examples of exam question styles are given throughout this book.

Unit G541 Psychological investigations

1 hour	The paper is divided into three sections: Sections A, B and C
Total 60 marks	All questions are compulsory.
30% of total AS mark	Each section is worth 20 marks and will focus on one of the four research techniques (observation, self-report, experiment and correlation). The full specification content for the Psychology Investigations is given on page 25 of this book.

You will be required to answer a variety of questions related to psychological investigations, such as:

- Identify aspects of a described study (e.g. identify the dependent variable, describe findings).
- Provide evidence of your knowledge (e.g. explain what a 'repeated measures design' is).
- Evaluate research techniques (e.g. strengths of the sampling method).
- Design certain aspects of a study (e.g. select appropriate behavioural categories for an observation).

How are the exam questions marked?

Some examples of how the exam questions are marked are shown on the right, taken from the specimen papers for the AS exam. Each mark scheme is adapted for a particular question but these mark schemes show you what you are aiming to achieve in order to gain high marks.

Unit G542 The Core Studies

2 hours	The paper is divided into three sections: Sections A, B and C
Total 120 marks	**Section A** Total 60 marks
70% of total AS mark	All questions in this section are compulsory.

Questions will be asked about specific detail of core studies, theories on which studies are based, research surrounding core studies, and methods used by the core studies. Questions will also be asked about issues and approaches raised by the core studies.

Section B Total 36 marks

You will be required to answer **one** question which will be about one core study. You will be given a choice of which core study you use. The question will require considerable depth and knowledge of one core study.

Section C Total 24 marks

You will be required to answer **one** question from a choice of **two**. Questions focus on approaches, issues and methods (as listed below), and refer to the core studies.

- *Approaches*: cognitive, developmental, physiological, social and individual differences.
- *Perspectives*: behaviourist, psychodynamic.
- *Methods*: experimental (laboratory and field), case study, self-report, observation and methodological issues such as reliability and validity.
- *Issues*: ethics, ecological validity, longitudinal and snapshot design, and qualitative and quantitative data.

In answering exam questions, it is essential for candidates to give answers which refer directly to the core study/or chosen study in the question. Often candidates forget to do this in their answers and lose marks unnecessarily.

Core studies

The 15 core studies have been selected to represent the five core areas of psychology (cognitive, developmental, physiological, social and individual differences).

For each core study you are required to know:

- the background to the studies (the context);
- theories on which studies are based;
- psychological perspectives applicable to the studies;
- other research pertinent to the studies;
- the information in the studies;
- the methods used in the studies;
- the way the results are analysed and presented; the conclusions that can be drawn from the studies;
- strengths and limitations of the studies;
- the general psychological issues illustrated by the studies;
- evaluations of all of the above.

For each core study you also need to have an awareness of the approaches/perspectives, methods and issues (listed on the left) that surround it. Turn over to page XIV and you will see how we have helped you with this.

Two mark question

For example, *What was the aim of your chosen study?*

0 marks	**No answer or irrelevant answer.**
1 mark	Aim is identified. Description is **basic** and **lacks detail**. **Some understanding** may be evident. **Expression generally poor.**
2 marks	Description of aim is **accurate**. **Detail** is appropriate and **understanding** is very good. Fine details may be added. **Expression and use of psychological terminology is good.**

Three mark question

For example, *Give **one** advantage of observational studies*

0 marks	**No answer or irrelevant answer.**
1 mark	Advantage is identified, with **little or no elaboration**.
2 marks	Description of advantage is **basic** and **lacks detail**. **Some understanding** may be evident. **Expression generally** poor.
3 marks	Description of advantage is **accurate** and has **elaboration**. **Understanding is good.**

Four mark question

For example, *Describe how the behaviourist approach could explain aggression.*

0 marks	**No answer or irrelevant answer.**
1–2 marks	Description is **generally accurate**, but is **basic** and **lacks detail**. **Some understanding** and/or **elaboration** may be evident. Expression generally poor.
3–4 marks	Description is **accurate**. **Detail** is appropriate and **understanding** is good. **Elaboration** (e.g. specific detail or example) is evident. **Expression and use of psychological terminology is good.**

Twelve mark question

For example, *Discuss the strengths and limitations of the social approach using examples from the Milgram study.*

0 marks	**No answer or irrelevant answer.**
1–3 marks	There may be **some strengths or weaknesses** which are appropriate or peripheral to the question, or there may be an imbalance between the two. Discussion is poor with **limited or no understanding**. **Expression is poor**. **Analysis is sparse** and argument may be just discernible. Sparse or no use of supporting examples.
4–6 marks	There may be **some strengths and weaknesses** which are appropriate to the question, or there may be an imbalance between the two. **Discussion is reasonable** with **some understanding** though **expression may be limited**. **Analysis is effective** sometimes and **argument limited**. Sparse use of supporting examples.
7–9 marks	There may be a **range of strengths (2 or more) and weaknesses (2 or more)** which are appropriate to the question, or there may be a balance between the two. Discussion is good with **some understanding** and **good expression**. **Analysis is reasonably effective** and **argument informed**. Some use of supporting examples. Maximum mark of 7 for strengths or weaknesses only.
10–12 marks	There is a **good range of strengths (2 or more) and weaknesses (2 or more)** which are appropriate to the question. There is a good balance between the two. Discussion is **detailed** with **good understanding** and **clear expression**. **Analysis is effective** and **argument well informed**. Appropriate use of supporting examples. The answer is **competently structured and organised**. Answer is mostly grammatically correct with occasional spelling errors.

Eight mark question

For example, *Outline the results of your chosen study.*

0 marks	**No answer or irrelevant answer.**
1–3 marks	Description of results is **very basic** and **lacks in detail** (e.g. one or two general statements are identified). **Some understanding** may be evident. **Expression generally poor**. The answer is **unstructured and lacks organisation**. The answer lacks grammatical structure and contains many spelling errors.
4–6 marks	Description of results is **accurate**. **Some omissions**. **Detail** is good. **Some understanding** is evident. **Fine details occasionally present**, but often absent. Expression and use of psychological terminology is reasonable. The answer has **some structure and organisation**. The answer is mostly grammatically correct with some spelling errors.
7–8 marks	Description of results is **accurate**. Very few or no omissions. Detail is appropriate to level and time allowed. **Understanding is very good**. **Fine details** may be added (such as numbers, or specific aspects). Expression and use of psychological terminology is good. The answer is **competently structured and organised**. The answer is grammatically correct with occasional spelling errors.

The common marking criteria are

- Accuracy
- Detail
- Elaboration
- Evidence of understanding
- Expression
- Use of psychological terminology.

For longer questions

- Structure and organisation are important.
- Analysis (being able to break the question/answer into smaller components).

The key to elaboration

Always think of the three-point rule:

S **State** your point.

E **Evidence** to support your point.

C **Comment** on the significance of your point, or add an explanation, or any further comment.

For example,

S One criticism of the study is that it lacks ecological validity.

E The study tested memory using a film of a car accident which doesn't reflect how eyewitnesses would actually experience an accident.

C Lack of ecological validity means you can't generalise the findings to everyday life.

S One strength of the physiological approach is that it has practical applications.

E For example, you can use evidence from Maguire's study to help people with brain damage.

C The evidence in the study suggests the brain can develop in response to demand so patients could be encouraged to exercise their brain to make it regrow.

If in doubt, stick it in

In some questions you may not be sure what is required. For example, in one question candidates were asked to describe how data were gathered in a named study – however, they did not gain full marks if they just described how; they also had to include a statement of what data were gathered. The moral of the story is – if in doubt, stick it in.

Introduction

Evaluating research and the key issues

The AS specification requires that you are able to evaluate all aspects of the core studies, and provides a list of the approaches, perspectives, methods and issues (see page XII). Throughout this book we have considered a number of **KEY ISSUES**. Some of these are from the specification (those that are emboldened in the left-hand column in the table below), and some are issues that we have selected ourselves because we feel they are important (the ones that are not emboldened in the table below!).

The table also lists all the core studied across the top so you can see which key issues are relevant to the study. In some columns you can see a number – this is the page where you can find the detailed spread about the key issues.

What is evaluation?

'Evaluation' literally means to 'establish the value of something'. There are many ways to do this, such as using the key issues. An important part of knowing about a research article is being able to evaluate it. Evaluation is a personal business. We can tell you the facts of the study but deciding whether the study is good or bad is up to you.

Throughout the book we have provided you with the tools to evaluate studies – the key issues. As well as being listed below for each core study we have helped you further by providing, within each study, a list of possible evaluations for that core study and some questions to help you think about the issues.

> There are suggested answers to these questions at
> www.a-levelpsychology.co.uk/ocr

	Psychological Investigations	Loftus & Palmer	Baron-Cohen et al.	Savage-Rumbaugh	Samuel & Bryant	Bandura, Ross & Ross	Freud	Maguire et al.	Dement & Kleitman	Sperry	Milgram	Reicher & Haslam	Piliavin, Rodin & Piliavin	Rosenhan	Thigpen & Cleckley	Griffiths
Cognitive approach		x	x	x	x	x										
Developmental approach			x	x	x	x										x
Physiological approach			x	x	x											
Social approach						x					x	x	x			
Individual differences			x				x							x	x	x
Behaviourist perspective				60		x										x
Being sceptical		40	x	x	x	x	x	x	x	x	x	x	x	x	x	x
Case studies			x				x			x	x			x	210	x
Ecological validity		x	x	x	x	x	x	x	x	x	x	x	x	x	x	x
Ethics		x	x	x	x	x	x	x	x	x	x	x	180	x	x	x
Ethnocentrism												x		200		
Experiment		x			x	x		x	x	x		x	x	x		x
Free determinism and will						x	x	120		x	x	x				x
Longitudinal and snapshot				x	80	x	x								x	
Nature and nurture			x	x		90	x	x			x	x			x	
Observation				x	x	x				x		x	x	x	x	x
Personality and situation						x	x				160	x	x	x	x	x
Promoting human welfare	x	x	x	x	x	x	x	x	x	x		170				
Psychodynamic perspective							100								x	
Psychology as a science	22	x	x	x	x	x	x	x	x	x	x	x	x	x	x	x
Psychometrics		x		x			x		x	x		x			x	220
Qualitative and quantitative	x	50	x	x	x	x	x	x	x	x	x	x	x	x	x	x
Reliability and validity	x	x	x	x	x	x	x	x	130	x	x	x	x	x	x	x
Reductionism		x	x			x	x	x	x	140						
Self-report		x					x		x		x	x		x	x	x

This chapter looks at how psychologists conduct research. Like all scientists, psychologists use systematic techniques for collecting and analysing data in order to produce objective and verifiable data.

Psychological investigations

Introduction to psychological investigations

End of chapter review

We use research methods to *find out information* about the world. We try to collect information that will help understand our world a bit better. The alternative is to *make information up* – just guess why things happen; this is less likely to help our understanding.

The first way to find out things is to look at what is happening around you and record it. To start with we tell a story about what we see and then we try to put it in categories. This is the process of **observation**; we all use it in everyday life to make sense of our world. This intuitive method of 'research' has been developed by psychologists to increase our knowledge of the world. Sometimes they record things that are usual in everyday life, such as people's behaviour in a library, and sometimes they record rather unusual things that are rarely experienced, such as response to emergencies.

The main subject for psychological research is the behaviour and experience of people, and if you want to know what someone thinks, feels or does the first thing to do is to ask them. This gives us first-hand accounts called **self-reports**. These are excellent sources of data but not necessarily accurate. We are not always the best witnesses of ourselves because we forget what we did, or we want to put over a good impression of ourselves, or because sometimes we just don't know why we do things.

As we build up our evidence (from observations and self-reports) we start to develop theories which we want to test to see if they are right or not. For example, observations of autistic children led to the theory that children with this condition had a specific deficit in their way of interpreting the world. The study by Baron-Cohen *et al.* tested this theory using the 'eyes task' that examines how accurate we are at reading emotion in another person. They compared the judgements of people with autism against the judgements of other people. Psychologists use **experiments** to see if one factor (in this case autism) causes a difference in behaviour (in this case difficulty interpreting emotion). These results can then be used to challenge or support their theories.

Some issues can be explored by looking at differences between groups while others are better explored by looking for associations between scores. For example we might measure a person's level of stress and also their sense of control over their behaviour (locus of control). Our hypothesis might be that the more control we feel we have over our lives the less stress we will experience. We can examine this hypothesis using a test of **correlation**.

In this chapter we look at these four ways of collecting data and comment on the relative strengths and weaknesses of them.

Basics of scientific research

Scientific research starts with theories which explain things in the world about us. However for a theory to be any good it must stand up to being tested. For example, the science of phrenology was based on the idea that the shape of the brain determined personality. However this has not been supported by any evidence and so cannot be held to explain any facts.

Testable

If a result is sound it ought to be possible to repeat it. If it is not possible to get the same result again it raises a question about the original study. Sometimes studies are not repeated because of ethical issues, for example Milgram's study of obedience but the question still remains.

Replicable

Objective

If we are objective then we try to remove as much bias as possible from our study (the opposite is to be subjective and personal). We can do this by using controls and by, for example, recording exactly what we observe rather than our interpretations. Freud's study is a very subjective account of Little Hans' fears.

Valuable

Psychological research doesn't have to have direct benefit to the general public but many people think it should make a contribution to our understanding of ourselves and others. In other words it should be useful. Whatever criticisms are made of Milgram's study, it has provided a valuable insight into human behaviour.

Activity

Play with psychological methods

Why not use your phone or iPod to carry out some research? If you haven't got an iPod then just make one out of pink cardboard and white string; nobody will notice. You can *observe* people's behaviour with an iPod: do they make less eye contact in the street? Do they hum out loud, or move in rhythm? You can *experiment* whether people do better at simple tests when listening to the iPod than when not listening. Or you can compare the effects of different types of music on performance. You can make a *questionnaire* about iPod playlists or colours, or attitudes to people who have iPods. And you might *correlate* the amount of time people use shuffle (compared to listening to whole albums) with some personality variable (such as extraversion – find a questionnaire on the web).

The mobile phone has pushed us to develop a whole new range of behaviours. Do people use hand gestures when they are on the mobile phone? Why? You could compare the gestures and facial expressions of mobile phone users with the gestures and expressions of face-to-face conversation. And what about asking people about how and when they use it, how many texts they send, and whether they save any texts, if so from whom? You could send the same message to males and females and look at the different answers. People love to talk about their phones so a questionnaire should be easy enough.

Measurement in psychology – some things to think about

What to measure

A key element of any psychological enquiry is the collection of data. This commonly, though not always, involves measuring the variable we are interested in. We don't just want to say what something is, we want to compare it to other similar things. How many, how big, how often, how strong, how unusual, are all questions we might ask. But what do we want to ask about in psychology and what do we want to measure? The big questions in psychology are why do I think like this? why do I feel like this? and why do I behave like this? We usually phrase the question to focus on other people rather than ourselves (e.g. 'why do people think like this?') but the same principles apply. We look at these three areas of human life below and consider how we might get data and measure them.

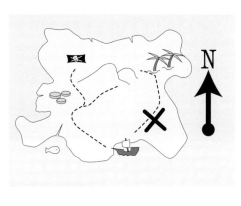

Mental treasure map

Measuring mental events can sometimes provide surprising insights. Kosslyn (1975) asked people to draw a map of a treasure island with some key features such as the beach, a hut, a coconut tree and buried treasure. When the drawing was finished Kosslyn asked the participant to close their eyes and imagine exploring the island. Kosslyn would choose a route, for example start at the beach and go to the hut. When they had reached the end they were asked to press a button which recorded how long they had been on the mental journey. Remarkably, the time taken to complete the mental journey was longer for items that were further apart. The mental world seems to have the same characteristics as the physical world and we move about it in the same way.

THINK

How can we measure what people are thinking? We can't see thinking although we sometimes believe that we can. "I know what you're thinking" we sometimes say to someone, but what gives us that belief? It comes from our observation of their behaviour. The changes in their facial expression or the pose they have adopted. We can't read or hear their thoughts but we can make an intelligent guess about what is going on inside their head.

We can measure thinking by asking people about their thoughts. Sometimes psychologists ask people to try and say out-loud what they are thinking as they think it. If you try to do this you'll realise how difficult it is. Griffiths used this technique in his gambling study. We can also measure thoughts by giving people puzzles to solve and seeing how they solve them and how successful they are. The autism study by Baron-Cohen et al. uses these sort of techniques.

A modern technique for measuring cognitive processes is an eyetracker which follows the movement of your eyes and records where you fixate on a scene or a page when you are looking at it. This technique has been especially useful in research on reading.

FEEL

Measuring feelings is no easier than measuring thoughts. We can see some of the physical changes that emotions bring about but as adults we are very skilled at hiding our emotions so people don't know what we are really feeling. If you know someone quite well then you can often tell their mood by observing them. You are able to compare how they look with how they usually look so you can spot whether their eyes look more steely than usual or their jaw is set tighter than usual.

When you observe these changes you are making a basic form of measurement by noting whether someone looks MORE or LESS tense than usual. Behavioural observations like these are one way to measure emotions. Another way is to take the obvious route and ask someone how they feel. We might get measures here by asking them to rate themselves on some emotion scales or to respond to a standard list of questions.

Emotions often bring about bodily changes and we can measure these changes. We might measure the galvanic skin response (GSR) which records the level of sweat and is commonly used as part of a lie detector test. We might also measure changes in hormones associated with stress and Haslam and Reicher used this technique in the prison study.

BEHAVE

This ought to be the easy one to measure. We can observe what people do and what people say and what people produce, and we can record this behaviour. With thinking and feeling we have to use other measures to try and estimate the variables we are interested in, but with behaviour we can measure the thing we are studying. But life is never quite that easy because just recording behaviour is sometimes not quite enough.

In the Bobo study (Bandura et al.,) the behaviour of the children was observed and recorded. But there is more to aggression than behaviour alone. We often give people a thump in a friendly way but if we did the same thing in anger we might not hit them any harder but the experience would be very different. Also, some people refer to passive aggression (a Freudian term) to describe awkward and obstructive behaviour that is used instead of confrontation.

Another issue for behavioural measures is that some behaviour is hidden from view. For example, we behave differently when we are alone and by being watched to when we are alone (unless we don't tell them). Also there are some social behaviours that are kept very private.

Activity

Use your common sense to suggest how you can investigate the following questions. When you've done that, try and connect your suggestions to the psychological methods you know about.

- What makes people happy?
- How do parents in Nottingham bring up their children?
- How does someone react to another person when they have a romantic interest in them?
- Do people get better after a series of therapy sessions?
- At what age do babies recognise a human face?

...Connections...

To understand any evidence you have to understand how the data was collected. You might ask the question 'How do you know that?', and throughout this text we have tried to answer that question. The 15 core studies illustrate a wide range of data collection techniques in psychology. We have our own views on which evidence is the strongest and which should be taken with a pinch of salt. We hope that by studying how the evidence was collected you can make up your own mind about which you think is most valuable.

Observation

The starting point for scientific enquiry is observation. We observe what is going on and then try and make sense of it. For example, people started to observe their surroundings thousands of years ago. They observed that the sun rose on one side of the landscape and set on the other and that this happened at regular and predictable intervals. They observed and recorded and then made the best sense of this, which was to belief that there was a bloke in a fiery chariot driving across the sky every day. Of course the conclusions were nonsense but the observations were sound.

The principles and problems are there in psychological observations. We observe behaviour, record it, look for patterns in the behaviour and then try and make sense of it. The first task is to make good observations and to devise ways of categorising it recording it that help our understanding. The tricky bit is to make sense of it and say what it means. What we are looking for is an explanation that tells us something we didn't already know about behaviour and does not involve flying blokes in flaming vehicles.

Activity

1. Unstructured observations

Aim

To investigate how to make observations.

Method

1 Work with a partner and take turns observing each other for five minutes. Person A should spend the time doing a piece of work, while Person B (the observer) should note down anything Person A does.

2 You can extend this study by making observations of other students in, for example, the library.

   - How will it affect their behaviour if you ask their permission beforehand?

   - If you do not seek permission beforehand, inform participants afterwards and ensure they are happy for you to keep the record of your observations.

2. Unstructured and structured observations

Aim

To consider individual differences in anxiety when speaking in public. (You could compare males and females).

Method

1 Pilot study: Begin by conducting an unstructured observation. Ask several volunteers (males and females) to stand up in front of your class and deliver a one-minute talk on any topic. The rest of the class should make a note of any nonverbal behaviours for example: scratching nose, licking lips, waving hands, saying 'um'.

2 Work in small groups to create a behaviour checklist (explained on right) from your preliminary observations. Each group can report back to the whole class with their ideas and the class can produce a table to record future observations, for example:

	Person 1	Person 2	Etc.
Extraneous vocalisation e.g. 'um'			
Hand touches face			
Etc.			

3 Record structured observations of people speaking using your behaviour checklist to score behaviours in a more structured way. Make a record for each speaker.

Results

Summarise your findings in a table showing totals for each behavioural category for each speaker. You can also illustrate the behavioural categories using a bar chart.

How to make observations

You might think that making observations is easy but if you tried one of the activities (on the left), you should now realise it is difficult:

1 To work out what to record and what not to record.

2 To record everything that is happening even if you do select what to record and what not to record.

Observational research, like all research, aims to be objective and rigorous. For this reason it is necessary to use observational techniques. We will look at some of these techniques.

Sampling observational data

An observer needs to decide when and how often to make observations. This may be continuous, where the observer records every instance of behaviour in as much detail as possible. This is useful if the behaviours of interest do not occur very often.

Usually continuous observation is not possible because there would be too much to record. Therefore observers use a systematic method such as:

Event sampling The observer keeps a count of each time a particular behaviour occurs.

Time sampling The observer decides on a time interval, such once a minute. At the end of the time interval the observer notes any particular behaviours that are being displayed by the target individual(s).

Unstructured observations

The researcher records all relevant behaviour but has no system. The behaviour to be studied is largely unpredictable. One of the core studies in this book is Rosenhan's study (sane in insane places)

Ethical issues

When participants are observed without their knowledge they clearly do not have the opportunity to provide **informed consent**, an important right for all research participants. One way to deal with this is to **debrief** the participants afterwards, explaining the aims of procedures of the study and asking permission to use their data.

Some observations may be regarded as an invasion of **privacy**. The issue of privacy is dealt with by the British Psychological Society (BPS) who advise that it is only acceptable to observe others without their consent in situations where participants would expect to be observed by strangers. In addition researchers should be aware that it is not acceptable to intrude upon the privacy of individuals who, even while in a normally public space, may believe they are unobserved.

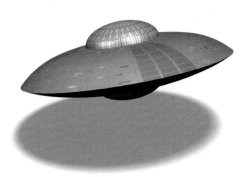

An example of a participant observation
In the 1950s the social psychologist Leon Festinger read a newspaper report about a religious cult that claimed to be receiving messages from outer space predicting that the end of the world would take place on a certain date in the form of a great flood. The cult members were going to be rescued by a flying saucer so they all gathered with their leader, Mrs Keech. Festinger was intrigued to know how the cult members would respond when they found their beliefs were unfounded. In order to observe this at first hand Festinger and some colleagues posed as cult followers and were present on the expected eve of destruction. When it was apparent that there would be no flood, the group initially became disheartened but Mrs Keech announced that she had received a new message from the aliens saying that the group's efforts had saved the day. Although some cult members soon left the cult others took this as proof of the cult's beliefs and became even more enthusiastic supporters. The question of just how involved the psychologists were, and how much they contributed towards the false beliefs, remains uncertain (Festinger *et al.*, 1956).

where unstructured observations were made. One problem with unstructured observations is that the behaviours recorded will often be those which are most visible or eye-catching to the observer. However, these may not necessarily be the most important or relevant behaviours.

Structured observations

One of the hardest aspects of using the observational method is deciding what you are going to record and how different behaviours should be categorised. This is because our perception of behaviour is often seamless; when we watch somebody perform a particular action we see a continuous stream of action rather than a series of separate behavioural components.

In order to conduct systematic observations one needs to break up this stream of behaviour into different categories, called **behavioural categories**. In order to do this a researcher has to break the behaviour being studied into a set of components. For example when observing infant behaviour, having a list such as smiling, crying, etc.

The categories are sometimes called a **behaviour checklist** or a **coding system** (when a code is invented to represent each category of behaviour). You can see an example of a behaviour checklist in the core study by Bandura *et al.* (aggression).

A behaviour checklist or coding system may be adopted from a previous research study or may be developed after first making preliminary observations. It should:

1   Be objective: the observer should not have to make inferences about the behaviour and should just have to record explicit actions.
2   Cover all possible component behaviours and avoid a 'waste basket' category.
3   Have no overlapping categories; if each category is not mutually exclusive observers may feel unsure which category to tick and this may reduce reliability.

Distinctions

Controlled and naturalistic
In a naturalistic observation behaviour is studied in a natural situation where everything has been left as it is normally. In a controlled observation some variables are controlled by the researcher, possibly in a lab, reducing the 'naturalness' of behaviour being studied.

Participant and non-participant
In many cases the observer is merely watching the behaviour of others and acts as a non-participant. In some studies observers also participate, which may affect their objectivity (see example above). This is not so much an either/or as a sliding scale of participation.

Disclosed and undisclosed
One-way mirrors can be used to prevent participants being aware that they are being observed. This is called undisclosed (covert) observation. This method was used in the study on aggression by Bandura *et al.* Knowing that your behaviour is being observed is likely to alter your behaviour.

Direct and indirect
On this spread we have considered direct observations. In some studies observations of human behaviour are made indirectly – of data that has already been collected, for example observing advertisements on TV or observing newspaper advertisements. This is called indirect observation and may use **content analysis** (see the example on the next spread).

Qs

1   Suggest **one** strength of using event sampling instead of time sampling as a method of collecting observational data.
2   Suggest **one** strength of using time sampling instead of event sampling.
3   In each of the following observations state which sampling procedure would be most appropriate and explain how you would do it:
   a   Observing the different activities young children engage in at a nursery school.
   b   Observing what dog owners do when they are walking their dogs in a park.
   c   Observing the products bought by shoppers in a supermarket.
4   Describe **two** strengths of using structured rather than unstructured observations in an observational study.
5   A university department undertakes an observational study of the behaviour of football fans at a live game.
   a   List **three** behaviours you might include in a behaviour checklist.
   b   Identify a suitable sampling procedure and explain how you would do it.
   c   How could you observe target individuals so that they were not aware that they were being observed?
   d   What ethical issues might be raised in this observational study?
   e   For each issue identified in your answer to (d), explain how you could deal with this issue and whether this would be acceptable.
6   A school decides to collect data about student behaviour in the cafeteria throughout the day. Answer questions a–e above.

Evaluating observational techniques

On this spread we will consider some issues related to the value of observational research and suggest some further activities for you to try.

Reliability

The term 'reliability' refers to how consistent any measurement is (**reliability** is discussed further on page 130). If you use a ruler to measure the length of a table you expect that ruler to be reliable so that if you used it again the measurement wouldn't change (unless the table suddenly got smaller!).

When making observations of a person (or animal or event) we require the observations to be something we can rely on. If they are reliable we would expect to end up with the same data even if the observations were made by a different person – two observers should produce the same record. This is called **inter-rater reliability**.

Assessing reliability

This can be checked by comparing the recordings made by two (or more) observers and calculating agreement.

Using time sampling a count can be kept for the number of times the observers agree with each other. A general rule is that if total agreements are more than 80% of the total observations made then the data have high inter-rater reliability.

Using event sampling, a correlation coefficient can be calculated for the data in each category, for example:

	Observer 1	Observer 2
Behaviour 1 (saying 'um')	10	3
Behaviour 2 (scratching face)	3	5
Behaviour 3 (nervous giggle)	1	2
Etc.		

The data above doesn't look like it would have high inter-rater reliability.

Improving inter-rater reliability

Reliability can be improved by making sure that observers are trained in the use of the behavioural checklist. It might also be necessary to review the checklist and see if some categories are unclear or need sub-dividing to make for more accurate coding.

Validity

Validity is the extent to which the research has measured what it intended to measure. This topic is discussed further on page 130. When making observations the main issue is **observer bias** – what someone observes is influenced by expectations. For example, if you think football fans tend to be quite aggressive this may lead you to 'see' more aggression than an observer who believes the opposite. This reduces the objectivity and validity of observations.

Improving validity

Observer bias can be dealt with by using more than one observer and averaging data across observers to balance out any biases.

It can also be improved by keeping observers naïve about the aims of the research in order to prevent their expectations biasing their observations.

Football fans are very aggressive. If you believe that they are aggressive you would probably produce biased observations of the behaviour of football fans – an example of observer bias.

Strengths and weaknesses of observational techniques

	Strengths	Weaknesses
Observational techniques in general	☺ What people say they do is often different from what they actually do so observations give a different take on behaviour.	☹ Observers may 'see' what they expect to see (*observer bias*).
	☺ A means of conducting preliminary investigations in a new area of research, to produce hypotheses for future investigations.	☹ Poorly designed behaviour checklist reduces reliability (low inter-rater reliability).
	☺ Able to capture spontaneous and unexpected behaviour.	☹ If participants don't know they are being observed there are ethical problems such as deception and invasion of privacy. If participants do know they are being observed they may alter their behaviour.
		☹ Observations cannot provide information about what people think or feel.
Participant observation	☺ Likely to provide special insights into behaviour, from the 'inside'.	☹ Objectivity may be reduced.
Structured observation	☺ Enables systematic observations to be made so important information not overlooked, otherwise observer may be overwhelmed by stream of information.	☹ Categories may not cover all possibilities and so some behaviours not recorded or placed in an 'other' category.
Time sampling	☺ Reduces the number of observations by using an objective means of sampling.	☹ Observations may not be representative.
Event sampling	☺ Useful when behaviour to-be-recorded only happens occasionally and might be missed if time sampling used.	☹ Observer may miss some observations if too many things happen at once.

When conducting your own studies try to include the following as useful preparation for exam questions:

- Summary tables and graphs.
- Draw conclusions.
- Comment on reliability and validity of measurements.
- Suggest improvements to design and the likely effects.

Examples of observations

Content analysis of TV ads

Various studies have looked at the way gender is portrayed in the media – magazines, books, TV and so on. Such studies are described as a **content analysis** because they make indirect observations of behaviour by looking at the content of communications produced by people.

Manstead and McCulloch (1981) looked at ads on British TV – 170 ads over a one week period, ignoring those that contained only children and animals. In each ad they just looked at what the central adult figure was doing and recorded frequencies in a table like the one on the right. For each ad there might be no ticks, one tick or a number of ticks.

In this study, women were found to be more likely than men to be portrayed as product users, to be cast in a dependent role, to produce no arguments in favour of the product and to be shown at home.

Observing everyday life

John Trinkaus is a giant in observational research. When something annoys him enough he takes the time and trouble to categorise and record it. He has published nearly 100 brief reports of observations of everyday life. For example, one study in 1993 looked at the number of shoppers in the express checkout line who had more than the permitted number of items. In his 1990 paper 'Exiting a Building: An Informal Look' he calculated the percentage of people who chose a door that was already open rather than one that was closed. In his 2003 paper 'Snow on Motor Vehicle Roofs: An Informal Look' he calculated the percentage of drivers who don't bother to brush the snow off their cars. For his careful appreciation of the little things in life, Professor Trinkaus was awarded the 2003 IgNobel Prize (see http://improbable.com/).

	Male	Female
Credibility basis of central character		
Product user		
Product authority		
Role of central character		
Dependent role		
Independent role		
Argument spoken by central character		
Factual		
Opinion		
Product type used by central character		
Food/drink		
Alcohol		
Body		
Household		

Shoppers exceeding the number of allowed items at the checkout – observing everyday life.

Qs

Answer the questions below for each of the studies described on the right.

1. Outline the procedure that the researcher might follow.
2. Give **one** strength and **one** weakness of using observational techniques to investigate the target behaviour.
3. With respect to the weakness that you mentioned, suggest a different way to conduct this study.
4. Explain what is meant by inter-rater reliability.
5. Suggest how the research could ensure that this observation has high inter-rater reliability.
6. Describe a possible threat to the validity of this observation.
7. Explain how the researcher could deal with this threat to validity.

Study A

A local zoo keeps some white tigers. For some time the zoo has been concerned about the effect people have on the tigers' behaviour. They employ a psychologist to conduct an observational study of the pair of animals when they are on their own (outside of zoo opening hours) and when they are being observed by the public.

Study B

The department of medicine at Nottingham University is conducting research about what makes a good GP. As part of this they wish to observe the behaviour of GPs when they are consulting with their patients.

Ideas for your own observational studies

Gender stereotypes

You could replicate the study on the left by Manstead and McCullough, or adapt their categories and look at magazine adverts.

People watching

You know you want to do this one. Well, you probably do it anyway for fun. Take a seat in a public space such as a town square and watch people go by. Try and describe what they are doing. Maybe choose to look at the bus queues. Devise some categories to capture most of this behaviour. Use the categories to see if there are differences in behaviour between different groups of people such as young and old.

Self-presentation on Facebook

A rich source of data can be found on the phenomenon which is Facebook. It is perfectly ethical because people have decided to place their personal information in the public domain, though you could always inform your friends about what you are doing.

One line of investigation might concern the way people present themselves in their photograph – some people have a face only portrait, others are pictured with friends or put in some other image. Work out your own way to code the various possibilities and, perhaps, compare males and females or look at age differences (even oldies like us are on Facebook!).

Observe your pet

If you are a pet lover (and have a pet) sit down and watch your pet, noting down any behaviours. Use this unstructured observation to produce a behaviour checklist and then observe the animal at different times. Is his or her behaviour different when there are lots of people in the room? Or at different times of day? Or different temperatures?

...Links to other studies and issues...

In this text the **Rosenhan** study gathers the bulk of its data from observational techniques and so is commonly referred to as an observational study. The study by **Bandura et al.** also uses observational techniques but the main question of the study is answered using an experimental hypothesis and so this study is commonly referred to as an experiment. If you think people are splitting hairs then you may well be right. It is probably best to think of observation as a technique for gathering data rather than as a research method.

Self-report

Observational studies provide insights into behaviour but they can't tell us what people are thinking or feeling. The most obvious way to find out what a person feels, thinks or does is to ask them. The term 'self-report techniques' refers to any data collection method that involves asking people to report on their thoughts, feelings or behaviour. This data can be collected by asking people to write about themselves (a questionnaire) or talk about themselves (an interview). Questionnaires/interviews can be structured which means that there are a set of pre-determined questions. Or they can be unstructured which means that questions are developed as the interview goes along. We will concentrate on structured techniques, and in particular on questionnaires. Commonly, questionnaires require short responses and allow us to easily compare the results between one person and another, and also to calculate average responses.

- **Questionnaires:** Respondents record their own answers.
- **Structured interview:** Pre-determined questions i.e. a questionnaire that is delivered in real-time (e.g. over the telephone or face-to-face).
- **Semi-structured interviews:** New questions are developed as you go along, similar to the way your GP might interview you. He or she starts with some pre-determined questions but further questions are developed as a response to your answers. For this reason this unstructured or semi-structured approach is sometimes called the *clinical interview.*
- **Unstructured interviews:** No questions are decided in advance.

Activity

Investigating dreams

Aim

To find out about people's dreams. Research questions: What do people dream about? Do people dream in colour? How often do people have nightmares?

Method

You can use the questionnaire below or extend it with some of your own questions. Brief all participants about the purpose of the questionnaire and what will be involved, and gain informed consent; hand out the questionnaire (or record the answers for an interviewee); debrief all participants.

QUESTIONNAIRE

What are your dreams like?

Think of a recent dream and answer the following questions related to your dream (you may tick more than one answer to each question):

1 What characters were in the dream?
- ❑ Known (e.g. family, friends)
- ❑ Generic (e.g. a policeman or a teacher but not a specific teacher)
- ❑ Animals
- ❑ Fantasy figure (e.g. angel, dragon)
- ❑ Other (please specify) _____

2 What kind of dream was it?
- ❑ Positive
- ❑ Negative

3 How meaningful was your dream?
- ❑ Can you remember a lot of details?
- ❑ Was the dream just fragments?
- ❑ Was it related to specific day-time events?

Results

You can use various **descriptive statistics** which are discussed on the next spread, such as stating the modal answer for each question and showing the answers to each question in a bar chart.

You could compare the content of male and female dreams, or dreams of teenagers and older people.

How to construct a questionnaire

Writing good questions

There are three issues to consider when writing questions:

1. Clarity

Questions must be written clearly so that the respondents can understand them. If a respondent doesn't understand the question he or she will given a meaningless answer, which reduces the validity of the data collected.

2. Bias

The way a question is phrased may lead respondents to give particular answers. For example, some questions contain a hint about the desired answer – 'Was that film interesting?' is likely to produce a different answer to 'Was that film boring?'. These are called **leading questions** – in the core study by Loftus and Palmer (eyewitness testimony) the leading question was asking 'how fast the cars were travelling when they smashed into each other'. The word 'smashed' suggests they were travelling fast. If the word 'contacted' is used instead, it suggests they were travelling at a slower speed.

An even greater problem is **social desirability bias** – people often prefer to answer questions in a way that makes them look better. For example, if you are asked 'Are you generally honest?', you might say 'yes' rather than 'no' because 'no' makes you look like a liar. Sometimes questionnaires include a *lie scale* to test how honest people are being – they ask questions such as 'Do you always think of other people's feelings?'. If a person agrees with such questions then it suggests that they are trying to show themselves in a good light rather than being honest.

3. Analysis

The way data is analysed depends on the kind of question asked:

Open questions invite respondents to provide their own answers and tend to produce **qualitative data,** i.e. data which can't be

---

Ethical issues

It is expected that researchers will obtain **informed consent** from all participants unless deception is necessary.

- Where deception is necessary all respondents should be **debriefed.**

Questions should not cause **psychological harm** (e.g. cause unnecessary embarrassment or loss of self-esteem), they should avoid where possible invasion of **privacy** (e.g. asking personal questions) and must respect **confidentiality.**

- Participants' names should not be recorded and their answers can only be stored if they have given their permission.

Briefing and debriefing

A brief is given to each participant prior to a study to explain to them what they will be required to do (standardised instructions) and inform participants of their right to withdraw from the study at any time. It should contain sufficient detail about the study for the participant to be able to provide **informed consent.**

Even with informed consent participants may not fully understand what is involved and only realise this once the study has started. That is why they also should be told that they have the right to withdraw at any time.

A **debrief** is conducted after the experiment for two reasons.

1 *Ethical*: If any deception took place then participants are told the true aims of the study and offered the opportunity to discuss any concerns they may have. They may be offered the opportunity to withdraw their data from the study.

2 *Practical*: The experimenter may ask for further information about the researcher topic. For example, they may ask why the participant found one condition more difficult, or may ask whether the participant believed the set-up.

A **pilot study** *is a small-scale trial run of a research design before doing the real thing. It is done in order to find out if certain things don't work. For example, participants may not understand the instructions or may guess what the experiment is about. They may get very bored because there are too many tasks or questions and not give truthful answers.*

immediately counted. Such questions are more difficult to analyse than closed questions because each respondent's answer may be different and therefore a researcher may look for trends rather than using descriptive statistics. The advantage of open questions is that they can produce unexpected information and allow respondents to express what they actually think rather than being restricted by preconceived categories.

Examples of open questions

1   What factors contribute to making work stressful?
2   How does it feel when you are in love?

Closed questions. Closed questions provide limited choices and provide **quantitative data** and the answers are easy to analyse. However such questions may not permit people to express their precise feelings and tend not to uncover new insights.

Examples of closed questions are shown on the right. Questions 3 and 4 are examples of **rating scales** where respondents are asked to give a rating for their answers.

(Qualitative and quantitative data are discussed on page 50).

Writing good questionnaires

When designing a questionnaire there are further issues beyond writing good questions. It is a good idea to conduct a pilot study to test out the clarity of the questions and any other difficulties that might be encountered.

A researcher also needs to decide on **sampling method** – the method used to select the respondents.

Examples of closed questions

1   Which of the following factors at work makes you feel stressed? (You may tick as many answers as you like)

    ❑ Noise at work   ❑ Lack of control

    ❑ Too much to do   ❑ Bored

    ❑ Workmates   ❑ No job satisfaction

2   How many hours a week do you work?

    ❑ 0 hours

    ❑ Less than 10 hours

    ❑ Over 10 hours but less than 20 hours

    ❑ More than 20 hours

3   Work is stressful (circle your answer)

    Strongly agree   Agree   Not sure   Disagree   Strongly disagree

4   How much stress do you feel in the following situations?

    (Circle the number that best describes how you feel)

At work	A lot of stress	5 4 3 2 1	No stress at all
At home	A lot of stress	5 4 3 2 1	No stress at all
Travelling to work	A lot of stress	5 4 3 2 1	No stress at all

---

Qs

A group of students decide to conduct research on the relationships adolescents have with family and friends.

1   One of the questions on the questionnaire is 'Who do you love most? Give **one** strength and **two** weaknesses of this question as a means of finding out about relationships.

2   Explain why the question in (a) is an open-ended question.

3   Write **one** closed question that the students could include in their questionnaire.

4   Outline **one** strength and **one** weakness of using this question.

5   The students' teacher suggests they could use a rating scale to gather information about the adolescents' different relationships. Describe exactly how this might be done.

6   Suggest **one** ethical issue that might arise when conducting this study and explain why it would be a problem and how the students might deal with the ethical issue.

7   Describe an alternative method of collecting data about adolescents' relationships rather than using a questionnaire.

8   Explain what effect this change might have on the results.

Sampling

Sampling

When studying any behaviour, such as obedience or what people dream about, researchers can't test everyone in the world or even everyone in your town. Therefore, when conducting research, psychologists select a **sample** from a **target population** (the group of people they are interested in – such as adolescents in the UK). Once the research is conducted the researcher hopes to be able to **generalise** from the study to the target population. In other words, if the study looks at the dreams experienced by a sample of adolescents, then the results will be used to make statements about all adolescents – making the assumption that all adolescents have experiences similar to those of the sample group.

It is OK to make generalisations about the target population from the sample only if the sample is representative of the target population. The aim of all sampling methods is to produce a **representative sample**.

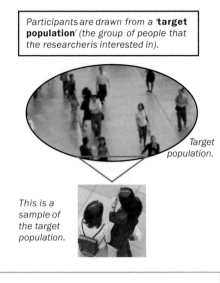

Participants are drawn from a **'target population'** (the group of people that the researcher is interested in).

Target population.

This is a sample of the target population.

Sampling methods

Opportunity sample

How to get an **opportunity sample** – for example, ask people walking by you in the street or people sitting in the school library, i.e. select those who are available.

- The easiest method because you just use the first participants you can find.
- Inevitably a biased method because the sample is drawn from a small part of the target population. For example, if you do an experiment using people in the street then the sample is selected from people walking around the centre of a town – not those at work, or those living in rural areas.

Self-selecting (volunteer) sample

How to get a **self-selecting sample** – for example, advertise in a newspaper or on a noticeboard.

- Access to a variety of participants.
- Sample is biased because participants likely to be more highly motivated and/or with extra time on their hands (= *volunteer bias*).

Random sample

How to get a **random sample** – for example, put names of the target population into a hat and draw out required number.

- Unbiased, all members of target population have an equal chance of selection.
- It is almost impossible to carry out a random sample unless your population is very small.
- May end up with a biased sample because not all Ps identified will participate.

> Many students mistake a systematic sample for a random sample. Don't make that mistake! In a systematic sample you select every nth person from a list.

Quota sample

How to get a **quota sample** – subgroups within a population are identified (e.g. boys and girls or age groups: 10–12, 13–14, etc.). Then a quota is taken from each subgroup (using an opportunity sample).

- More representative than an opportunity sample because equal representation of subgroups.
- Although the sample represents the subgroups, each quota may be biased in other ways, e.g. consist of people not at work.

[In a **stratified sample** the sample from each subgroup is obtained using a random method.]

How many?

The number of participants or respondents in any study varies enormously. When using questionnaires it is relatively easy to distribute them to hundreds if not thousands of people. When conducting an experiment numbers are usually much smaller, as few as twenty-five is acceptable (Coolican, 1996). Small samples can still be representative and may have advantages over using samples that are too big. For example, large samples can obscure important individual differences – consider a study looking at the effect of noise on memory, it might be that noise has no effect on most people's memory but does effect people with sensitive hearing; if you have a very large sample it may include enough people with sensitive hearing to affect the results so that it appears that all people's memory is affected by noise.

'You're very special'

Your mother has probably told you at some time or other that you are very special. And it's true, you are. In fact you are unique. There is no one quite like you (even if you are an identical twin).

We have to be careful about making generalisations because although we share common features with other people we are all unique and quite unlike anyone else.

Activity

Measure the height of 20 people in your class (alternatively make up 20 heights if you can't find a tape measure). Work out the average height by adding them together and dividing by 20. You now know the mean height of your population. This activity gives you a chance to try out the different sampling methods.

1 *Random samples.* Pick 10 names out of a hat and work out their average height (add them up and divide by 10). Do this 2 or 3 times.

2 *Systematic samples.* Pick out every other name on the list and work out their average height.

3 *Self-selecting sample.* Look at the heights of the first 10 people to be measured (the keen ones).

Look at the mean scores for each sample and compare them to the true mean (the one you originally calculated) and see which was the best way to select a sample.

Descriptive statistics are used to describe and summarise data. Psychologists also use statistical tests to check whether their results are significant, that is have not occurred by chance – however such tests are beyond the AS specification, you'll be glad to know!

Averages

There are three different ways to express the average or typical value of a set of data:

1 The **mean** is calculated by adding up all the numbers and dividing by the number of numbers. It is not appropriate for **nominal** data.

2 The **median** is the *middle* value in an *ordered* list. It is not appropriate for **nominal** data.

3 The **mode** is the value that is *most* common. It is the only method appropriate when the data are in categories (such as number of people who like pink) i.e. **nominal data**, but can be used for all kinds of data.

Graphs

A picture is worth a thousand words! Graphs provide a means of 'eyeballing' your data and seeing the results at a glance.

- **Bar chart**: the height of the bar represents frequency. Suitable for words and numbers.
- **Pie chart, pictograms**: illustrating frequency of data using slices of a pie or pictures.
- **Scattergraph**: suitable for correlational data (see page 20).

What are nominal, ordinal, interval and ratio data?

Nominal. *The data are in separate categories, such as grouping people according to their favourite football team (e.g. Nottingham Forest, Inverness Caledonian Thistle, etc.).*

Ordinal. *Data are ordered in some way, e.g. asking people to put a list of football teams in order of liking. Nottingham might be first, followed by Inverness, etc. The 'difference' between each item is not the same; i.e. the individual may like the first item a lot more than the second, but there might be only a small difference between the items ranked as second and third.*

Interval. *Data are measured using units of equal intervals, such as when counting correct answers or using any 'public' unit of measurement. Many psychological studies use plastic interval scales in which the intervals are arbitrarily determined so we cannot actually know for certain that there are equal intervals between the numbers. However, for the purposes of analysis, such data may be accepted as interval. In the example of our football teams we might compare the number of goals scored or the number of people they attract to their games.*

Ratio. *There is a true zero point and equal interval between points on the scale, as in most measures of physical quantities.*

Qs

We described a study about relationships on the previous spread.

1 Suggest a suitable sampling method for this study.

2 Describe how you would use this method to obtain your sample.

3 Outline **one** strength and **one** weakness of using this method to obtain a sample in this study.

4 Suggest which sampling method might be used to overcome the weakness identified in question 3, and explain why.

5 The students asked their respondents to identify the person they felt closest to: 34% said their boyfriend/girlfriend, 28% said their best friend, 15% said their mother, 2% named their father, and 11% said brother/sister.

   a. Place this information in a summary table.

   b. Sketch a bar chart to display the results.

   c. What conclusion(s) can you draw from your bar chart?

Don't draw meaningless graphs

Imagine that you did a study where there were two groups of 10 participants. One group were given a list of words organised into categories (items of food, precious metals etc.), the other group were given the same list of words in random order. The recall scores are shown in the graphs below.

The graph on the left is a participant-by-participant graph – it is meaningless, yet many students do this kind of graph. The bar chart on the right below may look too simple but it is all you need to present a clear summary of your results.

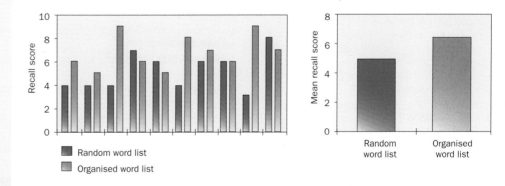

■ Random word list
□ Organised word list

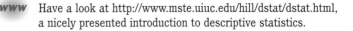

www Have a look at http://www.mste.uiuc.edu/hill/dstat/dstat.html, a nicely presented introduction to descriptive statistics.

Evaluating self-report techniques

We will now return to self-report techniques and consider issues of reliability and validity, as well as looking at the relative strengths and weaknesses of the different techniques.

Reliability

If the same questionnaire or interview or psychological test (such as a personality test) is repeated with the same person it should produce the same outcome. Reliability may be affected if different interviewers ask questions in different ways or the same interviewer behaves differently on different occasions – this leads to low **inter-rater reliability**.

Assessing reliability

Reliability can be demonstrated using the **test–retest method**, i.e. giving participants a test/questionnaire/ interview and then giving the same participants the same test a while later (so they have a chance to forget it) to see if the same result is obtained. The two sets of scores can be compared by calculating a *correlation coefficient* (see page 20).

Improving reliability

Reliability can be improved in the case of interviews, by training interviewers. In the case of other self-report measures inconsistency may be due to questions which are unclear so that answers vary from occasion to occasion. Therefore question clarity should be checked.

Validity

The validity of a questionnaire or interview or psychological test concerns whether it really measures what the researcher intended to measure. One way to assess this is **concurrent validity**, which can be established by comparing the current questionnaire/interview/test with a previously established one on the same topic. Participants take both tests and then their scores on both are compared using correlation.

Another means of demonstrating validity is **face validity**. The items on a questionnaire/interview/test should look like they are measuring what you intend to measure.

Improving validity

If the scores are not similar then the test should be revised by changing some of the questions. Researchers identify which questions are suspect by removing some questions to see if this improves the correlation with the existing measure. Then they can assume that these questions are not relevant.

Strengths and weaknesses of self-report techniques

Questionnaire

☺ Can be easily repeated so that data can be collected from large numbers of people relatively cheaply and quickly (once the questionnaire has been designed).	☹ Answers may not be truthful, for example because of *leading questions* and *social desirability bias*.
☺ Respondents may feel more willing to reveal personal/confidential information than in an interview.	☹ The sample may be biased because only certain kinds of people fill in questionnaires – literate individuals who are willing to spend time filling them in.

Structured interview

☺ Can be easily repeated.	☹ The interviewer's expectations may influence the answers the interviewee gives (this is called **interviewer bias**).
☺ Easier to analyse than unstructured interviews because answers more predictable.	☹ Reliability may be affected by the interviewer's behaviour.

Semi-structured or unstructured interview

☺ Generally more detailed information can be obtained from each respondent than in a structured interview.	☹ More affected by interviewer bias than structured interviews because the interviewer is developing questions on the spot which gives scope for them to ask leading questions.
☺ Can access information that may not be revealed by predetermined questions.	☹ Requires well-trained interviewers, which makes it more expensive to produce reliable interviews when compared to structured interviews.

Rating scales

☺ Enables respondents to represent thoughts and feelings quantitatively.	☹ Respondents may avoid using ends of scales and go for 'middle of the road', thus answers do not represent true feelings.

Open questions

☺ They can produce unexpected information.	☹ More difficult to analyse qualitative data produced and thus more difficult to draw conclusions.
☺ Allow respondents to express what they actually think rather than being restricted by preconceived categories.	

Closed questions

☺ Easier to analyse data.	☹ May not permit people to express their precise feelings.

Qs

1 If a questionnaire was described as 'unreliable', what does this mean?

2 Describe **two** advantages of using self-report measures and **two** disadvantages.

3 A researcher wishes to investigate internet use in 8–10 year olds.
   a. Why might it be preferable to use a questionnaire rather than an interview?
   b. Why might it be better to use an interview instead of a questionnaire?
   c. The researcher decides to use a questionnaire. How could the reliability of the questionnaire be assessed?
   d. If the reliability is low, how could the researcher improve it?
   e. How could the researcher demonstrate that the questionnaire is valid?

4 In another psychological study, researchers seek to find out about young people's experiences of eating problems.
   a. Would it be better to use a questionnaire or an interview? Explain your answer.
   b. Explain how the researcher might obtain a suitable sample and explain the reason for your choice.

Activity

Try the questionnaire below.

- Comment on its face validity
- Try assessing its reliability
- Check concurrent validity by comparing the results of the test below with an existing test (for example http://www.queendom.com/tests/access_page/index.htm?idRegTest=697)

How extravert are you?

Answer yes or no to the questions below

1 Do you prefer to make instant decisions rather than reflecting for a while on what to do?
2 Would you prefer to take up a course in sketching rather than karate?
3 At parties do you prefer to listen to people rather than do the talking yourself?
4 Do you work best in a quiet atmosphere?
5 Have you got a wide circle of friends?
6 Have you done something stupid just for a dare?
7 Is it quite hard to know you?
8 Do you avoid spending too much time on your own?
9 Do you make new friends easily?
10 Are you the life and soul of a party?
11 Do you feel it is important to say what you think rather than keeping some opinions to yourself?
12 Do you prefer staying in rather than going out?
13 Do you ever dream of flying?
14 Do you prefer to work independently?
15 Are you too shy to tell people what you really think of them?
16 Do you discuss your decisions with other people?

Score 2 if you answered yes to questions 1, 5, 6, 8, 9, 10, 11, 13, 16
Score 2 if you answered no to questions 2, 3, 4, 7, 12, 14, 15

A score above 20 Little Miss (or Mr) Extravert – you are one outgoing cool cookie, living life to the hilt and having fun. You are full of energy and everyone loves being around you – just make sure you don't burn yourself out, or turn out to just be too much for your friends.

Scores between 10 and 20 Little Miss (or Mr) Balance – you love people but you also don't mind your own company. You love a bit of daring and adventure but you're also happy curled up at home with a good book. Good on ya!

A score below 10 Little Miss (or Mr) Shy – you're an introvert, independent and cautious. Excitement is too much for you to cope with, scary rollercoaster rides freak you out. It pays to be careful but perhaps once in a while you should venture outside your shell. Remember all work and no play makes for a dull dude.

Examples of self-reports

HEALTH WARNING: It is easy and fun to devise your own tests and try them out on yourself and others. You can also use an established test from one of the sites below, but don't take any of them too seriously. They won't tell you anything about yourself that you don't already know. If you reflect on your own personality

you'll be able to say much more about it that any test can hope to do. Also remember, if you do a test on someone else, you should be sensitive about how they may feel about the results.

You can find lots of questionnaires and psychological tests to try out on the internet

- http://www.queendom.com/ Claims to be the world's largest testing centre, tests and questionnaires on everything.
- http://rand.org/health/surveys_tools.html Various health surveys and other scales.
- http://www.atkinson.yorku.ca/~psyctest/ Site providing access to copywrite psychological tests that can be downloaded and used by student researchers including dieting beliefs scale and self-esteem scales.
- http://ipip.ori.org/ipip/index.htm The International Personality Item Pool allows you to put together you own test using the subscales from loads of established psychometric tests.

Ideas for your own self-report studies

Ask your nan

Talk to an elderly relative and ask them about what they did at school. How long was the school day? What subjects did they do? How did the teachers treat them? What did they like about it and what did they hate?

There are all sorts of things to ask them about their time at school. Note it down and compare it to your own experience. You will probably find some things that seem better for you today but also some that seem worse.

What are you afraid of?

Find out what things people are most frightened of – is it snakes, or spiders, or roller coasters? The core study on Little Hans (Freud) is about phobias.

Are such fears innate or learned? There is good evidence that fears are inherited, for example identical twins are more similar in terms of their liking for roller coasters than non-identical twins. Also people are more likely to develop phobias if a close relative is also phobic. However, learning is obviously also involved because not everyone with a sister who is afraid of spiders also develops the same fears.

What is your identity status?

James Marcia (1966) investigated the formation of identity in adolescents. He asked them about their 'identity status' in areas such as occupation, religion, politics and attitudes about sex. Marcia concluded from his research that adolescents were in one of four possible identity statuses:

- *Identity diffusion.* Identity crisis not yet experienced.
- *Identity foreclosure.* Uncertainties avoided by committing self to safe, conventional goals (e.g. determined by parents) without exploring alternatives.
- *Identity moratorium.* Decisions about identity put on hold while various roles explored.
- *Identity achievement.* Individual emerges with firm goals, ideology, commitments.

You could construct a questionnaire to discover what identity stage your friends are at. You need to write statements that are typical of each status and ask people to rate the importance of each to them.

...Links to other studies and issues...

Many of the core studies use self report as at least one of their measures. The study of **Eve**, for example uses a range of psychological tests as well as the clinical interviews. These tests included personality tests, IQ tests and projective tests (see page 205). The prison study by **Haslam and Reicher** uses a number of tests to assess the thoughts and feelings of the participants. It is the sheer amount of data in this study that adds weight to their conclusions. The case studies of **Freud** and **Sperry** also use self reports as an essential part of their data. You might also argue that the **chimp** studies also use self report but that is, of course, open to debate.

The issues around self report questionnaires are also discussed elsewhere in this text, for example in the section on the **individual differences approach** and also in the issue on **reliability and validity**. And there is also the issue of the **Barnum Effect** (see page 221).

Experiment

When psychologists want to investigate causal relationships they use the experimental method. For example, if we want to know whether listening to music helps students study, we would have some students listening to music and some not (these are the two conditions or 'levels') and then give them a memory task (to assess quality of studying) to see who does better. It is logical and simple.

In this case we would be seeking to demonstrate that music is the cause of better (or worse) memory performance. The experimenter manipulates one variable – in this case music or not – which is called the **independent variable** (IV), and measures its effect on behaviour – in this case memory performance, called the **dependent variable** (DV).

There are two basic **experimental designs**:

1 **Repeated measures**: you test each individual in both conditions comparing their performance in both parts of the experiment.

2 **Independent groups**: you test one group of people in the first condition and a different group of people in the second condition, and then compare the two sets of scores.

Many people use the word 'experiment' quite loosely, as if an experiment was just another word for an investigation. It isn't. In an experiment, the experimenter:

- *Alters the levels of one variable (the IV).*
- *Observes the effects of the IV on the DV.*

Only by doing this can we discover a causal relationship because the experimenter can claim that any change in the DV must be due to the changes made to the IV – except if there are extraneous variables (see next spread for a discussion of control).

You actually conduct experiments without thinking. For example, when you start a class with a new teacher you might make a joke or hand in your homework on time (both IVs) to see if the teacher responds well (the DV). You are experimenting with cause and effect.

Activity

Here are some ideas of possible topics to study

- Music and studying – do people work as effectively if the work while music is playing? Do people who listen to quiet music study better than those listening to loud rock music?
- Weather and mood – are people in a better mood on a sunny day?
- Audience effects – do people get a better score at a computer game if they are being cheered on (or jeered) by an audience rather than when they play the game by themselves.

STEP 1 Work with a small group of other students and discuss how you might investigate one of the topics using the experimental method.

1 What will you need to measure?

2 Will you have two different conditions? What will you change across the two conditions?

3 Will everyone do both conditions? Or will you have two groups of participants, one doing each condition?

4 What will you expect to find out?

5 What will the participants do?

6 What do you need to control?

7 How many participants will you need and how will you get them?

STEP 2 When you have worked out what you will do, join with another group and explain your ideas to each other. The other group may ask useful questions which will help you refine your ideas.

STEP 3 Conduct your study. You may be able to do this in class or each member of your group could go away and collect some data.

STEP 4 Pool the data collected by your group and prepare a poster to present your results and conclusions.)

How to design an experiment

The activity on the left essentially takes you through the key steps in designing an experiment. The technical terms for each step are

1 Identify and *operationalise* the DV.

2 Identify and *operationalise* the IV.

3 Select *experimental* design (repeated measures or independent groups).

4 Write the *hypothesis*.

5 Decide on the *procedures*.

6 Decide on *controls* (discussed on next spread).

7 Choose *sampling method*.

Operationalisation

The term **'operationalise'** means to specify a set of operations or behaviours that can be measured or manipulated. For example, in the suggested experiment at the top of this page we want to know whether music helps students study. The IV is music and the DV is studying. We operationalised 'studying' by saying we would give the students a memory task and test their performance. In other words, we have specified how we will measure their ability to have studied well.

- How else could you operationalise or measure the ability of participants to have studied well? What task could you give them to do and how might you assess their performance?
- The IV is music. How could you operationalise this? You need to specify what music and for how long.

Hypotheses

At the outset of an experiment it is expected that the experimenter will state what they expect to discover. This is done in the form of a statement of what the experimenter believes to be true. In the case of our experiment:

People who listen to music while studying perform less well on a memory test than people who work in silence.

Qs

These questions relate to the study you did above – though you can answer most of them even if you haven't conducted the study.

1 Identify and operationalise the IV and DV in the study.

2 State a one-tailed alternate hypothesis for the study.

3 State a null hypothesis for the study.

4 What experimental design did you use (or could you use)?

5 Give **one** strength of using this method in this study.

6 Describe how you could have conducted this study using a different experimental design.

7 How might this have affected your results?

8 What sampling method did you use?

9 Give **one** weakness with using this method and describe a different method that you might have used.

10 How could you have investigated the same topic using a different research technique (i.e. not an experiment)?

11 How might this have affected your results?

When you look at a one-tailed cat you know which way it is going. A two-tailed cat could be going either way.

There are several things to notice about this **hypothesis**:

- The IV is clearly stated, including both levels of it (music and no music).
- The DV is also clearly stated (performance on a memory task)

This hypothesis states the expected direction of the results, that is we expect people who listen to music to perform less well. This is called a **one-tailed hypothesis**. The other possibility would be a **two-tailed** hypothesis, where the direction is not predicted:

People who listen to music while studying perform differently *on a memory test than people who work in silence.*

The alternate hypothesis and the null hypothesis

The hypothesis described above (which states what you believed to be true) is called the **alternate hypothesis** (H$_1$) because it is an *alternative* to the **null hypothesis** (H$_0$). The null hypothesis is a statement of no difference or no relationship:

There is no difference *between the memory test scores of people who listen to music or don't listen to music when studying.*

Note that the null hypothesis is not the opposite of the alternate hypothesis – it is null, that is a statement of nothingness! This seems very odd when you first come across the null hypothesis but we use it because that is what our statistical tests use to see whether we have a significant result.

Ethical issues

Some experiments involve **deception** because, if you tell participants the true aims of the experiment beforehand, this may affect how they behave in the experiment. This means that experimenters have to give false information (such as in the core study by Milgram).

- Experimenters can still obtain a form of **informed consent** because they can tell the participants as far as possible what they will be doing in order to help participants decide whether they are willing to take part.

Experimenters must avoid **psychological harm** – which includes embarrassment and loss of self-esteem, and also changing a person.

- The BPS code of ethics states that participants should experience no risks greater than encountered in their everyday lives.

Strengths and weaknesses of experimental designs

Repeated measures: order effects and counterbalancing

When using repeated measures, if you do Condition A first it might affect your score in Condition B. With staggering originality (but also clarity) this is called an **order effect**. Participants may do better on the second condition because of a *practice effect* OR may do worse on the second condition because of being bored with doing the same test again *(boredom effect)*.

One way to control order effects is to use **counterbalancing** which ensures that each condition is tested first or second in equal amounts. For example:

- Group 1: Participants study with music, do a memory test, study with no music, do a second memory test.
- Group 2: Participants study with no music first, do a memory test, study with music, do a second memory test.

Independent groups and participant variables

With independent groups design there are no order effects, however there is a different problem – **participant variables** are not controlled. It might be that the group of participants who did the no music condition happened to have better memories and this is why that group does better on the memory test (DV).

One way to deal with this is to **randomly allocate** participants to the different groups. Then you can assume that the same number of musically talented/untalented, people with good memories/poor memories, males/females, old/young people are in each group.

Activity

Aim: To investigate the effects of organisation on the recall.

Method 1: independent groups

1. Generate a list of 50 words in categories. For example, select food as one category and then think of four food items (gives you five words: category name plus four category words).
2. Create one version in categories and one version in random order.
3. Randomly allocate participants to the two groups: category list and random word list. Allow them five minutes to study the words and then test their recall.

Method 2: repeated measures

1. Create two lists of 25 words each – one organised in categories and one of a different 25 words in random order.
2. Counterbalance the conditions so that half the participants get the organised list then the random list, and the other half get the random list then the organised list. Give participants five minutes to study all 50 words and then test their recall.

Results for both methods

Calculate the mean number of words remembered in the organised condition and the random condition, and display this in a bar chart.

...Links to other studies and issues...

There are a number of experiments in this book. For example, the study by **Loftus and Palmer**:

- The cue word (smashed, hit, etc) is the IV.
- The estimate of speed is the DV.

Loftus and Palmer found that different cue words caused a difference in the estimate of speed. This causal conclusion is justified as long as the IV was the only thing that was affecting the DV. Were there *extraneous variables*?

Control in experiments

One of the key features of an experiment is control – which comes in various different shapes and sizes:

- *Control of the IV.* The experimenter *controls* the IV to see if changes in the IV lead to changes in the DV. This demonstrates cause-and-effect relationships.

- *Control over extraneous variables.* The experimenter aims to control **extraneous variables** (sometimes also called **confounding variables**). These are any variables other than the IV that might affect the DV. If changes in the DV are due to extraneous variables rather than to the IV, then the conclusions drawn from the experiment may be wrong.

- *Control as baseline.* If an experimenter wishes to find out if listening to music helps study, he (or she) might play music to a group of students and measure their studying (e.g. using a memory test). But how would we know whether the students' performance was better than without music? The experiment needs some form of *comparison line* or *baseline* – a **control condition** or **control group** (depending on whether repeated measures or independent groups design). The **experimental condition** (or **experimental group**) would involve the experimental treatment (in this case music) and the control condition/group involves no treatment (in this case no music). There isn't always a control condition/group. For example, the experiment might have two levels of the IV – rock music and classical music. In this case there are two experimental conditions and no control. The two experimental conditions provide the comparison.

Changes in the dependent variable (DV) may be due to an extraneous variable (EV) rather than being due to the independent variable (IV). Therefore you cannot conclude that the IV affected the DV.

Extraneous variables

Extraneous variables may be classed as **participant variables** or **situational variables**.

Participant variables

Characteristics of individual participants may influence the outcome of a study.

Age, intelligence, motivation, experience

Any personal variables might act as an extraneous variable – but only if an independent groups design is used because then people in one group may be more intelligent, more highly motivated, etc. than the people in the other group. When a repeated measures design is used participant variables are controlled.

One example of a possible extraneous participant variable in the experiment on music and studying might be music experience – participants who never listened to music might be more affected by the music than participants who listened regularly.

Gender

Women and men differ on some behaviours. For example research has shown that women are more compliant than men possibly because they are more oriented to interpersonal goals (Eagly, 1978). This means that if there are more women than men in one condition of an experiment this might mask the effects of the IV. However it is important to realise that gender doesn't always matter so there is no need to control gender unless there is a reason to suspect a gender difference in the behaviour being studied.

Controlling participant variables

Participant variables can be controlled by using repeated measures design – each participant acts as his/her own control.

Alternatively, when using independent groups design, experimenters can randomly allocate participants to groups and it is presumed that participant variables will be evenly distributed.

A further alternative is to use matching (**matched pairs design**) where participants are paired by matching them on key personal variables. This technique was used in the study by Bandura *et al.*

Situational variables

Any feature of a research situation which influences a participant's behaviour acts as a situational extraneous variable.

Order effects

In an experiment using repeated measures design order effects (see page 15) act as an extraneous variable – practice, boredom and fatigue effects.

Time of day, temperature, noise

Many environmental variables may act as extraneous variables but only under the following conditions:

- The variable does affect performance on the behaviour tested, e.g. if the task is a cognitive task and people who are tested in the morning always do better than those tested in the afternoon because people are more alert in the morning.

- The variable does vary systematically with the IV, e.g. participants in group 1 are all tested in the morning and those in group 2 are all tested in the afternoon.

Investigator or experimenter bias

Investigator bias is the term used to describe the effects of an investigator's expectations on a participant's behaviour. Any cues (other than the IV) from an investigator that encourage certain behaviours in the participant leading to a fulfilment of the investigator's expectations will act as an extraneous variable.

For example, an experimenter might be more encouraging on one experimental task so this would explain why participants do better on that task than another task, rather than the IV being responsible. Or an experimenter might be more encouraging to some participants which would explain why they do better. One study found that male experimenters are more pleasant, friendly and encouraging with female participants than male participants (Rosenthal, 1966), which could explain why some gender differences are found.

IN PSYCHOLOGICAL RESEARCH THERE ARE THREE KEY DEMANDS – control, realism and generalisability. The overall aim of any research in psychology is to provide insights into everyday human behaviour i.e. to make generalisations from a research study to everyday life.

Control – lab experiments aim to be highly controlled which means we can be more certain of demonstrating a causal relationship (reduced extraneous variables).

Control ←→ **Realism**

Realism – field experiments tend to be more like everyday life, however the more realistic the setting, the harder it is to control variables.

Generalisability

Generalisability – in order to generalise the findings from an experiment to everyday life, we need control (in order to be confident that it was the IV that changed the DV) and we want realism (so people behave more like they do normally).

Demand characteristics

Demand characteristics are cues in an experimental situation that communicate to participants what is expected of them and may unconsciously affect a participant's behaviour. People always seek cues about how to behave, particularly in a new environment, and particularly if a person knows they are in an experiment. The result is that participants may not behave as they would usually. See page 161 for more on demand characteristics.

Controlling situational variables

Order effects can be controlled by using an independent groups design. Environmental factors such as time of day and temperature etc. are controlled by keeping them constant – for example always conducting a study in the morning or making sure that all participants do the study in the same kind of room conditions.

Controlling investigator effects and demand characteristics is less easy. Some possibilities are:

- **Single blind** participants are not told the true aims of a study. This discourages them from seeking certain cues and altering their behaviour accordingly.
- **Standardised instructions** are a way of controlling investigator effects because they ensure that all participants have the same instructions and no hints can be given.

Different kinds of experiment

There are different kinds of experiment – greater/lesser control, greater /lesser 'realism':

- **Laboratory experiment** A lab is a special environment where causal relationships can be investigated under controlled conditions but such control may mean the set-up is contrived or artificial. Other problems include the fact that participants are aware they are being studied and therefore may respond to **experimenter bias** and **demand characteristics**. Note that some observational studies are conducted in labs.
- **Field experiment** An experiment conducted in a participant's natural environment, which means they may behave more like they do ordinarily. As with the lab experiment, the IV is still deliberately manipulated. However, unlike a lab experiment, in a field experiment participants are often not aware that they are participating in an experiment which again means they may behave more naturally. Note that a field *study* – as distinct from a field experiment – is a study conducted in a natural environment where no IV has been manipulated.
- **Natural** or **quasi-experiment** In a natural experiment, the experimenter does not manipulate the IV but takes advantage of a naturally varying IV. The reason for this is that there are some IVs that cannot be manipulated for practical or ethical reasons (such as giving a child a frightening experience to see what effect this has on development). The effects of the IV on the DV can be observed by the experimenter. Strictly speaking an experiment involves the deliberate manipulation of an IV by an experimenter, therefore natural experiments are not 'true experiments' (they are called *quasi-experiments*) because no one has deliberately changed the IV to observe the effect on the DV.

Qs

1   An experiment is conducted to investigate whether only children do better at school than children who have one or more siblings.
   a. Identify the IV and the DV in this experiment, and state how each could be operationalised.
   b. Suggest a suitable two-tailed hypothesis for this study.
   c. What kind of experimental design would be used – repeated measures or independent groups?
   d. Suggest **two** extraneous variables that you would need to control.
   e. Briefly describe how you would conduct the experiment.
2   Another psychological study looks at the effect of eating chocolate on moods
   a. Describe how you could investigate this by doing an experiment with a repeated measures design.
   b. How might experimenter bias affect the results of this study?
   c. Describe how demand characteristics might affect the results of this study.
   d. Describe how you could study this topic using a method other than an experiment.

Evaluating experimental techniques

On this spread we will consider some issues related to the value of experimental research and suggest some further activities for you to try.

Reliability

Experiments involve measurement of some kind. For example, in the experiment on music and studying, we decided to measure 'studying' by giving participants something to learn and testing their memory. In this case we would be concerned about the reliability of the memory test and the same considerations would apply as for any self-report measure, and we could assess this using the **test-retest method** (see page 12).

Alternatively we might simply have observed participants' behaviour when studying to see if it differed when studying with or without music. The IV would remain the same but in this case the DV might be a count of how often each participant looked away from their books. Reliability would be concerned with the consistency of the observations and, as in any observational study we could assess this using **inter-rater reliability** (see page 6).

Validity

The validity of measurements concerns whether an experimenter was testing what he/she intended to test. For example, you might decide to measure helping behaviour by dropping your scarf and seeing how long it took for people to pick it up in two different situations. Would this really test helping behaviour? If your answer is no, then the measurement lacks validity.

Another aspect of 'testing what an experimenter intended to test' concerns control. If an experimenter fails to control extraneous variables then changes in the DV may not be due to changes in the IV. This means that the findings would lack validity – the experimenter might claim a causal link was demonstrated between IV and DV but this would not be true.

A third issue concerns **ecological validity**, the extent to which the findings of a study can be generalised to everyday life. This is determined by a mixture of control, realism and participants' awareness of being studied. Ecological validity is discussed further on page 131.

Replication

One of the strengths of the experimental method is that experiments can be repeated because the procedures are well controlled. This is a way of demonstrating both reliability and validity. If an experiment is conducted again and produces the same result this suggests the original result was 'true' (i.e. did demonstrate a truth about human behaviour).

Strengths and weaknesses of conducting experiments

Lab experiments

☺	Manipulation of IV to observe effects on DV means causal relationships can be demonstrated.	☹	Artificial, contrived situation which may lack realism and participants may respond to experimenter's cues. This may mean that findings cannot be generalised to everyday life (low ecological validity).
☺	Well controlled, thus extraneous variables are minimised which increases certainty that IV did cause change in DV (high validity).	☹	Other problems may also affect generalisability, e.g. sample bias.

Field experiments

☺	IV manipulated therefore cause-and-effect may be demonstrated.	☹	Less control of extraneous variables, so you can't be sure that changes in the DV are due to changes in the IV (low validity).
☺	More natural environment and less awareness of being studied, thus higher ecological validity.	☹	Sampling can still be a problem.

Natural experiments

☺	Enables psychologists to study 'real' problems such as the effects of disaster on health (increased ecological validity).	☹	Cannot demonstrate causal relationships because IV not directly manipulated.
		☹	Participants may be aware of being studied, reduces naturalness.

Qs

1 A study by Rosenthal and Jacobsen is described on the right.

   a Write a suitable one-tailed alternate hypothesis for this study.

   b Name the experimental design used in this experiment and give **one** strength of using this design in this study.

   c Would it be possible to use an alternative experimental design? Explain your answer.

   d Describe **two** reasons why the validity of this study might be low.

   e How was the dependent variable measured?

   f Explain how you could check the reliability of this measurement.

2 A natural experiment by Charlton et al. is also described on the right.

   a One way of assessing the dependent variable (aggressiveness) would be to observe children during free play sessions at school. Describe how you would check the reliability of this measurement.

   b Suggest **one** other way to measure the DV.

3. Select one of the ideas for conducting your own experiment on the far right.

   a Suggest **two** controls that could be used in this experiment and state what you would be controlling.

   b What are the strengths and weaknesses of the use of control in your chosen study?

   c Evaluate the problems of **not** controlling variables in experimental research using examples of psychological studies other than the one you have chosen.

EXPERIMENT

Examples of experiments

Lab experiment

On the previous spread we looked at investigator/experimenter bias. One of the classic studies that demonstrated this was conducted with university students and rats! Rosenthal and Fode (1963) asked the students to train rats to learn their way around a maze. They were told that one group of rats was bred to be 'fast learners', whilst the others were 'slow learners'. In fact there were no differences between the rats – they had been randomly allocated to the conditions of maze bright and maze dull. Nevertheless the supposedly brighter rats actually learned more quickly. The only explanation can be that the students communicated their expectations to the rats' in subtle ways and this affected the rats' performance, an example of experimenter bias.

Field experiment

Rosenthal conducted other research on experimenter bias including another classic study sometimes referred to as *Pygmalion in the classroom* (Rosenthal and Jacobsen, 1966). This time the participants were teachers in a primary school. At the beginning of one school year the teachers were told that some of the pupils in each class were 'bloomers' – children whose IQs suggested they could be doing a lot better than they were. The children identified as bloomers had been selected randomly (i.e. they were actually no different to the other students). However, when all the children were assessed at the end of the year the bloomers had higher IQ gains than their classmates. This has been called the 'self-fulfilling prophecy' – things may turn out as you expected, not because you were right in your expectations but because your expectations altered subsequent events.

Natural experiment

This time we're looking at a different topic – TV and aggressiveness. Many people blame rising levels of aggressive behaviour on the fact that people watch a lot of violence on TV. Is increased aggression due to the TV? One way to investigate this is to take advantage of the fact that some communities in the world have only fairly recently received TV for the first time. One such community was the tiny island of St. Helena (47 square miles) in the Atlantic who tuned in to the likes of *The A team* for the first time 1995 (Charlton *et al.*, 2000). Before and after comparisons were made to see what affect the advent of TV had on the behaviour of children living there – therefore the IV is 'no TV' and 'TV', an IV that was not controlled by the experimenters but a naturally varying one that they took advantage of.

The vast majority of the measures used to assess anti-social behaviour showed no differences after the introduction of television. This outcome may be explained in terms of social norms. In St. Helena there was a community with a strong sense of identity and no reason to be aggressive whereas this is not the case in other communities where TV has been introduced and more anti-social behaviour was displayed.

Ideas for your own experiments

Are you only as good as your last CD?

There are two schools of thought as far as impression formation goes. One view is that people make up their minds about you as soon as they meet you and such impressions are quite enduring (a *primacy effect*). The other view is that what counts most is whatever you did more recently (people say 'he is only as good as his last CD' – a *recency effect*). A classic study by Solomon Asch (1946) looked at the primacy and recent effect in a lab experiment. Some participants were given a list of adjectives that described a target person: *intelligent, industrious, impulsive, critical, stubborn, envious*. Other participants were given the same list but in reverse order. All participants were asked to fill in a rating sheet to evaluate the target person – for example they were asked to rate how happy, sociable etc. the person was. The first group gave higher ratings presumably because their list started with positive descriptions, thus supporting a primacy effect. However other studies have found recency effects, for example Luchins (1957).

Smiling makes you happy

You might think that you smile because you are feeling happy but psychological research shows it works the other way round too. If you ask someone to tighten certain facial muscles (essentially making them smile) people say they feel happier and also rate cartoons as more funny, as shown in a study by Laird (1974) who told participants he was measuring facial muscular activity, attaching surface electrodes to participants' faces between their eyebrows, at the corners of their mouths, and on their jaws. Then participants were asked to contract their muscles at these points. By using this procedure, Laird was able, without ever mentioning an emotion or an emotional expression, to induce participants to either smile or frown. You obviously can't use electrodes but you can do a similar experiment just asking people to smile (or not) and then see if they rate cartoons as being funnier.

Right brain left brain

If you perform two tasks that occupy your left hemisphere you should be slower than when doing two tasks that involve separate hemispheres. Participants should tap their right finger while reading a page from a book (both involve left hemisphere) and repeat the same task without reading. Count the number of taps in 30 seconds in both conditions. You should counterbalance conditions.

...Links to other studies and issues...

Experiments are still the most common method used by psychologists so it is no surprise that many of the core studies use this method. Interestingly the **Milgram** study is commonly referred to as an experiment but is really a demonstration of obedience because it doesn't manipulate any independent variable.

Lab experiments: **Loftus and Palmer** (eyewitness testimony), **Baron-Cohen** *et al.* (autism), **Samuel and Bryant** (conservation), all use true experiments. The study by **McGuire** *et al.* compares the brains of taxi drivers with other drivers. And although the Bobo study (**Bandura** *et al.*) is often described as an observation it tests some tightly controlled experimental hypotheses.

Field experiments: The study by **Piliavin** *et al.* (subway Samaritan) is an example of a field experiment.

Natural/quasi experiments: The study by **Sperry** (split brain) is an example of a quasi experiment because you obviously can't allocate people randomly to the split-brain/whole brain conditions. No really, you can't.

Correlation

A correlation is a way of measuring the relationship between two variables.

Age and beauty co-vary. As people get older they become more beautiful. This is a **positive correlation** because the two variables increase together.

You may disagree and think that as people get older they become less attractive. You think age and beauty are correlated but it is a **negative correlation**. As one variable increases the other one decreases.

Or you may simply feel that there is no relationship between age and beauty (a **zero correlation**).

Activity

Assertiveness and watching TV

Aim
To see whether watching TV is related to assertiveness (because many programmes encourage such behaviour).

Method
You need to obtain two pieces of data from everyone in your class:

1   The number of hours they watched TV in the last 48 hours (presuming that the more TV watched, the more 'assertive' programmes were watched).

2   An 'assertiveness' score – each person should rate themselves (or be rated by someone else) on a scale of 1 to 10 where 10 is very assertive. Alternatively there's a short assertiveness quiz at http://www.queendom.com/tests/access_page/index.htm?idRegTest=675.

Results
Plot the scores for each person on a scattergraph.

Calculate a correlation coefficient to assess the strength of the correlation (see the Excel method, below).

You can collect both quantitative and qualitative data using observation or self-report techniques. In an experiment or correlation the data is strictly quantitative – though you can also collect qualitative data as part of the study, such as asking participants to comment on their experience (as Milgram did).

Scattergraphs

A **scattergraph** is a graph that shows the correlation between two sets of data (or **co-variables**) by plotting dots to represent each pair of scores. For each individual we obtain a score for each **co-variable**, in our case the **co-variables** are age and beauty.

The extent of a correlation is described using a **correlation coefficient**. This is a number between +1 and –1, +1 is a perfect positive correlation and –1 is a perfect negative correlation.

The correlation coefficients for the graphs on the right are .76, –.76 and +.002

The plus or minus sign shows whether it is a positive or negative correlation. The coefficient (number) tells us how closely the co-variables are related. –.76 is just as closely correlated as +.76, it's just that –.76 means that as one variable increases the other decreases (negative correlation), and +.76 means that both variables increase together (positive correlation).

Qs

A class of psychology students want to investigate whether there is any relationship between how hungry you feel and how good the food you are about to eat looks!

1   Write a suitable one-tailed hypothesis for this study.

2   In order to assess hunger the students devise a rating scale. Give an example of what this rating scale might look like.

3   Describe **one** problem with measuring hunger in this way.

4   The students find a strong positive correlation between the co-variables. Sketch a graph to show what this should look like.

5   One of the students concludes that hunger must have caused the food to look better. What is wrong with this conclusion?

6   Describe **one** ethical issue that might arise in conducting this study and say how it could be dealt with.

Strong or weak?

The benefit of using graphs to represent data is that you can 'eyeball' the results – you can see at a glance whether there is a strong or a weak correlation between co-variables. You may be asked, in the exam, to comment on the kind of relationship shown in a scattergraph and can use the table on the right to help you.

In order to get a 'feel' for scattergraphs and correlation coefficients you might have a go at constructing scattergraphs and seeing what correlation coefficients are produced. You can do this with the Excel method below or there are also a number of websites where you can enter data and a scattergraph will be produced with the correlation coefficient for you – try the excellent http://www.stattucino.com/berrie/dsl/regression/regression.html.

The closer a correlation is to 1 the stronger it is (remember the sign doesn't matter, +1 or as strong as –1)

Correlation coefficient	Type of correlation
1.0	Perfect
.80	strong
.50	moderate
.30	weak
.10	very weak

Activity

Playing with correlation coefficients: The Excel method

Using Excel (the Microsoft Office application) you can enter and alter pairs of numbers to see how this affects a scattergraph and correlation coefficient. Both are produced by Excel:

1   *Open a new document (select file new blank workbook).*

2   *Select insert chart XY (scatter) and press next.*

3   *Place cursor at very top left of the page, click and drag across 2 rows and then down 16 rows. Press next next finish.*

4   *Now enter your pairs of scores (these can be invented or you could try entering a real set of numbers to see if they are correlated – such as height and shoe size). Do not enter data in top row.*

5   *To calculate correlation coefficient: Place the cursor in an empty box. Select insert function. In top box type 'correl' and press 'go' and then OK.*

6   *Screen now says 'array1' and 'array2'. Click in 'array1' and then move cursor to top of first column of your numbers, click and drag to bottom of column. Do the same for array2.*

7   *Try changing some of the numbers and see how this alters your scattergraph and the correlation coefficient.*

The top graph illustrates a positive correlation. The middle graph shows a negative correlation. The bottom graph is an example of very little correlation.

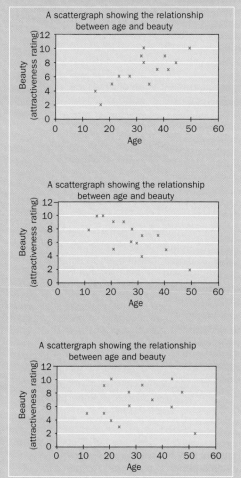

A scattergraph showing the relationship between age and beauty

A scattergraph showing the relationship between age and beauty

A scattergraph showing the relationship between age and beauty

Strengths and weaknesses of using correlational analysis

Strengths
☺ Can be used when it would be unethical or impractical to conduct an experiment.
☺ If correlation is significant then further investigation is justified.
☺ If correlation is not significant then you can rule out a causal relationship.

Weaknesses
☹ People often misinterpret correlations and assume that a cause and effect have been found whereas this is not possible.
☹ There may be other, unknown (intervening) variable(s) that can explain why the co-variables being studied are linked. For example, research studies have shown a positive correlation between amount of TV watched and aggressiveness. However it is wrong to conclude that watching TV is directly related to aggressiveness because it could be that a low boredom threshold was the cause of both of them, an intervening factor.
☹ Extraneous variables can lead to false conclusions. For example, the reason why watching TV is linked to aggressiveness may be because people who have aggressive tendencies do respond to TV in this way. Thus personality is acting as an extraneous variable.

Qs

A psychological study investigates whether there is a relationship between how well students do in exams and how highly motivated the students are, in order to see if motivation and performance are linked. Motivation is measured by assessing how much the students participate in class (for example, counting how often they answer a question in class or how much of class time is spent working).

1 Suggest **one** difficulty that might arise with the way class participation has been assessed.
2 Suggest a different way to assess motivation.
3 Describe how you could use time sampling to assess class participation, and give **one** strength of using this instead of event sampling.
4 At the end the researchers plot a scattergraph of average exam scores and level of motivation. Their graph looks like the one at top left. What would you conclude from this?

Ideas for your own investigations

Finger length
A number of studies have investigated the correlation between finger length and other factors. For example, Bailey and Hurd (2005) found that the shorter the index (pointing) finger is compared to the ring finger, the more physically aggressive a man will be. Another study (Brosnan et al., in press) found a positive correlation between children's scores on numeracy and literacy tests and the relative lengths of their index and ring fingers. The reason for this seemingly inexplicable link is that during prenatal development hormones have an effect on brain development and on finger length, therefore brain development and finger length are associated via this intervening variable.

IQ
There are many IQ tests on the internet (see, for example, http://www.queendom.com) and scores could be correlated with memory (give participants a word list to learn and test recall the next day), or with reaction time, or anything else you can think of. You can test reaction time using a metre ruler – one person stands on a chair holding the ruler in the air while the second person loosely holds the lower end. When person 1 drops the ruler and says 'Grab', person 2 has to grab it. The point at which the ruler is clasped equals reaction time. Alternatively go to http://mindbluff.com/reaction.htm.

...Links to other studies and issues...

Correlational analyses are commonly used in applied research. This is because it is often not possible to carry out controlled experiments in applied settings. For example, studies on health can't put people in health damaging situations but they can look at whether where someone lives can predict their long-term health (it does) or whether smoking 20 cigarettes a day is associated with shorter life span and more amputations (it is). Applied research is more the focus in A2 on this course and on the AS the chosen studies don't use correlation extensively.

One example is **Maguire et al.** who demonstrated the relationship between parts of the brain and highly developed spatial memories in London taxi drivers. They did this by correlating volume of brain matter with time spent as a taxi driver, and found a positive correlation in one region of the brain (the right posterior hippocampus) and a negative correlation in another region of the brain (the anterior hippocampus).

Another example comes from the study by **Dement and Kleitman** who correlated the length of REM episode with the number of words a person used to describe the dream experienced in that REM episode. The correlations were all positive and ranged between .40 and .71 for each participant.

Key issue: psychology as science

A debate that creates a lot of passion is whether psychology is a science. You might well ask whether this actually matters. Psychology is the study of human behaviour and experience and whether we call it a science or not seems to be largely irrelevant. However it does matter because psychologists want to place themselves alongside physical scientists like physicists and biologists rather than social commentators and authors such as journalists and novelists. All these people are trying to tell us about what it means to be human and how we can best understand our lives. The issue is where they get their information and how they construct their argument.

> **Science** is the observation, identification, description, empirical investigation, and theoretical explanation of phenomena.
>
> **Pseudoscience** is defined as scientifically testable ideas that are taken on faith, even if tested and shown to be false.

What is science?

The word science comes from the Latin word for knowledge. It is commonly taken to mean 'the observation, identification, description, empirical investigation, and theoretical explanation of phenomena'. Science is commonly divided into two classes, the natural sciences such as biology, physics and chemistry, which study natural phenomena, and the social sciences such as sociology, economics and anthropology, which study human behaviour and societies.

Psychology falls into both of these categories but commonly prefers to align itself with the natural sciences rather than the social sciences. This is for two reasons. First there is a long tradition in psychology of carrying out controlled laboratory experiments and if anything this work is expanding today rather than declining. The work of cognitive neuropsychologists in scanning brains (see for example the MacGuire study) is very close to medicine and biology. The second reason for aligning with natural science is more practical than theoretical in that there is more money available for science in universities and science students are funded at a higher level than social science students.

At one extreme of psychology, then, we have neuroscientists trying to map behaviour and thought to structures in the brain. At the other we have qualitative psychologists, such as discourse analysts, looking at text and conversation to try and interpret meanings. Some would argue that this latter type of psychology does not fall into the scientific tradition and has more in common with the type of critical analysis that is used to understand Shakespeare. At the moment however, most psychology departments in UK universities are able to happily contain both ends of this wide range of psychological research.

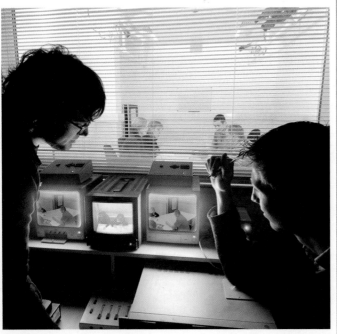

A modern psychology laboratory where group discussions are observed and recorded.

Activity

Draw up a table with two columns: science and pseudo-science.

Put as many entries as you can into each column. To get started put the following terms into the box you think is most appropriate; astrology, medicine, acupuncture, water divining, mind reading, geology, regression therapy (taking someone back to a previous life through hypnosis).

The scientific method

The distinguishing feature of science is how it gathers and interprets its evidence. The key to scientific enquiry is to be empirical. This means that we have to gather evidence that is open to scrutiny, is preferably replicable (we can repeat the study to get similar results) and is falsifiable. This last point sounds strange at first glance but is actually very important.

Science progresses in small steps. We are not able to prove anything, but only to come up with theories that offer the best explanation of the phenomena we observe. If we obtain new information in the future we might well find that there is a better explanation and so we then discard our original theory. Scientists have been aware of this for centuries; Isaac Newton, probably the UK's greatest scientist, famously wrote in a letter to Robert Hooke (of Hooke's law for the physicists) in 1676 *If I have seen farther it is by standing on the shoulders of Giants.'*

Knowledge is provisional. This means that we are not uncovering the truth but that we are inching our way to new understandings. What we 'know' today will be the chip paper of tomorrow. Newton's law of gravity is an example of this. The shock of being hit on the head by an apple helped Newton devise his law which stood for more than 200 years, until a better understanding of the movement of objects in the universe was devised by Einstein in his theory of general relativity. Our psychological theories can not expect to last as long as Newton's laws.

If we want our science to progress then we have to accept that what we believe to be true today might well be shown to be not true tomorrow. Our theories therefore have to allow for the possibility of disproof. One of the criticisms of the theories of Sigmund Freud are that they are not open to disproof. Psychoanalysis can seem to explain anything and there is no test that can be carried out that could possibly disprove the ideas. Being able to disprove a theory (*falsifiability*) is an important criteria of science.

The experimental method is often referred to as the cornerstone of science. It is what most people think of when they think of science, and the method is described on pages 14–19. However, it is not the only way to collect and analyse data in a scientific way, and research is accepted as being scientific as long as it follows the criteria described above.

Images of science

Science has been seen in different ways by the general public though there are common threads of awe and fear that run through those perceptions. We are amazed at the creativity of scientists to come up with new ideas, their intelligence to work through those ideas and test them and their ability to talk in a language that very few people can understand. On the fear side we have the recurrent image of the mad scientist who goes out of control and invents the nuclear disintegrator bomb and sits cackling in a corner as destruction is rained down on the innocents. Alongside this paranoia is a more realistic concern about the uses of science and whether scientists are taking account of the possible impact of their discoveries.

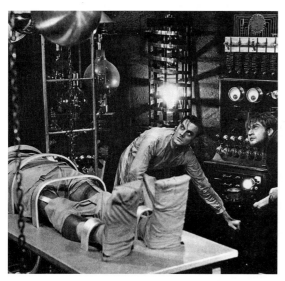

A common view of scientists is that they are brilliant but a little mad. We seem to fear that a Frankenstein is hiding behind every Einstein.

Science in psychology

The most common public image of psychologists is of the therapists and psychobabblers who appear on daytime television. The perceptions that come from this include (a) psychologists are a bunch of vacuous fame-seekers, and (b) psychology is mainly concerned with how we feel about our appearance and whether we can read body language. However, the tradition of psychology in universities is very different and most departments have a range of specialist laboratories and special kit to carry out controlled empirical studies. This kit includes brain scanners (page 112), eyetrackers (page 63), gaming labs and computer suites.

Science and pseudoscience

Science is a way of collecting knowledge about the world we live in that uses objective, verifiable methods and builds up coherent theories. It rolls back the clouds of superstition and ignorance to give us understanding and control of the world. Pseudoscience appears to use the techniques of science but does not produce verifiable evidence. Pseudoscience can be identified because it:

* Makes claims that cannot be verified.
* Makes claims that are not connected to previous research.
* Does not submit the data for review by other scientists.

Unfortunately, psychology is not free of pseudoscience though it is sometimes a matter of opinion as to which category some research falls into. For example, some suggest that Neuro-Linguistic Programming (NLP) has absolutely nothing to do with theories of biology (neuro), language (linguistic) or computers (programming), however NLP claims to be scientific and sells a lot of books. We leave it for you to decide, but beware of the fakers and charlatans.

Examples of pseudoscience

* Graphology: interpreting personality from samples of handwriting (see the Barnum Effect on page 221).
* Reiki therapy: the healing massage of spiritual energies without ever touching the body.
* Clairvoyance: predicting future events, though failing to make bucketloadsfull of money by selecting the right numbers in next week's lottery.
* Homeopathy: the multi million pound business of selling coloured water to the gullible.

Astrology: the art of convincing people that you can join the dots in the sky to make animal shapes, and that these animals will affect your day to day life like whether your piles will get better this week.

...Links to other studies and issues...

Many of the core studies use the experimental method, for example the Bobo study (**Bandura et al**) is a controlled experiment where variables are systematically manipulated and data recorded in a set and repeatable format. The work of **Maguire et al.** on brain scanning uses fancy technical equipment to compare the differences in brain structure between two different groups of people. A small number of the studies are more on the edge of what we think science is. For example the case study of Eve (**Thigpen and Cleckley**) collects data in a systematic way as a medical case history but the very personal nature of the record means that it is difficult to verify the data. The idea that people can have more than one personality remains controversial to this day.

There are also many links to the other issues, in particular **Being sceptical** which asks you to weigh up the information you are given. Things are often not what they seem and just because someone says they have scientific evidence it does not mean we should automatically believe everything they tell us. The scientific method is closely linked to **reductionism** as this forensic way of looking at problems is the most common way that scientists approach their work.

Qs

1 Select **one** core study and identify what parts of the scientific method are present and / or absent.

2 The work of Freud is often said to be unscientific though psychoanalysts claim that the theory is a scientific one. Look at the criteria of science (see 'The scientific method' on the left) and judge to what extent we can say that Freud's theory is scientific.

3 Is using the scientific method enough for work to be scientific? Describe **two** examples of work that uses scientific methods but can not be said to be scientific.

4 The natural sciences (physics, chemistry and biology) study natural phenomena. Is psychology a natural science? If so why? If not, why not?

Exam questions and answers

The example exam questions here are set out like the exam but there aren't as many. In the exam the total number of marks will be 60.

Section A

An experiment is designed to find out whether people like a product name because it is familiar. Participants were given a list of invented product names to read out loud. Some of the names appeared 10 times in the list whereas others only appeared once. After reading the list participants were asked to rate how much they liked each of the words on a rating scale from 1 to 10 where 10 represents 'like it a lot' and 1 is 'don't like it at all'. This was a repeated measures design.

The results are shown in the graph on the right.

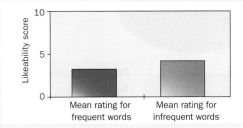

Bar chart showing mean ratings for likeability

1   Identify the independent variable and the dependent variable in this study.   [2]

Stig's answer

The IV is the words and the DV is rating.

Chardonnay's answer

The independent variable is whether the words were familiar or not, and the DV was the ratings for likeability given to the words.

Examiner's comments

Stig, you are a man of few words. Given that the question is only worth 2 marks your answers are not sufficient for any marks. You need to at least say 'frequency' of words to get 1 mark for the IV and some extra detail of the rating (e.g. 'rating of *likeability*' to get 1 mark for the DV. Chardonnay has given an operationalised description of each of the variables. Take care Stig, brevity is a dangerous course of action.

Stig (0 marks) Chardonnay (2 marks)

2   Outline **two** conclusions that could be drawn from the graph.   [4]

Stig's answer

One conclusion is that people didn't seem to like the words much at all. A second conclusion is that they liked the frequent words more.

Chardonnay's answer

1   You could conclude from the graph that in fact people actually like the infrequent words, on average, more than the frequent ones.
2   You could also conclude that this shows that people don't necessarily like things because they are familiar.

Examiner's comments

The question requires two conclusions which both students have provided. There are no marks for 'elegance' though Chardonnay's presentation makes for easier reading.

Stig, here each conclusion is worth two marks so brevity will be penalised. Neither of your conclusions will be worth 2 marks because they are each lacking detail. Your first answer is an unusual conclusion but actually a fair conclusion – the mean ratings for both groups of words were low. You would need to spell this out for full marks,

Chardonnay is again scooping up the marks with a thorough and clearly expressed answer.

Stig (2 marks) Chardonnay (4 marks)

3   The sampling method used was a self-selected sample. Suggest **one** strength and **one** weakness of the sampling method used in this study.   [6]

Stig's answer

The strength of a self-selected sample is that it is easy to obtain because people volunteer. The weakness is that you may get a biased sample because you only ask certain kinds of people (those who volunteer).

Chardonnay's answer

The strength of choosing this method was to get those people who would really want to take part so hopefully they would really think about the task. This is quite important when asking participants to rate something like likeability because they could just write anything. The weakness of choosing this method is that volunteers are not typical of all other people, they are possibly more highly motivated and more willing to please so the students who volunteered in this study might have tried to guess what the researcher wanted and realised it was to do with familiarity.

Examiner's comments

Stig, this is quite a short answer. You have essentially identified one strength and one weakness but you have not elaborated or explained further. Most importantly neither strength or weakness has been related to the study, as required by the question.

Chardonnay, for each strength and weakness you have identified it, explained it a little bit further and also, crucially, related it to the study. Generally speaking, if the question mentions 'in the study', you do have to ensure the answer is framed within the context of the study and not just any study!

Stig (1+1 marks) Chardonnay (3+3 marks)

Section B

An observational study was conducted of the behaviour of children in a school playground. Two researchers kept a record of acts of aggression by boys and girls using time sampling. They recorded a total of 43 acts by boys and 23 by girls.

1   Produce an appropriate summary table for this data.   [2]

Stig's answer

Aggressive acts

Boys	Girls
43	23

Chardonnay's answer

Table showing aggressive acts observed in a school playground

	Boys	Girls
Number of aggressive acts	43	23

Examiner's comments

You have drawn a table, Stig, and put the data in correctly but some important details are missing, as you can see if you look at Chardonnay's table. Maybe you thought the question just meant 'fill the data in a table', but the titles are an integral part of any table.

Stig (1 mark) Chardonnay (2 marks)

2   Suggest **one** problem with using time sampling in this study.   [3]

Stig's answer

It is difficult to do because there is so much you have to look at and you might not get it right.

Chardonnay's answer

The difficulty with time sampling is that at each observational moment you have to make a note of what all the children are doing and if there was a lot of children in the playground you could easily miss out some of the children which means that your observations wouldn't be very accurate.

Examiner's comments

Stig, it's good to be to the point and long answers are not always the best ones – but a bit too brief again here! Your answer suggests a good understanding but you need to explain yourself more clearly so the examiner can see that you do understand. For example, 'there is so much you have to look at' – what is the 'so much' you have to look at? And what do you mean by 'get it right'? Presumably you are talking about making an accurate record. Just a little more care would have meant a lot more marks.

Chardonnay, being the thorough student that you are, you have provided loads of detail and wisely used an example to aid your explanation.

Stig (1 mark) Chardonnay (3 marks)

3   How could the researcher check the reliability of the observations?   [3]

Stig's answer

One way to check the observations would be to use inter-rater reliability which means that you correlate each set of observations from each of the observers and the agreement should be better than 80%.

Chardonnay's answer

Reliability means how consistent you are. Reliability can be checked by looking at the observations made by both of the observers and seeing how much they agree with each other. They should agree with each other most of the time to show consistency.

Examiner's comments

Stig, you have finally outdone Chardonnay. Both of you have given clear answers but Stig has remembered the technical term, 'inter-rater reliability' and also remembered the level of agreement that would be expected. Such information adds up to a detailed response. Well done!

However, don't despair Chardonnay. You may not have produced the technical details but your answer shows a good knowledge of how reliability could be checked. You start off badly by providing general information about reliability – focused on 'what' instead of 'how' but sentences 2 and 3 are appropriate.

Stig (3 marks) Chardonnay (2 marks)

Section C

You have been asked to produce a questionnaire investigating the relationship between stress and health.

1   Outline the procedure you could use for collecting data.   [4]

Stig's answer

I could use a questionnaire from the internet on stress and then ask people how many times they were off school to measure their health. I would print 20 copies of this questionnaire and add some instructions for the participants about what to do, asking for their consent.

I would then give the questionnaires out to a range of people I know so that I got a good range of ages and both males and females. I would thank them for taking part at the end and ask if they had any further questions.

Chardonnay's answer

For this study I would create a structured questionnaire containing 20 questions, some open and some closed. The questions would be about how much stress people felt they were experiencing and also about their health (or illness). I would conduct a small pilot study to check that the questions were clear and make any changes necessary and then give the questionnaires out to a lot of different people. I would approach people and ask them if they could spare 10 minutes for my psychology project. I would then further explain the aim of the project to respondents so they could give their informed consent.

Examiner's comments

Stig, you have covered the basics of your procedure, but there are some details which would prevent me from replicating your study. Incidentally, a good way of checking your procedure is to get a friend to read it and see if they feel they could conduct a perfect replication of your study. If not, there is something missing and you will not get full marks. Here, I do not know where your respondents filled in the questionnaire, whether they were on their own or in groups, whether you gave them a time limit or not. As I do not have access to the questionnaire, it also might be useful if you gave a quick summary of the instructions!

Chardonnay, this is a good answer, covering all the main details to allow replication. You have included information given to the participants, location, time taken as well as the step-by-step information.

Stig (2 marks) Chardonnay (4 marks)

2   (a) Suggest an alternative way of measuring each of your variables.   [4]

    (b) Explain the effect these changes may have on your results.   [3]

Stig's answer

(a) I could have measured stress using a different questionnaire. Perhaps it might be a questionnaire for adolescents instead of one for adults which would have been more valid if I was just questioning adolescents. I could measure health by asking more detailed questions than just asking how many times people had been off school.

(b) The effect might have been to produce a different result. I might have found a correlation between the two variables because stress was measured more validly and because health was assessed more exactly.

Chardonnay's answer

(a) I could have measured stress by testing people's physiological reactions, such as blood pressure etc. I could have measured health also using objective physiological measures such as getting people to run on the spot and seeing how long it takes for blood pressure to return to normal.

(b) Physiological measures would be more objective and therefore you might get more valid data.

Examiner's comments

Stig – the alternative you suggest in (a) is plausible and in sufficient detail for the marks available. Your part (b) answer is fine, just not quite sufficient for three marks as you have not referred to how your changes might impact on the results, for example by saying that you might have found a *stronger* correlation with more precise variables.

Chardonnay, your part (a) is lacking some important details. The idea of measuring stress by taking blood pressure is good but you need to explain why, e.g. add 'People who are more stressed have higher blood pressure'. Your answer for part (b) is sound but too brief and again you have not related your answer to the effect the changes would have on the results.

Stig (4+2 marks) Chardonnay (3+1 marks)

3   Describe what psychologists mean by the term validity.   [2]

Stig's answer

It means that the psychologist found out what he was hoping to find out. The results were what he had predicted.

Chardonnay's answer

Validity means how true the results are. Are they really what happens in everyday life or did some aspect of the study mean that the results are meaningless. Validity is about whether you are testing what you meant to test.

Examiner's comments

Stig, this is not the right answer at all!

Chardonnay, you have got round to the right answer in the end (validity refers to whether you are measuring what you claim to be). Also, you have referred to a form of validity (ecological validity), by way of expansion. Thus, you have done (just) enough for two marks.

Stig (0 marks) Chardonnay (2 marks)

CHAPTER 2

This chapter looks at three core studies in cognitive psychology.

- Loftus and Palmer's work on memory for events.

- Baron-Cohen, Joliffe, Mortimer and Robertson's study of the thought processes of autistic adults.

- Savage-Rumbaugh, McDonal, Sevcik, Hopkins and Rupert's observations of chimpanzees experience of acquiring human language.

Cognitive psychology

Introduction to cognitive psychology

What is cognitive psychology?

Cognitive psychology is the study of all mental processes:

- How do we see the world?
- How do we store and recall information?
- How do we communicate?
- How do we think?

Cognitive psychology takes a mechanistic approach, which means that it largely looks at people as if they are machines. Modern research looks at human cognitive processes and compares them to those of a computer. Computers can do several of the things that people can do, and they can do some of them better. They can respond to the environment, store information, calculate and much more.

Activity

How do we see?

Think about these puzzles:

- Your eyes are moving all the time (stare into a friend's eyes to check this out) but your view of the world is stable.
- The screen at the back of your eye (the retina) is flat, but you see the world in 3D.
- The image on the retina is upside down and back to front, but you see things the right way round.
- Light never reaches the brain. It hits the back of the eye (the retina) and is transferred to your brains as electro-chemical messages.

Is the eye like a camera?

Yes and no. A diagram of the eye shows that it looks like a camera. It has a lens and a screen to collect the light, but if you could capture the images that appear on the retina they would not look like anything you would recognise. The eye is the first line of our battle to make sense of the world. It does not just record the information that comes in, it starts to interpret it. You might think of it as a bit of brain on a stick rather than a camera.

The puzzles of cognitive psychology

Making sense of the world is something we take for granted. Most of us are able to see, hear, think, taste, talk and listen (though many of us struggle a bit with the listening). But how do we do this? And what do we mean by seeing and hearing and thinking? In the items on these pages we are not trying to give you all the answers to these questions but merely trying to show you what the puzzle is. The more you think about it the more puzzling it becomes.

Take sound for example. What is it? If you did school physics then you'll know that our ears respond to changes in air pressure. These changes in air pressure are experienced by us as sound. You might well have come across the riddle 'if a tree falls in a forest and no one is there to hear it, does it make a sound?'. Certainly it creates some changes in air pressure but the experience of sound is your response to these changes so we would argue that the answer is no. Sound is in your head and is created by you. It's remarkable and almost unbelievable.

Sensation and perception

What is the difference between the physical stimuli that hit us (like light and sound) and the images that appear in our minds? The physical stimuli create *sensations* in our sense organs but we then use these sensations to create our *perceptions* of the world. We say that 'seeing is believing' but is what we see sometimes the invention of our minds? And are some of our memories also part invention?

Look at the two rows of characters. If you read the top row they are clearly all letters, and if you read the bottom row then it is a sequence of numbers. Look again and you will see that the second figure from the left in both rows is exactly the same. So what is it? The letter 'B' or the number '13'? In fact, it is neither and it is both. You understand the character

not just by the shape that you sense but also the meaning you perceive it to have. Your perception of the object is affected by the sensation the shape makes on your eye but this sensation is added to and interpreted by you to give it meaning.

The figure and ground phenomenon

We perceive one part of an event as the *figure* and the other as the *ground*. Edgar Rubin demonstrated the phenomenon by creating his classic example of an ambiguous figure–ground situation. In Rubin's figure, there is no *true* figure and ground. We can either see the dark piece as background in which case we see two faces, or we can see it as an object in which case we see a vase. We can't see both at the same time. Our perception makes sense of this figure and of the world by deciding what is figure and what is background.

This is the feature of perception that is played with when people want to camouflage an object or themselves. If you can blur the boundaries between an object and its background you make it less visible.

Visual illusions

Visual illusions show how our minds can be confused by sensations to create a false perception. Look at the images on any illusions website. You may well have seen some of them before but think how they are playing tricks on your mind. For a more dramatic demonstration go to Richard Gregory's website (www.richardgregory.org/) and look at the Charlie Chaplin mask. The remarkable thing here is that you know what is really there but you cannot see it. Your mind insists on seeing something that is clearly not there.

The Necker cube

This is one of the simplest illusions to create and one of the most puzzling. This figure is a flat drawing of two squares joined at the corners but it looks like a cube. And not just any cube. The orientation of the cube appears to change as you look at it. Sometimes it seems to point upwards and sometimes it seems to point downwards. You are seeing something that you know is not really there (a cube) and because it is not really there your mind's eye cannot decide which way round it is, so it tries out the different orientations and inverts it. Try keeping the cube in one position and you'll find it can't be done. You cannot stop seeing something that you know is not there.

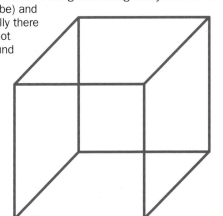

The Necker cube

The eyes of a child

What does a newborn baby see when it opens its eyes? We can never know this because they can't, or won't, talk to us. And when they can talk, they can't remember what it was like in the delivery room or the back of the car on the way home.

One of the most quoted views on this comes from the great US psychologist William James who wrote, *'The baby, assailed by eyes, ears, nose, skin, and entrails at once, feels it all as one great blooming, buzzing confusion.'* (James, 1890, p. 488). In other words babies don't see shapes or patterns, just a moving array of colours. Over time they start to see patterns in the confusions and eventually learn to build up the three-dimensional picture that greets most of us when we open our eyes.

We can't know what a baby sees but what if you find someone who has been blind all their life and then is given their sight as an adult? What will they see?

There are a few recorded cases of this including SB who was studied by Richard Gregory (you can read the story of SB at www.richardgregory.org/). Until the age of 52 SB lived a successful and active life as a blind man; advances in surgery meant that his sight could be restored. When the bandages were first removed, and SB could see, he heard the voice of the surgeon. He turned towards the voice but could only see a blur. Although he realised this must be a face he could not 'see it'. After a few days he was able to make sense of the visual information. He was best at recognising things he had been able to touch when he was blind. Some things surprised him, for example he had believed that a quarter moon would be like a quarter of a circle rather than a crescent.

People who recover their sight after blindness often experience depression. This was the case with SB and he found his new visual world brought him more sadness than happiness. He soon chose to spend a lot of his time in darkness.

Cognitive puzzles in everyday life

1. Why do my holiday snaps look so duff?
You were on the beach and saw this giant lizard. It was massive and you were really brave to get that close to take a picture, but when you get your photo back you can barely see it. And that giant ship on the horizon has become a dot. Is the camera rubbish? Probably not. Your mind's eye adjusts the size of objects so you perceive them to be bigger. The camera records what is really there, and your mind's eye distorts it to help you concentrate on the important objects.

Maybe your mind is monitoring all sorts of information below the level of your awareness and selects the important bits for you to attend to. But what is doing this monitoring and how does it decide what is important?

2. How do children learn language?
I was trying to make excuses for my lack of a foreign language by explaining to a Spanish friend that their language was difficult for English people to learn. My friend commented that this was remarkable because in his country there were many 5-year-olds fluent in it. Children do not need instruction to learn language, and in fact it is almost impossible to stop them developing language. Language is a complex set of sounds and rules that almost defy description yet we have no difficulty in developing them and being understood.

3. How do we tune in to conversations?
You are in a large group of people talking to a friend. You don't know what everyone else in the room is talking about but all of a sudden you hear your name from the other side of the room. Someone is talking about you. You immediately tune out of the conversation with your friend and listen to what is being said about you.

This is remarkable in itself. You don't have movable ears so the tuning in has taken place inside your head rather than outside. Even more remarkable is how you heard your name. If you weren't listening to that conversation how did you hear your name?

...Connections...

Cognitive psychology is about understanding how we make sense of our world and communicate within it. It has links to all the other areas of psychology in this text. In **Individual Differences** we look at the cognitive skill of intelligence; in **Developmental Psychology** we look at how children think; in **Social Psychology** we look at how people make social judgements, and in **Physiological Psychology** we look at how the brain carries out cognitive tasks. One of the fastest growing areas in psychology is cognitive neuroscience which focuses on the connections between brain structures and cognitive abilities.

Research into memory

Everybody has a tale about memory: how they forgot an important appointment, or the fact that their granny can remember everyone's name in the family over the last 200 years. Sometimes we surprise ourselves by what we can recall when we go back somewhere we haven't been for 30 years, or at an important moment in a quiz. 'How did I know that?' you ask yourself. Mind you, when you are in the exam room trying to answer the questions you are more likely to ask yourself why you can't remember things.

Two traditions

There are two routes to studying memory:

• The experimental study of mental mechanisms (see right).
• The study of everyday experience (see below).

The most commonly researched of these in psychology is the experimental study of mental mechanisms. This might seem a little disappointing because the interesting bits are the phenomena of everyday life. In fact, the cognitive psychologist Ulrich Neisser (1982) suggested that a basic principle of memory research was:

'If X is an interesting or socially significant aspect of memory, then psychologists have hardly ever studied X.' (p. 4)

Neisser goes on to make a more remarkable claim:

'I think that "memory" in general does not exist.' (p. 12)

This sounds ridiculous because it is obvious that we remember objects and events, but is there really a thing we can call a memory? There does not seem to be any one part of the brain that controls memories, so thinking of memory as a mechanism, like a DVD recorder, is probably not helpful. In fact it would be very misleading because, as we will see later, we do not store and recall exact records of events. Far from it: we recreate our memories and in so doing we distort them.

The experimental study of mental mechanisms

The earliest systematic work on the psychology of memory was carried out by Hermann Ebbinghaus at the end of the nineteenth century. He carried out a range of highly controlled experiments most commonly using himself as the sole participant. He measured his ability to remember nonsense syllables. These are three letter syllables that sound like words but mean nothing, for example 'wib', 'fut', 'wol', etc. He used nonsense syllables so that any past knowledge would not affect the results. The studies were methodical, and provided a wide range of findings which had a big influence on how memory research was conducted, and on theories of memory.

Bartlett (see below) criticised Ebbinghaus's work by noting that the use of nonsense syllables created a very artificial situation, and therefore lacked ecological validity. He also suggested that Ebbinghaus concentrated too closely on the material that was being remembered, and ignored other important features like the attitudes of the subject and their prior experience.

Later work developed a two-stage model of memory (long-term memory and short-term memory) which became a multi-store model as more boxes were added to the model. Although this research did not use nonsense syllables it commonly used word lists or other tasks that did not have much connection to everyday memory.

The study of everyday experience

In contrast to Ebbinghaus, Bartlett carried out a series of studies into the memory of meaningful material like stories and pictures. One of Bartlett's methods was to ask someone to look at some material and then recall it. This recalled material was then shown to someone else who had to recall what they had seen, and so on. This is called the method of serial reproduction.

Bartlett used another method (the method of repeated reproduction), where the same person is asked to keep remembering the same material over a period of time. An example of how the recall of an image changed over successive reproductions is shown on the right. The drawing is a representation of the Egyptian 'mulak', a conventionalised reproduction of an owl, which may have been used as the model for our letter 'M'. With each recall of the image the drawing changed and by the tenth version the person believed they had initially seen a black cat.

In his studies Bartlett (1932) found that memories change in a number of ways:

• *They become more conventional*: Drawings became more like common objects such as a cat in the example shown. Also when people were asked to recall stories these memories were also modified to be more conventional.

Flashbulb memory

Some events have a big effect on us and we are able to say where we were and what we were doing when we heard about the event or when we witnessed it. It is almost as if a flashbulb has gone off in our minds to highlight the scene and fix the image. Flashbulb memories are typically remarkably vivid and seem to be permanent. These memories are usually of very emotional and personal events in your life. Flashbulb memories can also be related to events that are public but affected you emotionally, such as the death of a famous person (like Princess Diana) or a dramatic news event (like the destruction of the Trade Towers on 9/11).

Maybe there is a flashbulb mechanism that is responsible for capturing these events and storing them in memory for an indefinite period of time. Maybe these memories are not encoded any differently from others but we remember them because we rehearse them by retelling them often.

A problem with much of the work on flashbulb memories is that data are not checked. If I say I remember I was in the bath when I heard the news that a famous person had died, how would you know this was correct? In fact, how would I know?

A flashbulb memory is a memory about what you were doing when you heard about something significant. It is not the memory for the event itself.

Neisser doubts whether these memories are any more accurate than our other memories and he carried out a number of studies including one on memories of the Challenger space disaster.

In 1986 the Challenger space shuttle exploded on take-off killing the entire crew. It was seen live on television and shown repeatedly on newscasts. The next day Neisser and Harsch (1992) asked students to give their recollections of the time when they first heard of the disaster. They went back to the same students two-and-a-half years later and asked them the same question. They discovered that at least 25% of them were wrong about every major detail. Only 10% gave all the same details. He also discovered that the students' confidence in the memories had no correlation with their accuracy. Students who had inaccurate recall were just as likely to be confident in their memories as students whose memories were unchanged.

The moment that The Challenger exploded. We think we remember where we were, but do we?

Activity

Try to draw both sides of a £1 coin. Then try to draw a £5 note. How many features can you get right? What does this tell you about memory?

- *They are simplified*: Stories and pictures become simpler when they are recalled.
- *Labels or names affect recall*: For example, in the images shown once a label 'cat' has been used, the recalls become more and more like a common view of a cat rather than the original image.
- *Elaboration takes place*: Some items are introduced into the story or the picture by the person remembering it. In the shown example a tail develops from one of the lines of the mulak but by the last drawing it has no connection to the original.
- *Emotional distortion takes place*: The way someone was feeling during the tests tended to affect the memory of the stories they were told.

Bartlett found that our memories are not exact recordings of events and images. This is obviously important when we look at evidence in court but it was more than 40 years before this idea was looked at again by Elizabeth Loftus (see next page).

Recall cues

We often have the experience of knowing something but not quite being able to recall it. This commonly happens in quizzes, examinations and when you forget to take your shopping list to the Co-op. What we need is a memory cue and then it all comes back to us. This is why advertisers use visual displays in shops that remind people of the TV adverts (see facing page).

One of the cues that helps us is the context in which we first came across the information. If we heard about something when we were on the bus then we might well remember it again when we next get on the bus.

The simple message here is that you should do your examination revision in a situation that is as close as possible to the exam room. So set yourself up with a wobbly desk and an uncomfortable chair and get your mum to walk up and down and keep staring at you.

...Link to the core study...

We are very confident about our own memories: 'I was there, I saw it, I know what happened.' Psychology tells us, however, that this is not the case and memory is far from an accurate record of events. Does this matter? Well, not if you are telling the story of a good night out, but yes if you are giving evidence in a court of law. Perhaps our memories are susceptible to suggestion and if so, the leading questions of barristers and police might have an effect on evidence given to them about a crime.

Elizabeth Loftus and John C. Palmer (1974) Reconstruction of automobile destruction. *Journal of Verbal Learning and Verbal Behaviour*, 13, pages 585–589.

(sidebar, vertical text) LOFTUS AND PALMER: EYEWITNESS TESTIMONY

Abstract

This study is concerned with the effect of leading questions on what people remember.

The study consists of two experiments:

Experiment 1
Participants were asked to say how fast a car is going. If the question contained the word 'smashed' ('How fast were the cars going when they smashed into each other') their estimates were higher than if other verbs were used (collided, bumped, contacted or hit). This shows that estimates of speed were affected by such leading questions.

Experiment 2
Does the critical word (e.g. 'smashed' or 'hit') change a person's subsequent memory of the event they witnessed? Participants were again shown slides of a car accident and asked how fast the cars were going when they smashed or hit each other. A week later they were asked some more questions including one about whether there had been any broken glass. There had been no broken glass but those in the 'smashed' condition (who tended to think the car was travelling faster) were more likely to say there was more glass.

Experiment 1: Aim

The aim of the first experiment was to investigate the accuracy of memory. People are quite poor at judging numerical details of a traffic accident such as time, speed and distance. Witnesses often give widely varying estimates and such estimates may be influenced by certain variables, for example the phrasing of a question to elicit a speed judgement. Some questions are more 'suggestive' than others; in legal terms such questions are called *leading questions* – a question that 'either by its form or content, suggests to the witness what answer is desired or leads him to the desired answer' (Loftus and Palmer, 1974, page 585).

The aim of the first experiment was to see if the estimates given by participants about the speed of vehicles in a traffic accident would be influenced by the wording of the question asked. For example, participants asked about how fast the cars were travelling when they *hit* each other would give different speed estimates and have different expectations than participants asked the same question with the word 'smashed' instead.

Experiment 1: Method

The participants in this study were 45 students.

The participants were shown seven film clips of different traffic accidents. The clips were originally made as part of a driver safety film.

After each clip the participants were given a questionnaire which asked them to describe the accident and then answer a series of specific questions about the accident.

There was one critical question: 'About how fast were the cars going when they hit each other?'. One group of participants was given this question. The other four groups were given the verbs 'smashed', 'collided', 'bumped' or 'contacted' in place of the word 'hit'. Thus there were five experimental groups in this lab experiment.

Biographical notes

Elizabeth Loftus is Distinguished Professor at the University of California, Irvine. She was born in Los Angeles, California in 1944 and planned to be a maths teacher but discovered psychology at university. She received her PhD from Stanford University in 1970.

She began her research with investigations of how the mind classifies and remembers information. In the 1970s, she began to re-evaluate the direction of her research. In 'Diva of disclosure' (Neimark, 1996) published in *Psychology Today*, she stated 'I wanted my work to make a difference in people's lives'. She began her research on traumatically repressed memories and eyewitness accounts and suddenly found herself in the midst of sexual abuse stories and defending accused offenders. Loftus has been an expert witness consultant in hundreds of cases on the unreliability of eyewitness testimonies based on false memories, which she believes to be triggered, suggested, implanted, or created in the mind.

Loftus has received numerous awards for her work from psychology and from other disciplines. She has received four honourary doctorates including one from the UK. She received the William James Fellow Award from the American Psychological Society, 2001 for 'ingeniously and rigorously designed research studies ... that yielded clear objective evidence on difficult and controversial questions'. She remains a respected and controversial figure in psychology and in a review of twentieth-century psychologists published by the Review of General Psychology she was the top-ranked woman on the list.

'I study human memory. My experiments reveal how memories can be changed by things that we are told. Facts, ideas, suggestions and other forms of post-event information can modify our memories. The legal field, so reliant on memories, has been a significant application of the memory research. My interest in psychology and law, more generally, has grown from this application.'

www Elizabeth Loftus' home page www.seweb.uci.edu/faculty/loftus

'Just because someone thinks they remember something in detail, with confidence and with emotion, does not mean that it actually happened, ... False memories have these characteristics too.'

Experiment 1: Results

The mean speed estimate was calculated for each experimental group, as shown in the graph below. The group given the word 'smashed' estimated a higher speed than the other groups (40.8 mph). The group given the word 'contacted' estimated the lowest speed (31.8 mph).

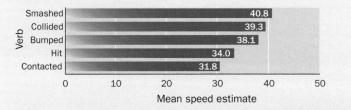

Verb	Mean speed estimate
Smashed	40.8
Collided	39.3
Bumped	38.1
Hit	34.0
Contacted	31.8

Experiment 1: Discussion

The results show that the form of a question can have a significant effect on a witness's answer to the question. In other words, leading questions can affect the accuracy of memory.

Loftus and Palmer propose two explanations for this result:

1 *Response-bias factors*: the different speed estimates occur because the critical word (e.g. 'smashed' or 'hit') influences or biases a person's response.

2 *The memory representation is altered*: the critical word changes a person's memory so that his/her perception of the accident is affected – some critical words would lead someone to have a perception of the accident being more serious.

If the second conclusion is true, we would expect participants to 'remember' other details that are not true. Loftus and Palmer tested this in their second experiment which is described on the next page.

How fast do you think the red truck was travelling when it hit the blue truck? How good do you think people are at estimating the speed a car is travelling? Does this mean they would be easily influenced by certain 'trigger' words in the question?

Activity

Before you turn the page, and look at experiment 2, try to think how you might design an experiment to work out which of the explanations suggested by Loftus and Palmer is 'correct'.

Work in a small group and plan all the details of your study (good practice for the Psychological Investigations Paper). This will include identifying an IV and DV, writing the alternate hypothesis, deciding on stimulus materials to be used and what experimental design (repeated measures or independent groups), writing down the procedure including your sampling method and considering any ethical issues.

A leading question is one that suggests to a witness what answer is desired or leads the witness to give the desired answers.

Do you get headaches frequently?

According to Loftus' research this is a leading question. People asked this question reported an average of 2.2 headaches per week whereas those who were asked 'Do you get headaches occasionally, and if so, how often?' reported an average of 0.7 headaches! The way the question was asked had a significant effect on the answer given.

Qs

1 Identify the independent variable (IV) and dependent variable (DV) in this experiment.

2 Write a suitable hypothesis for this experiment (make sure it is clearly operationalised).

3 Identify the experimental design used in this study and give **one** strength of using this design.

4 List the experimental groups in this study.

5 Why was it a good idea to ask 10 questions rather than just asking the critical question alone?

6 Each group of participants was shown the films in a different order. Why do you think this was done?

7 The participants all knew they were taking part in a psychology experiment. How do you think this might have affected their behaviour?

8 How do you think this also may have affected the results from the study?

9 Can you think of a way that this problem might have been overcome?

10 Describe a possible sampling method that might have been used in this study.

11 Give **one** strength and **one** limitation of this sampling method.

12 Outline **one** finding from experiment 1.

13 State **one** conclusion that can be drawn from this finding.

14 What did Loftus and Palmer decide to investigate in their second experiment?

Experiment 2: Aim

Loftus and Palmer conducted a second experiment to further investigate the effects of leading questions on memory, this time going one step further to see if the leading question altered subsequent expectations about the likely consequences. In particular they wanted to see if such questions simply create a response-bias (explanation 1) or if they actually alter a person's memory representation (explanation 2).

Experiment 2: Method

The participants in this study were again students but a new group of 150 students.

Part 1

Participants were shown a one-minute film which contained a four-second multiple car accident. The participants were asked a set of questions including the critical question about speed. There were three groups:

Group 1 was asked: 'How fast were the cars going when they smashed each other?'

Group 2 was asked: 'How fast were the cars going when they hit into each other?'

Group 3 was asked no question about the speed of the vehicles. This was a control group.

Part 2

One week later the participants were asked to return to the psychology lab. They were asked some further questions including 'Did you see any broken glass?' There was no broken glass in the film but, presumably, those who thought the car was travelling faster might expect that there would be broken glass.

Experiment 2: Results

Part 1

The results from Part 1 were the same as in experiment 1. Participants gave higher speed estimates in the 'smashed' condition, a mean of 10.46 mph compared with a mean of 8.00 mph for the 'hit' condition.

Part 2

In Part 2 (a week later) they found that participants in the 'smashed condition' were also more likely to think they saw broken glass. The table below shows the distribution of 'yes' and 'no' responses for the three conditions (smashed, hit, contacted).

Distribution of 'yes' and 'no' responses to the question about broken glass.

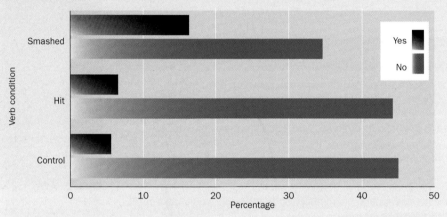

A calculation was also made of the probability of saying 'yes' or 'no' in relation to the three conditions (smashed, hit, contacted); the probability of saying 'yes' to the broken glass question is .32 when the verb was 'smashed' compared to a probability of .14 with 'hit'.

Verb condition	Speed estimate (mph)			
	1–5	6–10	11–15	16–20
Smashed	.09	.27	.41	.62
Hit	.05	.09	.25	.50

A probability table showing the probability of saying 'Yes' to the question 'Did you see any broken glass?' in relation to the original question asked about speed estimates.

> Draw a bar chart of the probability table on the left. This may help you understand the results of the study and what to conclude.

Qs

1. What is a 'control group'?
2. Why is it a good idea to have a control group in this experiment?
3. A possible hypothesis for experiment 2 would be 'Participants are more likely to report seeing broken glass when they are given the word 'smashed' in a previous question than when they have the word 'hit'. Is this a one-tailed or two-tailed hypothesis?
4. State a suitable null hypothesis for experiment 2.
5. Outline **two** findings from experiment 2.
6. What conclusions can you draw from the probability table above?
7. How do the aims for experiment 1 and 2 differ?

'The difference between false memories and true ones is the same as for jewels: it is always the false ones that look the most real, the most brilliant.'

Spanish artist Salvador Dali

'The past is a foreign country. They do things differently there.'

British novelist L. P. Hartley, in The Go-Between

Experiment 2: Discussion

The results from experiment 2 again show that the way a question is asked can influence the answer given. The results from Part 2 of the second experiment suggest that this effect is not due to a response-bias but because leading questions actually alter the memory a person has for the event.

Loftus and Palmer propose that memory is determined by two sources:

1 One's own perception gleaned at the time of the original event.
2 External information supplied after the fact (such as leading questions).

Over time information from these two sources is integrated in such a way that we are unable to tell which source any particular piece of information came from. All we have is one 'memory'.

In the second experiment the two pieces of information combine to form a memory of an accident that appears quite severe and therefore generates certain expectations, for example that there is likely to be broken glass.

Other research

This research can be linked to earlier studies of the way a verbal label given to an object alters the to-be-remembered form, such as in the study by Carmichael et al., 1932 – see below). A more recent study by Daniel (1972) found that participants' recognition of objects was similarly affected, and thus concluded that verbal labels cause a shift in the way information is represented in memory in the direction of being more similar to the suggestion given by the verbal label.

Carmichael et al. gave participants a set of drawings (central column) and then provided a verbal description (to left or right). When participants were later asked to redraw the image, the resulting object was typically affected by the verbal label.

Sample reproduced figures	Description presented	Figures presented	Description presented	Sample reproduced figures
	Curtains in a window		Diamond in a rectangle	
	Bottle		Stirrup	
	Cresent moon		Letter "C"	
	Beehive		Hat	
	Eyeglasses		Dumbell	
	Seven		Four	
	Ship's wheel		Sun	
	Hourglass		Table	
	Kidney bean		Canoe	

Evaluating the study by Loftus and Palmer

The research method
This study was a lab experiment. *What are the strengths and limitations of this research method in the context of this study?*

There are no simple answers. Evaluating a study requires you to think. We have provided some pointers here, linked to the KEY ISSUES covered through this book – see page XIV for a table of these key issues.

The sample
American students were used in this study. In what way is this group of participants unique? *How would the unique characteristics of the sample in this study effect the conclusions drawn?*

You might consider that America is an individualist culture, i.e. a society where its citizens are more concerned with individual gains than the 'common good'. This may affect their willingness to be led by leading questions. You might also consider the unique characteristics of students – they are more intelligent and tend to have good memories, and thus might be less likely to be affected by leading questions.

Qualitative or quantitative?
The data collected in this study were quantitative. *Explain in what way they are quantitative and explain the strengths and limitations of producing this kind of data in the context of this study?*

Representativeness
In this study eyewitness testimony was tested by showing participants video clips. *In what way is this different to a real-life accident?*

Real-life eyewitnesses may be feeling scared or anxious. *How do you think this might affect their memory?*

Ecological validity
The limitations of the sample affect the extent that we may or may not be able to generalise the findings of this study to other situations.

The contrived nature of the task also might affect the generalisability of this study. *In what way do you think the tasks in this experiment were contrived or artificial?*

To what extent do you think we can generalise the findings from this study to other situations, such as everyday life?

Applications/usefulness
How might the findings from the two experiments be used in real life?

How valuable was this study?

What next?
Describe **one** change to this study, and say how you think this might affect the outcome.

...Links to other studies and issues...

The issue of leading questions comes up elsewhere in this text.

- The study by **Samuel and Bryant** looks at the effect of questions on the responses of children to a simple cognitive task.
- The case study by **Freud** on Little Hans contains evidence from the child's father who put some very leading questions to Hans.
- Most controversial is the connection to **Thigpen and Cleckley's** study on multiple personality. Are the memories and the multiples created by the therapy?

Debate

What do you conclude about the ecological validity of the study by Loftus and Palmer?

Hold a 'mock trial'. One team has the task of arguing that this study has ecological validity and another team has to present the opposite case. You might do some extra research first.

What does your class conclude?

Memory research after the car crash studies

At first glance the topic of memory seems to be free from much controversy. Nothing could be further from the truth and this topic has become a hot issue. Seeing glass that wasn't there (in Loftus's second experiment) suggests that we invent memories or to put it another way we have some false memories. Now read on.

Mis-identification

Recent experiments have found that people can make errors when asked to identify someone who might have taken part in a crime. People were shown a grainy surveillance video of a man and told them that he had shot a security guard. Then they were presented with five mug shots and asked which one was the perpetrator. It was an impossible task, because none of the five mug shots really matched the man in the video. Nevertheless, every one of the 352 subjects identified one of the mug shots as the man they had seen (Wells and Bradfield, 1998). It seems that people are good at picking a criminal out of a line-up if he or she is there, but they are not good at being able to spot that he or she is not actually in the line-up.

False and recovered memories

Elizabeth Loftus is most famous today for her work on false memory. During the 1980s a number of therapists, mainly in the USA, reported that their adult clients had been recalling traumatic memories of childhood abuse that they had previously been unaware of. Many people were accused of child abuse as a result of these recovered memories and a number ended up in prison. Very few of the recovered memories were backed up with other evidence. Loftus, among others, became concerned about the type of therapy being offered and the quality of the memories. She came to believe that *some* of these memories were being created in the therapist's consulting room. It will not be a shock to the reader to say that this work is very controversial.

It is a sad fact of modern life that some children suffer abuse. They commonly find it difficult to talk about this and often only deal with it as adults, if at all. What Loftus is challenging is the memories that suddenly appear when the person is an adult and only in the therapist's chair. As she comments, people who suffer traumatic events have problems forgetting not remembering.

Lost in the mall

Can false memories be planted in people? Elizabeth Loftus believes so and conducted a study with her associate, Jacqueline E. Pickrell (1995) to see if they could demonstrate that memories can be planted. For ethical reasons they could not try to plant memories of childhood sexual abuse. They wanted to plant a memory that would have been distressing but had a happy ending. They decided to use a 'lost in the mall' story. They created a book for each participant that had stories from their childhood. Included in this was one made-up story about being lost in a shopping centre (mall) that was supposed to have been added by a close relative. It was, in fact, false. A quarter of their participants came to believe that this event had happened to them and they could recount features of the incident that were not part of the original planted story. In other words they had started to embellish the story and make it their own. The story was well and truly planted and started to take on a life of its own.

Loftus (1997) provides other evidence of false memories, from one of many cases from the US courts. Nadean Cool was a nursing assistant when in 1986 she received therapy to help her deal with a traumatic event that had happened to her daughter. The therapist used hypnosis among other techniques to dig out any hidden memories. The digging produced a remarkable haul of horrible memories. Cool came to believe that she had been in a satanic cult, that she had eaten babies and had sex with animals. She also came to believe that she had more than 120 personalities including children, angels and a duck. Some years later she realised that none of these events had happened and she sued the psychiatrist for malpractice. She was awarded $2.4 million in an out-of-court settlement.

Weapon focus

Loftus (1979) identified the 'weapon focus effect'. There were two conditions in her experiment. In both conditions participants heard a discussion in an adjoining room. In condition 1 a man emerged holding a pen and with grease on his hands. In condition 2 the discussion was rather more heated and a man emerged holding a paper-knife covered in blood. When asked to identify the man from 50 photos, participants in condition 1 were 49% accurate compared with 33% accuracy in condition 2. This suggests that the weapon may have distracted attention from the man and might explain why eyewitnesses sometimes have poor recall for certain details of a crime.

It might be that the witness focuses his or her attention on the weapon, so not attending to other features of the scene. This might be because of heightened arousal or because it is an unusual event (Wells and Olsen, 2003).

When people witness an event with a gun involved then they are less likely to be able to describe the characters than if there is no gun. You might well remember this page as the one with the gun.

Multiple choice questions

1 Which of the following was not a cue word in the experiment by Loftus and Palmer?
   a Smashed.   b Contacted.
   c Knocked.   d Hit.

2 The DV in the first experiment was
   a Estimate of speed.
   b The verb 'smashed'.
   c The question about broken glass.
   d The film.

3 In experiment 1, how many experimental conditions were there?
   a 1   b 3
   c 5   d 7

4 In experiment 2, how many experimental groups were there?
   a 1   b 2
   c 3   d 4

5 In experiment 2, participants were tested immediately and then asked to return for some more questions. How long afterwards was this?
   a 1 day.   b 3 days.
   c 1 week.   d 2 weeks.

6 In experiment 2, which group saw the most broken glass?
   a The 'smashed' group.
   b The 'collided' group.
   c The 'hit' group.
   d The control group.

7 Which of the following is true?
   a Experiment 1 and 2 were both repeated measures.
   b Experiment 1 and 2 were both independent groups.
   c Only experiment 1 was repeated measures.
   d Only experiment 1 was independent groups.

8 The conclusion drawn from experiment 2 was that
   a The leading question creates a response-bias.
   b The leading question alters memory.
   c a and b.
   d Memory is not affected by leading questions.

9 The participants in this study were
   a Children.   b Students.
   c Teachers.   d Adults.

10 A demand characteristic may act as an
   a IV.
   b DV.
   c Extraneous variable.
   d All of the above.

Answers are on page 65.

Exam questions

Section A questions

1 The study by Loftus and Palmer used film clips of car accidents. Outline **two** ways that this might affect the ecological validity of the study. [4]

2 Loftus and Palmer concluded, at the end of the first experiment, that there were **two** possible explanations for why leading questions affect the accuracy of memory. Outline these two explanations. [4]

3 Identify **two** conclusions that can be drawn about memory from the study by Loftus and Palmer. [4]

4 (a) Loftus and Palmer asked participants to estimate the speed of two cars in a traffic accident. They used different verbs in the questions they asked. Name **two** of the verbs. [2]
   (b) What was the effect of using the different verbs you identified in (a)? [2]

5 Loftus and Palmer used the same set of standardised procedures with each participant. Describe **two** of these procedures. [4]

6 (a) Explain the difference between the two experiments in the study by Loftus and Palmer. [2]
   (b) Explain the reason why a control group was used in this study. [2]

7 Loftus and Palmer concluded that leading questions do affect memory. Describe **two** findings that support this conclusion. [4]

> See page XII–XIII for notes on the exam paper and styles of question.

Section B question

(a) What was the aim of the Loftus and Palmer study? [2]

(b) Describe the sample used in the Loftus and Palmer study and give **one** limitation of it. [6]

(c) Describe how data was gathered in the Loftus and Palmer study. [6]

(d) Give **one** advantage and **one** disadvantage of lab experiments. [6]

(e) Outline the results of the Loftus and Palmer study. [8]

(f) Suggest **two** changes to the Loftus and Palmer study and outline any methodological implications these changes may have. [8]

Section C question

(a) Outline **one** assumption of the cognitive approach in psychology. [2]

(b) Describe how the cognitive approach could explain memory. [4]

(c) Describe **one** similarity and **one** difference between the Loftus and Palmer study and any other cognitive approach study. [6]

(d) Discuss the strengths and limitations of the cognitive approach using examples from the Loftus and Palmer study. [12]

Key issue: being sceptical

Nothing is as it seems

You can't open a newspaper or switch on the TV without someone trying to convince you about something. They have the knowledge and you don't. The title of 'expert' is given to almost anyone who is interviewed on the media, but how expert are they and how valuable is their evidence?

This key issue aims to help you look at evidence with a sceptical eye. That does not mean that you should rubbish it or dismiss it, but that you can try and come to your own view about whether to accept the evidence or not. This is a very useful skill for dealing with everyday information and it is also very useful for evaluating psychological evidence.

Sensible advice, but is it?

Some sensible advice is not all it cracks up to be. Take for example the following two government health messages

SMOKING KILLS: well it probably doesn't improve your health but does it kill you? For example, consider ciggie-loving Marie Ellis who died this year after living to 105 despite smoking nearly half a million cigarettes in her life. Marie also delighted in an unhealthy diet. She always had three sugars in her coffee, loved a drop of sherry and scoffed sweets and cakes, often refusing to eat savoury food. Throughout her life Marie remained incredibly healthy. She had all her teeth and never even suffered as much as a smoker's cough. The matron from her nursing home said: 'Our doctor used to raise his arms in bewilderment when he came to see her.' He'd say, 'Don't encourage her' – but she defied all medical reasoning. She had a lovely send-off. A couple of people had a smoke outside the chapel in her honour both before and after the service.'

This does appear to defy medical reasoning but only because that reasoning has a false idea about *cause and effect*. Smoking does not *cause* cancer, but it does something that raises the chances of developing it. This is very different and so people like Marie make health education messages seem silly and unbelievable.

And what about the **FIVE A DAY** campaign? The idea here is that if you have five portions of fruit and vegetables a day your will be healthier. But how could they know? Use all your research skills to design a research study that can test this hypothesis. You would need to feed some people 5 a day for, say, 10 years, and some other people to just eat no fruit and vegetables. And what about if you have just 4 a day, will that affect your health or if you eat 10 a day will you be overdosing? When you think about this claim it can only be a GUESS. The authors are convinced that in a few years time the health advice will change and we will be asked to eat more lard, chips, salt and beer in order to have a healthy life. We are currently doing controlled trials – we'll let you know the results.

Sceptic: someone who usually doubts, questions, or disagrees with assertions or generally accepted conclusions.

Superstition: an irrational belief that an object, action, or situation not logically related to a course of events can actually influence its outcome.

Cold reading: a set of techniques used by professional manipulators to get a subject to behave in a certain way or to think that the cold reader has some sort of special ability that allows him to 'mysteriously' know things about the subject.

Homeopathy: the multi-million business of selling coloured water to the gullible.

TOOLBOX FOR SCEPTICS

These are some key questions to ask about any evidence.

1. Who, or what, is the source?
Does the evidence come from someone with an international reputation for good work or did you overhear it in a sweet shop?

2. Where was the information published?
Was it in a scientific journal that has other scientists looking at the work before it is published or was it in *Heat*. This is not to say that *Heat* is a rubbish journal because it contains essential information but the claims it makes have probably not been verified by a review team.

3. What is the evidence?
Is it plausible and does it make sense?

4. What is the possible bias?
Is there any influence on the presentation of the evidence? So, for example if a lager company tells you their lager is probably the best lager in the world should we believe them or should we consider whether it is possible to actually tell the difference between their brand and any other?

5. Is there an alternative explanation?
Maybe we think the evidence is sound but we might not agree with the conclusions that have been drawn from it.

'... man will occasionally stumble over the truth, but usually manages to pick himself up, walk over or around it, and carry on.'
British Prime Minister Winston S. Churchill.

Activity

Look at the statements below which are some commonly held beliefs. Do you think they are true or false? (adapted from Della Sala, 1999)

1 Taking extra vitamin C will reduce you chance of getting a cold.
2 Cutting hair makes it grow more quickly.
3 Antibiotics kill viruses.
4 The brain operates on the same amount of power as a 10 watt light bulb.
5 Humans normally use only 10% of their brains.
6 A gifted person can bend spoons by thought alone.
7 There is a link between the MMR vaccine and autism.

Answers can be found on the facing page.

Derek Acorah

Derek Acorah is an author and performer who claims to have supernatural powers. On his website he describes how his first supernatural experience came as a child when the spirit of his late grandfather visited him. When young Derek told his grandmother she was not surprised as she herself was a medium. His early career was playing football with teams such as Liverpool Football Club and the premier Australian team USC Lion. He believes that his psychic powers were always with him and so in the early 1980s he became a full time spirit medium based at his home city of Liverpool.

Derek describes how he gets access to the spirit world though a guide called Sam. He first met Sam 2000 (yes two thousand) years ago in Ethiopia in a previous life. Interestingly, for **sceptics**, both Sam and Derek talk with strong Liverpudlian accents and don't know a word of Ethiopian. To find out more go to Derek's website – it's not hard to find.

If we use our **TOOLBOX FOR SCEPTICS** on Derek we have to ask:

1 Who is the source of information about psychic powers? Well, Derek himself. Nobody else can hear or see Sam.

2 Where was the information published? The evidence appears on TV shows such as *Most Haunted* and stage shows. It has not been examined by an independent panel of judges.

3 What is the evidence? Derek's evidence is his self reports of spirit possession (all over YouTube for the interested) and also the 'readings' he does with other people.

4 What is the possible bias? One obvious bias is that by maintaining a belief in a spirit world Derek maintains his living. The other bias is that many people want to believe in a spirit world. The loss of someone close to us is very hard to take and we want to believe that their lives had meaning and that they live on in some way. This wish for contact with people who have died makes us suspend our normal level of judgement.

5 Is there an alternative explanation? YES, most definitely. Many psychologists and magicians can demonstrate how to carry out a spirit reading and appear to read the thoughts of another person. Derren Brown, for example, is able to show how to fake a spirit reading and you can check this out on YouTube as well.

In the end, though, it's your call about whether Derek can make contact with dead people.

The Million Dollar Challenge

If you can demonstrate your paranormal powers you can win one million dollars. There's no trick. If you can read minds, bend spoons, talk to the dead, or levitate over mountains then the money can be yours. Just go to the website (http://www.randi.org/) and stake your claim.

The challenge, which is shown below, was first made by James Randi in 1996 and so far nobody has been able to claim the million dollars.

'At JREF (James Randi Educational Foundation), we offer a one-million-dollar prize to anyone who can show, under proper observing conditions, evidence of any paranormal, supernatural, or occult power or event. The JREF does not involve itself in the testing procedure, other than helping to design the protocol and approving the conditions under which a test will take place. All tests are designed with the participation and approval of the applicant. In most cases, the applicant will be asked to perform a relatively simple preliminary test of the claim, which if successful, will be followed by the formal test. Preliminary tests are usually conducted by associates of the JREF at the site where the applicant lives. Upon success in the preliminary testing process, the 'applicant' becomes a 'claimant'.'

To date, no one has even passed the preliminary test. I must remember to write to Derek about this. I'm sure he could use a million dollars.

Qs

1 Take **one** of your Core Studies and apply the Sceptic's Toolbox. Is the evidence convincing? If so why? If not, why not?

2 Make a list of irrational beliefs that you have, that is, things you believe to be true even though you have no direct evidence. For example, you might believe that the world is round, How do you know? Or you might believe that eating carrots gives you better eyesight, or if you buy a new pencil case just before the exams you will pass. That sort of thing.

3 Look at your list and consider how much evidence you have for each of these beliefs and if you have none, why do you believe in them?

4 Try to write a definition of an expert. What are you an expert in? Try not to boast – it's not attractive.

Activity answers

1. There is no evidence to support this and a lot to challenge it. 2. True 3. False 4. True 5. False 6. False 7. False (There is no evidence at all that links the MMR vaccine to autism. Despite this, a **superstition** *has developed in this country so the rate of children being given the vaccine has dropped).*

...Links to other studies and issues...

This issue links into a number of studies. Take for example the *Three Faces of Eve* (**Thigpen and Cleckley**) which tells us about someone who has a multiple personality. It is worth looking at this with a sceptical eye on two counts. First because the story is told to us by the therapist – the person who is bringing out the multiple personalities and the person who wrote a book and sold the film rights about the case. The second count is to do with the description of someone as having two personalities. The jury is out on whether this is a real condition or one that is created by the therapist. On a general point. many of the core studies have been carried out using the best scientific methods but there is a still a need for a sceptical eye, especially on the conclusions that people draw from the evidence. For example, the Bobo study (**Bandura *et al*.**) provides some excellent evidence but there is disagreement on what that evidence is telling us.

The sceptical agenda is also taken up in some of the issues such as **promoting human welfare** (see page 170) where we need to look at what psychologists are doing and judge whether it is a good thing, and also in the discussions about **ethics** (see page 180).

The history of autism

Leo Kanner

In the 1940s Leo Kanner, a psychiatrist at Johns Hopkins University in the USA, recognised that a number of children sent to his clinic displayed similar characteristics which he named 'early infantile autism'. The word autism comes from the Greek for 'self'. Kanner was able to describe the following features that were common to all of the autistic children:

- a lack of emotional contact with other people;
- intense insistence on sameness in their routines;
- muteness or unusual speech;
- fascination with manipulating objects;
- major learning difficulties but high levels of visuo-spatial skills or rote memory;
- an attractive, alert, intelligent appearance.

Kanner's pioneering work was slow to catch on but is now the focus of much international research.

Hans Asperger

Asperger was working at the same time as Leo Kanner and published a paper which described a pattern of behaviours in several young boys who had normal intelligence and language development, but who also exhibited autistic-like behaviours and marked deficiencies in social and communication skills. The condition, Asperger syndrome (AS), was named after Hans Asperger. Children with AS are deficient in social skills but, unlike other autistics, have a normal IQ and many individuals (although not all) exhibit exceptional skill or talent in a specific area.

Transporters

The Transporters are a series of stories for children that introduce them to emotions in faces and encourage them to pay more attention to human faces. The characters are based on transport which fascinates many children especially those with autism.

Theory of mind

'Theory of Mind' (ToM) is the ability to infer, in other people, a range of mental states, such as beliefs, desires, intentions, imaginations and emotions.

Baron-Cohen argues that having some difficulty in understanding other people's points of view is not the only psychological feature of the autistic spectrum, but it is the core feature and appears universal among individuals with autism. At one extreme, there may be a total lack of any theory of mind, a form of 'mind-blindness'. More frequently, autistics may have some basic understanding, but not at the level that one would expect from observed abilities in other areas.

Animal cognition

The psychologists who first coined the term 'Theory of Mind' (Premack and Woodruff 1978), were interested in animal cognition and believed that primates could read others' intentions. Subsequent research has shown that primates are quite sophisticated in their relationships: they can deceive, form alliances, and bear grudges for days. Chimpanzees can even tell what another chimpanzee can and cannot see. But after decades of studies, no one has found indisputable signs that chimps or other nonhuman primates have a theory of mind. It seems to be a unique human quality.

'Reality to an autistic person is a confusing, interacting mass of events, people, places, sounds and sights. There seems to be no clear boundaries, order or meaning to anything. A large part of my life is spent just trying to work out the pattern behind everything.'

A person with autism (www.nas.org.uk)

What are the characteristics of autism?

People with autism generally experience three main areas of difficulty; these are known as the triad of impairments:

- *Social interaction*: difficulty with social relationships, for example appearing aloof and indifferent to other people.
- *Social communication*: difficulty with verbal and non-verbal communication, for example not fully understanding the meaning of common gestures, facial expressions or tone of voice.
- *Imagination*: difficulty in the development of interpersonal play and imagination, for example having a limited range of imaginative activities, possibly copied and pursued rigidly and repetitively.

Other features commonly associated with autism are:

- Learning difficulties
- Obsessive interests
- Resistance to change in routine
- Odd mannerisms
- Repetitive behaviour patterns

Causes of autism

There is evidence that some people have a genetic predisposition towards autism. The condition appears to have family links but it isn't purely genetic. It is likely that autism develops as a response to environmental hazards though it is not clear at the moment what these hazards are. Currently a lot of research is looking at what happens during pregnancy and just after birth. The likely culprits are diet, hormones or vaccines (other than MMR – see below).

Rising rate of autistic spectrum disorders in the UK

For decades after Kanner's original paper on autism was published in 1943, the condition was considered to be rare with an incidence of around 2 per 10,000 children. Studies carried out over the last 100 years have shown an annual increase in incidence of autism in pre-school children. The data below show how dramatic this increase has been:

> 1966: 1 in 2,222
> 1979: 1 in 492
> 1993: 1 in 141
> 2004: 1 in 110
> (Source: National Autistic Society)

No one doubts that the diagnosis of autism is rising dramatically but there is some debate about why. Is this due to more cases and if so what is causing this? Or is it due to changing patterns of diagnosis so people are now receiving the label of autism who would not have done so in the past? There was a scare during the 1990s that the rise might be due to childhood immunisation (the MMR vaccine for measles, mumps and rubella) but there is no evidence to support this and a lot to challenge it (see the evidence at www.bmj.org).

Conclusion

The results of this study seem to provide evidence of ToM deficits in adults with autism or AS, contrary to previous research with adults. One criticism might be that the Eyes Task is not actually measuring ToM. However this can be countered:

- The target words are mental state terms.
- The terms are not just referring to emotions but refer to mental states.
- The pattern of performance on the Eyes Task was mirrored in the pattern of performance on the Strange Stories Task, providing concurrent validity.
- The performance on the Eyes Task was *not* mirrored in the performance on the two control tasks, suggesting that poor performance was not due to using eyes as stimuli, or to difficulties extracting social information from minimal cues, or to subtle perceptual deficits, or to lack of basic emotion recognition.

Finally it should be noted that some of the autism/AS group hold University degrees which suggests that this aspect of social ability is independent of general intelligence.

Ecological validity

This 'very advanced test' of ToM is still much simpler than real live social situations. One important difference is that the Eyes Task is a static one whereas in real life social situations are in motion. A more realistic task might involve making judgements of people in movies. Many of the participants with autism/AS reported that they found it very hard to comprehend what was going on in a movie – they couldn't work out who knows what and who doesn't, and why people laugh at particular points. The reason that movies were not used to test ToM is that comprehension of what goes on in movies involves more than *pure* ToM.

Mentalistic significance of the eyes

The Eyes Task involved interpreting the mentalistic significance of the eyes, which is similar to other problems exhibited by individuals with autism. For example, young children with autism have difficulty interpreting the direction of a person's gaze as a sign of what the person is thinking or intends to do.

Gender difference

The female advantage on the Eyes Task may be due to genetic factors or may be due to the way girls are socialised differently to boys, encouraging them to pay more attention to what people are thinking. Either way previous research has not found a gender difference on mindreading tests but this may be because previous tests showed a ceiling effect. Therefore the Eyes Task offers a new method of investigating this difference. (Baron-Cohen has increasingly become interested in such gender differences – see 'afters' on page 48).

Evaluating the study by Baron-Cohen *et al.*

The research method

This study was a quasi-experiment because the IV (autism versus normal) was not something controlled by the experimenter. What are the strengths and limitations of this research method in the context of this study?

> There are no simple answers. Evaluating a study requires you to think. We have provided some pointers here, linked to the KEY ISSUES covered through this book – see page XIV for a table of these key issues.

The sample

To what extent do you think the sample was representative of all people with autism/AS? How does this affect the conclusions that can be drawn?

Individual differences

The findings clearly show a difference between adults with autism/AS and the control groups, but there were individual differences – some of the autism/AS group were as good as the normal population. *What does this tell us?*

Quantitative and qualitative

The data collected in this study was mainly quantitative. *Explain in what way it is quantitative and explain the strengths and limitations of producing this kind of data in the context of this study?*

Some qualitative data was collected, related to the experience of the participants with autism/AS and watching movies. *Describe how this part of the study might be extended and explain the strengths and limitations of producing this kind of data in the context of this study?*

Ecological validity

The task used to assess theory of mind was simpler than the real demands of a live social situation. *What are the strengths and weaknesses of investigating theory of mind in a way that is not representative of everyday situations?*

To what extent can we generalise the findings from this study to other situations?

Applications/usefulness

The findings from this study might be used for theory or practice. *How do you think psychologists might apply the results from this investigation to developing new theories or to helping people in everyday life?*

> **Debate**
>
> How useful is this study?
>
> Take all the evaluations into account when deciding on its usefulness.

What next?

Describe **one** change to this study, and say how you think this might affect the outcome.

Many people with autism find going to the movies is a waste of time. The action moves too quickly for them to work out why one character did or said something, who knows what or who doesn't, and why the audience is laughing at a particular point. Movies require a theory of mind but they are not pure tests of theory of mind because understanding movies also involves central coherence and executive function.

...Links to other studies and issues...

The work on theory of mind is also relevant to the study on Kanzi by **Savage-Rumbaugh *et al*.** It is important for our understanding of the 'thought processes' of animals and machines. What do they understand? And what do they think we understand?

This study also illustrates the difficulties of studying children (see the studies in the Developmental Psychology section).

More studies on autism

The increase in the diagnosis of autism in this country has been matched by the expansion in research programmes in universities. Foremost among these is the Autism Research Centre (www.autismresearchcentre.com/).

The Lovaas programme

During the 1970s Ivar Lovaas developed an intensive behaviour therapy for children with autism and other related disorders. The treatment is widely used but remains controversial not least because of its expense but also because of questions about its effectiveness.

What does the programme involve?

Lovaas recommends that treatment should begin as early as possible, and ideally before the child reaches three and a half years. This is believed to be necessary in order to teach basic social, educational and daily life skills. It can also reduce disruptive behaviours before they become established.

The treatment takes place in the home and consists of 40 hours therapy a week. This therapy is on a one-to-one basis, six hours a day, five days a week, for two years or more. Because the therapy is so intense a team of therapists needs to be trained for each child. You can see why it is so expensive.

The intervention programme progresses very slowly from teaching basic self-help and language skills to teaching nonverbal and verbal imitation skills. The treatment then moves on to encourage the basics of playing with toys. When the child can do these tasks they learn the basics of expressing themselves and how to interact and play with other children.

As with many therapies much of the research on the Lovaas treatment is carried out by therapists using the treatment. A review of the research (Bassett *et al.*, 2000) came to the conclusion that intensive behavioural therapy with children with autism had some benefits but the claims that they developed normal functioning could not be supported.

Male brains?

Autism affects far more boys than girls. At the Asperger's end of the spectrum, the ratio is about 10 to 1. The sex difference, says Baron-Cohen, is *'one puzzle that has been completely ignored for 50 years. I think it's a very big clue. It's got to be sex-linked'* (quoted in Kunzig, 2004).

Baron-Cohen suggests that men and women think in different ways due to physical features in the brain. In particular there are two key abilities, empathy and systemising.

- *Empathising ability*: reading the emotional and mental states of other people and responding to them.

- *Systemising ability*: making sense of the world through categorising things, though this can take the form of a seemingly purposeless obsessions such as plane spotting, or memorising train timetables.

In brief, Baron-Cohen's most recent theory is that autism is characterised by low empathising ability and high systemising ability. Baron-Cohen's theory goes beyond people diagnosed with autism and includes all of us. The essential difference between men and women, according to Baron-Cohen, is that women are better at empathising and men are better at systemising. These are average differences and there are plenty of male brains in female bodies, and female brains in male bodies. There are even female autistics, but there are many more male ones: in Baron-Cohen's theory, autism is a case of the 'extreme male brain'.

Baron-Cohen developed a Systemising Quotient questionnaire. Here is an example item:

'When I read the newspaper, I am drawn to tables of information, such as football scores or stock-market indices. Strongly agree? Slightly agree? Slightly disagree? Strongly disagree?'

Facilitated communication

Which hand is doing the pointing?

There are many possible reasons why an individual doesn't communicate very well. It might be that they don't want to, or don't understand or they don't have the abilities to produce communications. The carers of people who are not communicating often hope that communication is in fact possible if only a way can be found to do it.

Facilitated communication (FC) is a technique which is used to allow communication by those previously unable to communicate by speech or signs due to autism, mental retardation, brain damage, or such diseases as cerebral palsy. It involves a facilitator who helps a patient use a keyboard by lightly balancing their hand above the letters; patients who have previously not communicated recite poems, carry on high-level intellectual conversations, or simply chat.

Parents are grateful to be told that their child does not have severe learning difficulties but is either normal or above normal in intelligence. FC allows their children to demonstrate their intelligence by giving them a new technique to express themselves with. But is it really their child who is communicating? Sometimes people using FC make quite startling claims about messages from God or, more worryingly, childhood abuse (see page 38 on false memories). Most scientific observers are sceptical about FC but carers are more willing to believe.

Another study by Baron-Cohen

In order to be able to arrange pictures into simple stories a child has to imagine what the story character is thinking. Baron-Cohen *et al.* (1986) tested the same three groups of children (autistic, Down's and 'normal') on three types of stories; autistic children found most difficulty with the belief story but did better than 'normal' children on the mechanical story.

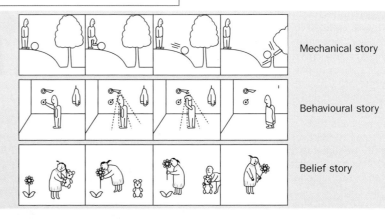

Mechanical story

Behavioural story

Belief story

Multiple choice questions

1. Earlier research showed that
   a. Adults with autism can pass second-order ToM tests.
   b. Children with autism can pass second-order ToM tests.
   c. Adults with autism did not pass second-order ToM tests.
   d. No participants with autism pass second-order ToM tests.

2. Which of the following tasks test ToM?
   a. Eyes Task.
   b. Strange Stories Task.
   c. Basic Emotion Recognition Task.
   d. Both a and b.

3. Which if the following is not true of individuals with TS?
   a. Have normal intelligence.
   b. Have suffered from a developmental disorder since childhood.
   c. Have experienced disruptions to their schooling.
   d. Are more likely to be male than female.

4. The control group in this study was
   a. Adults with AS.
   b. Normal adults.
   c. Adults with TS.
   d. Both b and c.

5. The participants were matched in terms of
   a. Age.   b. School experience.
   c. Gender.   d. All of the above.

6. The Eyes Task uses a form of questioning called
   a. Multiple choice questions.
   b. Open questions.
   c. Difficult questions.
   d. Forced choice questions.

7. Which of the following is a 'foil' word for 'friendly'?
   a. Repulsion.   b. Hostile.
   c. Happy reflection.   d. Disinterested.

8. The validity of the Eyes Task was confirmed using the
   a. Strange Stories Task.
   b. Gender Recognition Task.
   c. Basic Emotion Recognition Task.
   d. Both a and b.

9. The mean scores on the Eyes task was
   a. The same for all three groups.
   b. Groups 1 and 2 were similar.
   c. Groups 2 and 3 were similar.
   d. Groups 1 and 3 were similar.

10. A more realistic test of Theory of Mind than the Eyes Task might be
    a. The Strange Stories Task.
    b. Talking about your own feelings.
    c. Explaining what people were thinking in a movie.
    d. Both a and b.

Answers are on page 65.

Exam-style questions

See page XII–XIII for notes on the exam paper and styles of question.

Section A questions

1. (a) In the study by Baron-Cohen *et al.* why did they need to devise a new test of theory of mind? [2]
   (b) Explain what is meant by the term 'theory of mind'. [2]

2. In what way are individuals with autism the same as those with Asperger's syndrome, and in what way are they different? [4]

3. (a) From the study by Baron-Cohen *et al.*, describe **one** of the control tasks that was used. [2]
   (b) Outline the findings from this task. [2]

4. Identify **one** similarity and **one** difference between the participants in the autism/Asperger's group and the normal adults tested. [4]

5. (a) In the study by Baron-Cohen *et al.* theory of mind was tested using the Eyes Task. Describe this task. [2]
   (b) Describe a different way to test theory of mind. [2]

6. (a) Baron-Cohen *et al.* say that earlier tests of theory of mind produced ceiling effects if used with participants aged over 6 years. Explain the term 'ceiling effects'. [2]
   (b) Explain how such effects were avoided by the newer Eyes Task. [2]

7. (a) Explain what is meant by the term 'ecological validity'. [2]
   (b) Explain in what way the study by Baron-Cohen *et al.* may be described as lacking ecological validity. [2]

Section B questions

(a) What was the aim of the study by Baron-Cohen *et al.*? [2]

(b) Describe the samples used in the Baron-Cohen *et al.* study and explain the reason why each group was included in the study. [6]

(c) Describe how data was gathered in the Baron-Cohen *et al.* study. [6]

(d) Give **one** advantage and **one** disadvantage of the data collection method used by Baron-Cohen *et al.* [6]

(e) Suggest **two** changes to the Baron-Cohen *et al.* study and outline how these changes might affect the results. [8]

(f) Outline the conclusions of the Baron-Cohen *et al.* study. [8]

Section C questions

(a) Outline **one** assumption of the cognitive approach in psychology. [2]

(b) Describe how the cognitive approach could explain autism. [4]

(c) Describe **one** similarity and **one** difference between the Baron-Cohen *et al.* study and any other cognitive approach study. [6]

(d) Discuss the strengths and limitations of the cognitive approach using examples from the Baron-Cohen *et al.* study. [12]

Key issue: qualitative and quantitative

Qualitative data

Qualitative data are about 'qualities' of things. They are descriptions, words, meanings, pictures, texts, and so forth. They are about what something is like, or how something is experienced. Good examples of studies included in this book which are based on the collection of qualitative data are **Freud's** case study of Little Hans and **Reicher and Haslam's** prison simulation. Studies which mainly deal with qualitative data are in the minority in this book and this reflects the dominance of quantitative data in psychological research.

Quantitative data

Quantitative data are about 'quantities' of things. They are numbers, raw scores, percentages, means, standard deviations, etc. They are measurements of things, telling us how much of something there is. Most of the studies in this book deal with quantitative data. For example the memory study by **Loftus and Palmer** records estimates of speed and **Samuel and Bryant's** study of children's judgements records the number of children who make a particular judgement.

Quantitative data: data that represents how much or how long, or how many, etc. there are of something, i.e. behaviour is measured in numbers or quantities. You can analyse quantitative data using descriptive statistics (such as bar charts and other graphs) and inferential statistical tests.

Qualitative data: information that cannot be readily counted, for example about how you think or feel. Qualitative data can be summarised, and may be converted to quantitative data and then counted. Qualitative data typically comes from asking open-ended questions to which the answers are not limited by a set of choices or a scale, or from observations of behaviour without any pre-set categories.

Using the terms correctly

People sometimes refer to research methods as being either qualitative or quantitative. This is misleading, however, because it implies that certain methods always produce certain kinds of data. For example, experiments are usually referred to as 'quantitative' and textual analysis is usually described as 'qualitative'. Experiments, however, can sometimes produce both kinds. Milgram described the behaviour of his participants in some detail (qualitative), as well as measuring the extent to which they were prepared to comply with the demands of the experimenter (quantitative). On the other hand, textual analysis can be 'quantitative'. For example, the Savage-Rumbaugh study reports detailed observational data (qualitative) but the final analysis looks at how many words the chimpanzees learned (quantitative). For this reason it is more accurate to use the terms qualitative and quantitative to refer to 'data', rather than 'research method'.

Idiographic and nomothetic

The debate over the relative merits of qualitative and quantitative data has a long history in psychology. There has been a tension between those who put most value on studying individuals and those that look for common features in groups of people. The study of the individual is called the *idiographic* approach whereas *nomothetic* is more the study of a cohort of individuals.

- *Nomothetic* is a tendency to generalise, and is expressed in the natural sciences. It describes the effort to develop laws that explain objective phenomena, for example, in physics we have laws of motion. An example in psychology is the attempt to identify and measure underlying features in personality and cognition.
- *Idiographic* is a tendency to specify, and is expressed in the humanities. It describes the effort to understand the meaning of accidental and often subjective phenomena. In psychology, first-hand accounts of personal experience are a good example of this approach.

Qualitative and quantitative measures

*Many studies use both types of measure to make the best sense of the issue that is being studied. For example, the study of multiple personality by **Thigpen and Cleckley** starts off gathering qualitative data from the therapeutic interviews with Eve. During these interviews the therapists came to believe that they were dealing with more than one person. If this was the case then they might be able to confirm this by recording different scores for the different personalities on various psychological measures. They therefore used a range of quantitative measures to test the ideas they developed from their original qualitative measures.*

The table below gives a summary of the many measures used by the therapists and divides them into quantitative and qualitative.

Quantitative measures	Qualitative measures
Scores on personality tests.	Clinical interviews with patient(s).
IQ scores.	Interviews with family members.
Memory test scores.	Observations by therapists.
EEG measures of brain activity.	Letter sent to therapists.
	Responses to Rorschach test.

Activity

To Quant or Qual?

That is the question. Look at the terms below and figure out which applies best to qualitative or quantitative data.

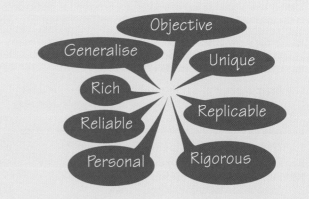

Objective · Generalise · Unique · Rich · Replicable · Reliable · Personal · Rigorous

The answers are not as straightforward as you might think and in some cases they are a matter of opinion. The debate between advocates of the two types is very fierce and often insulting. Maybe people use qualitative measures to cover up for not being able to use statistics, or do people use quantitative measures to avoid difficult questions and personal experience?

You can't explain the magic of the Ronettes in just numbers.

The magic of The Ronettes

How can we capture the richness of human experience? We want to record our experiences and compare them in some way. If we say one song is better than another then we have applied a simple form of measurement. If we want to create a top ten of music then we have to develop some measurement criteria to do that. We might want to use a combination of qualitative and quantitative measures. You might want to know who the best selling artist (quantitative) was but you also need to know what someone feels when they listen to the music. You can investigate this with measures of brain waves (quantitative) or changes in skin conductance (also quantitative) but will these measures be enough to provide an explanation of what the music makes us feel? The experience of music is very personal and rich and it is hard to see how numbers would be able to capture the full response to the greatest song ever performed which is *Be My Baby* by the Ronettes (*what do you mean you've never heard of it?*).

How do I love thee?

In one of the most famous love poems of all time Elizabeth Barrett Browning starts by asking

> *'How do I love thee? Let me count the ways.'*

If she had been looking for quantitative answers she might well have continued,

> *'Well I can think of three maybe four on a good day.'*

Although this would probably have been an accurate answer it would not have done much for the romance in the relationship. In fact she goes on to describe her experience in rich terms,

> *'I love thee to the depth and breadth and height*
>
> *My soul can reach, when feeling out of sight*
>
> *For the ends of Being and ideal Grace.'*

Our complex emotional and cognitive worlds can only be partly described with numbers but fortunately we have the richness of language to capture our experience.

Qs

1. Select **one** core study and give examples of quantitative and qualitative data collected in the study.
2. Outline the strengths and limitations of the quantitative approach in this study.
3. Outline the strengths and limitations of the qualitative approach in this study.
4. As you work your way through the core studies keep a running list of all the measures that they use. Identify (a) what they are trying to measure (b) how they do this (c) whether this is best categorised as being quantitative or qualitative.

Activity

Try and produce qualitative AND quantitative measures for the same material. Use the source given below as the material to work with.

1. Produce a *qualitative analysis:* One way that qualitative data can be summarised is by identifying repeated themes. These should be based on the participants' own meanings, that is they should be groupings as seen from the participant's perspective rather than ones imposed by the researcher. This enables the researcher to reduce the total material (hours of videotapes or pages of interview transcripts) to manageable proportions. The themes or patterns may be illustrated by using quotes from the participant(s).
2. Produce a *quantitative analysis* of the data. To do this you have to convert the data to numbers, for example count up how many times a particular theme is mentioned. You can then represent this data in a bar chart (see descriptive statistics on page 11).

Source for activity

Less than 36 hours into the experiment, Prisoner #8612 began suffering from acute emotional disturbance, disorganised thinking, uncontrollable crying, and rage. In spite of all of this, we had already come to think so much like prison authorities that we thought he was trying to 'con' us – to fool us into releasing him.

Prisoner #8612 told other prisoners, 'You can't leave. You can't quit.' That sent a chilling message and heightened their sense of really being imprisoned. #8612 then began to act 'crazy,' to scream, to curse, to go into a rage that seemed out of control. It took quite a while before we became convinced that he was really suffering and that we had to release him.

The only prisoner who did not want to speak to the priest was Prisoner #819, who was feeling sick, had refused to eat, and wanted to see a doctor rather than a priest. While talking to us, he broke down and began to cry hysterically, just as had the other two boys we released earlier. I took the chain off his foot, the cap off his head, and told him to go and rest.

While I was doing this, one of the guards lined up the other prisoners and had them chant aloud: 'Prisoner #819 is a bad prisoner. Because of what Prisoner #819 did, my cell is a mess, Mr. Correctional Officer.' They shouted this statement in unison a dozen times.

(from Zimbardo's prison study)

...Links to other studies and issues...

Measurement is a key part of any psychological study. You might well argue that it is the main puzzle for any researcher. How do I measure this behaviour or cognition or emotion so that I can best understand what is happening with it? If you want to measure aggressive behaviour, as in the Bobo study (**Bandura *et al.***), then you might count the number of physical acts or the number of shouts. This gives you one measure of aggression but sometimes people can create a very aggressive atmosphere without doing anything or saying anything. To capture this you would have to add first hand accounts of the situation to put alongside your quantitative measures.

One of the other issues that this one ties into very closely is that of **reliability and validity**. The argument for quantitative measures is that they can appear to be very reliable and very reassuring. If we are being prescribed a medication we might be interested to hear some recommendations of it by previous users but we want to know (a) how many people got better using it, and (b) how much better they got. The bottom line for most of the core studies is that they use a mixture of data in order to describe and analyse human behaviour and experience.

Animal language

Communication is inevitable. We can't stop sending messages to other people and interpreting their actions. Humans also have a remarkable way of communicating using symbols which we call language. But what is language and can other animals use it? It is clear that we can communicate with animals because they will respond to us and we will respond to them. There is no dispute about this, but what do animals understand during this communication, and what messages are they able to communicate back to us? In language we talk about things that aren't there, events that are not happening now and not in a place near here. Can animals or do they just communicate 'give me biscuit now!'?

Kanzi (left) and his mother, Matata, two of the chimpanzees in this core study.

Early attempts to teach language to chimps

Vicki

Virginia and Keith Hayes (1952) tried to train a chimpanzee, Vicki, to talk. Their intensive training sessions used rewards to encourage her to make sounds and imitate the lip movements of the trainers. The chimp learned a lot of skills but sadly not the skill of using language. She did learn four sounds, 'Mama', 'Papa', 'cup' and 'up', but her use of them was not very language-like and the sounds were not very convincing either (Hayes and Nissen, 1971). The clear finding is that chimps do not have the vocal apparatus to talk to us.

Gua

A different approach to language training was used by the Kelloggs (*they sound like a pair of flakes – ed.*) who brought up a chimpanzee called Gua with their son called Donald. As far as possible they treated the two alike. Gua seemed to treat the Kelloggs as his parents and showed a trait common in chimpanzees and children – disrupting their parents' love life. This meant that Gua was banned from the Kelloggs' bedroom though why he was ever let in is another matter. Sadly, Gua did not learn to talk. We have no information about Donald's tree climbing behaviour or liking for bananas (Kellogg and Kellogg 1933).

Sarah

Premack and Premack (1983) raised a chimpanzee, Sarah, and taught her to use different coloured and shaped discs to represent words. She placed these on a board to make sentences. First she learned the symbol for an object or concept (for example, apple), then she put symbols together to form sentences (first 'Mary + apple', next 'Mary + to give + apple', and finally 'Sarah + to give + apple + Mary'). At the end she had acquired 130 symbols and could make sentences up to eight units long. However, Sarah did not spontaneously use language to ask questions although she would practise sentences on her own.

Washoe

The breakthrough study in the field of animal language was of Washoe (Gardner and Gardner, 1969). Washoe was born in Africa, around September of 1965. She was taken to the US where Drs Allen and Beatrix Gardner adopted her for their research, naming her after Washoe County, Nevada where they lived. She was between 8 and 14 months old at the start of the project. Much later she moved with Roger and Deborah Fouts to Central Washington University where a special facility was set up for her and other chimpanzees involved in their language programme (see www.friendsofwashoe.org/).

Washoe has been claimed to be the first animal to acquire human language. She was taught American Sign Language and it has been reported that Washoe could reliably use about 250 signs. 'Reliable use' was established when a sign was seen by three different observers in three separate spontaneous instances in the correct context and used appropriately, and then seen 15 days in a row to be added to her sign list.

Chimpanzees are remarkable imitators, and in the early interactions, Washoe was encouraged to imitate the gestures of the humans. She would be rewarded for her efforts with tickles! Later in the programme, when Washoe made an incorrect sign or a badly formed sign, then she would be encouraged to imitate the correct one. However, if she was pressed too hard for the right sign, Washoe sometimes became diverted from the original task, or ran away, or went into a tantrum, or even bit the tutor.

The jury is still out on whether Washoe developed language or not. The Gardners pointed to the range of signs and the situations she used them in, but others noted that she never developed a regular word order which is a basic feature of any language. The controversy did not affect her celebrity status, however, and her progress was avidly followed by millions of people around the world.

Washoe died in October 2007, aged 42. It is reported on her website that she died at home surrounded by her family and friends. She was probably the best known and best loved primate ever – truly she was the people's chimpanzee (© T. Blair).

Language and communication

Language: A small number of signals (sounds, letters, gestures) that by themselves are meaningless, but can be put together according to certain rules to make an infinite number of messages.

Communication: The way in which one animal or person transmits information to another and influences them.

Everyone agrees that animals can communicate with each other. The disagreement is over whether they can use something similar to human language to do this.

Aitchison (1983) suggests there are ten criteria that distinguish communication from language including:

- arbitrariness of the symbols (the symbol is not like the object or the action it is describing);
- semanticity (the use of symbols to mean objects or actions);
- displacement (refers to things that are distant in time and space);
- it is used spontaneously;
- it involves turn-taking;
- it is structure dependent (the symbols are combined according to the rules of grammar).

ELIZA

Although Washoe and Kanzi respond to language it does not mean they understand it. For thirty years computers have been able to simulate conversation. For example in the 1960s Weizenbaum created a programme called ELIZA that was able to respond to a user's input as if it were a non-directive psychotherapist. Expert judges were not always able to tell the difference between ELIZA's responses and those of a real therapist (see Boden, 1977). If you want some therapy from ELIZA, then just do a search for her on the internet and start the consultation.

Naom Chomsky, the respected American linguist, on animal language.

'It is about as likely that an ape will prove to have language ability as that there is an island somewhere with a species of flightless birds waiting for human beings to teach them how to fly.' (cited in Terrace, 1979)

Samuel Pepys

'I do believe it already understands much English: and I am of the mind it might be taught to speak or make signs.' (Diary, 24th August 1661)

Animals and humans

What is the difference between animals and humans? Are humans just another animal that is a bit more intelligent or is there a qualitative difference between us and them? This is a question that challenges scientific and religious beliefs.

One of the crucial differences between humans and animals is that we have language, and it is argued that this shows our uniqueness. The work on Kanzi and the other chimpanzees is important because, if Sue Savage-Rumbaugh and her team can show that the chimpanzees have language, then it breaks down one of the last big divides between the species.

The chimpanzees, like many other animals, can communicate and respond to messages but is this the same as language? Linguists argue that a true language is one that can generate novel messages. To do this you need to have a set of rules (a *grammar* or *syntax*) to combine symbols. One example of a rule is the use of word order to change the meaning of messages. For example, 'the beer is on the table' has a different meaning to 'the table is on the beer'. If Kanzi can put words in order she is showing the rule of grammar. And if she makes spontaneous communications then that would be a further marker of language.

Monkey suit

When we look at an ape are we misinterpreting what we see? Do we see an animal or do we treat them as if they are a human in a hairy suit?

Anthropomorphism is the attribution of human characteristics to inanimate objects, animals, forces of nature, and others.

When we say dogs are loyal or foxes are cunning we are treating the animals as if they think and behave like humans. We often take this a step further and attribute human qualities to machines, for example talking to your computer as if it is deliberately messing you about.

When we are anthropomorphic we are assuming that the animals or machines have a theory of mind, that they know what they are doing and they are also responding to us (see the study on autism on page 44).

Thomas the Tank Engine is another example of anthropomorphism. We hope we're not spoiling anything if we tell you that tank engines aren't really alive.

Clever Hans

It is a common human error to overestimate the abilities of animals. Many dog owners will say things like 'he understands every word' about their pets. Unfortunately they are completely deluded as dogs do not understand language even though they learn to respond to 'walkies' and 'biscuit'.

There is a long history of making this mistake. In 1904 a scientific commission, including a psychologist, assembled to examine the intelligent horse known as Clever Hans. Russian aristocrat Wilhelm Von-Osten claimed to have taught Clever Hans basic arithmetic over a period of two years using skittles, an abacus and a blackboard with carrots for a reward. Hans gave the answers to problems by tapping his hoof on the ground. The commission were convinced by the demonstration.

Oskar Pfungst, however, carried out more tests on the horse and discovered that his skills were indeed clever, but not arithmetical. He found that Hans only got the questions right when Von-Osten knew the answer, and could be seen by the horse. Pfungst's studies showed that when Hans was counting with his hoof Von-Osten inclined his head downwards to see the hoof. When the correct answer was reached he would either straighten up slightly or raise an eyebrow or even slightly flare his nostrils. Pfungst himself was able to get the same level of performance out of Hans using these tricks himself. Von-Osten died a disillusioned man in 1909. It is not recorded what happened to Hans.

Clever Hans and his trainer Wilhelm Von-Osten enjoy some after-dinner chit chat about the runners in the 3.30 at Kempton Park.

...Link to the core study...

If only we could speak to the animals, what would they say? If **Savage-Rumbaugh et al.** can show that chimpanzees have the capacity for language they will have smashed the last great divide between people and other animals. Mind you, if they are successful it begs the question of why chimps don't use language on a daily basis. But then perhaps they do.

Savage-Rumbaugh *et al.*: the core study

Sue Savage-Rumbaugh, Kelly McDonald, Rose A. Sevcik, William D. Hopkins and Elizabeth Rupert (1986) Spontaneous symbol acquisition and communicative use by Pygmy Chimpanzees (Pan paniscus). *Journal of Experimental Psychology*, 115 (3), pages 211–235.

Abstract

Aim
To study human language capabilities in pygmy chimpanzees.

Method
The report focuses on two pygmy chimpanzees (Kanzi and his sister Mulika) and compares them to two common chimpanzees (Austin and Sherman).

Kanzi and Mulika learned to use lexigrams by watching through observation and also through natural communication with the experimenters, rather than being specifically trained.

A record was kept of Kanzi and Mulika's vocabulary use during the period of this report indicating (1) correctness and (2) whether it was spontaneous, imitated or structured. Behavioural verification was used to demonstrate that the chimpanzees did understand the symbols used. Reliability of observations was checked and the chimpanzees' vocabulary was also formally tested at the end to rule out the effect of cueing.

Results
Kanzi started using lexigrams when his mother went away. Mulika started using the lexigrams earlier (at 12 months), though not appropriately at first. Both chimpanzees first used a new term in an associative context, similar to the same process in children. In total, during the period covered by this report, Kanzi acquired 46 words and Mulika 37. Kanzi also produced an impressive total of nonimitative combinations (2,500). Kanzi and Mulika did well on the formal tests, being able to identify photographs when prompted with a lexigram (and vice versa) or spoken word. Kanzi was also able to lead a visitor who knew nothing of the forest at the Language Learning Centre to the various sites on request.

Discussion
This report records the entire body of symbol usage and comprehension for Kanzi and Mulika. It demonstrates a number of key differences between pygmy and common chimpanzees in (1) the ease of language acquisition, (2) the ability to comprehend Spoken English, (3) the specificity with which the lexigrams were used and (4) use of syntactical structure.

Overall the results suggest that it is possible for a chimpanzee to spontaneously acquire human language.

Aim

When learning language Lock (1980) has identified two steps:

1 *Associative symbol learning* – a child learns to *associate* specific sounds with specific objects, for example naming pictures in a book.

2 *Representational (or referential) symbol learning* – using the sounds to *refer* to the objects, for example being able to respond to the request 'get your ball' even if the ball is in another room (i.e. there are no contextual cues to provide association).

Past research with apes has supplied ample evidence of associative symbol learning but representational usage has only been demonstrated after extensive training with Sherman and Austin, two common chimpanzees (*Pan troglodytes*).

Understanding spoken English words
One of the barriers in training apes to use human language is their difficulty in producing speech. However they may still be able to comprehend it. True comprehension is more than just responding to words, for example a dog can respond to the command 'sit'. Children acquire true comprehension without any training, unlike dogs. Another characteristic of human language is the ability, when directed, to select a specific object from a group, i.e. provide a differential response on cue. Thus it should be possible to demonstrate human language capabilities in apes by (a) needing no training and (b) being able to provide differential responses on cue.

This report aims to demonstrate these abilities in pygmy chimpanzees.

Biographical notes

Kanzi (left) using a lexigram panel to communicate with Sue Savage-Rumbaugh at the Language Research Centre at Georgia State University which is a 55-acre forest for the apes' use. Kanzi, a pygmy chimpanzee *(Pan paniscus)*, was aged four at the end of this report. His name means 'treasure' in Swahili. The Centre has a number of other apes, some mentioned in this report. You can read all about the apes, and look at videos, on the website for the Great Ape Trust (see link below).

Dr. Savage-Rumbaugh's work with Kanzi, the first ape to learn language in the same manner as children, was selected by the *Millennium Project* as one of the top 100 most influential works in cognitive science in the twentieth century by the University of Minnesota Center for Cognitive Sciences in 1991.

Method

Subjects

The principal subject was a pygmy chimpanzee (Latin name *Pan paniscus*) called Kanzi who was aged 30–47 months during the time of this report. This particular species of great ape is rare both in captivity and in the wild. Observational studies of *Pan paniscus* suggest they are a more social species than other apes and display more highly developed social skills such as food sharing. Other research has also found indications that they might be a brighter species. This would suggest they might be better able to acquire language.

A second pygmy chimpanzee was studied, Kanzi's younger sister, Mulika, aged 11–21 months during the period of this report. Both spent several hours a day with their mother and were attached to her, but they appeared to prefer human company.

Two other chimpanzees (common chimpanzees – *Pan troglodytes*) are included in this study as comparisons – Austin and Sherman. They were part of earlier training programmes

The small number of subjects is inevitable because of the time required in conducting an in-depth longitudinal study.

www Great Ape Trust http://www.greatapetrust.org/research/srumbaugh/rumbaugh.php

Procedure

Communication system

Kanzi and Mulika used a visual symbol system consisting of geometric symbols (lexigrams) which brightened when touched. These symbols were on an electronic keyboard, or on a pointing board for use outside. A speech synthesiser was added when it became apparent that Kanzi could comprehend words, so the appropriate words were spoken when a symbol is touched.

Early rearing and exposure to lexigrams

Kanzi was exposed to the use of symbols, gestures and human speech from the age of 6 months as he watched the interactions between his mother (Matata) and her keepers. There was no attempt to train Kanzi directly. From the age of about one and a half years Kanzi started to show an interest in the symbols. He sometimes pressed a lexigram and ran to the food machine showing he had learned an association between touching symbols and the food dispensing machine, though he did not show an understanding that *specific* symbols were associated with specific foods. He did spontaneously start to use the *chase* lexigram to initiate a game of chase just shortly after he spontaneously started to use a hand gesture (hand clapping) for the same purpose.

Kanzi was separated from his mother Matata at two and a half years so Matata could take part in a breeding program. When she returned four months later Kanzi had developed a preference for human company. Kanzi's sister Mulika was born nine months later and Kanzi enjoyed spending time with her. At four months of age Mulika developed an eye infection and was taken away for treatment. When she returned she also chose to stay with human companions most of the time. Mulika did not observe Matata learning to use the lexigrams but she did observe Kanzi using them.

In contrast with Sherman and Austin, Kanzi and Mulika were not trained to use lexigrams. People around them modelled symbol use in the course of communicating with each other and the chimpanzees. They emphasised their activities vocally and visually by pointing to appropriate lexigrams. For example, if they were engaged in a tickling bout the teacher would say '[teacher's name] tickle Kanzi' via the keyboard and also vocally.

Naturalistic outdoor environment

During the warmer months of the year food was placed at 17 named locations within the 55-acre forest used by the Language Research Centre (see map on next page). The name of each site matched the food that was placed there (e.g. 'Raisins' and 'Hotdog'). To get food the chimpanzees had to go to these places. At first Kanzi was shown photos of various food items and asked to indicate which he wanted to eat, and then taken to the right location. Within four months Kanzi could select a photo and guide others to the right place, sometimes carrying Mulika on the way. Later he could use the symbols alone and Mulika too began to use the symbols to initiate travel.

The lexigrams were display on a computer or, when outdoors, the chimpanzees had a board with the lexigrams on it.

Data recording

When the chimpanzees used a lexigram indoors on the computer this could be automatically recorded. Outdoors the record was made by hand and entered into the computer at the end of each day. This meant there was a complete record of Kanzi's utterances from 30–47 months of age and for Mulika from 11–21 months.

Each utterance was classified as (1) correct or incorrect, (2) spontaneous (no prior prompting), imitated (if it included any part of a companion's previous utterance) or structured (initiated by a question, request or object). Structured questions were used to determine whether the chimpanzees could give a specific answer.

Vocabulary acquisition criterion

In order to count a word as being 'acquired' it was not sufficient that they produced context-appropriate words since this can happen without comprehension. What was required was a spontaneous utterance which could be verified on nine out of ten occurrences (= behavioural verification). For example, Kanzi might indicate he wanted to go to the treehouse and this would be verified if he then took the experimenter to this location, producing a positive concordance score.

In order to establish the reliability of the observations one block of 4½ hours of observations made in real time was compared with another set of observations made from a videotape of the same 4½ hours. There was 100% agreement with regard to the lexigrams used and their correctness but one disagreement about whether it was spontaneous or not. In addition the videotape observer recorded an extra nine utterances.

Tests of productive and receptive capacities

At the end of the period covered by this report, Kanzi and Mulika were formally tested on all the words in their vocabulary. This was done formally to ensure that their performance was not due to contextual cues or inadvertent glances. They were tested by (a) being shown photographs and then asked to select the right lexigram, or (b) listening to a word or a synthesised version of the word and then asked to select the right photograph or lexigram.

Qs

1 Explain the differences between the five chimpanzees in this report.

2 What symbol system did the chimpanzees use and how did they indicate their choice of symbol to the researchers?

3 How did the researchers communicate with the chimpanzees?

4 What was the purpose of using 'structured questions'?

5 Explain what was meant by 'behavioural verification' and 'concordance score'.

6 How did the researchers check the reliability of the observations?

7 What conclusions can you make about the reliability of the observations?

8 What were the formal tests and why were they necessary?

Activity

Try learning to use lexigrams yourself. Some people should be the researchers and others are chimpanzees. The researchers should create a list of made-up words such as 'TARK' and 'BLOP' and draw a symbol for each new word. They should also decide on the meaning for the word. Now try and teach your chimpanzees to use this vocabulary.

Results

Untutored gestures

Kanzi and Mulika naturally used gestures to communicate. Their gestures were often more explicit than those used by Sherman and Austin, for example, when Mulika wanted a balloon blown up she placed it in a person's hand and then pointed to the person's mouth and even pushed the balloon tow.ards their mouth.

First use of lexigrams

There was no direct attempt to teach Kanzi to use the lexigrams. Kanzi started using the lexigrams when his mother went away (age 2^1/$_2$ years). He immediately had a fair vocabulary which suggested that he had already learned the meaning of some of the lexigrams (by watching Matata using the symbols) though he hadn't shown this.

Mulika began using symbols at 12 months, much earlier than Kanzi. At first she used particular symbols (such as for milk) for a variety of all-purpose things such as asking to be picked up or requests for food or even for milk.

At about 14 months Mulika began using a number of lexigrams appropriately – her new words over the next few months were *milk, surprise, Matata, peanut, hotdog, cake, mushroom, melon, cherry, banana, jelly, go* and *blueberry*. Mulika occasionally reverted to using milk as an all-purpose communication.

Neither Kanzi or Mulika had difficulty identifying a lexigram when it was in a new position or on another keyboard.

Associative usage

It was observed that both chimpanzees started using a new term in an associative context first (see Lock's two steps in language acquisition at the start of this core study). For example, Kanzi first 'heard' the word strawberries when he was at the mushroom site. He and a researcher then went to the new *strawberries* site where he tasted some. Initially Kanzi's spontaneous usage of *strawberries* was restricted to the mushroom site, i.e. where the word was first imitated. Eventually this extended beyond the 'initial acquisition routine' to context-free situations. It seems likely that children go through the same initial process of associative usage before being able to use symbols independent of context.

Progress

In total, during the period covered by this report, Kanzi acquired 46 words and Mulika 37. Mulika's initial rate of acquisition was slower than Kanzi's . This was probably because Kanzi had actually acquired some words in the period before his mother's departure but not produced them. After his mother left Kanzi suddenly started producing words which he probably had

acquired before so it appeared that he learned more quickly. Comprehension preceded production in the case of 63% of the words.

Combinations

One of the key characteristic of human language acquisition is the ability to combine words to produce novel meanings. Kanzi's multisymbol expressions appeared quite early, within the first month of lexigram usage. Such combinations were far fewer than single symbol utterances. In total, over the 17 months, Kanzi produced 2,540 nonimitative combinations plus 265 which were prompted or partially imitated, and all but ten were judged to be appropriate and understandable; 764 were only ever produced once.

This is a lot less than Nim (another chimpanzee trained to use human language – see page 58) who produced 19,000 combinations during a similar period of time. Kanzi's three word utterances never referred to himself whereas all of Nim's did (e.g. 'more eat Nim'). Nim's most frequent combinations related to food whereas Kanzi's were more likely to relate to games (e.g. 'chase bit person').

Imitation

Like human children Kanzi and Mulika imitated most often when they were learning new words. The proportion of imitated to spontaneous utterances was similar to children's – about 15% of utterances were imitation and 80% were spontaneous. Imitation seems to be a strategy used by language learners when they don't know what to say.

Formal tests

The formal tests were described on the previous page. When Sherman and Austin were tested they were initially confused because they anticipated that, when they identified an object, they would then get the object (e.g. a banana). Kanzi and Mulika did well on the formal tests from the start. They could select photographs when prompted with the lexigram, and vice versa, and could also do either when prompted with the

spoken word. They had difficulty when the word was produced by a synthesiser (to cut out any cueing that might occur when giving vocal communication) but even the experimenters found it hard to identify the synthesised words.

Travel plans

When Kanzi was about three years old a 'blind' test was arranged with someone who had never been in the wooded area and therefore could offer no cues. Kanzi was able to choose a symbol or photograph from a selection and then go to the correct place.

When he was showing the 'blind' visitor around he directed him to the back of the 55 acres, an area where he was not usually allowed to go, presumably just to explore this area of dense bush. He then directed them back to the trail. There were two locations not selected by Kanzi; the visitor used spoken English to ask Kanzi to lead him to these places as well, which he was able to do.

This test was not given to Mulika because, at the time of this report, she did not like to travel without Kanzi.

General observations regarding symbol usage

Both Kanzi and Mulika made generalisations beyond the particular meaning of a word. For example, they used *tomato* to refer to different round red fruits.

Kanzi also used words in different ways. For example, if he said *juice* and then went to that location in the forest he didn't then look for the juice – indicating that he meant *juice* as the location and not the drink.

Sometimes Kanzi took the lexigram keyboard and went off by himself to use it, as if he wanted just to practise. Kanzi has also used the keyboard to indicate when he wanted *no play*.

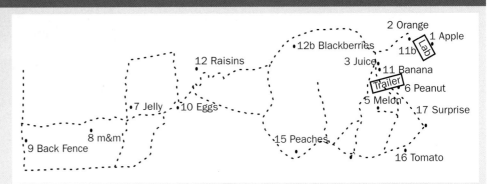

Map of the 55-acre forest at the Language Research Centre, showing Kanzi's food sites.

Discussion

This report is the first time the entire body of symbol usage and comprehension has been recorded for apes. Previous studies have been criticised because they included anecdotal records. For example, an ape might sign *coffee* when someone walks past with coffee (an appropriate usage) but might also sign the same word on occasions when it is inappropriate. Therefore it is not clear whether the ape has a true comprehension of the word. In this study the formal tests demonstrated usage and accuracy.

The number of apes studied means that it may be unreasonable to make generalisations. However some preliminary comparisons can be made between species.

Difference 1 regards the ease of language acquisition. Kanzi and Mulika acquired language with greater ease than Sherman and Austin, who required extensive training. It took three years for a clear concordance to develop between what they said and what they did, something that was spontaneously grasped by Kanzi and Mulika. Like normal children, Kanzi and Mulika usually used words appropriately from the start.

Matata did not acquire symbols spontaneously and required even more training than Sherman and Austin. This suggests that there may be a critical age for the development of language for these chimpanzees. In addition Sherman and Austin's difficulties might be due to their different learning environment (as compared to Kanzi and Mulika's learning environment).

Difference 2 is the ability to comprehend spoken English words. Kanzi and Mulika are the only chimpanzees recorded who have been able to respond to spoken language without any contextual cues. It is important to note that no one ever tried to specifically teach them to respond to English commands. They were spoken to normally at all times. This understanding of spoken English gave them an advantage with the keyboard because they understood the words first and then they just had to link the word to the lexigram in order to use the lexigram. This suggests that the way the pygmy chimpanzees acquire graphic symbols (lexigrams) is fundamentally different from the way the common chimpanzees learn to use symbols.

Difference 3 is in the specificity with which the lexigrams were used. Sherman and Austin were inclined to acquire broad differentiations, such as between *drink* and *eat*, whereas Kanzi and Mulika spontaneously learned to differentiate between specific words (e.g. between *juice* and *coke*). Even after Sherman and Austin were taught to differentiate, they often 'drifted' back into more general usage so that terms such as *juice* and *coke* were used interchangeably.

Difference 4 was that Kanzi could direct someone other than himself to do something (to request A to act on B where he was neither A or B). This is regarded as the beginnings of a use of syntax – the rules that govern the structure of sentences and enable us to understand the difference between 'Jim kissed Mary' and 'Mary kissed Jim' (the different structures tell a different story).

Conclusion

Further research is ongoing where infants of both species are being reared side-by-side in order to further examine the differences. From this study it appears that pygmy chimpanzees have a propensity for the acquisition of symbols. The possession of such a propensity is waiting to be tapped and it might be possible for one individual to push the behaviour of a group of wild apes towards language.

Evaluating the study by Savage-Rumbaugh *et al.*

The research method
This research could be described as a case study. *What are the strengths and limitations of this research method in the context of this study?*

It was also an observational study. What are the strengths and limitations of this research method in the context of this study?

There are no simple answers. Evaluating a study requires you to think. We have provided some pointers here, linked to the KEY ISSUES covered through this book – see page XIV for a table of these key issues.

The sample
Various chimpanzees were used in this study, belonging to different species. It was recognised as a small sample. *How would the size of the sample affect the conclusions that can be drawn from this study?*

Representativeness
Each chimpanzee may not have been representative of his/her own species, and may have had certain unique characteristics. For example Nim seemed more interested in food than Kanzi, who talked about games. *How might such individual differences affect the representativeness and generalisability of the observations in this study?*

Qualitative or quantitative?
Both qualitative and quantitative data was collected in this study. *Give examples of both kinds of data and the strengths of each kind in the context of this study.*

Ethical issues
Part of the process of teaching language to an animal is to enculturate them into the human world. *Is it ethical to teach human language to animals? [You might consider the costs and benefits.]*

Nature or nurture?
If animals can learn to use human language, then what can we conclude about the nature of human language?

Applications/usefulness
How might the findings from this report be used in real life?
How valuable was this study?

What next?
Describe **one** change to this study, and say how you think this might affect the outcome.

Debate

Can non-human animals use language?

Do some further research yourself on the language debate and prepare arguments for and against the view that research has been able to show that non-human animals can use language.

...Links to other studies and issues...

This study has clear links to the autism work of **Baron-Cohen** *et al.* because the aim of both strands of research is to unlock our understanding of an individual by developing ways for them to communicate.

Central to the work on animal language is the concept of theory of mind. Do animals have a sense of their own existence and can they create a mental model of another individual in their minds?

This study also uses the techniques of behaviourism outlined in the study by **Bandura** *et al.*

Just monkeying around

The jury is still out on animal language. There are strong supporters of the view that the chimps are using language and equally strong critics of this view. Maybe we want to believe in it too much (see the key issue on being sceptical).

Nim Chimpsky

Nim is another famous chimpanzee (mentioned in the core study). He was studied by Terrace (1979). Nim Chimpsky (named after the linguistics expert, Noam Chomsky) learnt 125 different signs and put them together in combinations. However, when Terrace examined the tapes of all of Nim's communications he was disappointed to find a marked difference between Nim's communication and child language.

1   There was no increase in the length of Nim's communications (children show a steady increase).

2   Only 12% of Nim's communications were spontaneous (children initiate more communications than they respond to).

3   Imitation increased (it declines in children) as language developed.

4   Nim made frequent interruptions and did not learn to take turns (very young children learn to take turns).

Although Terrace set out to replicate the Washoe study he was not able to find any evidence that Nim was using anything like human language. Nim could communicate to get things he wanted, but not to communicate ideas or thoughts or meanings. A pigeon could be taught the same skill using the techniques of operant conditioning (see page 61).

A good illustration of the limitations of Nim's communication can be seen in his longest recorded sentence, *'Give orange me give eat orange me eat orange give me eat orange give me you.'* It's not just that it doesn't resemble a Shakespearean sonnet, but it doesn't resemble the language of a toddler.

Terrace concludes his paper by writing:

'Sequences of signs, produced by Nim and by other apes, may resemble the first multiword sequences produced by children. But unless alternative explanations of an ape's combination of signs are eliminated, in particular the habit of partially imitating teachers' recent utterances, there is no reason to regard an ape's utterance as a sentence' (Terrace *et al.*, 1979).

The question of animal language remains controversial because replication studies are difficult to carry out. The key theoretical issue concerns whether the animals are learning the rules of a language or just learning to imitate for rewards

'That which distinguishes man from the lower animals is not the understanding of articulate sounds, for as everyone knows, dogs understand many words and sentences.' Charles Darwin *'Descent of Man'* (1871).

Kanzi or Can't he?

Remarkable animals have always been able to capture the public imagination. The example of Clever Hans (see page 53) shows how easy it is to overestimate what they can do. At the Kanzi website (www.greatapetrust.org/bonobo/meet/kanzi. php) it is possible to see another example of this. They claim that *'his vocabulary includes more than 500 words! His comprehension of spoken language is at least equivalent to that of a two-and-a-half-year-old child.'*

The most famous feature of bonobos is that they are very sexually active. Sex plays a big part in bonobo daily life and is used as a greeting, a way of resolving conflicts, a way of making up with another individual after a conflict and a form of bartering for food and treats.

Kanzi's social behaviour does not appear to be recorded on the website so we have no idea if he has used his communication skills to help make friends. We are told however that Kanzi's achievements are not limited to language, but include tool use and tool manufacturing. According to the great ape trust website, *'Kanzi has shown skills as a stone tool maker and he is very proud of his ability to flake Oldowan style cutting knives. Kanzi's stone knives are very sharp and he's able to cut hide and thick ropes with them.'*

The website goes on to say that Kanzi has also demonstrated his unspecified and musical skills, having played with Sir Paul McCartney and Peter Gabriel. It is not recorded what songs they played together nor whether he engaged with traditional bonobo behaviour with them afterwards.

Kanzi is supported by the Great Ape Trust and if you go to www.greatapestore.org you can buy a range of monkey-related products, our favourite being the PROUD TO BE A PRIMATE bumper sticker.

Talking to pets

Millions of pet owners will tell you their animal 'understands every word I say'. Check this out with the dog translation device. It is called the *Bowlingual* and it claims to be able to interpret about 200 phrases or words – grouped in six different emotional categories: fun, frustration, menace, sorrow, demand and self-expression.

The inventors of the Bowlingual were awarded the 2002 IgNoble Peace Prize (like a Nobel Prize, but not quite) for promoting peace and harmony between species (see www.improb.com).

So can other animals really acquire human language skills?
Despite the obvious fun of the Bowlingual the simple fact is that your pets can not communicate with you. They have no problems hearing words that we use and recognising them but they do not understand them. What they do is to learn an association (see the key issue on behaviourism) between specific words and specific activities (like going for a walk) or other rewards (like food).

This repertoire of words can become quite extensive, maybe even as much as 20–30 words or more but this is not language comprehension. For example if you say: 'Fang lets go out and have a nice walk in the park and chase rabbits', then what Fang hears is most likely 'FANG blah blah blah WALK blah blah blah' and this is enough to get Fang jumping all over the kitchen with excitement. And the fact that you picked up the lead and ball is also a big clue to the mutt.

Fang can also probably respond to the non-verbal emotional tones you use when you say the words and is able to make different responses to your different emotional states. It is a big jump to think that the animal understands your emotional state but it is clear that it can recognise the change and respond to it.

Our willingness to believe in the intelligence of our pets is another example of animism or anthropomorphism (see page 72).

Multiple choice questions

1 Kanzi belonged to which species
   a Old world chimpanzees.
   b Pygmy chimpanzees.
   c Forest chimpanzees.
   d Common chimpanzees.

2 Kanzi's mother was called
   a Mulika.   b Austin.
   c Matata.   c Mamosa.

3 The symbol system that was used with
   the chimpanzees was
   a Flexiforms.   b Lexiforms.
   c Flexigrams.   d Lexigrams.

4 Which of the following is not a name of
   one of the sites in the forest?
   a apple.   b campfire.
   c peaches.   d raisins.

5 In total Kanzi learned how many words
   during the period of this report?
   a 41   b 43
   c 46   d 53

6 Which chimpanzee had the fastest initial
   rate of acquisition of language?
   a Kanzi.   b Mulika.
   c Matata.   c Austin.

7 Which of the following is true for both the
   pygmy chimpanzees and children?
   a They imitated more words than they
     produced spontaneously.
   b A new term was used in an associative
     context first.
   c They preferred to use words related to
     games rather than food.
   d All of the above.

8 How many months old was Mulika at the
   end of the study?
   a 21   b 25
   c 30   d 47

9 One of the formal tests of comprehension
   required the chimpanzees to
   a Select the right lexigram for a
     photograph.
   b Combine lexigrams.
   c Lead a researcher around the forest.
   d Speak English.

10 Which of the following is not a difference
   between the pygmy and common
   chimpanzees?
   a The ease of language acquisition.
   b The ability to use lexigrams in a
     specific context.
   c The ability to understand spoken
     English words.
   d The ability to use lexigrams to
     communicate.

Answers are on page 65.

Exam-style questions

See page XII–XIII for notes on the exam paper and styles of question.

Section A questions

1 From the study by Savage-Rumbaugh et al. outline **two** methods that were used to record the lexigrams used by the chimpanzees. [4]

2 Describe **two** differences between the language acquisition of pygmy chimpanzees and common chimpanzees. [4]

3 Savage-Rumbaugh et al. claim that Kanzi and Mulika were exposed to language in a different way to Sherman and Austin.
   (a) Explain in what way this was different. [2]
   (b) How might this difference have affected their development of language? [2]

4 (a) Savage-Rumbaugh et al. conclude that Kanzi's use of language might be 'a precursor of syntactical structure'. Explain is meant by 'syntax'. [2]
   (b) Describe **one** other conclusion from the study by Savage-Rumbaugh et al. [2]

5 Identify **two** similarities between Kanzi's acquisition of language and the way children acquire language. [4]

6 (a) Savage-Rumbaugh et al. used formal tests with the chimpanzees. Why were such tests necessary? [2]
   (b) Describe **one** of the formal tests that was used to test Kanzi. [2]

7 In the study by Savage-Rumbaugh et al. explain the criterion used to decide whether a chimpanzee had acquired true comprehension of a word. [4]

Section B questions

(a) What was the aim of the study by Savage-Rumbaugh et al.? [2]

(b) Describe the sample used in the study by Savage-Rumbaugh et al. [6]

(c) Describe the way data was collected in the study by Savage-Rumbaugh et al. [6]

(d) Give **one** advantage and **one** disadvantage of conducting case studies. [6]

(e) Outline the conclusions drawn from the study by Savage-Rumbaugh et al. [8]

(f) Suggest **two** changes that could be made to this study and outline what impact these changes might have on the results. [8]

Section C questions

(a) Explain what is meant by both quantitative data and qualitative data, using examples from the study by Savage-Rumbaugh et al. [6]

(b) Discuss the strengths and limitations of using quantitative data with reference to the study by Savage-Rumbaugh et al. [12]

(c) Describe **one** similarity and **one** difference between the study by Savage-Rumbaugh et al. and any other study that used qualitative data. [6]

Key issue: behaviourism

Behaviourism was one of the great intellectual movements of the twentieth century. The term 'behaviourism' was first used by **John B. Watson** (1878–1958) in a paper written in 1913 in which he outlined a plan for behaviourism – an approach that was to dominate psychology for the next 50 years. It captured the public imagination because it suggested we are born equal, and the differences between us come from experience rather than breeding. This taps into the USA Declaration of Independence which states: *'We hold these truths to be self-evident, that all men are created equal ...'*

It is part of the American Dream that people can achieve because of their efforts and abilities rather than because of their class, and behaviourism gave scientific life to that dream.

Before Watson: Pavlov and Thorndike

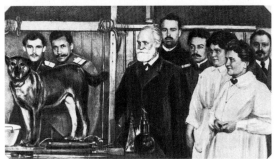

Pavlov and his associates at the laboratory.

In Russia, **Ivan Pavlov** (1849–1936) investigated reflex behaviour and discovered that dogs can learn to produce a reflex response to new stimuli. Most famously, he is reported to have trained dogs to salivate when they heard the sound of a bell because this was associated with food. This type of learning is called **classical conditioning.**

Pavlov discovered one of the ways in which animals learn. In this case they learn to perform reflex behaviours (ones they were born with) in response to new stimuli. In the famous example, the dogs were already able to salivate and Pavlov trained them to show this behaviour to a new stimulus. This is a very common experience as attested by one of the authors who regularly went to a local Asian restaurant where he would choose 'Hot Meat' off the menu. After a few visits to the restaurant he only had to read the words 'Hot Meat' on the menu in order to start salivating, and, in fact, just typing it now has brought about the same response.

Of course there is more to classical conditioning than salivating to food and it can explain how we develop a number of emotional and sexual responses. The principle of this type of learning is still used in psychotherapies today.

At the same time that Pavlov was getting his dogs to salivate, American psychologist **Edward Lee Thorndike** (1874–1949) was investigating how animals learn. In contrast to Pavlov, Thorndike was interested in how they learned new behaviours. In one series of observations he placed a cat in a 'puzzle box' and measured the time it took to escape. Over a number of trials the time taken to escape decreased yet the animal showed no sign of insight into the problem. It got out but it did not understand how it did it. From his observations he developed the Law of Effect which states that *the consequence of a successful behaviour is that it is more likely to recur in similar circumstances*. This provides a description of learning that does not require ideas such as 'the mind'.

Behaviourism is a school of thought which holds that the observation and description of behaviour is all that is needed to understand human beings, and that manipulation of stimulus-response contingencies is all that is needed to change human behaviour.

Classical conditioning is a form of learning which involves the pairing of a neutral stimulus with a reflex.

Learning is a change in behaviour, or the potential for behaviour, that occurs as a result of environmental experience, but is not the result of such factors as fatigue, drugs or injury.

Operant conditioning is the process of learning identified by B. F. Skinner, in which learning occurs as a result of positive or negative reinforcement of an animal or human being's action.

Watson and behaviourism

Before **John B. Watson** put forward his theory of behaviourism psychology was mainly looking at the internal workings of the mind. This work was making limited progress because it was difficult to get evidence on how the mind works because first there was no agreement on what the mind is and secondly there was no way to measure it or record what it did.

Watson suggested we should ignore concepts of intangible things like 'the mind' and concentrate on what we can observe and measure. The things people do (in other words, their behaviour) can be observed and measured and so Watson proposed that psychology should study this behaviour and record and analyse it using the techniques of science.

In brief Watson proposed:

- Studying behaviour rather than 'mind'.
- Using experimental and objective techniques.
- We are born with a tabula rasa (blank slate), and we develop our personality, intelligence, etc. through our experiences in life.
- Humans are like other animals and we can study animals to find out about human behaviour.

Psychology should aim to develop techniques that can control and alter human behaviour.

The behaviourist metaphor

The behaviourists believed that we can understand an animal or a person by thinking of it as a *machine*, and looking at what goes into the machine (stimulus or inputs) and measuring what comes out (responses or outputs). This view sees the animal or person as a passive puppet who responds to stimuli with no more control than we have to a reflex action like a knee jerk. Put in this way it sounds harsh and simplistic though it has led to a number of effective applications (see 'Modern uses of behaviourism' on facing page).

Issues with the behaviourist approach

Moral issues: the key moral issue is about control. If behaviourism can be used to control people and change their behaviour then who decides which behaviours should be changed and who controls the controllers?

Practical issues: the bottom line is, does it work? As ever the answer is not clear cut. The techniques can be used to change some behaviours but it doesn't always work and we are not sure how it works.

Theoretical issues: the theory can't explain all types of learning, for example, children learn to talk without any rewards and they learn to talk in their own style using a different style of speech to that which is used by adults. This can't be explained by behaviourism.

The general problem for behaviourism is that it deals with people as if they are a black box. It looks at what goes in and what comes out but does not pay much attention to all the processes that go on inside the box that might affect the output. The study of the gubbins inside the box was taken up by cognitive psychologists. This form of neo-behaviourism picked up the behaviourist baton and is still running with to this day.

After Watson: B. F. Skinner

Behaviourists such as **B. F. Skinner** explored the principles of learning using behaviour as the main focus of their study. A key concept is the role of reinforcement. This is commonly defined in terms of the effect on behaviour, so for example a stimulus is said to be reinforcing if the behaviour it is associated with appears more frequently, and a behaviour is said to be punishing if a behaviour appears less frequently. This is an important point because some things that might appear as punishment, for example shouting at a child who is behaving in an irritating way, might in fact lead to the behaviour appearing more frequently and so the shouting has to be seen as reinforcing rather than punishing.

Mrs Skinner views her daughter Debbie in a Skinner Box.

Skinner used the above procedures to explain an array of complex behaviours in humans believing that it was unnecessary to look for underlying causes of behaviour, but only the reinforcement contingencies that could be used to change that behaviour. This approach to the study of behaviour led to a certain view about people and the ways they make sense of the world.

Perhaps one of the most startling demonstration of the power of **operant conditioning** was the work by Skinner (1960) during the Second World War (1939–45) in developing a missile guidance system using live pigeons. He was able to train them to recognise landmarks on maps and to peck a screen so that a missile could be directed to its target. Sadly, although the system worked the military decided against sending the heavily armed pigeons out on active service. Can't think why.

'The major problems of the world today can be solved only if we improve our understanding of human behavior'.

B. F. Skinner, About Behaviorism *(1974)*

Activity

Try to mould the behaviour of a friend or family member by smiling at them every time they say a particular word, for example door or cabbage. See if you can increase the number of times that they say it through this simple reinforcement programme.

Qs

1 Use the principles of behaviourism to explain,
   (a) why cats always come running when they hear you using a can opener (at least mine do).
   (b) why shouting at a naughty child doesn't always stop them behaving like that.
2 Make a short list of behaviours that can be learned by simple rewards or punishments.
3 Make a short list of behaviours that *cannot* be learned by simple rewards and punishments.
4 Do you think that conditioning (classical and operant) can explain all our behaviour? Give reasons for your answer.
5 Look through the core studies and see how many of them use behavioural techniques.

Modern uses of behaviourism

It is possible to argue that behaviourism is psychology's 'big idea' because it has stood the test of time and, if anything, is growing in popularity today. Behaviourism offers a straightforward way to change behaviour and there is little doubt that it can be successful.

Therapies*: personal change is attempted through the use of classical conditioning techniques such as aversion therapy (where an unpleasant stimulus is paired with an unwanted behaviour), or desensitisation (where a pleasant feeling is paired with a feared situation). Modern therapies such as Cognitive Behaviour Therapy use a modified version of behavioural techniques to help people change the ways they think and behave.*

Advertising*: for example, classical conditioning is used to link up emotions with product. The UK's favourite advert (directed by film director Ridley Scott and available on YouTube) creates a feeling of warmth and nostalgia and pairs this feeling with a make of bread (Hovis).*

TV programmes*: there are a number of programmes such as Little Angels which offer behavioural techniques among others to change the way that people are behaving with each other. One favourite of this genre is Dog Borstal where the behavioural techniques of the trainers change the behaviour of the dogs in minutes but seem to take longer in changing the behaviour of their owners.*

The trainers of DOG BORSTAL use behaviourism and mean stares to change the behaviour of dogs and their owners.

...Links to other studies and issues...

Behaviourism is concerned with explaining why we do things (our behaviour) and how that behaviour can be changed if necessary. It is therefore relevant to all of the core studies in this text, and is used explicitly in a number of them, for example

- In the **Washoe** study (page 52), our furry friend was trained to make her first signs through the use of tickles as a reward. Everytime Washoe made a gesture that was close to the proper sign she was rewarded and in this way her signing was moulded (or shaped).

- The Bobo study (**Bandura et al.**) is an extension of behaviourism and looks at how behaviour is changed through observing other people.

Behaviourism also links to some of the other issues for example

- **Ethics**: if behaviourism can be used to control people and change their behaviour then who decides which behaviours should be changed and who controls the controllers?

- **Determinism**: behaviourism argues that much of our behaviour is not a choice but just a responses to rewards and punishments.

The cognitive approach

The cognitive approach is the dominant way of looking at people in modern psychology. The approach became the most popular approach in psychology departments once the problems with the behaviourist approach could not be ignored any longer. The behaviourists viewed people as a 'black box', and they studied what impinged on the black box (stimuli) and what came out of the black box (responses) but they did not pay much attention to what went on inside the black box. I know this will come as no surprise to most readers, but quite a lot goes on inside our heads and a lot of our behaviour can be affected by mental events as well as physical events.

The cognitive model of the mind is often influenced by the technology of the time. In the 1950's the most sophisticated information processing machine was a telephone exchange, and this was used as a template for describing how we process cognitive information.

Cognitive psychology still adopts a mechanical view of people but is prepared to admit that the machinery is quite complicated. As such, the cognitive approach is really neo-behaviourist, or to put it in other words, a reworking of the ideas of Watson and Skinner, but with a twist.

One of the most influential books was Ulrich Neisser's (1928–) *Cognitive Psychology* (1967) which helped to make the ideas more prominent. For Neisser, cognitive psychology is

'All the processes by which ... sensory input is transformed, reduced, elaborated, stored, recovered and used.' (p.4)

Mechanical models of human behaviour and thinking can only go so far. In the 1970's cognitive psychologists started to work more with a range of scientists including people who specialised in neurology (brain stuff), language, engineering, computers, as well as philosophers. *Cognitive science* is the result of this collaboration.

Cognitive science has developed theories of artificial intelligence, persuasion and coercion, cognitive bias and risk perception in psychology. It has also contributed theories to other subjects such as economics, mathematics and linguistics. Many people see cognitive science as the route to discovering the great secrets about human behaviour and experience.

Activity

The computer challenge

(a) Make a list of the things that computers and humans can do. To get you started there is: (i) storing information, (ii) calculating, (iii) recalling.

(b) When you've completed that list try to identify the differences between the ways that humans and computers do these tasks.

(c) Now try to make a list of the things that people can do that computers can't.

The history of cognitive psychology

The first psychology laboratory was set up by Wilhelm Wundt (1823–1920) in Leipzig, Germany in 1879. According to Wundt, psychology was the study of immediate experience – which did not include any issues of culture or social interaction. About half the work in the lab was on the topics of sensory processes and perception, though they also looked at reaction time, learning, attention and emotion. The main method that was used in the laboratory was *introspection*, which is a form of self-observation.

During the first half of the twentieth century, cognitive psychology was not as prominent as it is today, but we still draw work from psychologists in that time, for example, Jean Piaget (see the study by Samuel and Bryant) and Frederick Bartlett (page 32).

The cognitive revolution

Cognitive psychology came to the forefront of psychology in the 1950s. George Miller hosted a seminar in the USA in 1956 where Newell and Simon presented a paper on computer logic, Noam Chomsky (see the study on Kanzi by Savage-Rumbaugh) presented a paper on language, and Miller presented his famous paper on 'The magic number seven plus or minus two'. Each of these presentations defined their field and modern cognitive psychology is often dated to this event.

In the UK Donald Broadbent was a strong supporter of the information-processing models of cognition. These models were based on the communication technology of the time and were commonly represented as telephone exchanges to represent the way messages were sorted and distributed.

As technology developed so did the science of how people behave intelligently in the world. The models were now based on computer processes. This brings up a question about whether cognitive psychology is studying the cognitive processes of people or the cognitive processes of computers. It also brings up a much deeper question about what it means to be human and be alive. Can a computer think? Can it be aware of itself? Can it have a theory of mind? (For this last question see the study on autism on page 44.)

Artificial intelligence

One of the key strands of cognitive psychology is artificial intelligence (AI). It is the science and engineering of making intelligent machines, especially intelligent computer programs. The origins of AI can be seen in the work of British scientist Alan Turing in the 1950s on intelligent machines. Turing is particularly famous for his work on code breaking during the Second World War (1939–45) using the Enigma machines he helped to create.

Turing's claim

Turing held that in time computers would be programmed to acquire abilities that rivalled human intelligence.

As part of his argument Turing put forward the idea of an 'imitation game', in which a human being and a computer would be questioned under conditions where the questioner would not know which was which. This would be possible if the communication was entirely by written messages. Turing argued that if the questioner could not distinguish them, then we should see the computer as being intelligent. Turing's 'imitation game' is now usually called 'the Turing test'.

When is a robot not a robot?

The blurred lines between people and machines have been a recurring theme in fiction for years. Films such as Blade Runner, AI, Short Circuit and Star Trek explore the idea and challenge us to tell the difference between a living person and an intelligent machine. The robots behave like people and we feel the same way towards them as we do to human beings. Will we eventually build a machine that is so like a human being that we cannot tell the difference? And if so will it matter? Can we still switch them off or reboot them when we feel like it? Horror films of the past such as Frankenstein looked at attempts to create biological life, but perhaps we are much closer to creating cognitive life? Don't forget to switch off the computer tonight.

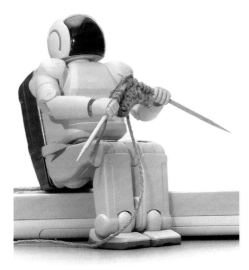

Will the study of artificial intelligence eventually create a robot that is indistinguishable from a human being?

Strengths and weaknesses of the cognitive approach

The cognitive revolution in the middle of the last century went further than changing the way psychologists look at the world. We all now pay attention to the way we think as well as the way we feel. Modern therapies such as cognitive behaviour therapy focus on the way we interpret the world. Cognitive psychology has told us a lot more about how the brain processes information and also the limitations of that processing. On the down side, the focus on thought has sometimes neglected the emotional side of our life. It has also concentrated on logical thinking (the way a computer works) rather than intuitive thinking (the way people often work). The future probably lies in the connection between cognitive psychology and brain science.

Recent work in cognitive psychology

There are two examples here of recent work, one is of an extraordinary phenomenon that has been recorded for centuries but little understood until recently, and the other is the modern technique of eyetracking.

Synesthesia

What is the colour of the letter M, or the number 6, or a prelude in E minor? How do red circles taste? What do they sound like? If you know the answer to one of these questions you probably enjoy (or suffer from) synesthesia. Most of us, however, do not and the questions therefore look very strange. Surely this is the road to madness if you can taste images or see colours in sounds. This is not the case, however, and we probably all have some small experiences like this.

Synesthesia (from the Greek syn = together, and aisthesis = perception) is the experience of a *cross-modal association*. In other words the stimulation of one of your senses causes a perception in one or more different sense. According to Baron-Cohen et al. (1996) at least 1 in 2000 of the population experiences synesthesia although many suspect it is more common. It is hard to obtain an estimate because many synesthetes are unaware that what they perceive is unusual.

The study of synesthesia helps us to learn more about how the brain processes sensory information and how it makes abstract connections between inputs that seem to be unrelated.

One of the most remarkable demonstrations of synesthesia has been carried out by V. S. Ramachandran on people who have phantom limbs. He investigated patients who had lost one arm and had experience of phantom limbs where the arm had once been. In some of the cases they experienced painful clenching sensations in the phantoms. It is obviously very difficult to treat pain in a phantom limb because, to put it bluntly, there is nothing there to treat. You can't use painkilling drugs or even rub it better. Ramachandran, however, developed an ingenious way to trick the brain and relieve the pain.

Ramachandran created a mirror box so the patients saw their good arm and a reflection of it that looked as if it was the phantom arm. When the good arm moved the patient could look in the mirror box and see its reflection moving and this looked as if the missing arm was moving. By exercising the good arm the patients felt that their phantom was also exercising and they were able to relieve the phantom clenching sensations.

(see http://psy.ucsd.edu/chip/ramabio.html)

Eyetracking

An eyetracker is a camera that records reflections of infrared light off the eye. It is fixed on a frame to a person's head and can show where someone is looking. By measuring eye fixations, which may be as brief as one tenth of a second, the equipment provides an online measure of human information processing.

Eyetrackers have been used to investigate how people read. The eyetracker can accurately time-lock the reading event as the eye moves through the text so it records the amount of time the eye spends on each word if indeed we do look at words one by one.

Eyetracking is being increasingly used for research in psychology, engineering, human factors and education. It is also being used by advertisers and market researchers to look at how long viewers' eyes remain focused on a particular ad or part of an ad; and animation and websites. This information will show designers which parts of a screen viewers show most interest in.

The future for eyetracking is almost limitless. As the technology becomes smaller and cheaper the eyetracker might help the way we interact with machines, such as computers. Professor Guang-Zhong Yang of the Department of Computing at Imperial College says *'Eyetrackers will one day be so reliable and so simple that they will become yet another input device on your computer, like a much more sophisticated mouse.'* (BBC website)

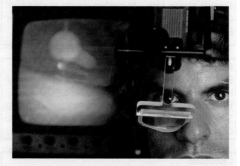

1   In the study by Loftus and Palmer, the subjects were shown film clips of car accidents.

   (a) Describe **two** differences between witnessing these film clips and witnessing a real accident.   [2]
   (b) For each difference, say how this might affect the results of the study.   [2]

Stig's answer

(a) One difference is that the film clips weren't real. Another difference is that people are scared in real life but wouldn't be scared in a lab.

(b) The fact that they weren't real means that people don't react like they would in real life. Being less scared might mean their memories could be better.

Chardonnay's answer

(a) The first difference is that which means that people don't behave like they do in real life.

(b) This means that the results can't be generalised to help us understand eyewitness testimony.

Examiner's comments

Don't just repeat the question, Stig. Of course the clips weren't real. Your suggestion about the absence of fear in the laboratory is a good point, so one mark for part (a). In the second part only the second sentence is creditworthy – the first doesn't say how the results would be affected.

Chardonnay, your answer for part (a) is OK but only just. You really should have referred to something in the study such as films clips or accidents whereas your answer could apply to any study. In parts (a) and (b) you have lost marks because there is no second difference. Other factors which would be important would include the effect of emotional arousal or being distracted by other events. Both of these might reduce the accuracy of recall – though some research suggests that emotion enhances memory (e.g. flashbulb memories).

Stig (1 + 2 marks) Chardonnay (1 + 1 marks)

2   Loftus and Palmer reported their results for the second experiment in a table similar to the one below. Describe **two** conclusions that could be drawn from this data.   [4]

Table 1. Response to the question 'Did you see any broken glass?'

Response	Verb condition		
	Smashed	Hit	Control
Yes	16	7	6
No	34	43	44

Stig's answer

More people were affected by the word smashed and less people were affected by the word hit.

Chardonnay's answer

Conclusion 1: Leading questions alter what we remember.

Conclusion 2: Even people who are not asked a leading question make mistakes in what they remember.

Examiner's comments

This is not two points, Stig. It is the same point said backwards. You could also be more specific than just saying they were 'affected'. Just look at Chardonnay's answer. She's got the right idea. She makes two good points, especially the second one which is commonly missed when people describe this study.

Stig (1 + 0 marks) Chardonnay (1 + 2 marks)

3   In the study by Baron-Cohen *et al.*, the autism/Asperger's syndrome group was compared with two other groups of adults.

   (a) Describe the other two groups of adults.   [2]
   (b) Explain why it was necessary to have these comparison groups.   [2]

Stig's answer

(a) The groups were autistic, normal and Tourette sydrome. In the first group there were 10 high functioning adults with autism or Aspergers. In the normal group there were 50 adults who were age-matched and the gender split was even. In the TS group there were 10 adults with more males to mirror the gender split in group 1. All participants had normal IQ.

(b) It meant you had a way of comparing the performance of the autistic/AS group on the Eyes Task.

Chardonnay's answer

(a) Normal adults and adults with Tourette syndrome.

(b) You needed to have other groups so you could see if the autistic spectrum participants were different in terms of theory of mind. The groups were all similar in age and intelligence so that couldn't be the explanation for any difference. The TS participants had a developmental disorder so that couldn't be an explanation. The only difference between the groups was the lack of social competence in the autism/Aspergers group.

Examiner's comments

Part (a) You're really doing well now, Stig. Unfortunately you only need to write a couple of phrases to get all the marks and you didn't need to include a description of the autism/Asperger's group. Chardonnay has saved precious time by answering the question simply but sufficiently for full marks.

Part (b) This isn't an easy question to answer – you may well understand but find it hard to put your thoughts into words (which is why practice is so important). Stig hasn't quite managed to explain himself clearly it but there is certainly enough for one mark. Chardonnay has expressed herself well for the full two marks. Comparison groups are used to control for extraneous variables that might act as an alternative independent variable, for example inability to score well on the Eyes Task might be due to general developmental delay therefore we need to control for this by having some participants (those with Tourette syndrome) with the same problem. It also might be that all adults find this task difficult therefore we need to control for this by having a group of normal adults as comparison.

Stig (2 + 2 marks) Chardonnay (2 + 2 marks)

4   In the study by Baron-Cohen *et al*. the Eyes Task tested theory of mind.

(a) Explain what is meant by 'theory of mind'.   [2]
(b) Describe **one** difficulty that might be experienced by someone in everyday life who does not have a theory of mind.   [2]

Stig's answer

(a) 'Theory of Mind' is having a theory about what is in someone else's mind, knowing what they are thinking.
(b) If you haven't got a theory of mind you don't know what other people are thinking.

Chardonnay's answer

(a) 'Theory of Mind' refers to the ability to represent the mental states of another person and understand what they are likely to be thinking.
(b) One difficulty that might arise would be having problems understanding what is going on in a movie, like understanding why someone has got annoyed with someone else.

Examiner's comments

Part (a) asks for a simple definition of 'theory of mind'. We can't know what someone else is thinking but we can build up a model in our heads so we can guess what people will think and say. Chardonnay's answer is clear and precise and worth all the marks. Stig has had a good go but maybe will only get 1 mark for part (a).

There are a number of everyday difficulties that arise if you do not have a theory of mind, for example social interactions with others or understanding a book or a movie. Stig has not given any example of everyday life – he really has just repeated his answer to part (a). Chardonnay's answer is correct and contains sufficient detail for two marks.

Stig (1 + 0 marks) Chardonnay (2 + 2 marks)

5   In the study by Savage-Rumbaugh *et al*. the chimpanzees communicated with the researchers using lexigrams.

(a) Why did the chimpanzees use lexigrams rather than spoken language?   [2]
(b) Explain **one** method used by Savage-Rumbaugh *et al*. to test the chimpanzees' ability to comprehend lexigrams.   [2]

Stig's answer

(a) They used lexigrams because chimps aren't very good vocally whereas they are very good with their hands so they should find it easy to point at the lexigrams.
(b) One way this was tested was to show the chimpanzees a range of photographs and lexigrams and they had to match them up.

Chardonnay's answer

(a) Because it is easy to learn to use the lexigrams and the chimps don't actually have to speak.
(b) Comprehension was tested in lots of ways, for example the chimps were shown a photograph and asked to select the correct lexigram, or they heard a word in spoken English and had to select the right photograph or lexigram.

Examiner's comments

Stig's answer is fine for part (a) but Chardonnay's doesn't explain why lexigrams might be easier than spoken language. Early studies found that chimps can't vocalise very well. They don't have the biology for it. They are, however, good with their hands.

In part (b) Chardonnay has given a lengthy answer covering more than the 'one method' required by the question. Stig's answer is along the right tracks but is not precisely right because at any time there was always just one item that had to be matched with a selection of lexigrams or photos.

Stig (2 + 1 marks) Chardonnay (0 + 2 marks)

6   In the study by Savage-Rumbaugh *et al*.

(a) Outline **one** similarity between the way that Kanzi acquired language and the way a child would acquire language.   [2]
(b) Outline **one** difference between the way that Kanzi acquired language and the way a child would acquire language.   [2]

Stig's answer

(a) It was similar because Kanzi first of all used words in an associative context which is like what young children do.
(b) It was different because she didn't learn that much in 17 months. Human children learn language very quickly and this is quite slow.

Chardonnay's answer

(a) One similarity was that Kanzi learned the lexigrams spontaneously without any specific training. He learned it just be watching his mother and also communicating with the researchers.
(b) One difference was that Kanzi didn't speak the words.

Examiner's comments

Both Stig and Chardonnay have provided clear similarities and would receive the full two marks. There are a large range of other similarities to choose from including the use of imitation and combination of words to form novel utterances.

In terms of the differences, Stig has provided an adequate answer (though he has made of the most common (though trivial) mistakes in referring to Kanzi as a 'she'. Kanzi is male). Chardonnay has slipped up. It is true that Kanzi didn't speak the words and children do – but the question focuses on a difference in the way language is acquired, not just a difference. With some elaboration this could have been turned into a fully creditworthy answer, for example 'One difference was that Kanzi had to be taught using symbols rather than listening to and producing spoken words'.

Stig (2 + 2 marks) Chardonnay (2 + 0 marks)

7 (a) Outline **one** assumption of the cognitive approach in psychology. [2]

(b) Describe how the cognitive approach could explain autism. [4]

(c) Describe **one** similarity and **one** difference between the Baron-Cohen *et al.* study and any other cognitive approach study. [6]

(d) Discuss the strengths and limitations of the cognitive approach using examples from the Baron-Cohen *et al.* study. [12]

Total [24]

Chardonnay's answer

(a) One assumption of the cognitive approach is that humans are like computers. In particular, the way the mind works is like a computer in that it has information inputted (stimuli), it does some processing (e.g. storing information) and it gives some output (e.g. recalling information).

(b) The cognitive approach would explain autism along the lines of a cognitive deficit. So, it wouldn't explain it in terms of genes, or biology or neurotransmitters, or brain areas, but in terms of some faulty thinking processes. For autism, a popular cognitive explanation is lack of Theory of Mind (ToM) as suggested by Baron-Cohen. This means that an autistic person is not able to infer in other people mental states such as beliefs and emotions. So, an autistic child might think that someone else is also thinking and feeling the same way as they do, and knows the same things.

(c) One similarity between Baron-Cohen et al. and Loftus and Palmer is that they both use a kind of experimental approach and this is a popular methodology for cognitive studies. In Baron-Cohen, the IV is whether the participant is autistic, Tourettes or normal. The DV is measured through a task (the Eyes Task). In Loftus and Palmer, the IV is the word given to the participants and again, the DV is measured through a task (recall of speed of the car in the video). One difference between Baron-Cohen and Savage-Rumbaugh is that Baron-Cohen uses a large sample whereas Savage-Rumbaugh uses a small sample and is therefore really more like a case study and not so generalisable.

(d) One strength of the cognitive approach is that it focuses upon what people think and this is really important to the study of psychology! For example, in Baron-Cohen's study, he has demonstrated how autistic people are not able to conceive of what other people are feeling as easily as non-autistic people i.e. not capable of 'mind reading'. This is shown because the autistic/AS participants scored less well on the eyes task than the non-autistic sample. This is useful research because it can help people know how best to communicate with and treat autistic children.

Another strength of the cognitive approach is that it is quite scientific. For example, in Baron-Cohen it is scientific because it uses the experimental method and there are many controls (e.g. matched ages, two control groups, standardised tasks etc.). This means we can be more sure that the findings are valid.

One weakness of the cognitive approach is that it ignores emotion. We do not know from this study how it feels to be an autistic child or person and what their experience is. This means that the cognitive approach is reductionist.

Another weakness of the cognitive approach is that really it is only guessing about how people think as you cannot directly observe thinking in the way that you can observe behaviour. So, in the Eyes task, we do not know why the autistic people did less well – it might not be because of poor Theory of Mind or it might have been for some other reason e.g. they didn't understand the adjectives, or they didn't concentrate etc. Really, we are only guessing because thought processes cannot be directly observed.

Examiner's comments

Overall, Chardonnay, your answer is about the right length and you have devoted proportionate time to each of the four question parts.

(a) You have accurately and clearly described one assumption of the cognitive approach.

(b) It is helpful to say how the cognitive explanation contrasts with alternative (e.g. biological explanations) and this shows that you clearly understand the focus of this cognitive explanation of autism. However, you could have provided more elaboration or detail. This could be achieved in many ways, such as providing an example of how lack of Theory of Mind might manifest itself in real life; or perhaps distinguishing between first and second order tasks.

(c) For this question, you really have to compare Baron-Cohen with one other study – here you used two other core studies, one for the similarity and one for the difference. Therefore, the examiner would mark the similarity, then mark the difference but you get only one of the marks, whichever is better.

For the similarity, the description is good, accurate and you have elaborated your point by detailing the IVs and DVs. Of course, some might argue whether Baron-Cohen is a 'true' experiment. It is really a natural experiment (or 'quasi' experiment); but essentially, you have made a valid point here and it is good enough for 3 marks.

For the difference, your description is just a little above basic (as well as being quite a superficial difference). You manage to push it out of the one mark category by referring (albeit briefly) to the fact that Savage-Rumbaugh's research is a case study nature and thus has doubtful generalisability – just enough for 2 marks.

Your answer for the similarity is better so you will get that mark only.

(d) I like the way you have structured this part to make it organised and clear. You have identified and explained two valid strengths and two weaknesses and your answer is reasonably balanced. This automatically puts you into one of the top two bands (7–9 marks and 10–12 marks). The rest hinges upon the detail of your discussion, the effectiveness of your analysis, use of supporting examples, and finally, the quality of your language. Thus, it is worth noting that your answer to part (d) is marked as a whole and not for each particular strength or weakness.

Certainly, your use of examples is, on all occasions, appropriate and there is evidence of analysis (e.g. in offering alternate interpretations of the Baron-Cohen results in your second weakness); but there is not much in the way of discussion... how much of a weakness/strength is this? Is there a counter-argument? You could discuss whether it is necessarily always a bad thing to ignore emotion; or whether controls necessarily have a negative impact upon ecological validity and so on.

Thus, while your use of examples is good, the lack of discussion prevents you from getting into the top band, and so you still get a very reasonable 9 marks.

Chardonnay (2 + 3 + 3 + 9 marks = 17/24 marks)

CHAPTER 3

This chapter looks at three core studies in developmental psychology.

- Samuel and Bryant's study of children's ability to conserve quantities.

- Bandura, Ross and Ross's demonstration of how aggression is learned through imitation.

- Freud's classic study of Little Hans and the Oedipus conflict.

Developmental psychology

What is developmental psychology?

Developmental psychology is sometimes understandably but misleadingly thought of as child psychology: understandably because the major part of the literature in developmental psychology is about children; misleadingly because it gives the impression that psychological development stops as the child enters adulthood. A truly comprehensive developmental psychology should concern itself with the whole lifespan of human development. Having said this, the studies in this chapter reflect the traditional preoccupation with children.

Activity

Make friends with your elderly relatives and ask them what they did when they were children. Try and sort out what was the same as your childhood and what was very different. How did they play? Who were their friends? What was school like?

Culture corner

Development is something that interests many people other than psychologists. They have observed how we go through different stages in our lives and they have recorded these changes in plays and pictures and novels. The speech from Shakespeare's As You Like It *suggests men go through seven stages in their progress from the cradle to the grave, and the picture by Hans Baldung Grien (*The seven ages of women, *above) shows a similar progression for women, though why they have to have their clothes off all their life is anyone's guess.*

What is a child?

This is not such a silly question as you might think. There have been many views of what childhood is in different cultures and in different periods of history. It is difficult to know how people saw the world 500 years ago but we can have an idea if we look at what they wrote and what they painted. For example, a lot of medieval pictures show children as little adults. They have the proportions of adults only smaller. In reality, children don't have the proportions of adults, for example, their heads are much larger in proportion to their bodies. Maybe the people who produced and looked at those pictures thought of children as being small adults. We know that children took on responsible roles from a young age and were commonly put to work.

What does a child know when it is born? What can it do? Can it make sense of the world when it opens its eyes? Does it have a range of instincts that develop as it grows? Alternatively, is it born with a 'blank slate' onto which experience will write the knowledge that gives the child its personality and cognitive skills? This nature–nurture debate has been live for over 300 years in this country and whatever answer is favoured has a significant effect on the social policies of the time for dealing with children.

Today we buy into the idea that children are immature humans and they require support and direction to develop into healthy adults. Although this seems like a modern idea it was proposed by the Greek philosopher Aristotle in the fourth century BC.

Attachment

One important research area in developmental psychology concerns the study of the strong emotional bond between two people, commonly referred to as *attachment*. This term is often taken to mean the emotional tie between a child and its adult caregiver. It is a popular belief in Western culture that the emotional experiences we have in our early years will have a critical effect on our adult behaviour and experience. This belief has been supported by Freud and also by John Bowlby.

John Bowlby

The social disruption caused by the Second World War (1939–45) created thousands of orphans across the world and prompted concern about the effects of bringing children up in institutions. Also, many thousands of children in this country were separated from their parents to keep them safe from the bombing that was happening in the cities. Parents were encouraged to send their children into the country. In 1951, Bowlby produced a report for the World Health Organisation (WHO) in which he suggested that '*mother love in infancy and childhood is as important for mental health as are vitamins and proteins for physical health*' (see Bowlby, 1965, p. 240). In the WHO report Bowlby put forward the concept of 'maternal deprivation' which is what happens when a child does not receive a '*warm, intimate and continuous relationship with his mother*'.

Although many children might experience mild deprivation Bowlby was most concerned with those who experience severe deprivation. This was said to occur when a child under the age of two and a half was deprived of its mother for a period of more than three months. Bowlby argued that research from orphanages and hospitals showed that such deprivation will have a dramatic and life-long effect on the child's emotional health and ability to form relationships.

Effects of this research

The clear implication of Bowlby's account is that mothers are a crucial part of a child's development and that many of the problems of later life can be traced back to inadequate mothering. In the 50 years since Bowlby's report research has confirmed the importance of a warm and stable emotional environment for a child; it has not supported the notion that this environment must be created by the biological mother. In fact Bowlby never suggested that mothering can only be done by a child's biological mother but his use of the terms 'mother' and 'maternal' led to this common misinterpretation. A *mother* is a woman who gives birth to a child, whereas *mothering* is a collection of activities that can be carried out by anyone, though most commonly this person is the child's mother.

Although Bowlby's work has been challenged over the years there is an acknowledgement that it led to a change in the way that children are cared for in institutions and helped to raise the standards of child care in this country (Tizard, 1986).

Different images of childhood

Babies in Zambia and the USA

Do babies from different cultures behave differently? Brazelton *et al.* (1976) studied the behavioural differences between a group of urban Zambian newborns, and urban North American newborns. They made extensive structured observations of ten newborn babies from each culture. The babies were measured in a variety of ways on the first, fifth, and tenth days of their lives. The most important measure was the Neonatal Behavioral Assessment Scale (Brazelton, 1973). This scale measures infants on more than 24 dimensions to do with interactive, perceptual, and motor abilities. Examples of these dimensions are: social interest in experimenter, motor activity, hand-to-mouth activity, alertness, following with eyes.

On day one the Zambian infants scored lower on a number of measures, mostly to do with alertness and activity. The researchers put this down to the relatively stressed intra-uterine environment of the Zambian babies, resulting in early dehydration and an overall lack of energy. By the tenth day, however, the Zambian group had started to score more highly than the US group on measurements of social interaction (for example, social interest and alertness).

The reason for this turnaround might be to do with the differences between the environments of the two groups of children. Due to the good health and diet of their mothers the US infants had a good physiological environment in the womb but after birth they had a '*relatively nonstimulating environment*' (p.106). The US babies were less likely to be handled than the Zambian infants and their mothers followed the '*cultural emphasis in the United States on quieting the infant and protecting him from external stimulation*' (p.106). In contrast, the Zambian infants improved as they began to be rehydrated and to receive nutrition by feeding from their mother. The increased social responsiveness of the Zambian babies may have been influenced by the more active, contact oriented, stimulating child-rearing practices of the Zambian women.

Not all childhoods are the same

It is estimated that there are 300,000 child soldiers worldwide (UNICEF website) in at least 18 countries. Although the term 'child soldier' commonly brings up a picture of gun-waving teenage boys the reality is a little different. A number of child soldiers are girls, maybe as many as 40% in some countries and many of the soldiers are as young as seven or eight. Not all of these children carry weapons but their roles as support to weapons units puts their lives in danger.

Some children take up arms to deal with poverty, abuse or discrimination. Some are seeking revenge for violence against themselves or their families. Sometimes they are abducted and forced to join armed groups, and sometimes they become separated from their families and the armies are the only source of food and shelter.

The effect of being a child soldier
However they came to be soldiers, children suffer from their involvement in military activity. It is an abuse of their right to be protected from the effects of conflict. Not only is their childhood destroyed, but they are also separated from their homes, communities and families. Children's education is brought to a brutal end and military activity damages them physically and mentally as many of them have witnessed or taken part in terrifying acts of violence – even against their own families and communities.

Child labour then and now

The exploitation of children was outlawed in the UK by a series of laws including the 1819 Cotton Mills and Factories Act which prohibited children under the age of nine years from working in cotton mills, and restricted those over the age of nine to a 12-hour day. The special status for young people in these laws reflected a changing view of childhood. Now if only all international clothing companies could follow suit today.

Romanian orphanages

It is now more than 15 years since the world found out about the thousands of children locked away in Romania's state institutions. When British teacher Monica McDaid first came across the orphanage in Siret she was horrified. '*One thing I particularly remember was the basement. There were kids there who hadn't seen natural light for years. I remember when they were brought out for the first time. Most of them were clinging to the wall, putting their hands up to shield their eyes from the light.*' (BBC website, 2005) Many children were adopted by families across Europe and the USA, but did they manage to adapt and recover? A group of these children, adopted by UK parents, has been studied by Michael Rutter from the Institute of Psychiatry in London. When they arrived in the country as babies, more than half the 165 children he studied showed severe delays in development compared with British children. Later he found that, even at the age of 11, many of these children had not caught up.
'*Contrary to popular opinion at the time, we found there were definite long-term effects from being in an institution,*' (Rutter, 2005) and the effects were more damaging the longer the child had spent in institutionalised care.

A child's mind is a blank book. During the first years of his life, much will be written on the pages. The quality of that writing will affect his life profoundly.' Walt Disney (Pinker, 2002).

...Connections...

The studies that are included in this chapter are not the only ones in this book that relate to developmental psychology. In a very real sense all psychology is developmental since it is the study of things (people and processes) which change and develop over time. For too long psychology as a whole has tended to study static snapshots of people, frozen in time and space, and thereby has risked missing some things which lie at the very core of human existence. Elsewhere in the book we look at the development of thought (**Baron-Cohen *et al.***), the development of language (**Savage-Rumbaugh *et al.***) and mental distress (**Thigpen and Cleckley**).

Samuel and Bryant: afters

Piaget revisited

Piaget's work has had a major effect on schooling in the UK and forms part of many teacher training courses. One consequence of this has been an army of student teachers heading off to primary schools equipped with beakers and plasticine.

SAMUEL AND BRYANT: CONSERVATION

Naughty Teddy

Another study that revisited Piaget's conservation tests was devised by McGarrigle and Donaldson (1974). In Piaget's test of conservation of number, he showed children two rows with equal number of counters and then spread the counters in one of the rows so the row looked longer. Children in the pre-operational stage tended to say there were more counters in the row that looked longer. There are a number of explanations for this including Piaget's (the child cannot conserve) and Samuel and Bryant's (the second question requires a different answer to the first).

Another possible reason might be in the task itself. Is it the way the counters are moved or even who does the moving that leads the children to make the mistake? To a child an adult has magic powers. Who knows where those powers end? Perhaps the child thinks that the adult can actually change the amount of counters?

McGarrigle and Donaldson used a naughty teddy puppet to mess up the counters rather than get an adult to do this. When Naughty Teddy did the messing up of the counters most of the 4–6-year-olds (70%) made the correct judgement about the rows (the quantities in each row are the same).

Very Naughty Teddy

It is not clear why they are more likely to make the correct judgement when the puppet is involved and M___ and Frye (1986) suggested the i_____ because the children w____ ___ the naughty teddy antics. ___ ___ e so distracted that they d__ ___ ___ hange.

Moore and Frye demonstra___ ___ getting Naughty Teddy to actually take away a counter as well as messing up the row. The children still said the quantities were the same even though now they weren't.

This all goes to show that it is very difficult to investigate children's thinking, and it also confirms Piaget's basic idea that children appear to have different thought processes to adults.

Cognitive development and culture

Does Piaget's theory describe how all children develop or just those in Western societies? To answer this we have to break down the question and look at three smaller questions:

Q: Do Piaget's stages occur in the same order in different cultures?

A: Probably yes.

A cross-cultural study of children in the UK, Australia, Greece and Pakistan found that children developed an ability to complete the conservation tasks in the same order (Shayer et al., 1988).

Q: Do children from different cultures go through the stages at the same age?

A: Probably no.

Various studies have found differences of up to six years in the age that children reach the third and fourth of Piaget's stages (Matsumoto, 1994). However, there is always an issue about whether the children were just doing badly on the task even though they actually had the ability to make the correct judgement.

Q: Do all cultures see scientific reasoning as the highest form of thought?

A: Clearly no.

Different societies place ___ ___ ues on styles of behaviour a___ ___ In the West we appear to think t___ abstract and hypothetical thought processes are the highest form of intelligence. Many other cultures, however, value thought processes that are more social and take other people into account (Matsumoto, 1994).

Children's drawings

Another illustration of the different way that children see the world to adults is in their drawings of people. The drawings follow a predictable developmental pattern that is nothing like the way adults draw people. Most remarkably, they start off by leaving out the body and draw the arms and legs coming out of a big head. This is like the famous Mr Men, but it is the Mr Men that copy children rather than children copying the Mr Men.

Another test of conservation

Miller (1982) designed a conservation experiment where no experimenter was involved in the transformation. It involved insects in one condition and boats in another. As the children watched, the insects/boats just drifted apart, so there was no experimenter doing anything. Despite the fact that the children were not distracted by an experimenter, they still failed the conservation task.

Multiple choice questions

1   This study was a replication of a study by
    a Piaget.
    b Samuel and Bryant.
    c Rose and Blank.
    d Both a and c.

2   What was the age range of participants
    in this experiment?
    a 4½ to 8½ years.
    b 5 to 8 years.
    c 5½ to 8 years.
    d 5 to 8½ years.

3   Which of the following were used to
    control for extraneous variables?
    a Different age groups.
    b Matching participants.
    c Fixed array task.
    d Both b and c.

4   Which of the following is true?
    a This was a repeated measures design.
    b This was an independent groups
       design.
    c This was a mixed groups design.
    d Both a and b.

5   What were the three kinds of material
    that were used in the experiment?
    a Height, number, volume.
    b Height, quantity, volume.
    c Mass, quantity, speed.
    d Mass, number, volume.

6   Which is the post-transformation
    question?
    a The question asked before the change
       was made.
    b The question asked while the change
       was made.
    c The question asked after the change
       was made.
    d All of the above.

7   Which of the following were IVs in this
    experiment?
    a Children's age.
    b Ability to conserve.
    c The three conditions (one question,
       two questions, control).
    d Both a and c.

8   Which of the kinds of material did the
    children find easiest to conserve?
    a Height.   b Number.
    c Volume.   d Mass.

9   Which group of children made most
    errors on the conservation tasks?
    a 5-year-olds.   b 6-year-olds.
    c 7-year-olds.   d 8-year-olds.

10 The results showed that
    a More children can conserve when only
       asked the post-transformation
       question.
    b Fewer 5-year-olds can conserve than
       8-year-olds.
    c Piaget underestimated what children
       can do in terms of conservation.
    d All of the above.

Answers are on page 105.

Exam-style questions

See page XII–XIII for notes on the exam paper and styles of question.

Section A questions

1   From the study by Samuel and Bryant on conservation, identify
    four factors that affect a child's ability to conserve.   [4]

2   Samuel and Bryant's study on conservation had three conditions.
    Briefly describe **two** of these conditions.   [4]

3   The study by Samuel and Bryant involved conducting interviews
    with children.
    (a) Describe **one** problem that psychologists have to consider
         when they interview children.   [2]
    (b) Suggest how psychologists might deal with this problem. [2]

4   Outline **two** conclusions that can be drawn from Samuel and
    Bryant's study into conservation.   [4]

5   Samuel and Bryant's study considered the validity of Piaget's
    methods of assessing conservation.
    (a) Explain what 'validity' means.   [2]
    (b) Outline **one** difference between the method used by
         Piaget and the method used by Samuel and Bryant.   [2]

6   From Samuel and Bryant's study on conservation, give **one**
    piece of evidence that supports Piaget's claims and **one**
    piece of evidence that challenges Piaget's claims about
    children's ability to conserve.   [4]

7   Outline **one** way the results from the study by Samuel and
    Bryant show that cognitive development has taken place.   [2]

Section B questions

(a) Identify an independent variable and dependent variable from
     the study by Samuel and Bryant.   [2]

(b) Describe the sample used in the study by Samuel and Bryant,
     and give **one** limitation of the sample.   [6]

(c) Describe how behaviour was measured in the study by Samuel
     and Bryant.   [6]

(d) Explain how the validity of these measurements could be
     assessed.   [6]

(e) Outline the results of the study by Samuel and Bryant.   [8]

(f) Suggest **two** changes to the study by Samuel and Bryant and
     outline how these changes might affect the results.   [8]

Section C questions

(a) Outline **one** assumption of the developmental approach in
     psychology.   [2]

(b) Describe how the developmental approach could explain
     conservation.   [4]

(c) Describe ethical issues that might arise in the study by Samuel
     and Bryant and explain why they are problematic.   [6]

(d) Discuss the strengths and limitations of the developmental
     approach, using examples from the study by Samuel and
     Bryant.   [12]

Key issue: longitudinal and snapshot design

How does behaviour develop and change during our lives? This is an interesting question for psychologists but it is difficult to get the evidence. One way to collect evidence is to study a group of people as they change and develop. This is called a **longitudinal study** and it involves repeated observations over long periods of time. The first obvious problem with this type of study is that it takes a long time to get any results because you have to wait for the people to age in real time. The alternative is to have a cross-sectional or **snapshot study** where different groups of people are studied at *different* stages of their development at one point in time. The clear advantage of this is that the data can be collected within a relatively short space of time but we can't know whether our results are due to the development of the behaviour or to differences in the experiences of the different groups.

Imagine a study into the skills of using computers. A study carried out today would probably find that people aged 15 would on average be brilliant at using computers, that people who are 35 would be pretty good at most aspects of computer use and that people who are 65 would on average be only fair to middling at computer use. Does this mean that computer skills decline with age? Probably not because there is a much better explanation – that people who are now 65 never used computers when they were 15 (personal computers were unheard of then) and so did not learn the skills, which would explain their low performance in their 60s.

Longitudinal study: observation of the same items over a long period of time. Such studies usually aim to compare the same individuals at different ages, in which case the IV is age. A longitudinal study might also observe a school or other institution over a long period of time.

Snapshot study: a study conducted at one point in time. Such a study may compare the behaviour of individuals of different ages.

Activity

Think about how your own psychological variables have changed over time. For example, think back 5 years and then 10 years and make a list of (a) the differences in the way you think, (b) the differences in the way you behave and (c) the differences in the way you feel. If that seems too tricky then try mapping out your tastes in (a) food, (b) music and (c) television.

Movies and snapshots

The difference between longitudinal and snapshot studies is like the difference between Flickr and YouTube.

Research studies that just take one set of data are sometimes referred to as snapshot studies. These studies have captured some aspect of behaviour or experience at one moment in time, like a snapshot. This is the most common way to collect data in psychology and the picture we get of behaviour is fine because we know *'every picture paints a thousand words'* (Telly Savalas). But if we explore the metaphor we can see some of the drawbacks to these psychological snapshots.

People pose for snapshots. Look through your photos. How many of your snaps have people smiling (usually cheesy and with their arms out)? Now look at how often people are smiling in their daily life. We smile when people look at us and when we think we are being observed. The rest of the time we rest our smile muscles. The snapshots you see on Facebook or Myspace would suggest that people are forever smiling to the point that their faces have got stuck in some hideous rictus like *The Joker*. If you just use snapshots as evidence then you would think the whole world is riotously happy every minute of the day.

The moving image tells a different story. It is harder to keep up the happy image when the cameras roll continuously as Jade found out on *Celebrity Big Brother*. It is possible to smile for the *Heat* photographer but once the snapshot ends and the smile fades the hideous bullying begins.

Movies can give a unique insight into people but a good portrait can still catch the depth of a person. What about if you combined the two? On YouTube and elsewhere on the internet there are projects by individuals where they have taken a picture of themselves everyday and then combined them into a movie to capture how they have changed. For example look at Noah who took a picture of himself every day for six years.

http://uk.youtube.com/watch?v=6B26asyGKDo or look at the Simpson's version
http://uk.youtube.com/watch?v=r3_ux4trTos&feature=related

Social research

Longitudinal studies are used in social research to track such issues as poverty and health. This type of study can dig deeper into the issues. For example, say the proportion of people in poverty in the UK is 10% in 1990 and also 10% in the year 2000, we might want to know whether this 10% is mainly the same group of people or different people.

Longitudinal studies vary enormously in their size and complexity. At one extreme a large group of people may be studied over decades. For example, the longitudinal study of the Office of Population Censuses and Surveys collects data on a 1% sample of the British population that was initially identified at the 1971 census.

www You can check this out at the government's statistic website (http://www.statistics.gov.uk/about/data/methodology/specific/population/LS/default.asp)

This data is used to see what factors such as housing or employment can be shown to correlate with illness or early death. At the other extreme, some longitudinal studies follow up a single case over a period of time.

Qs

1. Select one core study that has used a snapshot design and discuss **two** advantages and **two** disadvantages of longitudinal design, using examples from your chosen study.
2. Suggest how you might use a longitudinal design in this study and say how you think this might affect the results of the study.
3. Select **one** core study that has used a longitudinal design and outline **four** problems that might have arisen in the study, using examples from your chosen study.
4. Suggest how you might use a snapshot design for this study and say how you think this might affect the results of the study.

Longitudinal studies

Picture of the same person as she (gracefully) ages.

Snapshot studies

Picture of three generations of the same family

	Longitudinal studies	Snapshot studies
Time	Longitudinal studies take a long time, which makes them more expensive and also requires patience because you have to wait a long time for the results.	Snapshot studies can be done much more quickly (in a few moments or a few months instead of many years).
Attrition	Attrition is a problem for longitudinal studies because some of the participants inevitably drop out. The problem is that it may be certain kinds of participants (e.g. the ones who are less motivated or more unhappy or who have done less well) which leaves a biased sample.	This is much less of a problem for studies that take place over a short space of time.
Participant variables	In longitudinal studies participant variables are controlled. Participant variables are characteristics such as IQ, sociability, interests and so on.	The groups of participants may be quite different. The participant variables in a snapshot design are not controlled in the same way that they are controlled in an independent groups design. This means that differences between groups may be due to participant variables rather than the independent variable.
Cohort effects	We may not be able to generalise the findings from a study that looks at only one cohort because of the unique characteristics of that cohort.	Cohort effects may produce spurious results. For example one snapshot study compared IQs of 20-somethings with 80-somethings and found the mean IQ of the latter group was much lower, concluding that ageing led to a decreased IQ. The reason, however, might well be because the 80-somethings had lower IQs when they were 20-something (e.g. due to poorer diet).

> occur when a group of people are all the same age. They share certain experiences, such as children born just before the war had poor diets in infancy due to rationing.

There's more than one way to do a longitudinal study

Cohort studies sample a cohort, which is commonly a group of people who have something in common (often born in the same place or at the same time) and studying them at intervals through time. Panel studies sample a cross-section of people and survey it at regular intervals. A retrospective study looks back in time, for example, a researcher may look back through medical records to look for a trend.

One of the most well know in the UK is the *Up Series* which has followed a groups of 14 children since 1964 when they were seven years old. The first programme was called '7 Up' and the most recent one broadcast in 2005 was called '49 Up'. The children were chosen to represent the widest range of backgrounds, some came from privileged homes and some from economically disadvantaged ones. The director of the series is Michael Apted and every seven years he makes contact with them all and films as many of them are prepared to contribute.

Behind the series is the idea that our personalities and path in life is pretty much set for us by the time we reach the age of seven. Famously the Catholic Jesuits are associated with the phrase 'Give me a child until he is seven and I will give you the man'. If this is so then we should be able to see the adult of 49 in the child of 7, and this series gives an outstanding opportunity to explore this idea.

When the first show was planned there was no suggestion that it would repeat itself every seven years. The interviews since '7 Up' have been voluntary, although the participants have been paid for their contributions. In the recent films, each of the contributors was filmed for about two days, and the interview itself took more than six hours. The director admits this is a long process, but a very necessary one. The filmmakers wanted to capture a rich picture of each of the contributors and find out what was important to them. When they had finished their filming the contributors were shown the edited footage and were able to request alterations if they chose.

The films largely show that class barriers are still very strong in this country. The children from the prep schools at 7 went to university and obtained professional jobs. The children from the working class schools did not have the same opportunities and their lives turned out very differently. The shows also had an effect on the people taking part as their lives became public knowledge. Some have declined to take part in the some of the follow-up shows.

Cohorts

People (like Phil and Cara) who grew up in the 1960s have many shared experiences and attitudes which makes them different to, say, people who are teenagers in the twenty-first century. They remember Sergeant Pepper as if it was yesterday. They were brought up in a world without computers, sat nav, cheap foreign travel or even Pot Noodles. This means that a study of adolescents in the 1960s might have different findings to a study conducted today because of the very different experiences of these people. This is called a cohort effect.

...Links to other studies and issues...

Among the core studies that take measures over time are the case studies of Little Hans (**Freud**) and Eve (**Thigpen and Cleckley**). In the case of Eve, the report by Thigpen and Cleckley reads as a summary of several months of therapy. The story is much longer even than that and is told in Eve's own account of her life. It is an interesting postscript to Freud's study that Hans came to see Freud when he was a young man and appeared to have no recollection of the issues that form the basis for the powerful description in the case study.

There are also links to other issues covered in this text. The key ones concern the quality of the data that we get from these types of study. Are the data **reliable** and **valid**? How can we ensure the quality of our data over time because it is difficult to maintain our control of all the variables in the study.

Learning

How do we learn? Some of our behaviour is moulded by reinforcement. We do things that bring about pleasant consequences (rewards), such as warmth or praise or money, and we do things to avoid unpleasant consequences, such as cold or disapproval. Some of our learning comes through trial and error, but we also appear to learn by watching other people. It is, after all, safer to let others make the mistakes. When any behaviour appears to have positive consequences, we store it away for an appropriate occasion and then try it for ourselves.

When we are successful we become more confident (self-efficacy). As we interact with our environment, it becomes a two-way process: as we change the environment, the environment changes us (reciprocal determinism). Learning is therefore a combination of watching, thinking and trying. We learn most from people with whom we identify. When we are very young this is our parents; later it is peers, and later still it is attractive and famous people as well as people in authority.

History

Learning has been one of the key topics in psychology for over one hundred years. It can be defined as:

a relatively permanent change in behaviour (or potential behaviour) as the result of experience.

John B. Watson (1878–1958) was the first to study how the process of learning affects our behaviour, and he formed the school of thought known as Behaviourism. Behaviourists are basically interested in explaining behaviour simply in terms of the stimuli in the environment. Although it can explain some examples of human learning there is a lot of behaviour it cannot explain.

Social learning theory

The behaviourism of Watson took on a more human dimension with the publication of the book *Social Learning* and *Imitation* (Miller and Dollard, 1941). This approach added imitation to the known principles of learning. The book was written to explain how animals and humans imitate observed behaviours (a process called 'modelling'); in other words you don't just learn because you have been rewarded but because you see someone else rewarded and store this memory for future reference. You then may imitate or model the behaviour given appropriate circumstances and will only continue to repeat it if directly reinforced. Social learning theory explains human behaviour in terms of a continuous interaction between cognitive, behavioural and environmental influences. It is now most closely associated with **Albert Bandura**.

Why are people aggressive?

Aggression has a lot of forms. It can be giving someone a funny look, or it can be shouting at them or it can involve physical violence. Sometimes we think aggression is a good thing, such as in sport where we want sports people to show controlled aggression. Some people believe it is important to fight and even kill people for your beliefs. Mostly, however, we judge aggression to be a bad thing, though strangely we appear to enjoy watching violence and murder for entertainment.

Is aggression learnt?
Perhaps we are born with the potential to be peaceful and calm but learn how to be aggressive as we grow up. This is where the work of Bandura comes in.

Why road rage?

Is aggression an instinct?
A lot is made of research into animal aggression and one influential book was On Aggression by Konrad Lorenz (1966). He defined aggression as 'the fighting instinct in beast and man which is directed against members of the same species' (page IX).

Is aggression cathartic?
Catharsis is the cleansing effect of releasing intense, stored emotion. The term was used by Freud to describe the effect of releasing painful memories during therapy. It is suggested that being aggressive will release the tension and make someone less likely to engage in further violence.

Role models

The idea of role models is one of the most overused concepts in popular psychology. It is often used to criticise people who are in the public eye. For example, the wife of the former British Prime Minister, Cherie Blair, was blamed by psychologist Sandi Mann for being too successful and so causing stress to ordinary mothers who tried to copy her. 'Whilst Mrs. Blair is a very impressive lady,' said Dr Mann, *'she may not necessarily be the best role model for women if the perception is that she rarely gets time to take any time out for herself.'* (BBC, 2000). England footballer Wayne Rooney was banned from coaching kids at a schools match because he was not considered a 'good role model' by the English Schools Football Association (Manchester Evening News, 2005).

These two examples illustrate the power of the role model and how the idea is used to attack the behaviour of people in the news. It is a common feature to put pressure on women to be less successful in their careers, and on young working-class men not to get above their presumed station in life.

What is aggression?

This is harder to define that you would think. Not least because what one person sees as being aggressive another person might see as a bit of a laugh. One definition is

'any behaviour directed toward another individual that is carried out with the proximate (immediate) intent to cause harm. In addition, the perpetrator must believe that the behaviour will harm the target and that the target is motivated to avoid the behaviour.'
(Bushman and Anderson, 2001, page 274)

The important issue is intention. If you injure someone accidentally by tripping on the carpet and throwing a cup of coffee on them this would not be seen as aggressive. But if you stood in the middle of the room and deliberately threw it at them, this would be an aggressive act. The action is the same, the injury is the same but the intention is different.

Is aggression a response to frustration?

Dollard, for example, made the assertion that 'the occurrence of aggressive behaviour always presupposes the existence of frustration' *and that the* 'existence of frustration always leads to some form of aggression' *(Dollard et al., 1939, page 8).*

Biographical notes on Albert Bandura

Albert Bandura (1925–)

Albert Bandura was born on December 4, 1925 in the province of Alberta, Canada. He studied at the University of British Columbia and of Iowa. In 1953, Bandura accepted a teaching position at Stanford University, USA where he continues to teach today.

He is most associated with the development of 'social learning theory' which he has recently renamed 'social cognitive theory' to take in further developments of the theory. In 1986 Bandura wrote *Social Foundations of Thought and Action* which outlines his social cognitive theory. Bandura has made a large contribution to the field of psychology, as seen in the many honours and awards he has received including several honorary degrees from universities all over the world.

To introductory psychology students, however, he is still best known for the Bobo studies. Recently he wrote of this,

'In my earlier life, I conducted research on the power of social modeling. ... The studies of aggressive modeling were conducted over 40 years ago. But the Bobo doll continues to follow me wherever I go. The photographs are published in every introductory psychology text and virtually every undergraduate enrols in introductory psychology. I recently checked into a Washington hotel only to have the clerk at the registration desk asked, "Did you do the Bobo doll experiment?" I explained that "I am afraid that will be my legacy." He replied, "Hell, that deserves an upgrade. I will put you in a suite in the quiet part of the hotel." So there are some benefits to the wide exposure.' (Bandura, 2004, page 626)

Superman: a role model to copy or to be put off by?

How do people learn not to be aggressive?

One example can be found in the behaviour of the !Kung people of the Kalahari Desert described by Draper (1978). The parents were observed to have some distinctive ways of dealing with conflict between children:

1 *'When two small children argue or begin to fight, adults don't punish or lecture them; they separate them and physically carry each child off in an opposite direction. The adult tries to soothe and distract the child and to get him interested in other things.'* (p.36).

2 *'[P]arents do not use physical punishment, and ... aggressive postures are avoided by adults and devalued by the society at large.'* (p.37)

3 *'Adults consistently ignore a child's angry outburst when it does not inflict harm. A child's frustration at such times is acute, but he learns that anger does not cause an adult to change his treatment of the child, and the display of anger does not get the adult's attention or sympathy.'* (p.37–8)

So does this have an effect on adult behaviour? According to Draper, the !Kung were very successful in discouraging harmful and malicious behaviour in young people. During the twelve months she lived with the !Kung she saw no conflicts between adults, which resulted serious injuries.

Oh Superman…

In the popular imagination, role models inspire us to do more and achieve more, but is this always the case? What if you think you can't match up to the role model? It seems that Superman is too good a role model. Fans of the man from Krypton seem to compare themselves to the superhero, and realise they can't measure up. And as a result, they are less likely to help other people (Nelson and Norton, 2005).

In a study on decision-making, students were asked to list the characteristics of Superman, or alternatively superheroes in general, as part of a larger questionnaire. Later on the students were given the opportunity to volunteer for a fictitious community programme. Students who had been prompted to think about Superman volunteered less often than those who had thought about other superheroes. One explanation for this is that thinking about someone exceptional makes you think about your own shortcomings and think about what you can't do rather than what you can.

...Link to the core study...

This study looks at how aggressive behaviour develops in children. It is now over 40 years old but it still attracts a lot of attention and is still quoted in many texts. The study addresses two key questions, first, 'is aggression an innate feature of our behaviour or do we learn it?' Our answer to this question affects how we develop social policies to deal with aggressive behaviour. The second question, which follows on from the first, is 'if aggression is learnt then how is it learnt?'

Bandura *et al.*: the core study

Albert Bandura, Dorothea Ross and Sheila A. Ross (1961) Transmission of aggression through imitation of aggressive models. *Journal of Abnormal and Social Psychology*, 63 (3), 575–582.

BANDURA ET AL.: AGGRESSION

Abstract

A bobo doll is an inflatable doll about 5 foot tall. There is a weight in the bottom that makes it bob back up when you knock him down. If this experiment was repeated today they might use a Darth Vader doll.

The aim of the study was to see if learning that took place in one situation would be generalised to other situations.

Method
The experiment sought to answer these questions by comparing the behaviour of three participant groups of 24 each, matched for aggressiveness:

1   Observed an aggressive model.
2   Observed a non-aggressive model.
3   No model.

Groups 1 and 2 were further split into four separate groups each: boys with male models, boys with female models, girls with male models and girls with female models.

Procedure
1   *Modelling*: Children watched a model playing with toys.
2   *Aggression arousal*: The children briefly played with attractive toys but then had to stop.
3   *Delayed imitation*: Children observed playing with toys.

Results
The children who observed the aggressive model were more likely to exhibit the same specific acts of violence as shown by the model than the other two groups were, and also were generally more aggressive.

The boys were more affected by same-sex models than girls. Both boys and girls were more affected by the male models in terms of physical (but not verbal) aggressiveness.

Discussion
The results showed that children do imitate behaviour of models beyond the specific situation where the behaviour was viewed.

The aggressive models affected behaviour in two ways: they provided information about specific behaviours and they also generally increased levels of aggression.

Male models appear to have a stronger influence possibly because aggression is a masculine-type behaviour and therefore boys and girls attend more readily to male models.

Introduction

Previous studies have shown that children will imitate behaviours they observe someone else performing in the immediate setting – but will they repeat such behaviours in a new setting when the model is no longer present? This is a more crucial test of the principles of imitative learning (or social learning theory).

Research predictions
1   Observing an aggressive model will lead a subject to reproduce aggressive acts similar to their models, whereas this will not be true of subjects who observed non-aggressive models or who observed no model.
2   Observing an aggressive model will lead a subject to behave in a generally more aggressive manner, whereas those who observed a non-aggressive model would be inhibited from behaving aggressively.
3   Subjects will imitate the behaviour of a same-sex model to a greater degree than a model of the opposite sex.
4   Boys will be more likely than girls to imitate aggressive behaviour because it is a highly masculine activity.

Method

Participants

The participants were children from a university nursery school (Stanford in California), 36 boys and 36 girls aged between 37 and 69 months (approximately 3 to 5 years). The mean age was 52 months (about 4½ years).

There were two adult 'models', a male and a female, plus a female experimenter.

Procedure

There were two experimental groups and one control group:

Experimental group 1: observed an aggressive model.

Experimental group 2: observed a non-aggressive (and subdued) model.

Control group: no exposure to any model.

Each of the experimental groups was subdivided into four groups: boys watching same-sex model, boys watching opposite sex model, and the same for the two girl groups (making a total of 8 experimental groups each with 6 subjects). There were 24 children in the control group.

This means that there were 3 IVs in this study: the behaviour of the model, the sex of the subject, and whether the model was male or female.

Controlling aggressiveness
In order to ensure that each group contained equally aggressive children (and thus control this potential extraneous variable), ratings were done of the children beforehand by an experimenter who knew the children well and one of the children's teachers.

On the basis of these ratings the subjects were arranged in triplets and assigned at random to one of the three groups.

1 Would you anticipate that there would be individual differences in the way people respond to aggressive models? Why or why not?

2 Why is it necessary to have two experimental conditions as well as the control?

3 What is the dependent variable (DV)?

4 In assessing aggressiveness, why is 'inter-rater agreement' important?

5 In what way could aggressiveness be an extraneous variable in this study?

6 What kind of design is used in this study (independent, repeated or matched)?

7 What aspects of this experiment might be harmful to a child?

8 What problem(s) might arise from using the male model as the observer? Could he be biased, and if so, in what way?

9 Besides the Bobo doll and the mallet, name a few other toys in the room. Why were they selected?

10 Why was it important that the children were taken to a very different setting for the 'aggression arousal'?

11 Why was it important that the toys were in the same position for every child?

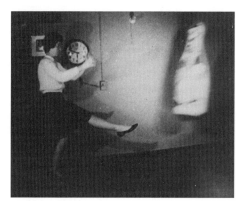

A female model kicking Bobo around the room. When Bandura et al. refer to a 'model' they don't mean a fashion model – the term 'model' is used in social learning theory to refer to anyone who is imitated. And when someone is 'modelling' a behaviour, it means they are 'imitating' it.

Phase 1: Modelling
Each child was taken individually by the experimenter to an experimental room in the main nursery building and the 'model' was invited to join them. The experimenter seated the child at a small table in one corner of the room and encouraged the child to design a picture using stickers and potato prints. Once the child was settled, the experimenter escorted the model to the opposite corner which contained a small table, chair, tinker toy set, a mallet and the Bobo doll. The experimenter then left the room.

A tinker toy set, one of the neutral toys available for the children to play with.

1 Non-aggressive condition: The model assembled the tinker toys in a subdued manner and ignored the Bobo doll.

2 Aggressive condition: The model spent the first minute playing quietly but then turned to the Bobo doll and spent the rest of the time being aggressive towards it. This included specific acts which might later be imitated, namely laying the doll on its side, sitting on it and repeatedly punching it on the nose. Then picking the doll up and striking it on the head with the mallet, throwing the doll in the air and kicking it about the room. This was done three times accompanied by various comments such as 'Hit him down', 'Pow' and 'He keeps coming back for more'.

3 Control: The report does not say what treatment these children received.

The experimenter re-entered the room after 10 minutes and informed the subject that it was time to go to another game room.

Phase 2: Aggression arousal
Before testing the children's imitation of the models it was necessary to mildly provoke them. This was done partly because observing aggressive behaviour may reduce the probability of behaving aggressively, making it less likely that those observing the aggressive model would behave aggressively. It was also done because the children who watched the non-aggressive model might be inhibited from behaving aggressively because of what they observed.

The children were taken to an anteroom in another building that contained some attractive toys (e.g. fire engine, jet fighter plane, colourful spinning top, complete doll set with a wardrobe, and baby crib). The subject was allowed to play with the toys but, after about two minutes the experimenter said that she had decided to reserve the toys for the other children. The experimenter and child then moved to the adjoining experimental room.

Phase 3: Test for delayed imitation
This room contained a variety of toys:

- 'Aggressive' toys, that could be used to express aggression, including a mallet, dart gun, tether ball with a face painted on it hung from the ceiling, and a 3-foot Bobo doll.
- Non-aggressive toys including a tea set, crayons and paper, a ball, dolls, cars and plastic animals.

The experimenter sat quietly in the corner working while the child played for 20 minutes. The child was observed through a one-way mirror by the male model and, some of the time, by another observer. The observers did not know which condition the child had participated in (except if the child had been in one of the sessions with the male model).

The observers recorded what the child was doing every 5 seconds (giving 240 observations). Responses were recorded in the following categories and provided an 'aggression score':

1 Imitative aggression responses
- *Physical*: Any specific acts which were imitated.
- *Verbal aggression*: Any phrases which were imitated, such as 'Pow'.
- *Non-aggressive verbal responses*: Such as saying 'He keeps coming back for more'.

2 Partially imitative responses
- *Mallet aggression*: uses mallet on toys other than Bobo.
- *Sits on Bobo doll* but doesn't behave aggressively.

3 Non-imitative aggressive responses
- *Punches Bobo doll*: strikes, slaps, pushes the doll.
- *Non-imitative physical and verbal aggression*: aggressive acts directed at toys other than Bobo, saying hostile things not said by the model.
- *Aggressive gun play.*

Results

In brief, children imitated the models they saw both in terms of specific acts and in general levels of their behaviour.

- **Complete imitation** Children in the aggressive condition imitated many of the models' physical and verbal behaviours, both aggressive and non-aggressive behaviours – in fact about one-third of their imitations were of non-aggressive verbal behaviour. In contrast, children in the non-aggressive condition displayed very few of these behaviours; 70% of them had zero scores.

- **Partial imitation** There were differences for partial imitation in the same direction as those found for complete imitation.

- **Non-imitative aggression** The aggressive group displayed more non-imitative aggression than the non-aggressive group, though the difference was small.

- **Non-aggressive behaviour** Children in the non-aggression condition spent more time playing non-aggressively with dolls than children in the other groups.

The graph summarises some of the results, showing that in all conditions children behaved aggressively but children only displayed imitative aggression (physical and verbal) when the model was aggressive.

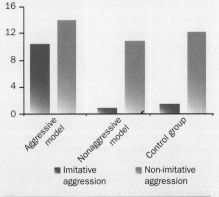

Was the little girl imitating the model's act of kicking the doll (see previous page)? Or was this behaviour due to demand characteristics – an inflatable doll kind of 'invites' being kicked or punched?

Gender effects

- **Same-sex imitation** There was some evidence of a 'same-sex effect' for boys but not for girls. The male models had a greater influence in general than the female models.

- **Gender** Boys imitated more physical aggression than girls but the groups didn't differ in terms of verbal aggression.

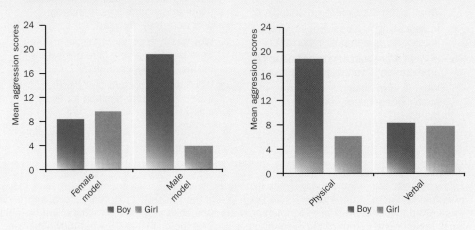

> ### Activity
>
> The actual data produced in the report of this study are shown in the table below. It is interesting to examine these data for yourself and decide on what conclusions you would draw.
>
> For example, it is interesting to note that the children with the aggressive model were sometimes less aggressive than the children with the nonaggressive model.
>
> How would you explain that?
>
> There were also occasions when boys were *more* aggressive with a female model rather than the male model.

Raw data from study by Bandura *et al.*, mean aggression scores (page 578)

Response category	Experimental groups				Control groups
	Aggressive		Nonaggressive		
	F model	M model	F model	M model	
Imitative physical aggression					
Female subjects	5.5	7.2	2.5	0.0	1.2
Male subjects	12.4	25.8	0.2	1.5	2.0
Imitative verbal aggression					
F	13.7	2.0	0.3	0.0	0.7
M	4.3	12.7	1.1	0.0	1.7
Partially imitative: Mallet aggression					
F	17.2	18.7	0.5	0.5	13.1
M	15.5	28.8	18.7	6.7	13.5
Partially imitative: Punches Bobo doll					
F	6.3	16.5	5.8	4.3	11.7
M	18.9	11.9	15.6	14.8	15.7
Non-imitative aggression					
F	21.3	8.4	7.2	1.4	6.1
M	16.2	36.7	26.1	22.3	24.6
Non-imitative: Aggressive gun play					
F	1.8	4.5	2.6	2.5	3.7
M	7.3	15.9	8.9	16.7	14.3

Eugenics

One of the reasons that the nature–nurture debate is so controversial is because of where it can lead. One of the destinations for the debate is eugenics. Eugenics refers to the attempt to improve the quality of human beings through selective breeding, so for example, if we wanted to improve the general level of intelligence in the country we would encourage intelligent people to have lots of children and unintelligent people to have none. Of course this only works if the factors that lead to differences in intellectual performance can be inherited.

There are many problems with the eugenics approach to intelligence including,

- it is not clear that intelligence can be reliably and validly measured;
- it is not clear that intelligence is a fixed quantity that cannot be improved;
- it is not clear that the differences in intelligence between people are mainly due to genetic factors;
- it is not clear that there is a single human quality that we can call intelligence. The alternative is that we have many different types of skilled behaviour.

It is a well rehearsed argument that the idea of eugenics leads to destructive and brutal social policies, and the strength of the argument around intelligence testing is to do with this. Psychologists are not always on the side of the angels here. For example, Lewis Terman who introduced the IQ test to America while he was professor of psychology at Stanford University, USA wrote,

'If we would preserve our state for a class of people worthy to possess it, we must prevent, as far as possible, the propagation of mental degenerates' (Lewis Terman, 1921, cited in Kamin, 1977).

The big words disguise the sentiments of the quote. To paraphrase Terman, he is saying we must stop poor and uneducated people from having children. All this would seem unpleasant but unimportant were it not for that fact that over half of the states in the USA brought in sterilisation laws for the *'feeble minded'* and carried out tens of thousands of operations.

This is not an argument that is going away. In fact it is likely to get even more difficult as genetic screening becomes more developed and allows parents to select the characteristics of their unborn children. If you had the choice would you choose not to have a child that might have a disability, or a low IQ, or an unattractive face?

Let's have a heated debate

Although people don't commonly use the terms nature and nurture in everyday speech they use the concepts in a whole range of conversations. For example, think about the arguments on why some young people engage in violence or substance abuse. Are young people bound to behave because of their genetics or is it due to how they were brought up? Are people born to be aggressive and selfish and is that why we have the economic system we have? Why are some people more successful at cognitive tests than others? Are they genetically superior in intelligent tasks?

It doesn't take a rocket scientist to recognise that the answers to these questions are very political. They will shape social policy and affect the lives of all of us.

David Beckham and son.
If you believe that footballing ability is inherited then place your bets now that the boy will play for England (or, of course, sing in a band).

Qs

1 Look at the following list of characteristics and put them in order from 'mostly nature' to 'mostly nurture'. (There is no right answer to this but it should help you think through the issues and maybe start another heated debate.)

   cheerfulness, intelligence, artistic, musical, height, hair colour, depression, friendliness, fearfulness, religiousness, greediness, kindness, aggression, mathematical thinking, common sense, compassion

2 Select **one** core study that illustrates the nature side of the nature–nurture debate, and describe what it tells us about how behaviour is inherited.

3 Select **one** core study that illustrates the nurture side of the nature–nurture debate, and describe what it tells us about how behaviour is learned.

4 Outline **two** strengths and **two** limitations of conducting research on the nature–nurture debate, using examples from these studies.

...Links to other studies and issues...

The debate about nature and nurture is present in many of the core studies although it is not always explicitly discussed.

The work by **Milgram** on obedience looks at how people will behave when instructed to harm another person. In later work Milgram went on to consider why people obey authority and speculated that we have a genetic tendency to be obedient. The argument is not very convincing because many people make the choice not to obey sometimes and it is difficult to see how this fits into the genetic theory.

The Bobo study (**Bandura et al.**) asks the question whether children are born to be aggressive or whether they learn how to do it. The importance of this debate centres on what we should do about aggressive behaviour that we think is inappropriate. If it is genetic then the solution will have to be medical but if it is learned the solution will be through training.

The nature–nurture debate also links to some of the other issues such as **free will and determinism** because if our behaviour is largely controlled by genetic influences there is very little we can do about it and we have relatively few choices in life.

It also links to the way that psychology might **promote human welfare**. The issue here is how the findings of our research might be used. The argument that some groups of people are superior to others can lead to eugenic solutions (see left).

FREUD: LITTLE HANS

Psychoanalysis

You can't get more interesting or more controversial than this. Basically it's about sex and death, two topics that we obsess about but find it difficult to discuss in a sensible way. The name of Sigmund Freud will always get a reaction. Many people seek to dismiss his work and many others will argue that he was the greatest thinker of the last century. Love him or hate him, you can't ignore him.

It is nearly 70 years since Sigmund Freud died in London but he is still one of the most influential thinkers in the Western world. Type his name into Google and you'll get more than 2 million hits. Site after site gives summaries of his work, interprets it, applies it to life, the universe and everything, and carries on arguments with other sites about what the theory means. In this text it is only possible to hint at the importance of the theory so if you are interested then check out the many websites.

The unconscious mind

Perhaps Freud's most important contribution to the way we think about ourselves has been the unconscious mind. He didn't invent the concept but developed the idea and applied it to a wide range of events. Freud proposed that our awareness is in layers and there are thoughts occurring below the surface. He suggested that the power of the unconscious can be seen in dreams which he called the 'royal road to the unconscious'. Dreams may appear to be nonsense but they are meaningful and reveal your hidden thoughts, feelings and desires. We hide the true meaning of the dream in symbols. The trick is to interpret the symbols and find the cause of the dream.

Psychic structure

Freud developed the idea of the unconscious by proposing a 'psychic structure'. This structure is divided into the id, ego and superego.

You are born with a mass of pleasure-seeking desires (I want it, and I want it now!). This is the id. As you become socialised your ego develops and controls the desires of the id. Finally you take on the ethics of other people and these appear in your mind as the superego. One way to think of the superego is as your conscience or maybe as the voice of your mother, which you can hear even when she isn't there. The task of the ego is to maintain a balance between the id and the superego. Too much id and you get in all sorts of trouble, too much superego and you get consumed by guilt. Much of the id is in the unconscious because if you had half an idea of what your desires are telling you to do you'd die of shock.

The talking cure

Freud believed that the answer to a number of psychological and physical problems lay deep in the unconscious mind. The task of the therapist was to help the patient get access to these unconscious thoughts and feelings. After he studied with Charcot in Paris, Freud briefly used hypnosis to achieve this. He later moved on and developed the method of free association, which is one of the techniques used in psychoanalysis – commonly called 'the talking cure' – to get people to say whatever is going through their minds. He believed that if he could guide his patients to a relaxed mental state their thoughts would automatically drift towards any areas of conflict and pain.

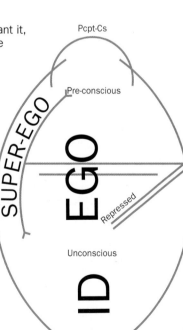

Freud sketched out a diagram of his conception of psychic structures as shown here.

The couch

When Freud carried out psychoanalysis on his patients he got them to lie on a couch. In fact, Freud's original couch can be seen at the Freud Museum in London. Many psychoanalysts still use a couch with their patients. They believe it is useful because when lying down the patient will focus less on objects in the environment and more on images and feelings that come from their own minds. Also they are unable to see the reaction of the analyst which prevents them playing the game of trying to guess what the analyst is thinking or feeling. Maybe the lack of eye contact also helps the patient to relax and be less concerned by the reaction to what they are saying (Ross, 1999).

Ego defence mechanisms

We can protect ourselves from a full awareness of unpleasant thoughts, feelings and desires with 'defence mechanisms'. They are ego defences because the ego (our rational, conscious mind) uses them to protect itself from anxiety. For example:

Denial is the refusal to accept reality and to act as if a painful event, thought or feeling did not exist.

Displacement is the redirecting of thoughts feelings and impulses from an object that gives rise to anxiety to a safer, more acceptable one. For example, being angry at the boss and kicking the dog.

Projection means placing your undesired impulses onto someone else. For example, an angry spouse accuses their partner of hostility.

Repression is the blocking of unacceptable feelings or memories from consciousness. However, things which are placed in the unconscious mind are expressed through, for example, dreams or neurotic behaviour such as phobias. This is a key theme in the study of Little Hans – he repressed his anxieties about his mother, father and sister; this anxiety was then attached to something else (horses) which made him fearful of horses.

Isolation is sometimes called *intellectualisation* and means that in certain situations or when recalling particular memories, a person will show no emotion or feeling. They may recall painful events without recalling the emotion that they felt at the time. An example may be that the person recalls how they were abused as a child, but acts as if it meant nothing to them.

Regression is where a person behaves in a way that in the past may have brought about relief from the anxiety-provoking situation. An example may be of an older child reverting to sucking their thumb when another child is born into the family. Or an adult may throw a tantrum if things aren't going the way they want them to.

Biographical notes on Sigmund Freud (1856–1939)

Sigismund Schlomo Freud (later shortened to Sigmund by himself) was born to a middle-class Jewish family in Freiberg in central Europe. When he was four years old the family moved to Vienna where he stayed until 1938 when he was forced to leave the city to escape the Nazi regime. The anti-Semitism that he had lived with all his life finally drove him out of Vienna. Four of his sisters were subsequently unable to get out and died in the death camps.

During his childhood Freud had some hostility towards his father but was very close to his mother. This family dynamic is thought by some to have influenced his later theories of, for example, the Oedipus complex.

He studied medicine and became a respected neuropathologist. One condition that interested him was hysteria, where patients would exhibit extreme physical symptoms such as paralysis without an obvious physical cause. A visit to the French neurologist Jean-Martin Charcot convinced him that hysteria was caused by mental events rather than physical ones. He started to explore the mental reasons for hysteria and developed his techniques of free association. With Joseph Breuer he published *Studies in Hysteria* in 1895.

Freud continued to develop and publish his theories for the next 40 years. 'The Interpretation of Dreams' (1900) and *Three Essays on the Theory of Sexuality* (1905) made Freud famous. They also made him very controversial especially because of his views on infantile sexuality. He developed his theories from his clinical work and some of his case studies are published, including the story of Little Hans. He also engaged in a lot of self-reflection and analysis.

Freud tackled the big questions about life and came up with many uncomfortable answers. He attracted devoted followers though there were many splits in the community of psychoanalysis. Wider society recognised the extraordinary contribution Freud made to our understanding of the human mind and in 1935 he was appointed Honorary Member of the Royal Society of Medicine.

Sigmund Freud (1856–1939)

In Memory of Sigmund Freud
by W. H. Auden (extract)

He wasn't clever at all: he merely told
the unhappy Present to recite the Past
like a poetry lesson till sooner
or later it faltered at the line where
long ago the accusations had begun,
and suddenly knew by whom it had been judged,
how rich life had been and how silly,
and was life-forgiven and more humble,
able to approach the Future as a friend
without a wardrobe of excuses, without
a set mask of rectitude or an
embarrassing over-familiar gesture.

The Oedipus complex

Freud believed that children are born with powerful emotions and drives. As a child develops, the drives focus on different parts of their body. After birth, the focus is on the mouth and children explore the physical and emotional world through it (this is called the oral stage). As children start to gain control of their bodily functions they move into the anal stage where they get pleasure from retaining or expelling faeces. Then comes the phallic stage where the focus is on their genitals. Between the ages of 7 and 11 Freud suggested children go through a latency period where sexual feelings are repressed before moving into the adult genital stage at puberty.

The part of this theory most relevant to the study of Little Hans is the phallic stage and, in particular, the Oedipus complex: *'I want a girl, just the girl that married dear old dad.'*

Part of the Greek myth of Oedipus refers to a child who is brought up not knowing who his parents are. As a man he goes to the city of Thebes where he kills the tyrant king and marries the queen. Unfortunately for Oedipus he then discovers that the king was his father and the queen, now his wife, is also his mother. Well it would upset anyone.

Freud saw the story as describing a childhood drama for all little boys. Their mother is their first source of affection and is the focus of their erotic feelings. During the phallic stage of development the boy wants to possess his mother and recognises a competition with his father. He fears he will be punished for such wishes by castration but resolves the conflict by 'identifying the aggressor' and taking on the values and behaviour of his rival.

Book burning

It's difficult to imagine in the UK today that a government would organise events to burn the books of people they believed had degenerate views. This is what happened to Freud among others during the 1930s in Germany.

Freud (1933) commented: 'What progress we are making. In the Middle Ages they would have burned me. Now they are content with burning my books.'

Anti-Semitism

'My language is German. My culture, my attainments are German. I considered myself German intellectually, until I noticed the growth of anti-Semitic prejudice in Germany and German Austria. Since that time, I prefer to call myself a Jew.' (Freud, 1925)

Freudian slips

Freud became interested in the trivial errors of everyday life such as forgotten appointments or saying the wrong thing. Freud believed that these events were not due to chance but were the result of unconscious attitudes, for example he quoted Charles Darwin who always made a written note of research findings that disagreed with his own ideas because he found that these facts and ideas were more likely to slip the memory than those that agreed with him. Today we use the term *Freudian Slip* to describe those occasions when we say something we didn't mean to but what we say actually reflects what we really believe or are thinking about. Commonly they involve saying a sexual word by mistake.

...Link to the core study...

Freud used case studies as evidence for his theories. Much of his theory on children was based on the recollections of adults which are, of course, coloured by their subsequent experiences. Little Hans is one of the few children that Freud had direct experience of, and even then most of the contact was made indirectly through interviews with Hans' father. The full study is the length of a short novel and we recommend that if you don't enjoy reading you look it out.

Freud: the core study

Sigmund Freud (1909) Analysis of a phobia in a five-year-old boy. In J. Strachey (ed. and trans.)
The Standard Edition of the Complete Psychological Works: Two Case Histories (vol. X), pages 5–147. London: The Hogarth Press.

FREUD: LITTLE HANS

Abstract

The case study of Little Hans is divided into three parts.

Part I. Introduction: Hans' early life
Hans' father recorded Hans' early childhood and used Freud's theory of psychoanalysis to analyse events.

Part II. Case history and analysis
This section blends evidence and analysis of that evidence.

- The *source of his anxieties,* mainly his parents and sister.

- The *development of his phobia* about horses, which changed from being a concern about white horses biting him to a fear of horses with laden carts. The phobia was related to his anxieties.

- The *fantasies* which represented his anxieties, including the 'two giraffes', criminal fantasies and the origin of babies.

- The final fantasies which enabled him to *resolve his anxieties,* including one about his own make-believe children.

Part III. Discussion
Freud offered a discussion of the case dealing with three major issues:

- Support for Freud's theory of sexuality.

- The nature of phobias and how they develop.

- Views on life and the upbringing of children.

A reproduction of a drawing made by Hans. He asked his father to add the widdler but his father said "Draw it yourself".

Aim

Freud spent his time treating adult patients and using their recollections as the basis for his theory of child development. The case study of Hans gave him the opportunity to test his theory about infantile sexuality and the Oedipus conflict on a 'real' child.

There was a second aim for this study. During the period when Hans' father was recording observations, Hans developed an intense phobia of horses. This provided Freud with an opportunity to also test his explanation of the genesis of phobias.

Method

Participant
The participant in this case study is a boy called Little Hans who was aged between three and five during the period of this case study.

Procedure
Hans' father recorded events and conversations with Hans and sent these regularly to Freud. Both Freud and the father offered interpretations of Hans' behaviour. On one occasion Hans was taken to meet Freud. Hans' father was one of Freud's closest 'followers' and was keen to put Freud's ideas of psychoanalysis into practice. Psychoanalysis involves the interpretation of a patient's thoughts and fantasies so that the patient can come to understand them himself.

Part I. Introduction: Hans' early life

Little Hans and his 'widdler'
Just before he was three, Hans started to show a lively interest in his 'widdler'. Hans observed that animals had big ones, especially an animal like a horse. He assumed that both his parents must have big ones because they were fully grown.

He got pleasure from touching his widdler and also from excretion. Later, when he imagined having his own children, he imagined he would help them widdle and wipe their bottoms – performing those things which had given him much pleasure. He kicked about when weeing/defecating showing the pleasure associated with such activity.

His mother found him playing with his penis: 'If you do that, I shall send for Doctor A. to cut off your widdler'. This led to acquiring a castration complex (fear of having his penis removed) which meant he had to repress his feelings of pleasure. Hans also felt sexual desire for his mother, which was repressed and expressed as an interest in other girls and wanting to kiss them.

Death wish towards his father and baby sister
During his summer holiday at Gmunden, Hans spent much time alone with his mother while his father returned to work in Vienna. Back home, Hans had to share his mother once again with his father and wished his father to be permanently away.

Hans expressed his conflicting aggression and love towards his father by hitting him and then kissing the spot.

When Hans was 3½ his baby sister Hanna was born (October 1906), further separating him from his mother and reminding him of the attentions he used to receive from his mother when he was a baby. Hans admitted that he had watched his sister having a bath and wished his mother would let her go. This unconscious desire to see his sister drown became translated into a fear that his mother might equally let Hans go. Baths were womb-like and so also related to the process of being born.

Sources of his anxieties
In summary, Hans felt anxious about his:

- *Mother* He had sexual fantasies about her but these resulted in anxieties, for example she had threatened that his penis would be cut off and that led to castration anxiety.

- *Father* Hans saw his father as a rival for his mother, and wished him dead. But at the same time he loved his father and this created conflict and feelings of anxiety.

- *Sister* He wished Hanna would drown, which led to anxiety and a fear that his mother would drop him.

Part II. Case history and analysis

The phobia starts (January 1908)

When Hans was 4½, he developed a fear that a white horse would bite him – Hans referred to his fear as 'my nonsense'. Freud felt that Hans' real fear was that he would lose his mother; his anxieties had been repressed into his unconscious mind and eventually expressed as a phobia. Freud explained the links between his anxieties and horses:

1. It was partly based on a real event. Hans heard a father warn his daughter that a white horse might bite her if she touched it.

2. This was linked to his mother telling him that it would not be proper if she touched his penis – Hans had asked her to touch his widdler once when she was drying him after a bath. The link was: if you put your finger on a white horse it will bite you, if someone put their finger on your widdler this was not proper.

3. This created a sense of anxiety because his mother might leave him because she disapproved of his request. Hans' desire for his mother was a product of his sexual libido (his sexual drive). His sexual desire was now linked to a sense of anxiety. A coping mechanism would be to transfer his anxiety from his libido to the horses and therefore he became afraid of a white horse biting something that touched it.

4. Horses also represented his father (see Hans' visit to see Freud) and the anxiety associated with his father.

5. His anxiety was exacerbated because his father told him that women have no widdlers. This would lead Hans to think – 'My mother had a widdler before and now she hasn't. It must have been cut off. She said mine might be cut off if I touched it. She obviously wasn't joking because it happened to her'. This would lead to castration anxiety.

Hans visits Freud (March 1908)
Freud proposed that a horse might be symbolic of Hans' father because the black around the horses' mouths and the blinkers in front of their eyes might be symbols of his father's moustaches and glasses – symbols of manhood (i.e. things that Hans might envy because he wanted to be grown up and able to have his mother's love).
Freud told Hans that he was afraid of his father because he was so fond of his mother. Freud's revelation appeared to release Hans and enable him to deal more directly with his phobia. He started to be able to go out into the street again and to the park. However, soon another phobia developed, the fear of horses pulling heavy carts.

A conversation recorded by Hans' father which shows how he often used 'leading questions' (questions which may 'suggest' a certain answer from the respondent – see study by Loftus and Palmer for more on leading questions)

I:	*Did you often get into bed with Mummy at Gmunden?*
Hans:	*Yes.*
I:	*And you used to think to yourself you were the Daddy?*
Hans:	*Yes.*
I:	*And then you felt afraid of Daddy? Can you remember the funeral at Gmunden? You thought then that if only Daddy were to die you'd be Daddy.*
Hans:	*Yes.*

(From Freud, 1909, page 90)

Hans played with dolls and had one that he named 'Lodi', the word for 'sausage'. His father pointed out that a sausage is like a lumf (the word Hans used for faeces). 'When you sat on the chamber and a lumf came, did you think yourself you were having a baby?' Hans said yes 'You know when the bus-horses fell down? The bus looked like a baby-box, and when the black horse fell down it was just like...' Hans finished the sentence '...like having a baby'. And the noise of the horses' hooves was like Hans' noise he made with his feet when on the chamber.

(Conversation from page 95)

Further horse anxieties

A new fear developed of horses pulling heavily laden carts or a bus. This again was related to an actual event: Hans recalled an occasion when he was walking with his mother and they saw a horse pulling a bus fall down and kick its legs about. This terrified Hans because he thought the horse was dead. However the fear also represented many repressed anxieties:

- Hans secretly wished his father would fall down dead. Seeing the horse fall over increased his anxiety about this death wish.

- Hans had become preoccupied with bowel movements ('lumf'). A laden cart was like a body full of faeces. Lumf falling in the toilet made a noise similar to the noise of a horse falling.

- A heavily laden cart was also like a pregnant woman and babies are also lumf-like. Therefore all the laden vehicles represented pregnancy. When they fall down it represents giving birth. This was linked to Hans' repressed feelings about his sister.

- Hans was particularly concerned about the horse 'kicking about' when it fell over which was linked to his own behaviour when defecating.

The phobia also served a real purpose of keeping him at home with his mother.

Continued on next page

Qs

1. Briefly outline Hans' feelings towards his sister, mother and father.

2. Give an example of a 'leading question' from the conversation between Hans and his father.

3. Give **two** explanations for Hans' castration anxiety.

4. Explain why Hans came to fear having baths.

5. Give **two** reasons why Hans developed a fear of being bitten by a horse.

6. Suggest **one** reason why Hans might have been afraid of a horse pulling a laden cart.

7. Give an example of Freud's search for 'deep meanings' (i.e. hidden meanings).

8. What is the link between anxiety and phobia?

Timeline

Year	Hans' age	Event
1903		Hans born.
1906	3–3¾	First reports.
	3¼–3½	Summer holidays, first visit to Gmunden.
	3½	Castration threat.
	3½	Hanna born.
1907	3¾	First dream.
	4	Removal to new flat.
	4¼–4½	Second visit to Gmunden, episode of biting horse.
1908	4¾	Episode of falling horse, start of phobia.
	5	Recovery, end of analysis.

Part II. Case history and analysis (continued)

Fantasies
Hans reported many fantasies or 'dreams' which each expressed different aspects of his anxieties

The dream about giraffes
A week or so before they visited Freud, Hans told his father the following 'dream' of two giraffes – *'In the night there was a big giraffe in the room and a crumpled one; and the big one called out because I took the crumpled one away from it. Then it stopped calling out; and then I sat down on top of the crumpled one.'* Hans' father perceived that the big giraffe was him (the father) or his penis, and the crumpled one was his wife's genital organ.

The scene is a replay of what happened on recent mornings – Hans came into their bed in the morning, welcomed by his mother but his father would warn her not to do this (this is the big giraffe calling out). Hans stays a little while (sits on the crumpled one). In the night Hans experiences a longing for his mother and comes to see her for that reason. The whole thing is a continuation of his fear of horses.

Criminal fantasies
Hans dreamt about doing forbidden things with his father. He dreamt, for example, that he went *'with [my father] in the train, and we smashed a window and the policeman took us off with him.'* This represented wishing to do something forbidden to his mother which his father was also doing.

Origin of babies
When Hanna was born Hans was told that the stork brought her but he didn't believe this and made up his own story that she had been like a lumf (faeces) inside his mother and giving birth was like defecating (pleasurable).

The resolution
Hans had several fantasies which enabled him to express his repressed feelings and finally fully recover from his phobias.

1 The plumber
Hans related the following to his father *'I was in the bath, and then the plumber came and unscrewed it. Then he took a big borer and stuck it in my stomach.'* Hans' father interpreted this to mean: 'I was in bed with Mummy. Then Daddy came and sent me away. He pushed me away with his big penis.'

Hans also had another fantasy: *'The plumber came and first he took away my behind with a pair of pincers, and then he gave me another, and then the same with my widdler.'* Presumably both the new backside and widdler were bigger, like Daddy's.

These fantasies showed that Hans was now identifying with his father by (apparently) wanting a behind and a widdler as well as a moustache like his father's. Thus Hans was becoming more conscious of his feelings about his father and resolving those feelings.

2 Knowing where babies came from
Hans' continued fear of baths represented an unconscious understanding of where babies come from, and his interest in laden carts represented his own answer – he called them 'stork-box carts' because his parents told him a stork brought the baby – the box that brings the baby, i.e. the mother's womb (Freud called this the pregnancy complex).

Hans' parents finally explained where babies really came from – from inside 'Mummy'. This meant he no longer had a need for the cart analogy. After this he played outside, not fearing the carts.

3 Becoming the daddy
Hans had always had an ongoing fantasy about his own children and how he was going to look after them. One day he was playing a game with these imaginary children and his father asked 'are your children still alive?' Hans replied that boys couldn't have children, he had been their mummy but now he was their daddy. And Hans' father was the grandaddy. So he had worked out a solution where his father was still part of the family and both were married to Hans' mother.

This led Freud to conclude that Hans had at last overcome his Oedipus complex and was able to identify with his father.

After this he managed to go all the way to the park, no longer fearing horses and thus demonstrating that he had fully overcome his phobia.

Postscript
Freud reported that Hans was interviewed when he was 19 and at that time appeared entirely normal and had experienced no difficulties during adolescence. He had no recollection of the events of his childhood.

The real Little Hans, Herbert Graf (1903–1973), who became an opera producer in America.

Qs

1   In what way were Hans' fantasies important?

2   What might have led both Freud and Hans' father to draw biased conclusions?

3   List at least **two** different methods that were used to collect data in this case study.

4   Freud says that children do not respond to the therapist's 'suggestion'. What does this mean?

5   How did Freud respond to the two criticisms of the study (see top right)?

6   Summarise the conclusions made by Freud (right).

7   How does this study support Freud's theory of sexuality?

8   Psychodynamic theory is dynamic. Give an example of this from this case study.

9   Do you think Little Hans would have recovered without Freud's help? Why or why not?

Part III. Discussion

Freud divided his discussion of the case into three sections

I. Support for Freud's theory of sexuality
There are two criticisms:

1 If Hans was 'abnormal' we can't draw conclusions about normal development.

2 The analysis was conducted by his father and lacked objective worth.

Freud's response was

1 That such neuroses in early childhood are relatively normal.

2 That, even if a response is triggered by suggestion, it is not arbitrary. In any case Hans did sometimes disagree with his father's suggestions, and there were benefits of the close relationship (for example, more intimate details would be revealed).

Freud concluded that the case study of Hans provided support for his ideas about infant sexuality, for example Hans' interest in his 'widdler'. He also was a perfect example of a 'little Oedipus'. Hans had a wish to be close to his mother and to engage in sexual relations with her. His father was his rival whom he wished dead, but also loved deeply.

II. Understanding phobias
Freud explained phobias as the conscious expression of repressed anxieties. Hans' case fitted this well. In order to help Hans, Freud's task was to throw out hints so that Hans could obtain a conscious grasp of his unconscious wishes.

Hans' phobias were triggered by real events but represented unconscious anxieties created by conflicts over his feelings towards his mother and father. Freud traced Hans' initial anxieties to his sexual feelings towards his mother, her rejection which led Hans to fear losing her, Hans' castration anxiety and his jealousy of his father. Freud told Hans that his fear of horses biting him represented a fear of his father. This enlightenment enabled Hans to delve deeper into his other fears – the fear of horses falling down and a new fascination with 'lumf' which was variously associated with pleasure in defecation, pregnancy, understanding where babies come from and laden carts. The final bath/plumber fantasy was again a composite one which *'exhausted the content of the unconscious complexes which had been stirred up by the sight of the falling horse'* (page 131).

III. Views on life and the upbringing of children
Freud suggested that Hans' conflicts were relatively 'normal' and therefore the same could be said of the phobias. Freud concluded that it might be generally useful to apply the same principles of psychoanalysis to all children to free them of repressed wishes that inevitably arise during childhood.

Evaluating the study by Freud

The research method
This study was a case study. *What are the strengths and limitations of this research method in the context of this study?*

The research technique
Hans' father collected data about Hans by observing what Hans did and said. *What are the strengths and limitations of observation in the context of this study?*

Hans' father also questioned Hans (interviewed him). *What are the strengths and limitations of interviewing in the context of this study?*

The sample
Hans and his family were the participants in this study. Hans was a middle European boy from an intelligent middle-class family and from a specific period of time (circa 1900). *In what way might these characteristics affect the results and conclusions drawn from the study?*

Ethical issues
What ethical issues should have concerned the researchers in this study, and how might they have dealt with these issues?

Qualitative or quantitative?
What kind of data were collected in this study? What are the strengths and limitations of producing this kind of data in the context of this study?

Validity
Hans' father may have influenced the information Hans provided by using leading questions. *Explain how this might affect the validity of this study.*

Hans' father and Freud explained Hans' behaviour. *In what way were these explanations biased and thus might lack validity?*

Applications/usefulness
Freud used the results from this study to support his theory of personality and also to enhance our understanding of the development of mental disorder (phobias). *How valuable do you think this study was?*

What next?
Describe **one** change to this study, and say how you think this might affect the outcome.

> *There are no simple answers. Evaluating a study requires you to think. We have provided some pointers here, linked to the KEY ISSUES covered through this book – see page XIV for a table of these key issues.*

Debate

Many people are not very convinced by Freudian explanations for behaviour.

Conduct a debate in class to decide whether Freud still has a place in modern psychology. Do his explanations stand the test of time? Were they ever any good?

...Links to other studies and issues...

Such is Freud's influence that there are links all through this text. The work of Elizabeth **Loftus** looks at repressed and false memories; the case study of **Thigpen and Cleckley** deals with the unconscious mind. Freud contributes to our understanding of moral development in children and offers an opposing view to the social learning theory of **Bandura**.

The legacy

It is hard to think of many people who have had such a deep and enduring effect on the Western world as Sigmund Freud. It is also difficult to think of people who have inspired such strong feelings both for and against their work. The theories and practice of psychoanalysis are still fiercely debated. What is undeniable is that Freud has affected the ideas we hold about identity, memory, sexuality and childhood. A brief search of the internet will find a wealth of resources on the man and his work. Like him or loathe him, you can't really ignore him.

Freud merchandise

Can't afford a therapist but want someone to talk to? You can get the Sigmund Freud Beanbag Doll ('Soft, squeezable, and oh so smart! Great gift for anyone in the mental health field'), or maybe the Freud and Couch finger puppet, or the ever popular movable Freud action figure ('captures Freud in a pensive pose, holding a distinctly phallic cigar. Put him on your desk or nightstand to inspire you to explore the depths of your unconscious and embrace the symbolism of your dreams'). You can even buy Freudian Slippers.

These items and others available from The Unemployed Philosopher's Guild (www.philosophersguild.com)

The legacy

Since Freud first published his theories whole forests have been destroyed printing what people have to say about them. Bookshop shelves still groan with texts about Freud and by people following his ideas. In mainstream psychology, however, Freud does not feature very highly in UK university courses and many psychologists would not cite Freud as an important influence on the modern subject. Having said that, he still has the greatest recognition of any psychologist and when students were asked to identify the most important psychologist in a recent survey (Banyard and Kagan, 2002) they gave Freud twice as many votes as his nearest rival.

Freud's influence is massive both in psychology and beyond. Most obvious is the effect on therapy. Although traditional psychoanalysis is relatively rare in this country, the ideas about the importance of the first five years, the role of the unconscious and the power of defence mechanisms influence many therapists. Freud is commonly cited in texts on critical theory and his influence is seen in literature and the arts.

Freud's family continue to be prominent in British life and the diversity of their work perhaps reflects the enduring influence of the man.

The Freud dynasty

The only one of Freud's children to continue his work as a therapist was Anna who came to the UK with him in 1938. Famous in her own right, her legacy is the Anna Freud Centre in Hampstead, London dedicated to the well-being of children and their families.

Of Freud's grandchildren, Lucian Freud is one of Britain's most famous (and expensive) living artists. His daughter is the fashion designer Bella Freud.

Lucian's brother is Clement Freud who has been a broadcaster for 40 years. He was a Liberal Party MP for the Isle of Ely between 1973 and 1987. His daughter Emma Freud is a British broadcaster and cultural commentator. She is married to the writer Richard Curtis which therefore gives us a link from Freud to *The Vicar of Dibley*. He'd be so pleased.

Emma's brother Matthew Freud is one of the most powerful PR men in London. He has close connections to the Labour Government and his clients include companies such as Pepsi, BT, and BskyB. He is married to Elizabeth Murdoch (Rupert's daughter) who is a media executive.

The careers of the family members reflect the areas of life that continue to be influenced by Freud: therapy, broadcasting, the arts, advertising and public relations.

Anna Freud with her Dad.

Farting as a defence against unspeakable dread

Psychoanalyst Mara Sidoli was famous for her willingness to deal with difficult cases. She took on a severely disturbed 'latency boy' (named from Freud's latency period between the ages of 7 and 11 years) called Peter who frankly didn't smell too good.

According to Sidoli (1996) 'Peter held loud conversations with imaginary beings and made loud anal farts as well as farting noises with his mouth whenever he became anxious or angry.' He also tended to soil himself when anxious. Sidoli describes this behaviour in terms of Freud's defence mechanisms and suggested he was testing his parents' commitment to him.

After a year of therapy that seemed to be having little effect Sidoli took the nuclear approach and started to make farting noises herself. This so surprised Peter that it finally broke through the defences and he was able to express his dread, affection and humour about his parents in a less noxious way.

For this report and for her courage and tenacity Mara Sidoli was awarded the 1998 igNoble Prize (like the Nobel Prize but not really) for literature.

Behaviourist explanation of phobias

Freud's explanation of Little Hans' phobia is not the only possible explanation. The behaviourist Hobart Mowrer (1947) analysed the same situation using the learning theory concepts of association and reinforcement. According to this behaviourist view a fear is learned when something that was previously neutral (such as a horse) is paired with something that provokes fear (the experience of watching the horse fall down dead). Once this association has been learned other things reinforce it. In this case the fact that Hans' phobia meant staying away from horses and thus spending more time at home with his mother was reinforcing.

Multiple choice questions

1 How old was Hans when his father started recording the case study?
   a 2 years old.   b 3 years old.
   c 4 years old.   d 5 years old.

2 When Hans was 3½ what important event occurred?
   a He developed a phobia.
   b His sister Hanna was born.
   c He worked with a plumber.
   d All of the above.

3 In the dream of the giraffes, Hans dreamed that the big giraffe called out because:
   a He sat on the big one.
   b He sat on the crumpled one.
   c He took the crumpled one away.
   d He hit the big one.

4 What animal represented his father?
   a Horse.   b Giraffe.
   c Lion.   d Both a and b.

5 What is a 'castration complex'?
   a Fear of becoming a man.
   b Fear of having one's penis removed.
   c Fear of sexual rejection.
   d All of the above.

6 What kind of horse was Hans afraid of?
   a Large horse.   b White horse.
   c Spotted horse.   d Police horse.

7 Hans used his own word for his phobia, which was his
   a Troubles.   b Illness.
   c Babble.   d Nonsense.

8 What did a laden cart represent?
   a His father.
   b A full stomach.
   c A pregnant woman.
   d All of the above.

9 The term 'lumf' referred to
   a Faeces.   b Horses.
   c Mountains.   d A penis.

10 The final fantasy Hans had was about:
    a Giraffes.
    b Breaking into a train.
    c A plumber.
    d His pretend children.

Answers are on page 105.

Exam-style questions

> See page XII–XIII for notes on the exam paper and styles of question.

Section A questions

1 Freud suggested that Hans' fear of horses symbolised his fear of his father. Outline **two** pieces of evidence that support this suggestion.   [4]

2 In Freud's study of Hans, several dreams or fantasies are described. Outline **two** of these.   [4]

3 Freud describes Hans as a 'little Oedipus'.
   (a) Explain briefly what the Oedipus complex is.   [2]
   (b) Give **one** example from the study by Freud of how Hans was a little Oedipus.   [2]

4 Freud suggested that boys go through a phallic stage in the course of their early development.
   (a) Identify **two** features of the phallic stage which were shown by little Hans.   [2]
   (b) Give **one** weakness in the evidence that used to support this conclusion about Little Hans.   [2]

5 The study by Freud of Little Hans provided an explanation of how a phobia develops.
   (a) Outline Freud's explanation of the development of Hans' phobia of horses.   [2]
   (b) Suggest an alternative explanation of Hans' phobia of horses.   [2]

6 The study by Freud contains the following extract of a conversation between Hans and his father:
      Father: *When the horse fell down did you think of your daddy?*
      Hans: *Perhaps. Yes it's possible.*
   (a) Explain why Hans might think of his father when the horse fell down.   [2]
   (b) Give **one** problem with this type of questioning.   [2]

Section B questions

(a) Describe the aim of the study by Freud.   [2]

(b) Describe how data was collected in the study by Freud.   [6]

(c) Give **one** advantage and **one** disadvantage of the method used to collect data in the study by Freud.   [6]

(d) Describe **two** ethical issues that are important in the study by Freud.   [6]

(e) Outline the conclusions of the study by Freud.   [8]

(f) Suggest **two** changes to the study by Freud and outline how these changes might affect the results.   [8]

Section C questions

(a) Outline **one** assumption of the psychodynamic approach in psychology.   [2]

(b) Describe how the psychodynamic approach could explain the development of phobias.   [4]

(c) Describe **one** similarity and **one** difference between the study by Freud and any other developmental study.   [6]

(d) Discuss the strengths and limitations of the psychodynamic approach, using examples from the study by Freud.   [12]

Key issue: psychodynamic perspective

The **psychodynamic** approach tries to explain all human behaviour and experience in terms of the inner conflicts of the mind. The approach concentrates on the structure of the mind which has parts we are aware of (the conscious) and parts we are unaware of (the unconscious). The approach comes initially from the work of Freud but also includes ideas from the many people who developed Freud's ideas.

The psychodynamic approach sees the individual as being in continual conflict with the various drives inside them and that good mental health is achieved by resolving these conflicts as best you can. The approach goes further than looking at individuals to explain how societies develop and function, and comments on governments, religion, families and just about everything. To the believers it can explain everything, and to the non-believers it can explain next to nothing.

The approach (a way of explaining events and experiences) is often mixed up with Freud's theories and there is a good reason for this because there is considerable overlap. It is not possible to understand the approach without having some basic idea of the theories (see also page 92).

(see also page 92).

Defence mechanisms are protective strategies that the mind uses to defend itself against unwelcome or disturbing information.

Hypnosis is a temporary trance-like state that can be induced in healthy individuals and is sometimes used in stage shows to encourage people to behave like a chicken.

Libido is Freud's concept of internal motivational energy commonly taken to mean the sex drive.

Psychoanalysis is Freud's theory of personality which describes how human behaviour is affected by unconscious thought and feelings.

A **psychoanalyst** is a therapist who is trained in psychoanalysis and employs its methods in treating emotional disorders (commonly with a beard and a central European accent).

Psychodynamic refers to explanations which focus on factors that motivate behaviour.

Psychosomatic: the mind and body

The term psychosomatic is commonly used but little understood. The two parts of the term refer to the mind (psycho) and the body (somatic) and suggest a connection between the two. This was a revolutionary idea at the end of the nineteenth century and Freud was one of the people who developed it.

In 1885 Freud went to Paris to visit the French neurologist Jean-Martin Charcot who specialised in treating patients who were suffering from a variety of unexplained physical symptoms such as paralysis that had no obvious medical cause. Charcot believed that his patients were suffering from a form of hysteria which had developed from their emotional response to a painful (traumatic) event in their past. They suffered, in his view, not from the physical effects of the event, but from the idea they had formed of it. Under **hypnosis**, Charcot was able to relieve the symptoms. Freud returned to Vienna and started to use hypnosis with people who were showing symptoms of hysteria to see if he could get to the mental causes of the disorder. It is hard to convey quite how dramatic this idea was at the time, but it is part of Freud's legacy that we take it for granted today that there is a connection between our state of mind and the general health of our body.

The causes of psychosomatic disorders

Freud took a forensic view of psychological disorders and looked for the cause. He soon abandoned hypnosis in favour of the 'talking cure' where patients would be encouraged to let their thoughts run towards the things that gave them emotional disturbance. He would often find a painful event from the patient's past hidden deep in their memory – gone but not forgotten. Freud reported that when the patient was able to recall the traumatic event and live through it again, the symptoms would disappear. The patients were suffering from hidden memories of unpleasant or troubling event.

The aim of the talking cure was to find the hidden emotion from the past that was bottled up and was having a bad effect on the person. This is another legacy from Freud that we take for granted today, that blocked up emotions will bring all sorts of problems, Whether this is true or not is still fiercely debated but what is undeniable is the popular belief that it is true.

Over the course of many interviews with many patients Freud discovered a recurrent and disturbing theme. When the talking cure unravelled the various troubling events they finally ended up at a childhood sexual experience. Freud initially suggested that many instances of adult mental disturbance were caused by sexual experience (abuse) as a child. The word controversial does not do justice to the response that this idea provoked. Freud later retracted the theory and suggested instead that the children had imagined the sexual contact but never actually experienced it. This second idea is even more controversial today because we are much more ready to accept that children experience unwanted sexual advances from adults.

'Freud considered laughter the conservation of psychic energy. Then again, Freud never played Friday night, second house, at the Glasgow Empire', British comedian Ken Dodd.

Anatomy is destiny

Freud claimed that *anatomy is destiny*, that is, your sex determines your main personality traits. Men are men and women are women. This idea has created a lot of debate with, for example, one of Freud's colleagues, Karen Horney (1885–1952) who took the opposite view. She said that culture is more important than biology as the main influence on personality. Psychoanalysis does not seem to understand women as well as it does men. For example Freud wrote, *'Nor will you have escaped worrying about this problem – those of you who are men; to those of you who are women this will not apply – you are yourself the problem'* (1933).

Karen Horney suggested that psychoanalysis appears to understand men better than women because the psychodynamic approach has been dominated almost exclusively by male thinking and has therefore evolved into a masculine enterprise.

Dreaming

'You should bear in mind that the dreams which we produce at night have, on the one hand, the greatest external similarity and kinship with the creations of insanity, and are, on the other hand, compatible with complete health in waking life' (Freud, 1910).

Freud's idea that dreams are essential for good mental health has received a lot of support over the years. If you were not allowed to dream then it is likely that you would soon start experiencing different mental states that might well include paranoia and anxiety.

Many of us remember our dreams and sometime puzzle on what they mean. Freud believed that all dreams are meaningful and, in fact, the meaning is the cause of the dream. The issue is figuring out, by looking at the symbols in the dream, what it means. Freud also suggested that all dreams are the fulfillment of wishes, that is something that we want to happen, but those wishes are sometimes so shocking to us that we disguise them in many ways.

'Sometimes a cigar is just a cigar'. In his analysis of dreams and symbols Freud suggests that many of the things we dream of are symbols for sex. In particular anything long and thin, or capable of getting bigger is seen as a phallic (penis) symbol. A cigar can be a classic phallic symbol but Freud recognised that sometimes you might just want to smoke some tobacco.

Life and death

In his later writing Freud developed the idea of two competing instincts inside us, one struggling for life (Eros) and one struggling for death (Thanatos). He summarised his view by writing *'The goal of all life is death'*. It sounds very strange to us that we should have an internal urge to die but if we look at it in a broader way then it makes more sense. The drive for life is a drive for activity, action and unpredictability (chaos). Although we might have a lust for life and seek out exciting events and people we don't want this all of the time. Sometimes we want to chill out (young people talk) or take it easy and have a cup of tea (old people talk). When we chill out we are looking for less stimulation, we want the world to be slower, quieter, more predictable and less demanding. If you take this to its obvious conclusion then we are most at peace and least troubled when we are dead. The drive for peace and quiet is ultimately the drive for final peace and quiet.

Little Red Riding Hood, *the most analysed fairy tale character ever.*

Fairy tales

Why do some stories have a big effect on us? Freud would suggest that they tap into some deep fears or wishes. Take for example the story of Little Red Riding Hood (Hoodie for short). This is a fairy story of a little girl who goes into the wood to see Granny. Sadly Granny has been eaten by a Wolf who takes her place in Granny's bed. When Hoodie arrives she does not realise that her Granny has been replaced by a Wolf. How can this be? Is she blind? How can there be a problem telling the difference between a wolf and your granny? The story is quite ridiculous but as children we suspend our disbelief and go along with the story. To see how ridiculous it is change the part of the Wolf to a talking Banana, and when you get to the bit that Hoodie can't tell the difference between Granny and Banana the story falls apart.

A Freudian answer to this puzzle is that to the child the Wolf and Granny are in fact one and same person. To a child, adults are very unpredictable. Sometimes they are kind and caring and give you treats and sometimes they get angry and shout at you. The reasons for these changes are not obvious to the child who sees the adult as having two sides – Granny and the Wolf.

Qs

1   Take **one** of the core studies (other than Little Hans) and look at it from a psychodynamic perspective. For example why were children aggressive in the Bobo study and why did Eve develop more than one identity?

2   Compare the psychodynamic approach to the behavioural approach. Which one gives the better explanation for why children sometimes behave badly?

3   Are your dreams full of things and events that are symbols for sex? Make a list of everyday events or objects that can symbolise some part of sexuality. Is Freud correct in suggesting that when we dream of these things we are really dreaming about sex?

4   Describe a trivial mistake you have made recently, or a dream you have recently experienced and try to analyse it within Freud's ideas.

'Time spent with cats is never wasted'. This is perhaps the most controversial thing Freud ever wrote, especially to the many cat haters in this country.

...Links to other studies and issues...

Some would argue that all psychology and in fact all human life can be explained from a psychoanalytic perspective. The common view, however, in UK university psychology departments is that Freud is only of historical interest. You are more likely to study him if you take English at university than if you take psychology. That being said, it is possible to see his influence in many of the core studies and in many of our public services. The study of Eve (**Thigpen and Cleckley**) highlights her inner conflicts and her early life experiences as an explanation for her adult behaviour. It is possible to see the obedience (see **Milgram**) of some people as their responses to the relationship they had with their father, and so on.

The psychodynamic approach is also best understood by comparison to other approaches such as **behaviourism** or the **cognitive approach**. These broad views on life try and look for the common threads that can be used to explain our behaviour and experiences. You might also like to look at the issue that considers **case studies** as much of the theory of psychoanalysis is based on case study evidence.

The developmental approach

The developmental approach looks at the changes that individuals go though during their lives. It has commonly focused on child development but the approach is actually interested in how we develop from the 'cradle to the grave'. In fact, modern scientific techniques mean that we can track development even before the cradle and so we should really say from 'conception to the grave'. Some psychologists see the changes as developing steadily and progressively, and some describe the changes as going through a series of stages. The interest for all developmental psychologists is in the things that bring about these changes.

Questions for developmental psychologists

Psychologists take a range of different approaches to the study of development.

Similarities or differences: Psychologists can look for the features that all children share and are important to the development of any child, or they can look at the features that are different between one child and another.

Stages: If children develop bit by bit then we do not need to talk about stages, but if development involves reorganisation and the emergence of new strategies and skills then it is more useful to talk about stages. For example, in everyday speech we commonly refer to informal stages such as the 'terrible twos'.

Key issues

Here are two key issues for developmental psychologists. One is the nature–nurture question (see page 90) which explores how much of a behaviour is the product of genetically determined factors (nature) and how much from experience (nurture). We clearly share some characteristics with our parents but how much is that due to being brought up by them or how much to sharing their genetic structure? One way of checking this is to study children brought up by people who are not their biological parents.

Baby showing the diving reflex, an innate (inherited) behaviour.

The second key issue is about the timing and plasticity of development. Are there key times for certain behaviours to develop and what happens if that development is disrupted? For example, babies up to the age of about 6 months display a diving reflex which means that if they go under water they automatically hold their breath and make swimming like movements. This reflex fades by the age of one.

Plasticity refers to the amount that a behaviour can change and adapt or how rigid it will be once it has developed.

Pablo Picasso: *'All children are artists. The problem is how to remain an artist once he grows up.'*

The history of developmental psychology

Modern developmental psychology is commonly said to have been kick started by William Preyer's book *The Mind of the Child* which was published in 1882. Like many of the developmental psychologists that followed him, he based his work on observations of his own child. What distinguished Preyer's work and what set the pattern for developmental psychology was the use of scientific procedures, in particular accurate and thorough recording of behaviour and the identification of patterns of change in that behaviour.

Cognitive development

In Europe one of the pioneers of developmental psychology was Alfred Binet (1857–1911) who looked at how children think. Binet is most famous for developing the IQ test which has become a way of classifying a child's intelligence by providing a single number. This outcome does not reflect Binet's approach because he was interested in the many diverse ways that children think and he was trying to explore how they learn to learn.

The tradition that has grown from Binet's work has been about the development of thought in psychology. This is labelled cognitive development and the most famous psychologist in this tradition is **Jean Piaget** (see pages 72–73) provided an account of how children pass through various stages of thinking as they progress towards adult thought. More recently psychologists in this tradition have looked at children who show unusual patterns of thought. One such pattern is labelled as autism and many psychologists including Simon Baron-Cohen (see page 44) have carried out studies to investigate the nature and causes of this.

Emotional development

A different tradition in developmental psychology has focused on emotional development rather than cognitive development. The most cited figure in this tradition is Sigmund Freud (see page 93) who, like Piaget, proposed a stage theory of development. According to Freud a child develops their adult personality by resolving a number of basic and inevitable emotional conflicts during the first five years of life. This concern with the emotional life of the child can be seen in the work of **John Bowlby** and **Mary Ainsworth** on attachment (see page 70).

Behavioural development

A third tradition in developmental psychology comes from the behaviourists (see page 60). **John Watson** carried out a number of studies on children and although he is most famous for the rather quirky Little Albert study he also carried out studies on children in nurseries to observe how their behaviour developed. The underlying principle here is of the effect of rewards and punishments on behaviour. If a child responds to these (and they do) then it is important that we reward the behaviour we want the child to develop and punish or ignore the behaviour we don't want to see again. You can watch this being played out on the many child behaviour shows on television. In the behaviourist tradition the most famous and enduring study is **Bandura's** Bobo doll experiment.

Different stories of parenting

Every Child Matters

A major policy initiative of the UK government is *Every Child Matters* (www.everychildmatters.gov.uk) which aims to improve the quality of life and wellbeing of every child in the UK. In his foreword to the discussion document on this initiative, then Prime Minister Tony Blair showed the importance our society places on this when he wrote, *'For most parents, our children are everything to us: our hopes, our ambitions, our future.'*

The policy identifies five outcomes for children that are seen as being key for well-being in childhood and later life:

- being healthy,
- staying safe,
- enjoying and achieving,
- making a positive contribution to society, and
- achieving economic well-being.

Save the nanny, save the world

The principles of behaviourism are demonstrated in many programmes on television that try to change people's behaviour. The family therapy shows such as Supernanny set out to change the behaviour of children but the most effective way to do this is to change the behaviour of the parents who are moulding the behaviour of children.

Cinderella: is it all true?

One of the strongest themes in fairy tales is of the wicked stepmother. The story of Cinderella has been around in many cultures for centuries. It is estimated that over 350 versions of it exist starting with one recorded in the ninth century in China. In this version Cinderella doesn't have a fairy godmother but is helped by a magical fish (a glass kipper perhaps?). The story has developed over the centuries but the role of the wicked stepmother remains constant.

Is the story so powerful because it relates to a truth we know but daren't speak about? There is an uncomfortable line of research developing that points to the negative effects of being in a step-family. We'll put in the usual caveats and say that many children in step-families have a perfectly acceptable life though Bowlby is recorded as saying *'The myth (of the wicked step-parent) has some validity to it. A step-parent is a very unsatisfactory parent for a child to have. It is nobody's fault. It's a fact.'* (Maddox, 1998).

Evolutionary psychologists go a step further and suggest that we are going against thousands of years of evolution when we try to nourish and support our partner's children as if they were our own. On the front cover of their book *The Truth about Cinderella* Daly and Wilson (1998) state *'having a step-parent is the most powerful risk factor for severe child maltreatment yet discovered.'* You can see why this work is controversial.

Fathers 4 Justice campaigning for more access to their children and better fitting superhero suits.

New families

The pattern of family life is changing in this country. At least one in three children will experience parental separation before the age of 16. Most of these children go through a period of unhappiness; many experience low self-esteem, behaviour problems, and loss of contact with part of the extended family. Children are usually helped by good communication with both parents, and most settle back into a normal pattern of development (Dunn and Deater-Deckard, 2001). Many children have experience of being in a step-family. Becoming part of a step-family seems to be helpful for younger children but to be harder for older children to adapt to (Hawthorne *et al.*, 2003). Older children seem to appreciate step-parents more when they act in a supportive and friendly way rather than being involved in discipline or control.

There are also issues around the role of fathers in successful parenting and some fathers argue for greater access to their children. The group called 'Fathers 4 Justice' campaigns for a child's right to see both their parents and all their grandparents. One of the consequences of Bowlby's work was that in divorce cases the courts started to give custody to mothers rather than the traditional placement with fathers. The result of this has been that fathers (and grandparents) have sometimes been cut out of the child's life and been allowed only limited access.

Black, white or mixed race?

Racially mixed couples are no longer a rare phenomenon. It is estimated that a third of British people of African-Caribbean origin under the age of thirty who are currently married or co-habiting, have white partners. Tizard and Phoenix (1993, 2001) explored the issue of mixed race identity by interviewing young people from a range of social backgrounds, all of whom had one white and one African or African-Caribbean parent. The interviews looked at adolescents' perception of their racial identity, its role in their lives, their feelings about having one black and one white parent, their attitude to black and white people, allegiance to black and white cultures, their experience of, and ways of coping with racism. They found that many young people have very positive dual identities, as both black and white, and resist demands from others about the kinds of identities they should have.

Developmental core study 1: Samuel and Bryant (conservation)

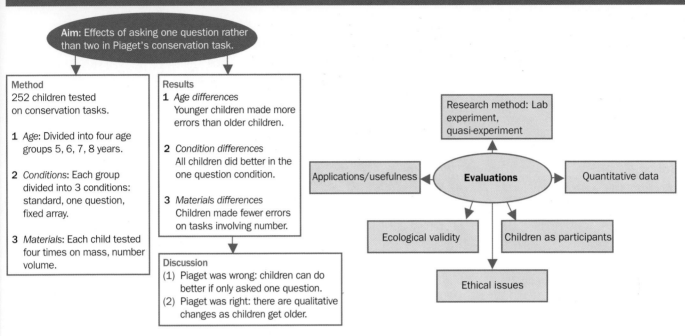

Aim: Effects of asking one question rather than two in Piaget's conservation task.

Method
252 children tested on conservation tasks.

1 *Age*: Divided into four age groups 5, 6, 7, 8 years.

2 *Conditions*: Each group divided into 3 conditions: standard, one question, fixed array.

3 *Materials*: Each child tested four times on mass, number volume.

Results
1 *Age differences*
Younger children made more errors than older children.

2 *Condition differences*
All children did better in the one question condition.

3 *Materials differences*
Children made fewer errors on tasks involving number.

Discussion
(1) Piaget was wrong: children can do better if only asked one question.
(2) Piaget was right: there are qualitative changes as children get older.

Research method: Lab experiment, quasi-experiment

Applications/usefulness

Evaluations

Quantitative data

Ecological validity

Children as participants

Ethical issues

Developmental core study 2: Bandura *et al.* (aggression)

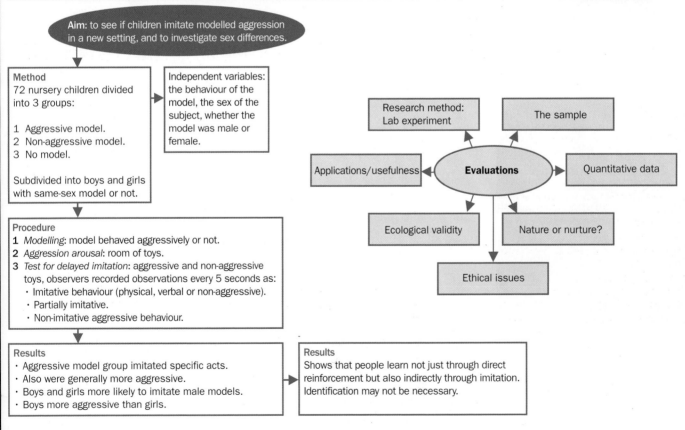

Aim: to see if children imitate modelled aggression in a new setting, and to investigate sex differences.

Method
72 nursery children divided into 3 groups:

1 Aggressive model.
2 Non-aggressive model.
3 No model.

Subdivided into boys and girls with same-sex model or not.

Independent variables: the behaviour of the model, the sex of the subject, whether the model was male or female.

Procedure
1 *Modelling*: model behaved aggressively or not.
2 *Aggression arousal*: room of toys.
3 *Test for delayed imitation*: aggressive and non-aggressive toys, observers recorded observations every 5 seconds as:
· Imitative behaviour (physical, verbal or non-aggressive).
· Partially imitative.
· Non-imitative aggressive behaviour.

Results
· Aggressive model group imitated specific acts.
· Also were generally more aggressive.
· Boys and girls more likely to imitate male models.
· Boys more aggressive than girls.

Results
Shows that people learn not just through direct reinforcement but also indirectly through imitation. Identification may not be necessary.

Research method: Lab experiment

The sample

Applications/usefulness

Evaluations

Quantitative data

Ecological validity

Nature or nurture?

Ethical issues

Developmental core study 3: Freud (Little Hans)

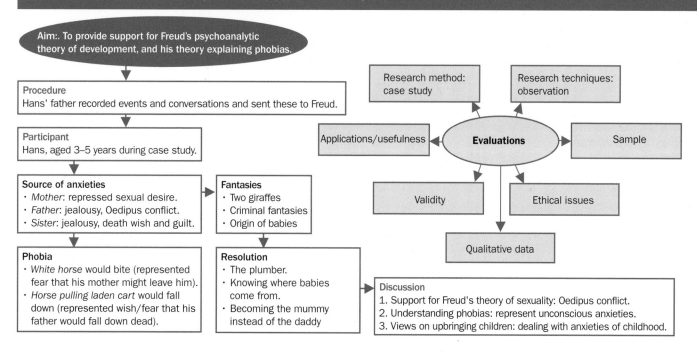

Aim:. To provide support for Freud's psychoanalytic theory of development, and his theory explaining phobias.

Procedure
Hans' father recorded events and conversations and sent these to Freud.

Participant
Hans, aged 3–5 years during case study.

Source of anxieties
- *Mother*: repressed sexual desire.
- *Father*: jealousy, Oedipus conflict.
- *Sister*: jealousy, death wish and guilt.

Fantasies
- Two giraffes
- Criminal fantasies
- Origin of babies

Phobia
- *White horse* would bite (represented fear that his mother might leave him).
- *Horse pulling laden cart* would fall down (represented wish/fear that his father would fall down dead).

Resolution
- The plumber.
- Knowing where babies come from.
- Becoming the mummy instead of the daddy

Research method: case study

Research techniques: observation

Applications/usefulness

Evaluations

Sample

Validity

Ethical issues

Qualitative data

Discussion
1. Support for Freud's theory of sexuality: Oedipus conflict.
2. Understanding phobias: represent unconscious anxieties.
3. Views on upbringing children: dealing with anxieties of childhood.

Further reading and other things

There is so much material on developmental psychology that it is difficult to know where to start. You might try some of the books that cover unusual childhoods such as *Genie: A Scientific Tragedy* by Russ Rymer (Penguin 1994) which tells the story of a young girl brought up with very little human contact for the first 12 years of her life. Another possibility is *The Forbidden Experiment* by Roger Shattuck (Kodansha International, 1995) which tells the story of the 'Wild Boy of Aveyron' who appeared from the woods in the year 1800 in France and had the behavioural characteristics of an animal. An account of a more recent child that is a popular read is *Dibs in search of self*, by Virginia Axline (Penguin, 1990) which tells the story of a boy who could not connect with other people.

If you go away and read one book then choose this next one: *As Nature Made Him: the boy who was raised as a girl* (P.S.), by John Colapinto (2006, Harper Perennial). This text tells how psychologists can sometimes interfere in the lives of ordinary people and become so concerned with their theories and research that they lose sight of the humanity around them. It's one of those books that is hard to put down once you start it. And if you read it, you won't feel the same about psychologists again. For other accounts of development then just pick any biography or autobiography because they commonly give interesting accounts of how events during childhood

shape the adult. If you want a suggestion then what about *The Autobiography of Malcolm X*, by Malcolm X, Alex Haley and Paul Gilroy (Penguin 2001). With this book you get two stories for the price of one; the story of the Black civil rights leader as told by himself and also by others.

Samuel and Bryant
- Original article can be found on PsychExchange (http://www.psychexchange.co.uk/file124.html)
- Some interesting background reading relating to Piaget is in the class book by Margaret Donalson *Children's Minds*.

Bandura et al.
- Original article at http://psychclassics.yorku.ca/Bandura/bobo.htm
- Albert Bandura's website http://www.des.emory.edu/mfp/Bandura/index.html

Freud
- Freud's case studies read like novels rather than clinical accounts. The Little Hans case study is published along with another case history (the Rat Man) – see full details in reference section on page 94 (Freud, 1909).

MCQ answers	
Bryant and Samuel (MCQs on page 79)	1d 2d 3c 4b 5d 6c 7d 8b 9a 10d
Bandura *et al.* (MCQs on page 89)	1a 2c 3d 4d 5d 6b 7d 8a 9b 10d
Freud (MCQs on page 99)	1b 2b 3c 4d 5b 6b 7d 8c 9a 10d

1 The study by Samuel and Bryant showed that younger children were less able to conserve than older children.

(a) Explain what the ability to 'conserve' is. [2]

(b) Describe **one** of the methods used by Samuel and Bryant to test whether the children could conserve or not. [2]

Stig's answer

(a) They mean that children are able to work out that something stays the same even if it looks like it is different.

(b) You can test for conservation using mass, volume or number – counters in a row. You show a child two identical rows of counters and then space the counters out in one row so it looks longer and see if the child says they are the same or different.

Chardonnay's answer

(a) The same quantity of water may look more or less in a shorter or taller glass but it doesn't actually change.

(b) One way to test for conservation is using volume – a liquid in two beakers.

Examiner's comments

Stig, you are showing off now. These are two sound answers. Although part (a) could be more tightly phrased, it is accurate. Part (b) is very clear.

Chardonnay, you talk about conservation of water ... which is actually conservation of volume. You're a bit confused. You're not wrong, but you're not totally right either. In part (b) for full marks you need to describe and not just identify, you have just said that there was a liquid in two beakers but not actually said what is done to test conservation (the liquid from one beaker is poured into a taller and thinner one and the child asked whether they are the same).

Stig (2 + 2 marks) Chardonnay (1 + 1 marks)

---

2 Samuel and Bryant's study on conservation compared Piaget's original method of testing conservation (two-question condition) with a 'one-question'.

(a) Outline a key difference between these two conditions in terms of the results. [2]

(b) Explain why Samuel and Bryant thought the children would do better on the one-question condition. [2]

Stig's answer

(a) In Samuel and Bryant's study young children did less well when they were asked only one question than when they were asked two questions.

(b) One reason is that they might have been confused. Being asked two questions could be confusing.

Chardonnay's answer

(a) In Piaget's original experiment (with two questions) he found that younger children did less well than those over the age of 7. In the one-question experiment more of the younger children got the question right but there were still differences.

(b) The reason why more younger children did better with only one question might be due to demand characteristics. They might have thought that when they were asked a second question they were supposed to give a new answer.

Examiner's comments

Hmm, Stig you have got it the wrong way round. Children did better in the one-question condition, making fewer errors on the conservation task. Despite getting part (a) wrong, you strangely are on the right lines for part (b). You would need further explanation – why does asking two identical questions cause confusion?

Chardonnay's turn to show off now. Part (a) is a very full answer and you also talk about one-question/two-question in terms of another IV – age. This is almost surplus to the requirements for 2 marks for this question. Part (b) is also very strong! You have identified 'demand characteristics' as one reason for doing better and then explained this concept in the context of the question asked.

Stig (0 + 1 marks) Chardonnay (2 + 2 marks)

---

3 When studies are conducted with children researchers need to consider ethical issues especially carefully. Outline **two** ethical issues that were important in the study by Bandura *et al.* on the imitation of aggressive behaviour.

Stig's answer

The children should not have experienced harm and there were two ways they could have been psychologically harmed. First the children who watched the aggressive model might have been stressed and they also learned to be violent. They also were made to feel aggressive because the toys they were playing with were taken away.

Chardonnay's answer

One issue is of informed consent. The younger children couldn't give their own informed consent. Their parents must have been asked and they might not have wanted to take part. A second issue is that they might have felt distressed because of the frustration of having the toys taken away from them.

Examiner's comments

This is all true Stig, but you have, sadly, not identified two separate ethical issues as both stress and mild aggression arousal relate to the same issue – protection from harm.

Chardonnay has outlined two different ethical issues. However, informed consent is not strictly speaking, according to the ethical guidelines, a problem here. As the parents and carers gave consent, the guidelines indicate this is acceptable. The second issue is fine – identified and outlined.

Stig (2 + 0 marks) Chardonnay (1 + 2 marks)

4   (a) Explain how **one** of the controls was used in the study by Bandura *et al*.   [2]
    (b) Give **one** reason why it is difficult to generalise from the findings of this study to aggression outside the laboratory.   [2]

Stig's answer

(a) One control that was used in Bandura's study was that the children were matched for their aggressiveness.

(b) It's difficult to generalise from Bandura's findings because the study was done in a lab.

Chardonnay's answer

(a) Bandura had a control group who did not observe any aggression. This controlled for the fact that the children may have behaved aggressively even if they didn't see any aggression.

(b) One reason why it might be difficult to generalise from this study is because the children were American children and they might be more aggressive than other children.

Examiner's comments

Stig, you have identified a control used in the study, and this automatically gets you one mark. However, the question asks you to 'explain how', so you are required to give a brief (1–2 sentences) description of how they were matched. In part (b) you haven't provided enough for two marks as you have only identified the reason. For two marks you could have added 'and children might not behave in the same way in everyday life'.

Chardonnay, in part (a) you have identified a control and explained how it was used. So, 2 marks. In part (b) you have identified that they were American, so limiting generalisability to other cultures. Another point you could have made is that the nursery was for the children of university staff, who were probably middle-class, thus limiting generalisability to other groups. Anyway, you have written enough for 2 marks.

Stig (1 + 0 marks) Chardonnay (2 + 2 marks)

---

5   In Freud's study of Little Hans, one of the main events was the birth of his sister.

    (a) Describe what Hans felt about his sister?   [2]
    (b) What explanation did Freud give linking Hans' sister and Hans' fear of death?   [2]

Stig's answer

(a) Hans did not like his little sister. He wished she hadn't been born and was dead.

(b) The connection was that his wish that his sister was dead made him fear that he might die too.

Chardonnay's answer

(a) Hans had mixed feelings about his sister. He loved her but also wished her dead because she was a rival for his mother's affections.

(b) I think it might be due to the bath and Hans' worries that his mother would let him go and he would drown. This was because he wished that she would let his sister go.

Examiner's comments

A bit too simple, Stig. Hans did appear to have a bit of a 'deathwish' thing going on with his little sister, but it wasn't necessarily a conscious wish. We do not know if Hans liked his little sister or not. Chardonnay has provided the examiner with a fuller picture and brought in the important theme of jealousy and rivalry for his mother's affections.

Part (b) for both Stig and Chardonnay is good enough to attract full credit.

Stig (1 + 2 marks) Chardonnay (2 + 2 marks)

---

6   From Freud's study of Little Hans, Hans' father recorded what Hans said and did, sometimes asking Hans questions about his behaviour. Outline **one** strength and **one** weakness of the way in which the data were gathered.   [4]

Stig's answer

One strength is that this was a study about a normal child rather than Freud's usual work with patients who were mentally ill. One weakness is that there were lots of different ways the data could be interpreted. Freud's way is only one possibility, not necessarily the right one.

Chardonnay's answer

One strength about the way the data were collected is that Hans knew his father well and therefore felt freer to tell him everything. On the downside his father talked to him a lot and often gave 'leading questions' about the meaning of what Hans did or said, and this might have led him to give answers that were what his father expected.

Examiner's comments

Stig, I don't really think that you were concentrating on the question. The key phrase here is 'the way in which data were gathered' and this is different from the sample or the interpretation. The question is asking about how the data were collected from Hans. Your first answer is not appropriate to the question (it is related to the aims of the study rather than to *how* the data were collected). Your second answer is about how the data were interpreted, so again it is not appropriate.

Chardonnay's answer is along the right lines and contains sufficient elaboration for the full marks. A key issue in this study (though Freud was in denial about this!) was that the person collecting the data (Hans' dad) was biased, being instilled with Freudian ideas, and this is apparent in his use of leading questions.

Stig (0 + 0 marks) Chardonnay (2 + 2 marks)

7 (a) Outline **one** assumption of the developmental approach in psychology. [2]

(b) Describe how the developmental approach could explain conservation. [4]

(c) Describe ethical issues that might arise in the study by Samuel and Bryant and explain why they are problematic. [6]

(d) Discuss the strengths and limitations of the developmental approach, using examples from the study by Samuel and Bryant. [12]

Total [24]

Chardonnay's answer

(a) One assumption of the developmental approach is that as we get older, we change and develop.

(b) The developmental approach would say that conservation is something which changes according to age – so that while some children under, say, age 7 cannot conserve, in general, those aged more than 7 will be able to conserve. Developmental theories often use stages and the ability to conserve is something which indicates whether a child has reached concrete operational stage or not. Ability to conserve is, according to Piaget, whether a child has the logical operations to understand that just because, e.g. something looks longer or taller, it doesn't necessarily mean it is bigger – in other words being logical and not just going on the appearance of things.

(c) One ethical issue is consent. While, according to the BPS code, children do not need to themselves give consent, is it ok for just their parents or the teachers to give consent? We do not know from the study whether the parents gave consent – it might have just been teachers and they might not really be good enough to give consent especially as some of the children were quite young.

Another ethical issue is harm. There is not too much harm here but children are very keen to get things right and in this study, they might feel upset because it is quite difficult to get the question right especially in the fixed array condition and especially if they are young. This might make them a bit upset and this would be harm.

(d) One strength of the developmental approach is that it is a particularly useful branch of psychology. If we can better understand how children learn and develop, these can become strategies and policies in nurseries and schools in order to improve people's lives and help education. For example, in the Samuel and Bryant study, because we know that by asking children the same question twice (as in the standard judgement condition), this encourages them to give the wrong answer, teachers should avoid doing this in class and people who set Key Stage 1 tests should avoid this sort of thing. However, some might say that this is all obvious and most of developmental psychology is common sense.

One weakness of the developmental approach is that it focuses too much on children. The developmental approach should really be a life-span approach, from the cradle to the grave, and while a lot of developmental psychologists do believe this, most of the research has been done on childhood development. For example, in the case of cognitive development (e.g. Samuel and Bryant) most of the theories and studies are about changes in childhood. This ignores any changes in patterns of cognition in adulthood and assumes that it all remains the same after 18.

Another weakness of the developmental approach is that it ignores individual differences between children and looks instead at overall patterns. For example, in Samuel and Bryant, even though it wasn't true that all 7 year olds could conserve all of the time, the study isn't interested in why some children can and some children cannot – is it personality, education, nature, intelligence which explains this? Therefore, developmental psychology overgeneralises.

Examiner's comments

(a) Chardonnay, your answer is to the point, brief, and true. However it is lacking in detail or fine points that are necessary for the full 2 marks. You could have mentioned different aspects of development – emotional, cognitive, attachment, learning, for example.

(b) You clearly understand conservation itself and how it fits into Piaget's theory of cognitive development. Certainly, it was perceived as a key test of whether a child had reached the concrete operational stage or not. You use terminology appropriately and there is a good level of detail. Therefore, full marks here.

(c) You seem to know that this is really not the most unethical study – but of course there are always ethical issues to think about, especially where children are the participants. Your description of the first issue shows that you understand that children themselves are not required to give consent (a common mistake), though you could have given a bit more detail such as the age of the children.

The second issue you identify is well explained and well related to the study. However, for both issues you could have explained more why these issues are problematic. So, 2 + 2 marks here.

(d) Chardonnay, you have one strength and two weaknesses. In fact, you need at least two of each to be able to get more than 6 of the 12 available marks here and the mark scheme is very specific about this requirement. This is a real shame, because the quality of your answer otherwise, is very good – relevant examples, detailed discussion, clear expression, effective analysis, and well structured and organised. All your points are coherent and show excellent understanding. As I said, a real shame... had you supplied a second strength of the same calibre, this would have certainly been a top band response. But as it is, it can only get the maximum of 6. Sorry.

Chardonnay (1 + 4 + 4 + 6 marks = 15/24 marks)

CHAPTER 4

This chapter looks at three core studies in biological psychology.

- Maguire et al.'s study of the role of specific brain structures in memory for places.

- Dement and Kleitman's research into the link between REM sleep and dreaming.

- Sperry's investigation of what happens when you deconnect the two hemispheres of the brain.

Biological psychology

Introduction

What is biological psychology?

Biological psychology explores human behaviour and experience by looking at people as if they are biological machines. This idea has some value because it is clear that our biology affects our behaviour and experience. On a simple level we know that certain foodstuffs, such as coffee or alcoholic drinks, will affect the way we see the world and the way we behave. Also, it has been observed for a long time that damage to the brain and nervous system can have an effect on behaviour and experience. So the action of chemicals and the structure of the nervous system are the two main themes of biological psychology. However, the question that arises is how much does our biology affect us and what other factors intervene to affect the response.

The selection of studies in this chapter look at the structure and function of the brain. They also look at how we can map biological processes onto biological changes. The goal of the biological psychologist is to map all behaviour onto chemical and neurological changes.

Golgi stains

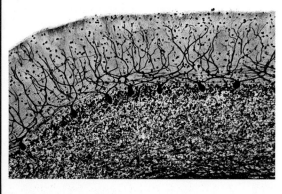

Our knowledge of the brain has advanced as scientists have found new techniques for viewing and recording its structure and functions. Camillo Golgi discovered a technique to stain nerve tissue so that the structure of nerve cells could be seen and investigated. This enabled scientists to map the paths of nerve cells in the brain for the first time. The Golgi stain, as it is now called, highlights a few cells in their entirety and creates striking images such as the one shown above. It is not fully understood even today how this process works.

Physiological research

An international team of brain scientists used the EEG technology (see page 125) to look at the effects of chewing different flavours of chewing gum (Yagyu et al., 1997). Twenty volunteers had to chew three different flavours of gum while being attached to an EEG machine. The three flavours were plain (with no sugar or flavourings), Relax Gum (a popular Japanese brand) and Relax Extra (with added green tea). Each chewing session went through a strict routine of chewing to strict time, opening and closing eyes when told and strict rest periods. They found two things: first it is possible to measure brain waves while someone is chewing gum and second that the EEG showed different patterns for the three flavours.

Brain and behaviour

We now know that what goes on in our brains will affect what we think, what we feel and what we do (our cognitions, our emotions and our behaviour). The relationship between the brain and our behaviour is still only partly understood but the research gives us some fascinating questions that make us think about who we are and what makes us tick.

Brains and personality

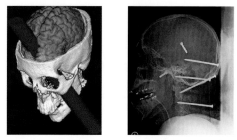

An artist's impression of Phineas Gage's skull with the metal rod that was fired through his head (left) and x-ray of Isidro Mejia's head with nails embedded (right).

The case of Phineas Gage is often cited as an example of the effects of the brain on personality. Gage was a US railway worker in the nineteenth century who had an industrial accident in which a large bolt was blasted through his skull and blew a hole in his brain. The bolt was 1 m in length, over 3 cm in diameter and weighed over 6 kg. It blasted through Gage's left cheek bone and came out of the top of his head. It is reported that Gage regained consciousness after just a few minutes.

The story of Phineas Gage appears in many psychology texts because of the changes that were then observed in the man. His behaviour changed dramatically after the event and he stopped being a conscientious worker. The railway company who had been employing him would not give him his job back when he regained his health because of these behavioural changes. The changes are described below in an account written at the time of the incident by a doctor.

'Gage was fitful, irreverent, indulging at times in the grossest profanity (which was not previously his custom), manifesting but little deference for his fellows, impatient of restraint or advice when it conflicts with his desires, at times pertinaciously obstinate, yet capricious and vacillating, devising many plans of future operations, which are no sooner arranged than they are abandoned in turn for others appearing more feasible. A child in his intellectual capacity and manifestations, he has the animal passions of a strong man. Previous to his injury, although untrained in the schools, he possessed a well-balanced mind, and was looked upon by those who knew him as a shrewd, smart businessman, very energetic and persistent in executing all his plans of operation. In this regard his mind was radically changed, so decidedly that his friends and acquaintances said he was "no longer Gage".' (Harlow, 1868)

Some of the details of the case are disputed but the incident highlights the question of how much our behaviour is affected by our brains. Was Gage a different man because some of his brain had gone or had the shock of being injured and then rejected by his employer changed his world view? Whatever the explanation the case shows how the brain can continue to function even when some parts are damaged.

A more recent version of Gage story was reported recently when Isidro Mejia of Los Angeles had a nail gun accidently discharged into his head. He survived the major brain injury with some loss of speech and other functions but has made a good recovery (BBC, 2004).

Brains and emotions

Emotion and the brain

There are a range of brain structures that are associated with emotions. Perhaps the most researched is the series of small structures hidden deep in the brain called the *limbic system*. It is this system that is the difference between mammals (us) and reptiles (crocodiles) – well, that and the teeth of course.

The discovery of the importance of these structures in emotion was made by Papez (1937) by looking at the brains of people and animals that had suffered emotional disorders.

Bulls

Two structures are particularly important; the *hypothalamus* which controls the bodily changes associated with emotion and the *amygdala* which has an effect on aggression. This has been demonstrated by a range of experimental and case study evidence. For example, the Spanish psychologist, Jose Delgardo is a pioneer in the implantation in the brain of radio activated electrodes. His ability to find an exact spot in the animal's brain is so precise that he has trusted his life to it in dramatic demonstrations. He implanted an electrode in the amygdala of a bull and then got into the bullring with it. When the bull started to charge, Delgardo activated the electrode and the bull halted its charge. After repeated experiences of this, the animal became permanently less aggressive. Not many people would put their science on the line in his way.

No need to fear a charging bull – if its amygdala is disabled.

Murderers

What if our behaviour can be changed by small changes in our brains? Would we become a different person and do different things? One curious case which raises these questions is the story of Charles Whitman. On August 1st 1966, Charles Whitman murdered his mother, drove home and murdered his wife then climbed the tower at the University of Texas with a high velocity rifle. For several hours he shot at everything he saw, killing 14 people and wounding 31 before he was gunned down by police. After the tragedy it was found that Whitman had sought psychiatric help for bad headaches and violent feelings. In a diary he requested an autopsy to be carried out after his death. This autopsy discovered a tumour the size of a walnut pressing on his *amygdala* which is a small area of the brain associated with aggressive behaviour.

The case illustrates the question of making connections between biological changes and behavioural changes. The more you read about the Whitman case the more confusing it gets (if you are interested just Google his name). Whitman had been experiencing a depressed mood over a long period of time and had even told his therapist of his dreams of shooting people from the tower. On the day of the murders he was observed to be very calm and left long diary entries describing the reasons for his actions.

One explanation of his behaviour focuses on the brain tumour and therefore sees the man having only limited control of his actions. Another explanation, however, focuses on the history of poor behaviour in the army and at college including firearms offences. So was it the tumour? Or something else?

On the fiddle

Our experience of emotion is affected by our judgement of our bodily reactions. So if we think we look nervous this will make us more nervous. So if we can control our bodily changes can we control our emotions?

This was tested in an experiment by Ian James (1988) with six young violinists. The musicians were filmed and assessed in conditions designed to increase stress. They played one piece in the morning and another in the afternoon. Before the afternoon recital half of the musicians were given a drug while half were given a placebo (a substance which has no pharmacological effects). The drug was a 'beta-blocker' which stops the action of adrenalin. There are two types of receptor sites for adrenalin – alpha and beta. When the beta sites are stimulated the heart accelerates, blood vessels dilate in the skin and muscles, and the muscles of the intestine and bladder are relaxed. Many of our responses to danger or stress are switched on through such receptors. The beta-blocker blocks the beta receptors and stops adrenalin having its usual effect.

The violinists who were given the beta-blocker gave a noticeably better performance in the afternoon. The drug also reduced the feelings of anxiety as well as the symptoms. The violinists noticed this, one reported that in the afternoon *'I was less nervous both physically and mentally'*, and another said *'...the beta-blockers made you relax more, mentally and physically'*.

...Connections...

Many psychologists will argue that all psychology will eventually be biological psychology. They believe that concepts such as **free will** or consciousness will be found to be controlled by simple biological processes when we have unlocked more secrets of the brain. Other psychologists are more **sceptical** about what we are able to discover about the brain. Elsewhere in this text **Piaget** and **Freud** both look to biological explanations of behaviour and Milgram argued that being obedient is our destiny because it is part of our nature. The biological approach also gives us explanations for unusual behaviours such as **autism** (**Baron-Cohen et al.**) and **mental illness** (**Rosenhan**) and for other individual differences such as intelligence or personality. There is no doubt that biological explanations have contributed to our understanding of a range of conditions but if we follow the argument too far we arrive at biological solutions for all our social problems.

Maguire *et al.*: starters

Brain scanning: a new technology

In the final quarter of the twentieth century, scanning technology stimulated a dramatic breakthrough in brain research. Before scans there were EEGs but these only provided general information about electrical activity in the whole brain. And before EEGs, the only way to investigate brains was to deal with the real thing. This meant operations where the brain was altered in some way by the use of surgery or chemicals or electrical stimulation. The work of Sperry and also Penfield (see page 133) was part of this. There were also studies that were carried out on people with brain injuries though, in such cases, the final analysis often had to wait until the person died and their brain could be fully examined. Phineas Gage (see page 110) and the Texas tower murderer (see page 111) are examples of this evidence. This type of early research on brain function is clearly limited because it can't really see the brain at work.

Scanning allows scientists to view the brain while it is working. The advent of such techniques meant that scientists could now study the brain without cutting it open. A whole new world appeared to be available to them. But things are never so simple and the issue is to be able to interpret what the scans tells us and recognise what they can't tell us.

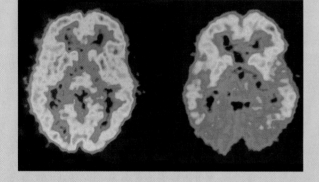

The images above show two PET scans. The normal brain on the left shows a lot of activity throughout the scanned area; the one on the right is the scan of a person with Alzheimer's Disease, showing far less activity.

Different kinds of scanning technique

Types of scan include:

CAT (computerised axial tomography)
CAT scans are built up from taking a series of x-rays 180 degrees around the head. The images show areas of damage and will highlight, for example, the area where a person has experienced a cerebral haemorrhage (a type of stroke).

MRI (magnetic resonance imaging)
People are slid into a machine looking like a giant pencil sharpener and subjected to a strong magnetic field which is turned on and off rapidly in the presence of a radio wave. The atoms of the brain change their alignment (spin) because of the magnetic field when it is on and produce characteristic radio signals when it is turned off. A detector reads those signals and, using a computer, can map the structure of the tissue. There are no radioactive materials used in an MRI.

fMRI (functional magnetic resonance imaging)
fMRI scans are the most recently developed forms of brain imaging and the scan of choice for psychologists. The scans use MRI technology to measure the changes in the blood oxygen levels that are connected to neural activity in the brain or spinal cord.

PET (positron emission tomography)
Patients are injected with slightly radioactive glucose (sugar). The most active brain tissue uses the glucose and so attracts the radioactive substance. Radiation sensors detect where the radiation is greatest and so build up a picture of activity in the brain. The scans take between 10 and 40 minutes to complete and are painless. Mind you, there is the slight issue of radioactive substances in your brain.

The data from the scan is usually presented as a coloured picture where the 'hot' colours such as orange and red are used to represent the areas where there is greatest activity and the 'cold' colours such as green and blue represent the areas with least activity. The scans tell us which bits are busy but not what they are doing.

The 10% myth: 'Scientists say we use only 10% of our brains'

The 10% brain myth is one of the most persistent and most puzzling errors that people make about the brain. For a start we don't seem to be able to find the scientists who say this, if it was ever said at all. A bit of logic is called for here along with some findings from brain studies:

- If 90% of the brain is unused then many parts of the brain could be damaged without causing any problems. This is not the case, and damage anywhere in the brain is likely to cause problems.

- If we only used 10% then brain scans would show a lot of quiet areas, but in fact most of the brain appears to be active most of the time.

- Research has built up a complex picture of what different parts of the brain do (localisation of function). There are few, if any areas that are not associated with any activity.

Early studies of the visual system (e.g. Riesen, 1950) found that if you don't use it you lose it. To put it more technically, when animals were kept in the dark for several months after birth their visual system did not develop and when they were later allowed into the light they had restricted vision.

All in all there is no scientific evidence to support the idea that we only use 10% of the brain. The writers who have bought into this myth tend to be trying to sell us something that will help us use the missing 90% and so turn into geniuses.

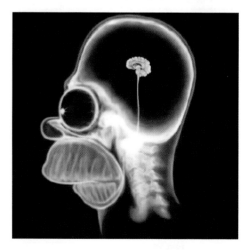

Evidence for the ten per cent hypothesis?

The Knowledge

Some of the participants in this core study were London taxi drivers. To obtain an 'All London' taxi licence you need to acquire The Knowledge. This means you must have a thorough knowledge of London, including the location of streets, squares, clubs, hospitals, hotels, theatres, government and public buildings, railway stations, police stations, courts, diplomatic buildings, important places of worship, cemeteries, crematoria, parks and open spaces, sports and leisure centres, places of learning, restaurants and historic buildings; in fact everything you need to know to be able to take passengers to their destinations by the most direct routes.

'I had a brain surgeon in the back of my taxi the other day...'

The 'All London' licence requires you to have a detailed knowledge of the 25,000 streets within a six-mile radius of Charing Cross with a more general knowledge of the major arterial routes throughout the rest of London. The difficulty here is that the centre of London is still based on a medieval road map and there are numerous small paths and tortuous routes. It is very easy to get lost and lose you sense of direction. The Knowledge is a unique skill that requires learning a very detailed mental map of the area.

Drivers are assessed by means of an initial written test which determines whether they have reached the required standard to start 'appearances'. These are a series of one to one oral examinations conducted by a qualified Knowledge of London Examiner. The examiner grades each applicant according to his or her performance. The higher the grade on each appearance, the quicker the applicant can expect to receive a licence. Some applicants pass The Knowledge with as few as 10 or 12 appearances while others take longer. The whole process usually takes between 2 and 4 years. And you thought A Levels were tough! (www.taxiknowledge.co.uk/).

Alzheimer's disease and memory

The hippocampus is believed to be one of the areas that is damaged in Alzheimer's disease, leading to severe loss of memory. The Spanish film director Luis Bunuel watched his mother develop the disease and wrote,

'You have to begin to lose your memory, if only in bits and pieces, to realise that memory is what makes our lives ... Our memory is our coherence, our reason, our feeling, even our action. Without it we are nothing ... we can only wait for the final amnesia, the one that can erase an entire life, as it did my mother's.'

The case of HM's hippocampus

HM is very famous in psychology; '...*he has probably had more words written about him than any other case in neurological or psychological history*' (Ogden and Corkin, 1991, page 195). HM is always given those initials to protect his identity, though that might seem ironic after you read about what the psychologists did to him. He was born in 1926 and had a head injury at the age of seven that started a lifetime of epileptic seizures. These seizures got worse over the years and in his mid 20s he was having uncontrolled grand mal attacks (health threatening seizures). It was proposed to attempt a brain operation to a cure the epilepsy. At that time there were some surgeons who were very enthusiastic about brain surgery and William Scoville was one of these, having carried out hundreds of lobotomies (an operation to sever connections to the brain's frontal lobe). These operations, based on minimal theory and with limited or no success, were used to change the behaviour of people thought to be aggressive or psychologically disturbed.

Experimental brain surgery

Scoville carried out an experimental piece of surgery on HM to reduce his epilepsy. Among the brain tissue he removed were parts of a small structure named the *hippocampus*. On the good side, HM survived the operation and his epilepsy was now less damaging, but on the very big down side he had profound retrograde and anterograde amnesia. More precisely, he had lost much of his memory for the ten years prior to the operation (anterograde amnesia), and even more damagingly, he had lost the ability to store new information (retrograde amnesia). He had a memory span of just a few minutes, so he was effectively waking up every few minutes not knowing where he was or who he was talking to.

This was clearly a disaster for HM though he probably never understood that because he could never remember what happened to him, or if he did he would forget it within a couple of minutes. This tragedy for HM was a great opportunity for psychologists who became aware of the case. They queued up for the next 40 years to study HM's memory, assessing it with all kinds of tests and checking out a wide range of hypotheses concerning the theoretical distinctions between long-term and short-term memory, and between explicit and implicit memory. They used all sorts of stimuli including electric shocks and white noise (for a review see Corkin, 1984, or Parkin, 1996).

HM and ethics

The story of HM is commonly presented without comment in psychology books but ask yourself this, how did HM give consent for the 40 years of constant experimentation? He did not know what was being done to him or even who was doing it. Is this ground breaking science or cruel exploitation of a man whose life has been ruined by experimental brain surgery?

> **...Link to the core study**
>
> The core study by Eleanor **Mcguire**'s team at University College London is an excellent example of the remarkable discoveries that we can find from modern scanning technology. They help us to map the brain and find out more about the way that activities are distributed around the brain. Some studies, such as this one, take pictures of the structure of the brain (the bits) while others take pictures of the functions (the brain in action). This type of research is fascinating and frustrating in equal measure because it raises as many questions as it answers.

Eleanor A. Maguire, David G. Gadian, Ingrid S. Johnsrude, Catriona D. Good, John Ashburner, Richard S.J. Frackowiak and Christopher D. Frith (2000) Navigation-related structural changes in the hippocampi of taxi drivers. *Proceedings of the National Academy of Science, USA,* 97, pages 4398–4403.

Abstract

To demonstrate that the hippocampus is the region of the human brain associated with spatial memory and navigation.

Method

London taxi drivers were used because their work involves spatial memory and navigation. This experimental group of sixteen men (mean age 44, mean experience of taxi driving 14.3 years) was age and gender matched with a control group.

MRI scanning was used to assess how the taxi drivers brains had changed in response to their jobs. Two methods of image analysis were used:

- *VBM* produced a measure of the density of grey matter throughout the brain.
- *Pixel counting* produced a measure of hippocampal volume as a function of total brain size. 24 photograhic slices through the brain were examined from anterior, body and posterior regions.

Results

Results from VBM showed more grey matter in both left and right hippocampi of taxi drivers than controls but this was restricted to the posterior region. The controls had relatively more grey matter in the anterior region.

Results from pixel counting showed greater volume for the controls in the anterior and body of the hippocampi, and in both cases the right was larger than the left. In the taxi drivers the posterior hippocampi had greater volume than in the controls. Overall there was no difference in total volume of the hippocampi in the controls and taxi drivers.

There was a positive correlation between time spent taxi-driving and volume of the right posterior hippocampus and a negative correlation between time and the volume of the anterior hippocampus.

Discussion

The results suggest that a 'mental map' is stored in the right posterior hippocampus which fits with data from previous studies. This shows functional differentiation within the hippocampus which is the outcome of experience. It may well be the result of reorganisation at a cellular level within the hippocampus. These results have implications for the rehabilitation of patients with brain damage.

Aim

Past research has indicated that the hippocampus plays a role in spatial memory, i.e. the ability of animals and humans to remember locations in space and navigate between them. For example research studies have found that:

- Small mammals and birds who engage in exceptional behaviours requiring spatial memories (such as food storing) have increased hippocampal volume (relative to their brain and body size) when compared to animals who do not use spatial memories.
- Hippocampal volume increases in some species during seasons where demand for spatial ability is greatest.
- There are structural brain differences in healthy human brains, such as differences between males and females, and musicians and nonmusicians.

There are several questions which have not been answered by past research:

1 Are brain differences predetermined or is the brain capable of changing in response to environmental stimulation – i.e. is it nature or nurture?

2 What is the precise role of the hippocampus? Studies that have involved lesioning (severing links in parts of the brain) and brain scanning (neuroimaging) have shown that the hippocampus plays a role in spatial memory and navigation but they have not demonstrated its precise role.

3 Does the human brain respond to experiences requiring spatial memory in the same way as the brains of lower mammals and birds? Previous research found structural changes in the brain in response to behaviour requiring spatial memory. The present study will look at *morphological* change in the healthy human brain associated with spatial memory and navigation. (Morphology is the study of the form and shape of things.) The prediction is that the hippocampus is the most likely region to show morphological changes.

Biographical notes

Eleanor Maguire and her team won the 2003 IgNobel medicine prize 'for presenting evidence that the brains of London taxi drivers are more highly developed than those of their fellow citizens' (http://www.improbable.com/ig/ig-pastwinners.html#ig2003). In fact the research didn't show that the taxi driver's brains are more developed – but this seems to be a typical media exaggeration of the research findings.

Dr Maguire works in London as the Professor of Cognitive Neuroscience at the Wellcome Trust Centre for Neuroimaging, University College London, UK. She first became interested in the neural basis of memory while working with patients with brain damage.

Method

Participants

An ideal group to use in studying spatial memory and navigation are London taxi drivers. They have to undergo extensive training to acquire 'The Knowledge' – learning to navigate between thousands of places in London. Learning this knowledge takes an average of two years culminating in a very stringent set of police examinations.

All sixteen participants were right-handed London taxi drivers, mean age 44 (range 32–62). There was an even spread of participants in each age group (e.g. 31–40, 41–50, 51–60) and all had been licensed drivers for more than 1.5 years (mean 14.3 years, range 1.5–42 years). All of the taxi drivers had healthy medical, neurological and psychiatric profiles. Participants were excluded if they were younger than 32 or over 62, and also if they were females or left-handed males, or had any health problems.

There was a control group of sixteen men none of whom were taxi drivers. The mean age and age range were the same for the control group as for the experimental group of taxi drivers.

The hippocampus and the seahorse

The Latin name for 'seahorse' is 'hippocampus' (hippo = horse). The structure in the brain was called hippocampus because it was thought to look like a seahorse. See what you think.

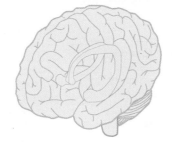

A sketch of what the hippocampus looks like.

The hippocampus is located deep inside the brain as shown in the diagram below.

Use a cauliflower to label the key areas of the brain (see page 132) just to get a 'feel' for it! Later you can attach new labels showing what the study found for each of these key areas. Finally, you can add a few onions and make a stir fry – education and nutrition!

Qs

1   Give **one** reason why Maguire *et al.* predicted that the hippocampus was the region most likely to show changes related to spatial memory.
2   Why did Maguire *et al.* use taxi drivers in this study?
3   Explain the reason for having a control group.
4   Why was it important that the control group was age matched with the experimental group?
5   The report of the study gave details of mean age and also age range. Why is it useful to know the range as well as the mean?
6   In what way is this study a quasi-experiment?
7   Identify the IV and DV in this experiment.
8   The VBM was described as 'unbiased'. What does this mean?
9   Why were the images analysed by someone 'blind' to whether a participant was a taxi driver or control?
10 Two measures were made of each participant's brain. In essence what was the purpose of each measure?
11 Which three regions of the hippocampus were studied?

Procedure

Data was collected using structural MRI scans and then these scans were analysed using two techniques.

Image analysis method 1: VBM
VBM stands for 'voxel-based morphometry'. This technique enables every point of the brain to be examined in an objective and unbiased way. Traditionally, brain volume is measured by focusing on specific regions and calculating the volume enclosed. However, this is time consuming and can only provide measures of large areas. Smaller differences in volume may be overlooked.

VBM identifies differences in the density of grey matter in different parts of the brain. 'Grey matter' describes some parts of the brain – there is grey and white matter. Grey matter lies on the surface of the brain and also deep inside in structures such as the hypothalamus and hippocampus. It is the part of the brain that is most dense in neural connections and therefore associated with higher order thinking.

Image analysis method 2: Pixel counting
Hippocampal volume was calculated using a well-established pixel counting technique. A pixel is a single point on a graphic image ('pixel' stands for pix + element). The pixels were counted in the images produced by the MRI scans. Each scan was of a photographic slice made through the hippocampal region of participants' brains (see diagram on the right). There were at least 26 contiguous slices (i.e. slices lying next to each other). Each slice was 1.5 mm thick, therefore covering a total length of approximately 4 cm.

The images were analysed by one person experienced in the technique who counted the pixels in each slice. This person was blind to whether a participant was a taxi driver or control, and also blind to the VBM findings.

In the final analysis only 24 slices were used. Total hippocampal volume was calculated by adding up the pixels from each slice and multiplying this by the distance between adjacent slices (i.e. 1.5 mm). Finally a correction was made in relation to the total intracranial volume (ICV – the area within the cranium or skull). This was done to account for the fact that some people have larger brains than others and therefore we would expect their hippocampi to be correspondingly bigger.

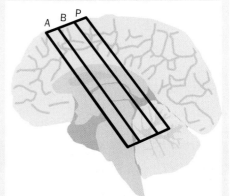

The diagram above shows where the photographic slices were taken through the brain. The slices cut through the length of the hippocampus covering three regions:

A – anterior hippocampus (6 slices)
B – body hippocampus (12 slices)
P – posterior hippocampus (6 slices)

Results

VBM

Comparing the taxi drivers to the controls there were only two brain regions with significantly increased grey matter – the right and left hippocampi. No differences were observed anywhere else in the brain.

In the taxi drivers the increase was limited to the posterior hippocampi. In the controls there was relatively more grey matter in the anterior hippocampi than there was in the brains of the taxi drivers.

Pixel counting

There was no significant difference between the taxi drivers and the control group in terms of (1) intercranial volume and (2) total hippocampal volume.

However there were differences in specific regions of the hippocampus:

Controls

- **Anterior right hippocampus** larger on right than left (i.e. had a greater volume) than in taxi drivers.
- **Body of the hippocampus** larger on the right than the left.

Taxi divers

- **Posterior hippocampus** larger than controls.

Graphs showing the mean of the cross-sectional area measurements for the three regions of the hippocampus.

Left hippocampus.

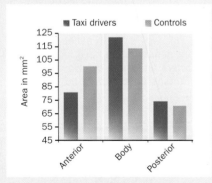

Right hippocampus.

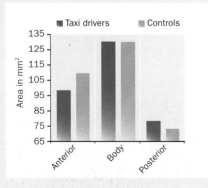

The brain scans above show the additional grey matter (coloured in yellow) in the posterior left hippocampus (LH) and posterior right hippocampus (RH) in the taxi drivers as compared to the controls.

	Left hippocampus	Right hippocampus
Anterior		CONTROL
Body		CONTROL
Posterior	TAXI DRIVERS	TAXI DRIVERS

The table shows the regions of the brain that had the largest volume for each group of participants based on pixel counting e.g. control participants had largest volume in the anterior right hippocampus.

Changes with navigation experience

Correlations were examined between the amount of time spent as a taxi driver (including both training to be a taxi driver and time spent as a qualified driver) and volume of specific brain regions.

Time spent as a taxi driver was

- Positively correlated with the volume of the right posterior hippocampus.
- Negatively correlated with the volume of the anterior hippocampus.

(The technique of correlational analysis is explained on pages 20–21).

Qs

1. Explain what the term 'intercranial volume' means.
2. Write at least **two** conclusions that can be drawn from the graphs on the left.
3. What evidence was used to argue that the observed differences between taxi drivers and controls was due to experience (nurture) rather than predisposition (nature)?
4. The discussion on the right includes a quote from the article about plasticity. Explain this quote.
5. Describe **one** finding from previous research that supports the results of this study.
6. One of the conclusions is that the results demonstrate functional differentiation within the hippocampus. Explain this conclusion.
7. Explain what a 'mental map' is and state where it is stored.

Discussion

The results from both methods of data analysis indicate a difference between taxi drivers and controls – in the taxi drivers there was significantly greater volume in the posterior hippocampus whereas in the controls there was significantly increased volume in the anterior hippocampus. This suggests a relationship between navigational skills and the relative distribution of grey matter in the hippocampus.

Nature or nurture

The question is whether this distribution is an *effect* of spending time navigating or whether this particular arrangement of hippocampal grey matter is present in some individuals and *predisposes* them to take up a job that requires navigational skills.

This possibility was tested by looking at the correlation between hippocampal volume and time spent as a taxi driver. The fact that right hippocampal volume was significantly correlated with driving experience suggests that such changes are acquired. There was an increase in posterior hippocampus (positive correlation) and a decrease in anterior hippocampus (negative correlation). This implies there is *'local plasticity in the structure of the healthy adult human brain as a function of exposure to environmental stimuli'*.

Previous research and current conclusions

These findings are supported by other research:

- Rodent and monkey studies have found the posterior hippocampus was involved in spatial navigation.
- In rats the posterior hippocampus is richer in *place cells* than other areas of the hippocampus – these are cells related to spatial perception.
- Studies in humans using functional neuroimaging (fMRI) show that the posterior hippocampus is active when recalling or using previously learned navigational information.
- Patients with damage to the hippocampus which has spared the posterior region can still recall routes learned before damage occurred.

The posterior hippocampus seems to be related to *previously learned* spatial information. The anterior hippocampus may be more involved in encoding *new* information (which would also involve the posterior region. This demonstrates *functional* (morphological) differentiation within the hippocampus.

The results of this study suggest that taxi drivers store a 'mental map' of London permitting increased understanding of how routes and places relate to each other. The consequence of this is an increase in tissue volume.

These findings challenge the traditional view that the hippocampus has only a transient role in memory. The hippocampus is an 'old' part of the brain, that is if we look back through evolution this was a part of the brain that was present in very primitive animals. The need to navigate would be an important behaviour for all animals and therefore it is not surprising that it is the function of this part of the brain. Undoubtedly in humans the hippocampus has evolved to take on other functions, such as *episodic memory* (memory for events, places, associated emotions, and other conception-based knowledge in relation to an experience; as distinct from, for example, *procedural memory* which is memory for how to do things).

Right and left hippocampus
The study found differences between the right and left hippocampus. Left hippocampal volume did not correlate with taxi-driving experience. This suggests that the left hippocampus has a different role in spatial memory and navigation than the right hippocampus. It is possible that the role of the left hippocampus is to store memories of people and events (episodic memories) associated with the context of taxi driving. This would complement the role of the right hippocampus which integrates information into an existing map.

The data in this study are not at a microscopic level but one might speculate about how the observed changes take place. The simplest explanation is that the cells of the hippocampus are re-organised in response to the increased demand to store navigational information. The increase in grey matter in the posterior region would 'borrow' material from the anterior region to cope with the demand.

The demonstration that normal activities can bring about changes in the relative volume of grey matter has important implications for rehabilitating people who have suffered brain damage – by making demands on the brain it may respond by enlisting the use of grey matter from other regions. However, this study only demonstrates such plasticity in the hippocampus and it remains to be seen whether other regions of the brain respond to experience in a similar way.

There are no simple answers. Evaluating a study requires you to think. We have provided some pointers here, linked to the *KEY ISSUES* covered through this book – see page XIV for a table of these key issues.

Evaluating the study by Maguire *et al.*

The research method
This study was a quasi-experiment because the IV (taxi driver or not) was naturally varying – the participants were not assigned to being a taxi driver or not. *What are the strengths and limitations of this research method in the context of this study?*

Research techniques
Behaviour was measured using MRI scans and assessments of grey matter density and hippocampal volume. *What are the strengths and limitations of these methods in the context of this study?*

Qualitative or quantitative?
What kind of data were collected in this study? What are the strengths and limitations of producing this kind of data in the context of this study?

Nature and nurture
What evidence is there from this study to support the nature or nurture side of the debate?

Validity
Taxi-driving may represent a very specific form of navigational ability. *How do you think this would affect the validity of the results?*

Determinist
This study suggests that certain aspects of our behaviour are determined by the brain. *What are the strengths and limitations of determinism in the context of this study?*

Applications/usefulness
Maguire *et al.* suggest how the results from this study could be used. *Describe this application and say how valuable you think this study was.*

What next?
Describe **one** change to this study, and say how you think this might affect the outcome.

Debate
Studies such as this suggest that our behaviour can be reduced to activity in the brain.

Such reductionist and determinist arguments have advantages but also have disadvantages.

Divide your class into groups and assign each group with the task of either preparing arguments for or against the view that reductionism and/or determinism leads to important advances in our understanding of human behaviour.

...Links to other studies and issues...
This study maps some cognitive processes to specific areas of the brain. The attempt to map psychological changes to physical areas in the brain is creeping into all aspects of psychology. Any identifiable group of people, for example gamblers (see the core study by **Griffiths**) can be examined to see if their brains show any measurable differences from non-gamblers. Likewise people with autism (**Baron-Cohen et al.**) and people with mental health issues (**Rosenhan**) have been studied in this way. This particular brain scanning study tells us something very specific about memory and so links to the study by **Loftus and Palmer**.

Scan on

The future is clearly in brain scanning as psychology departments fall over themselves to buy scanners and take ever more pictures of people's brains. The jury is still out, however, on how much value we will get from all these pictures

Scanning race

Scanning techniques are now being used to investigate social issues and social judgement. Which parts of our brain are being used when we laugh or when we are attracted to someone or when we meet someone different to us? Jennifer Eberhardt is a prominent researcher in racial stereotyping, prejudice, and stigma imaging race. Recently she has been examining brain scans to see what they tell us about racism and racial differences (Eberhardt, 2005).

Jennifer L. Eberhardt

Working in the USA, Eberhardt's research team have used fMRI to study the face recognition of people of the same and different race to the viewer. Previous studies have shown that people find it easier to recognise faces from the same race as themselves and that this effect is stronger for European American than African American participants. The researchers were able to identify differences in brain activity that correlated with the race of the face they were identifying (Golby *et al*., 2001).

Other work (Richeson *et al*., 2003) found a relationship between frontal lobe activity and racial prejudice, and that the greater the brain differences in the face recognition task the greater the level of prejudice.

This work sounds very interesting if difficult to interpret but there are dangerous issues that can be raised by scanning studies on race. For example, what if you looked for differences in the average scans of different racial groups? There is little doubt that any scientific argument would soon be drowned under the weight of social prejudice. The history of brain science is littered with attempts to prove one group superior to another.

Adrian Raine and the search for the murderer's brain

One line of investigation with brain scans has been to look for differences in the brains of people with mental health issues or a history of criminality. An influential figure in this research is the British psychologist Adrian Raine (www-rcf.usc.edu/~raine/). Raine is confident that he has discovered that the brains of murderers are different to those of non-murderers (hopefully most of the population). He writes,

'There are now 71 brain imaging studies showing that murderers, psychopaths, and individuals with aggressive, antisocial personalities have poorer functioning in the prefrontal cortex – that part of the brain involved in regulating and controlling emotion and behaviour.

More dramatically, we now know that the brains of criminals are physically different from non-criminals, showing an 11% reduction in the volume of grey matter (neurons) in the prefrontal cortex.

Violent offenders just do not have the emergency brakes to stop their runaway aggressive behaviour. Literally speaking, bad brains lead to bad behaviour ... One of the reasons why we have repeatedly failed to stop crime is because we have systematically ignored the biological and genetic contributions to crime causation.' (Raine, 2004)

You will not be surprised to know that a lot of people do not agree with Raine and think he is greatly overstating the case. For example, Steven Rose puts forward an alternative view (see http://news.bbc.co.uk/1/hi/programmes/if/4106217.stm).

The main concern with the brain scanning work like this is that it seems to propose some very simple solutions to very complex problems. The bottom line is that we know very little about why people choose to be violent or passive, or whether they choose to murder someone or count to ten and have a cup of tea instead. The recent history of psychosurgery (brain surgery to change behaviour) has not been a positive one and that is why many people urge caution with this research.

The man with no brain

It's a great headline and even though it is not quite true it does describe one of the remarkable findings of the brain scan revolution. John Lorber was a neurosurgeon in Sheffield who was interested in people who had survived hydrocephalus as a child. This condition (hydro = water, cephalus = head) can be fatal if not treated as the ventricles (spaces) in the brain fill up with cerebro-spinal fluid.

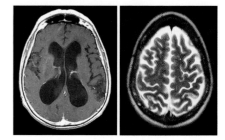

Scan of a hydrocephalus patient (left) and a normal brain (right). The dark areas are fluid and the grey areas are the brain.

A young man in perfect health was referred to Lorber because he had a slightly larger than average head which can be a sign of hydrocephalus. When Lorber looked at the CAT scans he found that the man's brain was a thin smear around the skull and the bulk of his head contained spinal fluid. According to all theories of brain structure the man should not have been alive, but not only was he alive but he had a degree in maths and economics. Lorber went on to scan more than 600 people with hydrocephalus and found numerous cases where the ventricles were filling more than 50% of the head with fluid (Lewin, 1980).

Lorber liked to give dramatic talks and entitled his paper on this topic 'Is your brain really necessary?' Partly because of his style of presentation and partly because the results are difficult to explain the work does not appear in many textbooks.

Decade of the brain

In 1990 President George Bush (the first) designated the 1990s as the Decade of the Brain: 'to enhance public awareness of the benefits to be derived from brain research'. In so doing he gave a lift to brain research in the USA. It is not known which body organ his son designated this decade to.

The two President Bushes enjoy the joke about the decade of the brain.

Multiple choice questions

1 The method of brain scanning used in this study was:
   a CAT scan.   b PET scan.
   c MRI.   d VBM.

2 The control group was matched with the taxi drivers on the basis of:
   a Age.   b Gender.
   c Experience.   d Both a and b.

3 The method of VBM was used to calculate:
   a The amount of grey matter.
   b The density of grey matter.
   c The volume of the hippocampus.
   d Both b and c.

4 The method of pixel counting was used to calculate:
   a The amount of grey matter.
   b The density of grey matter.
   c The volume of the hippocampus.
   d Both b and c.

5 The thickness of each cross-sectional scan was:
   a 1.5 mm   b 2.5 mm
   c 1.5 cm   d 2.5 cm

6 When co-variables are negatively correlated:
   a They both increase together.
   b They both decrease together.
   c As one increases the other decreases.
   d There is no relationship.

7 Which of the following is *not* true?
   a The hippocampus is a newer part of the brain.
   b There are two hippocampi in a person's brain.
   c The hippocampus is named after a sea horse.
   d The hippocampus is divided into three regions.

8 The hippocampal volume in the control participants was:
   a The same as the taxi drivers.
   b Greater in the anterior hippocampus than taxi drivers.
   c Greater in the posterior hippocampus than taxi drivers.
   d Both a and b.

9 Which side of the hippocampus correlated with taxi driving?
   a Right.
   b Left.
   c Right and Left.
   d We don't know.

10 Maguire *et al.* concluded that:
   a Taxi drivers are born with an enlarged hippocampus.
   b Observed differences in the hippocampus are due to experience.
   c All parts of the brain have the same plasticity as found in the hippocampus.
   d Both b and c.

Answers are on page 145.

Exam-style questions

See page XII–XIII for notes on the exam paper and styles of question.

Section A questions

1 (a) Explain why Maguire *et al.* used taxi drivers in their study of spatial memory. [2]
   (b) Identify **two** criteria used to select the taxi-drivers as participants in this study. [2]

2 (a) Describe **one** finding from this study. [2]
   (b) Suggest how the findings from this study might be used. [2]

3 Outline **two** major ideas of the biological approach to psychology that are in the study by Maguire *et al.* [4]

4 Outline **one** control that was used in the study on brain scanning by Maguire *et al.* and explain why it was important to use this control. [2]

5 The study by Maguire *et al.* used the biological technique of brain scanning.
   (a) Describe **one** commonly used brain scanning technique. [2]
   (b) Suggest **one** reason why results gained from such biological scanning techniques should be treated with caution. [2]

6 (a) In the study by Maguire *et al.* describe **one** method used to analyse the brain scans. [2]
   (b) Describe **one** result obtained using this method. [2]

7 Maguire *et al.* found a positive correlation in their study of taxi drivers's brains.
   (a) Explain the term 'positive correlation', using examples from this study. [2]
   (b) State **one** conclusion that can be drawn from this result. [2]

Section B questions

   (a) Identify the aim of the study by Maguire *et al.* [2]
   (b) Describe the sample used in the study by Maguire *et al.*, and give **one** limitation of the sample. [6]
   (c) Describe how behaviour was measured in the study by Maguire *et al.* [6]
   (d) Explain how the reliability of these measurements could be assessed. [6]
   (e) Outline the results of the study by Maguire *et al.* [8]
   (f) Suggest **two** changes to the study by Maguire *et al.* and outline how these changes might affect the results. [8]

Section C questions

   (a) Outline **one** assumption of determinism in psychology. [2]
   (b) Describe how the biological approach could explain navigation. [4]
   (c) Describe how the approach taken by Maguire *et al.* is an example of determinism. [6]
   (d) Discuss the strengths and limitations of determinism, using examples from the study by Maguire *et al.* [12]

Key issue: determinism and free will

Determinism is the idea that every event including human thought and behaviour is causally determined by an unbroken chain of prior events. According to this idea there are no mysterious miracles and no random events.

Newton's cradle is a demonstration of the idea. The movement of one ball has an effect on the others. Their motion is determined by the movement of the first ball. It is cause and effect.

The idea of determinism appears to contradict the personal experience we have of free will. We experience ourselves as making choices and deciding what to do rather than just responding like automatons to previous events. Our choices are obviously limited but we feel as if we are making choices about what we do, what we say, what we wear and so on.

The issue with determinism is that if our behaviour is a response to previous events then we have little or no control over it. In which case we can not be held responsible for the things that we do.

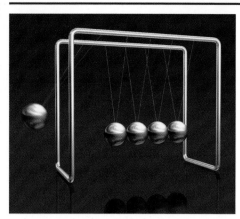

Newton's Cradle illustrating the principles of determinism. As the ball on the left swings in and hits the stack of stationary balls the energy of the impact passes through them and propels the end ball away from the stack. The movement of the end ball is determined by the movement of the ball at the other end.

Is free will an illusion?

Sigmund Freud claimed that most of the causes of our behaviour are largely hidden from us and unconscious, thus we may think we are acting freely but in fact our behaviour is determined by unconscious forces and is predictable.

The behaviourist B. F. Skinner argued that we think we are free but that is because we are not aware of how our behaviour is determined by reinforcement. There is modern belief that one way to encourage people to behave in a socially responsible way is to improve their self-esteem and self-image. Skinner challenged this when he wrote,

'The real issue is the effectiveness of techniques of control. We shall not solve the problems of alcoholism and juvenile delinquency by increasing the sense of responsibility. It is the environment which is "responsible" for the objectionable behaviour, and it is the environment, not some attribute in the individual which must be changed.' (Skinner 1971, pages 76–77)

Humanistic psychologists

Humanistic psychologists believe that behaviourists and Freudians overlooked the important role of free will in human behaviour, and the drive of humans to be self-determining.

Carl Rogers, one of the founders of humanistic psychology and also the 'inventor' of counselling, proposed a very simple personality theory, in contrast with Freud's very complex theory. The theory is built on the actualising tendency – the tendency in each individual to develop his/her potentials to the fullest extent possible. Rogers suggested that taking responsibility for oneself is the route to healthy self-development. As long as you remain controlled by other people or other things, you cannot take responsibility for your behaviour and therefore cannot begin to change it.

Determinism is the idea that every event, including human cognition and behaviour, decision and action, is causally determined by an unbroken chain of prior occurrences.

Free will refers to the power of making free choices that are unconstrained by external circumstances or by an agency such as fate or divine will. It is our capacity to be self-determining; in other words to exercise our own will.

The behaviourist John Watson argued that it is possible to use training techniques to mould a person into whatever you want them to be.

'I should like to go one step further now and say, "Give me a dozen healthy infants, well-formed, and my own specified world to bring them up in and I'll guarantee to take any one at random and train him to become any type of specialist I might select – doctor, lawyer, artist, merchant-chief and, yes, even beggar-man and thief, regardless of his talents, penchants, tendencies, abilities, vocations, and race of his ancestors." I am going beyond my facts and I admit it, but so have the advocates of the contrary and they have been doing it for thousands of years.' (Watson, 1924, page 104).

Watson is saying that we are not born with artistic skills or with high intelligence or with a sunny personality but that these qualities are developed through the experiences we have in life. This view disputes the determinism of our biology and replaces it with the determinism of our environment.

Chaos theory

Chaos theory proposes that very small changes in initial conditions can eventually lead to major changes, sometimes called 'the butterfly effect'. A butterfly flapping its wings in Bristol can, in theory, produce a tornado in Kansas. Like a snowball going downhill the consequences of the initial event get bigger and bigger. Although this does not look like a determinist explanation it is because you can trace the tornado back through an unbroken chain of events to the butterfly. Clearly if we want to stop tornados we have to find that butterfly and stop it flapping its wings.

Determinism versus responsibility

Determinist ideas have been given a new boost in recent years with the development of brain scanning studies. These studies match up changes in the brain to changes in behaviour and commonly propose that the brain changes are the cause of the behaviour.

Adrian Raine has reported a large number of brain scan studies in particular on people who have been involved in criminal behaviour or who have psychiatric conditions. In one study he found that men who had antisocial personality disorder (APD) had a deficiency in the frontal lobe of their brains. Raine posed the question: 'Assuming these people are not responsible for their own brain damage, should we hold them responsible for their criminal acts?' (Raine, 2000).

This argument has already been presented in court in the USA (for example Stephen Mobley, see left) where people charged with serious offences have argued their behaviour was determined by inherited tendencies and so therefore was not their fault.

Among the arguments against Raine are first, the diagnosis of APD is controversial with the suggestion being that it is no more than giving badly behaved people a label, and the things we judge to be bad behaviour change with each generation. Second, the abnormalities are very individual and it is not possible to look at a scan and predict whether someone will be a criminal or not.

Stephen Mobley killed a pizza shop manager in 1981. His lawyers argued that he was not accountable for his aggressive tendencies because he was 'born to kill' as evidenced by a family history of violence. He should not be sentenced to death for the crime because, in effect, he was not responsible for his actions. His lawyers' argument was rejected, and Mobley was sentenced to death.

Minority Report

The Tom Cruise film Minority Report *(based on a book of the same name by Philip K. Dick) looks at the issue of determinism and free will using a science fiction crime story. The story imagines a world where a group of people with special powers are able to predict future crime. These 'precogs' operate in groups of three and if one disagrees with the other two you obtain a minority report.*

The detective played by Tom Cruise is predicted by the precogs to be about to kill someone he doesn't know. Will knowing about this possible future help him change it or will it actually ensure that it happens. And if we could predict that someone is likely to commit a crime what should we do about it? Can we lock someone up because they may do something criminal in the future? This is a very real issue today as debates rage about what to do with people diagnosed with personality disorders or people identified as possible terrorists.

The case against determinism

The idea that behaviour has simple causes is very plausible and, on the surface, appealing. The case against it includes the following arguments:

(a) We experience our daily life as presenting us with a number of choices. We can choose to be good or bad; to eat fruit or to eat a kebab; to help an old lady across the road or to swipe her handbag. We experience these events as choices and other people act towards us as if we are making those choices. It therefore does not make sense to go along with a theory that denies our daily experience.

(b) Not all events in nature can be described in terms of cause and effect. For example, the atomic decay of matter is so predictable that it is possible to create very accurate clocks based on this decay. The problem for determinists is that although we have an accurate measure of the half-life of this material (the time it takes for exactly half of it to decay) we have no way of predicting which bits will decay when. If we select one small piece then it might decay in the next few seconds or in a thousand years time.

Free will, not the same as Free Willie.

Qs

1 Select **one** core study and describe what it tells us about how our behaviour is influenced in everyday life.

2 Think of an event like a violent assault. What are the possible *causes* for the behaviour of the attacker? How much control do you think the attacker has over these possible causes?

3 Try a similar analysis with helping behaviour. Why do people help each other? How much control do we have over this behaviour?

4 Briefly discuss the usefulness of studying how we are influenced in everyday life.

...Links to other studies and issues...

The idea of determinism most commonly surfaces in psychological studies when we discuss how much control a person has over their behaviour. For example, **Milgram's** study of obedience suggests that the participants' behaviour was caused by the situation they were in rather than their spontaneous choice. Another study that looks at issues of individual control is the one by **Griffiths** on addictive behaviours. The fruit machine players, like many people with addictive behaviours, don't seem to be able to control their behaviour to the point where it has a negative impact on their life.

Determinism also links to some of the other issues. The discussion about the effect of **personality and situation** on behaviour looks at whether it is the situation that brings about our behaviour or whether it comes from something inside ourselves. Mind you, the thing that is inside ourselves might also be a deterministic argument if we believe that we are largely controlled by our genetics and our chemicals. Determinism is also closely linked to arguments of **reductionism**.

Sleep and dreams

Sleep does not mean switching off and closing down the body's activity. Far from it. Sleep is a very active state, both physically and mentally. Our bodies move frequently and, more interestingly for psychologists, our brain activity is even more varied during sleep than it is during the normal waking state.

Measuring sleep

Sleep researchers commonly look to three measures to describe the stages of sleep. First, gross brain wave activity, as measured by an electroencephalogram (EEG). This machine provides the summary of electrical activity from one area of the brain. Second, the electrical activity of a muscle is measured with an electromyogram (EMG). Third, eye movement is recorded via an electro-oculogram (EOG).

Stages of sleep

Awake

In an awake state the pattern of our brain waves (measured by EEG) are typically beta waves. However, when you become relaxed, your brain waves become slower and more regular and have a greater amplitude (the height of the wave). This pattern is called an **alpha wave** which can be observed during meditation.

Asleep: stages one and two

As you go to sleep, your brain waves slow down further (greater wave frequency – the distance from the crest of one wave to the next) and the amplitude also becomes greater. This wave form is called a **theta wave**. The transition from relaxation to stage 1 and then stage 2 sleep is quite gradual. This is very light sleep and a sleeper, awoken at this time, will often say that they weren't actually asleep. The brain waves in stages 1 and 2 are also characterised by sleep spindles and K complexes which are sudden increases in wave frequency and wave amplitude respectively.

Asleep: stages three and four

Deeper sleep is characterised by the **delta waves** of stages 3 and 4. These waves are the slowest and have the highest amplitude. It is very difficult to wake someone up from deep sleep and if you do rouse them, they will be quite confused and disoriented. However, the brain is not dead to the world and will respond to significant noises such as if a mother hears her baby crying this will wake her. Delta sleep is also when sleepwalking and sleeptalking are most likely to occur.

REM sleep

There is another form of sleep, REM or **rapid eye movement sleep**, named after the darting eye movements that occur during this stage (measured by the EOG). This sleep stage is associated with the experience of dreaming. It is also characterised by a lack of muscle tone (measured by the EMG) which results in temporary paralysis (which explains why you sometimes can't move in a dream). This stage is also associated with a unique brain wave pattern – fast, desynchronised EEG activity resembling the awake state.

Normal night

At the start of a night a sleeper progresses through the four sleep stages ending up in deep sleep. This is followed by a return back through the stages from 4 to 3 to 2 but then, instead of stage 1, REM sleep occurs. This cycle is repeated through the night taking approximately 90 minutes . During the course of the night the length of REM episodes increases and the length of delta sleep decreases in each cycle. By the end of the night there is no delta activity at all.

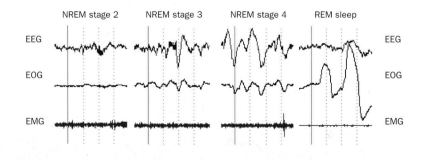

The puzzle of dreams

Dreams have puzzled people for centuries. Why do we dream, and what do they mean? Some people believe that dreams can prophesy the future, some think they tell us about our emotions and some think they are just random firing of the brain that mean nothing.

Dream worlds and real worlds

When I am dreaming then I feel as if I am there. I get scared or I get happy depending on what is happening in my dream world. But it is not real and when I wake up I know that. But do I really know that? Maybe this is all a dream and one day I will wake up from this. What is the difference between the awake world and the dream world? When I'm awake I use the sensations I get and my experience of the past events to create a perception of the world. This 'real' world is as much in my head as my dream world. So how do I tell the difference?

Shakespeare had a lot to say about dreams in his plays and he ponders on this idea in *The Tempest* (IV, i) when Prospero says

We are such stuff
As dreams are made on, and our little life
Is rounded with a sleep.

'Do androids dream of electric sheep?'

If dreams are just the random thoughts of a mind that is switched off then do computers dream? The little red light is on and it sometimes whirrs and gurgles. Is it dreaming and if so what is it dreaming of? Possibly the best ever title for a science fiction book asks the question, Do Androids Dream of Electric Sheep? The book, written by Philip K. Dick, was adapted to make the cult film *Blade Runner*.

The sidewinder sleeps tonight

The band R.E.M., formed in 1980, got their name when Michael Stipe picked it out of a dictionary while searching for something that the band members would all accept. 'How about REM?' he said. 'What does it mean?' they asked. 'Rapid eye movements,' Stipe was said to have replied.

Method 3 Eye movement patterns and visual imagery of the dream

There was great variation in eye movements during REM periods and it was proposed that the movements might correspond to where and at what the dreamer was looking. To investigate this the participants were woken when their eye movements were mainly vertical or horizontal or both or neither, as shown in the table below:

Type of eye movement	Content of dream reported by participants
Mainly vertical *There were 3 such dreams reported*	Standing at bottom of cliff and looking at climbers at different levels. Climbing ladders and looking up and down. Shooting at a basketball net and looking down to pick up the next ball.
Mainly horizontal *1 dream*	Two people throwing tomatoes at each other.
Both vertical and horizontal *10 dreams*	Looking at things close to them, e.g. talking to a group of people, fighting with someone.
Very little or no movement *21 dreams*	Watching something in the distance or just staring fixedly at some object.

Effects of practice

The table below compares performance in the first half of the tests with the last half, showing that participants didn't recall more dreams as they got more practiced.

| | First half | | Second half | |
	Dream recall	No recall	Dream recall	No recall
DN	12	1	5	8
IR	12	5	14	3
KC	18	2	18	2
WD	19	2	18	3
PM	12	3	12	3
Total	73	13	67	19

Discussion

This study showed that dreaming is accompanied by REM activity. It cannot be stated with complete certainty that dreaming doesn't occur at other times. The few instances of NREM dreaming can be best explained by assuming that the memory for a dream persisted for some time and thus appeared to occur during NREM sleep.

Previous research had found REM activity to be absent in some participants but Dement and Kleitman suggest that this may have happened because REM periods occurred between when the samples were taken or that REM activity was minimal because the dreams were about distant activities.

It seems reasonable to conclude that an objective measurement of dreaming may be accomplished by recording REMs during sleep.

Evaluating the study by Dement and Kleitman

There are no simple answers. Evaluating a study requires you to think. We have provided some pointers here, linked to the *KEY ISSUES* covered through this book – see page XIV for a table of these key issues.

The research method
This study could be considered a laboratory experiment – because the experimenter controlled when the participants woke up. It could also be considered to be a natural or quasi-experiment because the IV (REM/NREM sleep) wasn't controlled by the experimenter. *What are the strengths and limitations of a lab or quasi-experiment in the context of this study?*

The research techniques
One of the techniques used in this study was self-report measures. *What are the strengths and limitations of this research technique in the context of this study?*

The sample
In what way are the participants in this sample unique? To what extent were the participants different in terms of their recall in REM sleep? How does this affect the conclusions drawn from the study?

Qualitative and quantitative
Both quantitative and qualitative data were collected in this study. *Give examples of each. What are the strengths and limitations of producing each kind of data in the context of this study?*

Ecological validity
Participants slept in a lab with electrodes on their head and were awakened throughout the night. *To what extent does the behaviour in this study reflect 'normal' sleep and dreaming? How might this affect the conclusions drawn from the study?*

Applications/usefulness
How valuable is this study? Find out more about sleep research in general and consider all the benefits (or not) of this landmark study.

What next?
Describe **one** change to this study, and say how you think this might affect the outcome.

Debate

Is REM activity the same as dreaming?

The research by Dement and Kleitman was ground-breaking in establishing a link between REM sleep and dreaming but some psychologists don't see dreams as a physiological state. Conduct some further research into explanations for dreaming and conduct a debate in class.

...Links to other studies and issues...

This core study makes an interesting link to **Freud's** approach to dreaming. In the Little Hans study he makes use of some dreams that Hans has to interpret the boy's feelings for his parents. This core study also links to the work of **Rosenhan** because of the well-established connection between sleep deprivation and symptoms of mental disorder. This core study has a methodological simplicity used to look at the seemingly very complex phenomenon of dreaming. This same methodological simplicity can be seen in the study comparing taxi driver's brains with those of non-taxi drivers and also the experiment on eyewitness testimony by **Loftus and Palmer.**

Dream on

The work of Dement and Kleitman was the spark for an avalanche of research into sleep and its effects. Much of this work has been used to good effect but as you can see on this page, this is not always the case. This research has only answered some of the many questions about sleep. If we know a lot more about sleep because of psychological research it is also fair to say that we know only a little more about dreaming. What are dreams and nightmares? When we dream at night we have fragmentary experiences over which we have very little control. People appear and disappear, change into giant frogs and then start eating your left leg. Before you know what has happened you're buried up to your waist on Skegness beach and you've just married Gary Neville. At which point, of course, you wake up screaming. These dream events are strangely powerful and can stay with us for years. The great Italian artist Leonardo Da Vinci mused *'Why does the eye see a thing more clearly in dreams than the imagination when awake?'*

Sleep and torture

Barney the purple dinosaur sings 'I Love You'. But how would you feel if you had to listen to it for 24 hours non-stop?

World record

So how long do you think you can stay awake? The world record was set in 1964 by Randy Gardner in San Diego, USA. He wanted to enter a science fair and decided to make a project of a world record attempt at sleep deprivation. His attempt attracted a lot of attention and after a week William Dement (yes the very same) got in touch.

'I immediately called Randy's home, explained to him and his parents who I was, and asked if I could observe him attempt to break the record.' (Dement, 2001).

Gardner had to be watched all the time to make sure he did not fall asleep and Dement took his turn in keeping him awake.

'If [Gardner] began to fall asleep, I would hustle him outside to the small basketball court in his backyard or drive him around the deserted San Diego streets in a convertible with the top down and the radio playing loudly.'

Dement spent the tenth day of the attempt walking around the town with Gardner and records how the teenager was able to beat him on arcade games and also at basketball. On the eleventh day Gardner hosted a press conference where he spoke without slurring or stumbling over his words and appeared to be in excellent health. At 6:04 a.m. he finally fell asleep having set a world record for sleeplessness that has never been broken.

The remarkable aspect of this achievement is Gardner's apparent good health throughout the time without sleep. This has not been observed on other attempts where people quickly show severe psychological effects including hallucinations. One possible explanation is that he was able to indulge in 'microsleep' – small periods of sleep during the day which allow some physiological recovery to take place.

Sleep debt

Surveys in the UK find that young adults report sleeping about 7–7.5 hours each night. A hundred years ago the average person slept nine hours each night. This means that today's population sleeps one to two hours less than people used to sleep (Webb and Agnew, 1975).

The key change is probably artificial light which triggers wakefulness. People probably sleep 500 hours less each year than they used to and this might well be less sleep than evolution intended. When people go out of their daily routine, for example on holiday, they tend to sleep longer. In fact, in less industrialised societies, the total daily sleep time tends to still be around nine to ten hours (Coren, 1996).

A group of researchers spent a summer above the Arctic Circle where there is continuous light 24 hours a day (Palinkas et al., 1995). All their watches, clocks and other timekeeping devices were taken away, and they chose when to sleep or wake according to their 'body time'. At the end of the study, the participants' overall average daily sleep time was 10.3 hours. Every member of the team showed an increase in sleep time, with the shortest logging in at 8.8 hours a day, and the longest at almost 12 hours a day.

People who are living with a sleep debt are less efficient and the common effects of a large sleep debt are lapses in attention, reduced short-term memory capacity, impaired judgement and having 'microsleeps' which the sleeper is commonly unaware of – obviously not good if you're driving. It is estimated that 20% of UK motorway accidents are caused by sleepiness (Home and Reyner, 1995) and over 300 people are killed each year by drivers falling asleep at the wheel (THINK 2004).

There is now evidence that many major disasters have been due to sleep-debt effects. The evidence shows that these include the oil spill of the Exxon Valdez, the nuclear accidents at Chernobyl and Three Mile Island, and the loss of the space shuttle Challenger (Coren, 1996).

Sleep deprivation has been used by many countries as an interrogation technique. For example, prisoners in Iraq have been deprived of sleep by playing them loud heavy metal music for long periods of time. The US Psychological Operations Company (PsyOps) reports that their aim was to break a prisoner's resistance through sleep deprivation and playing music that was culturally offensive to them (BBC, 2003).

To say this is controversial is to understate the issue. Amnesty International, for example, says these techniques may well be psychological torture and therefore breach the Geneva Convention.

Sergeant Mark Hadsell, of PsyOps, comments *'These people haven't heard heavy metal. They can't take it. If you play it for 24 hours, your brain and body functions start to slide, your train of thought slows down and your will is broken. That's when we come in and talk to them.'*

Sergeant Hadsell's favourites are said to be 'Bodies' from the *XXX* film soundtrack and Metallica's 'Enter Sandman'. The theme tune from the US children's programme *Sesame Street* and songs from the purple singing dinosaur Barney are also on his hit list.

One US serviceman said *'In training, they forced me to listen to the Barney "I Love You" song for 45 minutes. I never want to go through that again.'* (BBC, 2003).

To be fair, it is argued by members of PsyOps that these tactics only have temporary effects on the prisoners. For example, Rick Hoffman in an interview with the BBC said *'There have been other kinds of non-lethal, non-harmful techniques, such as sleep deprivation... which leave no long-lasting effects but do have the end result of breaking down the individual's will to resist questioning.'* It is a fine line between using pressure on people and straying into torture (BBC, 2003).

Multiple choice questions

1 REM stands for:
   a Random Eye Movements.
   b Random Eye Motion.
   c Rapid Eye Motion.
   d Rapid Eye Movements.

2 How many participants were studied intensively?
   a 3   b 5
   c 7   d 9

3 Which of the following are characteristics of REM activity?
   a No EEG activity.
   b Different kinds of EEG activity.
   c Relatively fast EEG activity.
   d Relatively slow EEG activity.

4 In this study, the recall of dreams was:
   a The DV.
   b The IV.
   c An extraneous variable.
   d A confounding variable.

5 Which of the following procedures acted as a 'control' in this study?
   a Participants reported their dreams without direct contact with the experimenter.
   b Participants were not told if they had been woken from REM activity or not.
   c The study was conducted in a laboratory.
   d All of the above.

6 Almost all of the dreams reported in NREM sleep were reported within how many minutes of REM activity?
   a 2   b 4
   c 6   d 8

7 At what time of the night were REM episodes absent?
   a At the beginning.
   b In the middle.
   c Towards the morning.
   d REM episodes were always present.

8 At what time of the night were REM episodes longest?
   a At the beginning.
   b In the middle.
   c Towards the morning.
   d The duration of REM did not differ during the night.

9 On average REM episodes lasted:
   a 10 minutes.
   b 20 minutes.
   c 30 minutes.
   d 40 minutes

10 The most unusual form of REM activity was:
   a Mainly vertical movement.
   b Mainly horizontal movement.
   c A mixture of horizontal and vertical.
   d Little or no movement.

Answers are on page 145.

Exam-style questions

See page XII–XIII for notes on the exam paper and styles of question.

Section A questions

1 Dement and Kleitman's study on sleep linked REM activity to dreaming. Describe **two** pieces of evidence that supported this link. [4]

2 In the study of sleep by Dement and Kleitman there was some evidence that dreams also occurred in NREM sleep.
   (a) Explain how they collected this evidence. [2]
   (b) How did they explain the dreams being reported in NREM sleep? [2]

3 Dement and Kleitman used an electroencephalogram (EEG) to record sleep activity.
   (a) Explain what the EEG shows. [2]
   (b) Describe **one** limitation of using an EEG to investigate dreaming. [2]

4 (a) Identify **two** of the controls used by Dement and Kleitman in their study of sleep and dreaming. [2]
   (b) Outline why controls are used in psychological research. [2]

5 In the study of sleep by Dement and Kleitman, participants were told to abstain from two substances on the day of the experiment.
   (a) Identify these **two** substances. [2]
   (b) Outline **one** problem with this instruction. [2]

6 (a) Identify **one** of the hypotheses of the Dement and Kleitman's study on sleep and dreaming. [2]
   (b) Outline the results of the study in relation to this aim. [2]

Section B questions

(a) State a suitable hypothesis for the study by Dement and Kleitman. [2]
(b) Describe the sample used in the study by Dement and Kleitman, and give **one** limitation of this sample. [6]
(c) Describe the measures of sleep used in the study by Dement and Kleitman. [6]
(d) Explain how the validity of these measurements could be assessed. [6]
(e) Outline the conclusions of the study by Dement and Kleitman. [8]
(f) Suggest **two** changes to the study by Dement and Kleitman and outline how these changes might affect the results. [8]

Section C questions

(a) Outline **one** assumption of the biological approach in psychology. [2]
(b) Describe how the biological approach could explain the experience of dreaming. [4]
(c) Describe **one** similarity and **one** difference between the study by Dement and Kleitman and any other biological study. [6]
(d) Discuss the strengths and limitations of the biological approach, using examples from the study by Dement and Kleitman. [12]

Key issue: reliability and validity

How do psychologists ensure quality control? When we read about a set of findings, how confident should we be about them? Psychologists set up a number of measures to ensure the quality of their research including the process of peer review where, before a study is published, it is examined by other psychologists to see whether it is sound or not. Among the many things that will be examined are the **reliability** and **validity** of the evidence.

Reliability

Another word for reliability is consistency. If we are measuring something we want to know whether our measuring instrument will always give us the same result. If you use a ruler to measure the height of a chair today and check the measurement tomorrow, you expect the ruler to give you the same result. It is unlikely that the height of the chair has changed very much though you might make an error in reading the scale. When we try to measure people, however, the process becomes more difficult because the thing we are measuring changes, sometimes as we are measuring it.

Imagine trying to measure the number of people in the UK. Even if you could count everyone, and this is not possible, the number would be changing every minute as people came in and went out of the country. We are only ever able to obtain an estimate of the number. In this case it is important to have some idea of the tolerance limits of the measurement, or in other words we could say the number of people in the country is somewhere between x million and y million. Obviously we would like the gap between these numbers to be as small as possible.

When it comes to psychological measures we have further problems. We are often trying to estimate a psychological quality by measuring something else. For example, if we want to measure a person's memory capacity we may give them a list of words to learn and count up how many they remember. We are not measuring their memory but their *performance* on a task to investigate memory. All sorts of things can affect this performance such as being distracted during the learning process, their past associations with some of the words or whether they can be bothered to try. These factors are all further possible sources of error in our measurement.

Psychologists assess the reliability of their measures with a range of techniques including

1. *Test–retest*: in this case we carry out the measurement on two occasions and compare the scores using a correlation technique. Test-retest reliability is affected by a number of factors including changes in the participants between the two measurements, and, if the time between the two measures is brief then the participants might remember their original responses.

2. *Internal consistency*: This is often used with questionnaire measures that have several questions and we compare two parts of the test to see how similar the scores are.

3. *Inter-rater reliability* (also known as *inter-observer reliability*): This is a check to see whether different users of the measurement tool get similar results using it. Two people should be able to administer the same scale to the same group of people and get the same or similar scores from them. Equally, when using an observational or behaviour checklist, observers who are working independently should be able to get the same pattern of recorded observations as each other. Inter-rater reliability is also discussed on page 12.

Reliable, but not valid   Not reliable, not valid   Reliable and valid

Being reliable is being consistent (far left and far right); being valid is being on target, in relation to what you are aiming to do (far right).

Validity, in general, is about the legitimacy of results. It is a measure of the extent to which something tests or measures what it aims to test/measure.

Reliability refers to whether a measuring device or assessment is consistent.

Ecological validity The ability to generalise a research finding beyond the particular setting in which it is demonstrated to other settings. It is established by considering representativeness and generalisability.

The amazing PSYCHOMEASURE. Yes, you too can measure your intelligence. Just wrap the PSYCHOMEASURE around your forehead and read off the value.

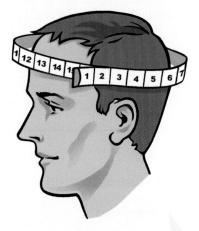

Available from SCOOBY ENTERPRISES for only 3 monthly payments of £19.99

Is the PSYCHOMEASURE reliable?
Is the PSYCHOMEASURE valid?
Give reasons for your answers.

Replication

Another way to ensure the reliability of our evidence is to repeat the study to find out if we get the same results. This is referred to as *replication* and it is seen as an important test of any scientific evidence. This means that an independent researcher should be able to copy the procedure of a given research study, and obtain the same pattern of results. This is why it is so important to be explicit about the details of how a research study was conducted. Sometimes replications are exact: in other words, they are conducted in exactly the same way as the original study, with the same type of participant sample. More often, however, they are designed to be slightly different in order to further develop the ideas in the original study. One example of this is the study by **Samuel and Bryant** which is a part-replication of Piaget's work and part critique.

Validity

As well as wanting to ensure our measures are reliable (consistent) we want to ensure that they measure what we want them to measure. This is not as easy as it sounds. Does our memory test actually measure memory or does it measure how hard someone is trying to remember something? We might be measuring motivation rather than memory. Also, think about AS and A Levels. What do they measure? Will the results give us a good measure of how clever a person is, or maybe how hard they work or whether they went to a good school or whether they are lucky? The answer is difficult to establish.

With our psychological measures we want them to give us an accurate assessment of the variable we are studying. So, for example, in the study by **Bandura *et al*.** we want our measure of aggression to give us an estimate of how aggressive a child is. A measurement technique is said to be valid if it measures what it claims to measure. This is linked to the concept of reliability. For a measure to be valid it must first of all be reliable (it cannot be valid if it gives inconsistent measurements of the same thing), but it must also have other properties.

There are a number of ways in which researchers try to examine the validity of their operational definitions and measures, including:

1   *Face validity*: This simply means asking the question of whether, 'on the face of it', this measure looks valid. Does the measuring tool look like it is measuring the variable you are interested in? This is a fairly weak form of validity but very important because as long as it looks as if you are doing the right thing many people will be convinced that you are in fact doing the right thing (*This is a good rule for life – Ed.*).

2   *Construct validity*: By far the most important type of validity is construct validity which refers to the theoretical foundations of what you are doing. Does the measurement make sense within the theories of psychology that you are testing? The idea that you can predict a person's personality from asking them about their favourite colour might be fun to discuss on daytime television but has no theoretical basis and therefore has no construct validity.

3   *Ecological validity*: The degree to which the behaviour observed in a study reflects behaviour that occurs in everyday settings. A study which examines the behaviour or experience of people in their natural settings is often high in ecological validity (that is, high direct relevance to everyday life – see **Rosenhan** for example). Studies which take place under highly controlled, artificial conditions (in a laboratory, for example) are often low in ecological validity (see **Loftus and Palmer**).

Ecological validity is associated with generalisability, which is the extent to which findings can be generalised to the real world. It is also concerned with representativeness, which is the extent to which a study mirrors conditions in the real world.

In virtually all studies there is a trade-off between control and ecological validity. The greater the control the greater the danger of compromising the ecological validity. When we study people in a laboratory their behaviour is clearly affected by the laboratory environment and the tasks they are required to do are often very contrived. If we study them in their daily life it is usually impossible to do this in a controlled way and then extraneous variables may affect our results.

The topic of control and generalisability validity is considered on page 17.

Qualitative data

Reliability and validity are usually discussed using examples of quantitative research (see page 9). Researchers who deal with qualitative data, however, are also required to demonstrate that their findings are trustworthy, but they do not have the traditional statistical procedures for doing this. They are often less concerned with the idea of reliability as described on the left, preferring instead to talk about the richness, diversity and changeability of human behaviour and experience. They are often not looking for consistent measures but for the uniqueness of human beings.

Validity, however, is something that can not be ignored and the core question for them is the same as for quantitative researchers, 'Why should we believe your findings?'.

Error

'All measurement is befuddled with error' (McNemar, 1946)

When we measure anything our reading is made up of two components, the true score and error.

Observed value = True score + Error

What psychologists try and do is to minimise the error and then to estimate it so that they can judge how close their observe value is to the true score, or in other words, how accurate their measurement is.

---

*The study by **Piliavin** et al. collected data from a real life situation on a New York subway train. This gave the research high ecological validity but reduced the amount of control they had over the experiment. Interestingly, they obtained a different result to similar studies carried out in laboratories.*

Qs

1   Take **one** of the core studies and assess how reliable the data is and how valid it is.

2   Select **one** core study and describe in what way the task that participants were required to do was different from everyday life.

3   In what way does this affect the results from the study?

4   Identify some of the problems psychologists might encounter if they studied the same behaviour in everyday life.

...Links to other studies and issues...

Reliability and validity are key issues for all research in psychology. Some of the core studies illustrate particular problems with this quality control. For example, the case study work of **Freud** is challenged because we do not know how reliable his measures are. Would his patients have said the same things to someone else? **Qualitative** researchers would argue that this is not a problem because Freud is trying to capture something unique so he was not looking for reliability. If we look at the Bobo study (**Bandura et al.**) we can see that the behaviour of the children was observed by more than one person and when they compared their observations there was close agreement. This shows high inter-observer reliability. On the other hand you might wonder whether just by watching behaviour you are getting a full picture of aggression because aggression isn't just something we do, but also something we feel.

Many of the studies in this text have been selected because they have clear relevance to issues of everyday life and so would be judged to have high ecological validity. Even these studies, however, have to make some compromises in order to carry out controlled investigations. For example, the memory study by **Loftus and Palmer** avoids the common problem of memory studies. Such studies often lack representativeness because they test memory with word lists which doesn't tell us much about memory for an accident. It is clearly not possible to stage accidents for people to view so they have to be viewed in picture or video formats. This means there are limits to how much we can generalise the results.

One brain or two?

The brain is a truly remarkable organ. Think about it. The brain creates our world for us every time we wake up. Roger Sperry said, '*Before brains there was no color or sound in the universe, nor was there any flavor or aroma and probably little sense and no feeling or emotion.*' (Sperry, 1964). All these qualities only exist in our brains. I know you think a tree is green and the sky is blue and Rudolf's nose is red but it isn't so. The world is full of radiation of different wavelengths and it is our brain that senses that radiation and creates the colours we use to interpret our surroundings. It's almost too amazing to think about.

During his career Sperry made some startling discoveries about the brain, none more so than the ones described in this core study. I think this study challenges what we know about ourselves and what we can become.

A lot was already known about the brain before Sperry's study and some of that is summarised on this spread. There is also a summary of the development of brain research on pages 110–111. Every year sees our knowledge of the brain growing with the promise of finding out more about why we do the things we do. Brain scientist Wilder Penfield (see below right) believed that the brain represented the most important unexplored field in the whole of science and it is hard to argue with him. We have only scratched the surface in our understanding of the brain.

Activity

Right eyed or left eyed?
Which is your dominant eye? Test it out for yourself. Look at a distant object such as a clock on a wall or a tree on a hill. Now line up one finger with the object so that the finger is blocking it. Then close one eye and then the other. What happens? When you close one of your eyes the object will still be blocked, only even more so. When you close the other eye the finger will appear to jump.

What the brain does

The brain has two relatively symmetrical halves (left and right). The illustration shows a brain that has been cut down the middle. You can see that the top third of the brain (i.e. the cortex) is not joined to its other half: the only part that has been cut through is where the two halves are joined – at the commissural fibres, which include the corpus callosum.

Cerebral cortex

This is the clever bit of the human brain and the largest part. The cerebral cortex actually covers the brain like a tea cosy and is highly wrinkled which increases the surface area and probably increases its power. Structures that are 'sub-cortical' lie under the tea cosy. Such sub-cortical structures are concerned with more basic processes like emotion and are present in all animals, whereas the cortex is specific to higher animals such as mammals.

The cortex is divided into four lobes which are believed to control different functions:

- **Frontal lobe** (front of the brain, above the eyes): reasoning, planning, parts of speech, movement, emotions, and problem solving.
- **Parietal lobe** (top, towards the back): movement, orientation, recognition, perception of stimuli.
- **Occipital lobe** (back): visual processing.
- **Temporal lobe** (sides): perception of auditory stimuli, memory, and speech.

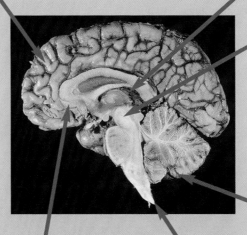

Thalamus

The simple story is that the thalamus (a sub-cortical structure) is a 'relay station' for signals from the senses (skin, stomach, eyes, ears but not the nose) to the cerebral cortex. The real story is more complicated, because the thalamus does more than just send the signals on – it also does some initial analysis of the signals.

Hypothalamus

This is located below the thalamus (hence hypo-thalamus). It is the size of half a baked bean but plays a very important role as the major control centre for a range of essential functions. For example it controls body temperature, hunger and thirst. It also appears to be involved in emotional and sexual activity. A lot of work for half a baked bean.

Corpus callosum

The corpus callosum connects the left and right cerebral hemispheres and carries most of the communication between the two halves of the brain. A number of claims have been made about sex and racial differences in the corpus callosum. The idea is that the greater the traffic across the two halves the greater the person's intelligence (favouring women and white people). Such claims are made in popular magazines but they have little scientific support (Bishop and Wahlsten, 1997).

Cerebellum

The cerebellum, or 'little brain', is similar to the cerebral cortex in that it has two hemispheres and has a highly folded surface or cortex. This structure is associated with regulation and coordination of movement, posture, and balance.

Brain stem

The brain stem is the stalk of the brain below the cerebral hemispheres. It is the major route for communication between the forebrain and the spinal cord and peripheral nerves. It also controls various functions including respiration and regulation of heart rhythms.

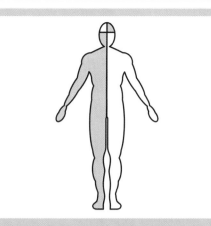

Cross-wired

The left side of the body and the left visual field are controlled by the right hemisphere, and the right side of the body and the right visual field by the left hemisphere.

Control of the auditory fields is more complex, while our sense of smell, the most neurologically ancient of the senses, is not crossed over at all, each nostril being 'wired' to the hemisphere on the same side of the body.

Wilder Penfield (1891–1976)

Penfield was a Canadian surgeon and researcher who was interested in finding cures for epilepsy and other brain disorders. With his colleagues, Penfield developed a new surgical approach in which he was able to examine the exposed brain of a conscious patient using just a local anaesthetic. As the patient described what they were feeling, Penfield pushed a probe into sections of the brain and located the damaged tissue that was the source of the epileptic seizures. The damaged tissue was removed and many patients then had relief from their seizures.

Of course, once you have an open brain in front of you, it is only natural to poke about a bit to see what is going on. This is exactly what Penfield did and he made some astounding discoveries. For example, he found that careful administration of a mild electric shock to one of the temporal lobes could make some patients recall precise personal experiences that had long been forgotten.

This brain technique also allowed him to create maps of the sensory and motor areas of the brain. These maps are commonly represented as distorted models of a person that show how much of the brain area is associated with each part of the body (if you find it difficult to visualise this then Google 'Penfield homunculus'). He first published this work in 1951 and it is still being used today. Penfield's research also gave us a lot of information about how different areas of the brain have different effects on our behaviour and experience (lateralisation of function).

Penfield's research into the structure and function of the brain was prompted by his desire to discover a physical basis for the belief in the human soul, an idea that was followed up some years later by V.S. Ramachandran (see his website).

Penfield's work has captured the imagination of many people and he gets a mention in number of works of fiction. For example, in the science fiction classic Do Androids Dream of Electric Sheep? *by Philip K Dick (also filmed as* Bladerunner*) characters use a household device called a Penfield Mood Organ to dial up emotions on demand.*

Sperry's animal experiments

It is an uncomfortable part of medical science that many advances come from research on animals. Pictures of animals in painful apparatus illustrate one side of the story and life-saving medicines illustrate the other.

It can be no surprise that Sperry carried out a lot of research on animal brains before he operated on people. Those of a nervous disposition should stop reading now.

Sperry was able to show that a number of functions are 'hard-wired' into the nervous system and cannot be learned. For example he swapped wiring round on a rat's foot so that when it tried to move its left foot the right foot moved instead. The rat was not able to adapt to this new arrangement. He also cut the optic nerves of salamanders and then rotated them before allowing the nerves to regenerate and reconnect to the eye. The salamander then saw the world upside down and it was not able to adapt to this. And of course, the split brain technique of severing the corpus callosum was tried out on cats and monkeys before being used on people.

The full gory details of the animal work does not make good reading and many readers might object to the zoo full of animals who had their brains rearranged by Sperry. On the other hand, the patients with epilepsy who had the split brain operation were better able to live an ordinary life and so might disagree. It's a moral maze.

Epilepsy

Epilepsy is the term given to a collection of disorders that are associated with uncontrolled seizures. The severity of the seizures can differ from person to person. Some people will just experience a trance-like state for a few seconds, or minutes, whereas others will lose consciousness and have convulsions (uncontrollable shaking of the body). Epilepsy is a relatively widespread condition affecting around 456,000 people in the UK. The condition usually begins during childhood but it can start at any age. Around 1 in every 280 children is affected by epilepsy. Modern medications can usually control epilepsy but not cure it and surgery is still sometimes used in difficult cases.

St. Valentine, patron saint of lovers and people with epilepsy.

It is not clear what causes epilepsy though one of the main risk factors (common to many other disorders) is being poor. Parts of the world that are less developed than the West have up to twice the incidence of epilepsy.

A common myth about epilepsy is that it is brought on by flashing lights, but around only 10% of people with epilepsy are sensitive to lights in this way.

Epilepsy in history

The split brain operation used in this study was performed as a means of treating severe epilepsy. Epilepsy has been recognised as a condition for many centuries and people have tried to explain it in a number of ways. In the fourteenth and fifteenth centuries seizures were commonly seen as being a curse or the work of demonic forces. People with seizures made pilgrimages to the Priory of St Valentine, a monastery on the border between France and Germany, for spiritual healing. They went there because, as well as being the patron saint of lovers, Valentine moonlights as the patron saint of people with epilepsy.

In the Middle Ages epileptics were pointed in the direction of medical 'cures' ranging from blood-letting to burning.

Treatments and attitudes are much better today but it is fair to say that people with epilepsy still experience discrimination and negative responses in the UK.

www If you are interested to find out more about the brain then you might start your exploration at the whole brain atlas (www.med.harvard.edu/AANLIB/home.html)

...Link to the core study...

The idea of splitting a person's brain in half is shocking and fascinating. You just have to know what happens. If your personality is merely something in your brain, rather than in a mystical idea like a soul, then maybe cutting the brain in half will create two personalities. Of course you can't do this to people just for the sake of investigating this question but sometimes extreme surgery is the only option. In this study the split brain operation was done to relieve epilepsy, but also afforded scientists the ideal opportunity to assess the psychological effects of splitting the brain.

Roger Wolcott Sperry (1968) Hemispheric disconnection and unity in conscious awareness. *American Psychologist*, 23, pages 723–733.

SPERRY: SPLIT BRAIN

Abstract

The study demonstrates some interesting things about the way the human brain is organised by comparing the performance of split-brain patients with normal behaviour. Specially designed apparatus was used which:

* Presents information to left and right visual fields (LVF and RVF) for very brief periods (0.1 seconds).
* Allows hands to examine objects while out of sight.
* Relays visual and manual information to left and right hemispheres (LH and RH).

Example results	Conclusion that can be drawn
If a $ sign is flashed to the LVF and ? sign flashed to RVF the patient will draw (using his left hand) the figure ($) shown to LVF but will tell you that he saw the sign shown to RVF (?).	LVF linked to RH and RVF linked to LH. Left hand linked to RH (and LVF), right hand linked to LH (and RVF). Language centres are in LH. The function of the corpus callosum is to enable communication between RH and LH.
If visual material is projected to the LVF the participant says he did not see anything or there was just a flash of light on his left side.	RH has language limitations.
Patients can select objects, with their left hand, that are related to a pictured item presented to LVF, e.g. selecting a wrist watch when wall clock was shown.	RH is not completely 'word blind'; shows some language comprehension.
If a pinup picture is shown to the LVF there is an appropriate emotional reaction (such as a giggle) but says he saw nothing or just a flash of light.	The right hemisphere is still characteristically human because it demonstrates an appropriate emotional response (and also spatial awareness) but has no language.
If two objects are placed simultaneously one in each hand and then hidden in a pile of objects, both hands then search through the pile and can select their own object but will ignore the other hand's objects.	We effectively have two minds. Split brain patients are two rather than one individual.
Patients continue to watch TV or read books with no complaints; intellect and personality are unchanged. They coped better with dual processing tasks. However they had short term memory difficulties.	Split brain patients cope relatively well with everyday life.

Biographical notes

Roger Sperry, who was one of the premier neurobiologists of his time, started out as an English undergraduate and only later took an interest in psychology. Like many remarkable people he had a range of interests and talents: he was a star athlete in javelin and played basketball at University, was an avid fisherman, and an exceptionally talented sculptor, painter and ceramicist. He also was a keen paleontologist who collected prehistoric molluscs from around the world and, according to one colleague, was known for hosting great parties where he served his special 'split brain' punch.

Sperry had a profound effect on the progress of physiological psychology specifically and brain science generally. He revolutionised neuroscience. In later years he turned more and more to philosophy and formulating a non-reductionist view of consciousness. He proposed that consciousness emerges from the activity of cerebral networks as an independent entity.

'The great pleasure and feeling in my right brain is more than my left brain can find the words to tell you.' Roger Sperry (1913–1994)
Sperry received the Nobel Prize in Medicine in 1981, one of only a few psychologists to receive the award.

Aim

To study the psychological effects of hemispheric disconnection in split-brain patients, and to use the results to understand how the right and left hemispheres work in 'normal' individuals.

Previous split-brain studies with humans (e.g. Akelaitis, 1944) found that there were no important behavioural effects whereas split-brain studies with animals produced many behavioural effects (e.g. Myers, 1961).

Method

Participants

The participants were a group of patients who suffered from severe epileptic seizures which could not be controlled by medication. The split-brain operation is a possible remedy; it involves cutting through the cerebral commisures which connect the left and right hemispheres of the brain. Note that the operation was not done for the purpose of this experiment, which would have been unethical. For most patients the operation reduced the frequency and severity of their seizures.

Procedure

The main setup for testing the behavioural effects of hemispheric deconnection is shown on the right. It means that information can be presented selectively to the left hemisphere (via the right visual field) or to the right hemisphere (via the left visual field).

www Try the split-brain game: *http://nobelprize.org/medicine/educational/split-brain/index.html*

Qs

1   What structures were cut in the split brain procedure?
2   Akelaitis conducted earlier studies of split brain patients. What effect did he find the procedure had on the behaviour of patients?
3   In what way was Sperry's study a natural experiment?
4   Why might it be considered unethical to perform a split-brain operation just for the purpose of this experiment?
5   Suggest a hypothesis for this study.
6   Why do you think Sperry projected the slides so briefly?
7   In a split-brain patient if information is presented to the left visual field only, why wouldn't they be able to report what they are seeing?
8   Why can normal individuals say what they see in the left visual field?
9   Why couldn't participants recognise material presented to the left visual field with their right hand?
10 Why was it important that participants couldn't see their hands?

Activity

Right brain left brain

It is possible to demonstrate right and left field advantages in normal individuals (without split brains).

Present two words (one on the right and one on the left) on a computer screen for less than 100 milliseconds. Participants should show a preference for reporting the word on the right.

If you present two pictures (one left and one right), there should be a preference to report the picture on the left because the right hemisphere is better at analysing pictures.

Apparatus for studying split-brain patients

The participant has one eye covered and is asked to gaze at a fixed point in the centre of a projection screen. Visual stimuli are back-projected onto the screen, either to the right or left of the screen, at a very high speed – one picture every 0.1 (1⁄10) second or less. This means that the eye only has time to process the image in the visual field where it was placed (i.e. if the image was shown to the left visual field there is not time for the participant to move their eye or head so that the right visual field might also receive the image). Below the screen there was a gap so that the participant could reach objects but not see his or her hands.

Results

Baseline results

- If a projected picture is shown and responded to in one visual field, it is only recognised again if it appears in that visual field.
- If visual material appeared in the right visual field (processed by left hemisphere), the patient could describe it in speech and writing as normal.
- If the same visual material is projected to the left visual field (right hemisphere) then the participant says he did not see anything or there was just a flash of light on his left side. (Language centres are in the left hemisphere.)
- If you then ask the same participant to use his left hand (right hemisphere control) to point to a matching picture or object in a collection of pictures/objects, then he points to the item he just insisted he couldn't see.

These results confirm that the right hemisphere cannot speak or write (called aphasia and agraphia respectively).

Results continued on next page.

Activity

Role play

Two right-handed people should sit next to each other (on one chair if possible) in front of a table with a screen on it, divided into left and right with an X in the middle. The volunteer on the left (Person A) represents the left hemisphere and the one on the right (person B) represents the right hemisphere.

The two volunteers should put their outer hands behind their back. They should place their inner hands on the table and cross them over (ideally under the screen). The two hands represent the split-brain patient's left and right hands.

Members of the class should act as experimenters and conduct Sperry's mini-experiments. The volunteers should try to react as a split-brain patient.

EXAM TIP

When you get into the exam, write this down:

RVF ⟶
left hemisphere (LH) ⟶
right hand / left nostril

LVF ⟶
right hemisphere (RH) ⟶
left hand / right nostril

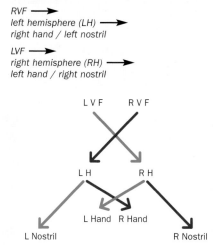

SPERRY: SPLIT BRAIN

Results continued

$ and ? signs

If a $ sign is flashed to the left visual field (LVF) and ? sign flashed to RVF the participant can draw the $ figure with his left hand (perceived by right hemisphere) but will tell you that he saw the ? sign which was shown to RVF (left hemisphere). Sperry says *'the one hemisphere does not know what the other hemisphere has been doing'* (p. 726).

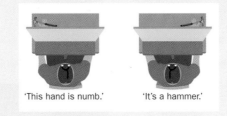

What do you see?

Partcipant draws a $ with left hand

What do you see?

I see a "?"

Composite words

When words are flashed partly to the LVF and partly to the RVF, the letters are responded to separately. For example if 'keycase' is projected ('key' to the LVF and 'case' to the RVF) then a participant would

- Select a key from the collection of objects with his left hand (LVF goes to right hemisphere which controls the left hand).
- Spell out the word 'case' with his right hand (RVF goes to left hemisphere which controls the right hand).
- Say 'case' if asked what word was displayed (RVF goes to left hemisphere which controls speech).

What do you see?

Participant selects a key with left hand

What do you see?

'The word is "case"'. Participant spells the word with right hand

Using touch

Objects placed in the right hand (left hemisphere) can be named in speech and writing. If an object is placed in the left hand participants can only make wild guesses and may seem unaware that they are holding anything. However, if the same object is placed in a grab bag with other objects, the participant can find the original object with his left hand. They cannot retrieve the object with their right hand if it was first sensed with the left hand.

When asked to name objects held in their left hand (such as a hammer) participants said something like 'This hand is numb' or 'I don't get messages from that hand'. If they successfully identified an object with their left hand they would comment 'Well, I was just guessing' or 'I must have done it unconsciously'. In other words, they had developed a way of explaining their rather strange behaviour to themselves. Of course they could easily give a verbal identification of the object if it was held in their right hand.

'This hand is numb.'

'It's a hammer.'

Dual processing task

If two objects are placed simultaneously one in each hand and then hidden in a pile of objects, both hands can select their own object from the pile but will ignore the other hand's objects. Sperry said *'It is like two separate individuals working over a collection of test items with no cooperation between them'* (p. 727).

Everyday effects

In everyday life split-brain patients don't usually notice that their mental functions are cut in half. They continue to watch TV or read books unaware of the separate visual input. This is because all the problems described in the study only arise when visual material is displayed very briefly. In everyday life deconnection can be overcome by moving the eyes or saying an answer out loud so information is shared between right and left hemisphere.

However, this doesn't mean split-brain patients are better off in their 'deconnected' state. It is true that their IQ scores and personality were little changed; however, in most complex activities people with cooperating hemispheres appear to do better, for example all the patients had some problems with short-term memory and had limited attention spans.

On the other hand, there are some tasks that are actually performed better by split-brain patients. They could carry out a double reaction-time task as fast as they could carry out a single task. In normal patients the introduction of a second task causes interference.

Abilities of the right (minor) hemisphere

Before Sperry's research little was known about what the right, 'silent' hemisphere could do. Tests with the split-brain patients revealed a range of higher-order mental abilities, including some verbal comprehension. These capacities are described in the table on the right. In fact there are some abilities that are dominant in the right hemisphere, such as spatial awareness and emotion.

Qs

1. Explain the outcome of the mini-experiment using the $ and ? signs.
2. Explain why the two halves of the split brain represent two minds.
3. How do you think that split brain patients manage to watch the TV without noticing their abnormal visual input?
4. Identify **three** things controlled by the left hemisphere.
5. Identify **three** things controlled by the right hemisphere.
6. Why is the right hemisphere referred to as the 'minor' hemisphere?
7. Sperry pointed out the fact that there were important individual differences. What is the importance of this for interpreting the study's results?
8. What does 'lateralised' mean?

Closing statements

Patients appear to have two independent streams of consciousness, each with its own separate memories, own perceptions, own impulses to act; in a sense two minds in one body.

Sperry ends the article by saying *'The more we see of these patients and the more of these patients we see, the more we become impressed by their individual differences'* (p. 733). Such differences might explain the contrasting results collected by different investigators. For example some patients display some ipsilateral control (right hemisphere can communicate with right hand, i.e. same side of the body). Such patients would not display some of the behavioural effects described here.

This table shows some of the things the right hemisphere could do in the split-brain patients.

Human mental capacities	If a patient is holding an object in their left hand, they can then point to the name of the object displayed in their LVF. This demonstrates that the right brain has some distinctly human mental capacities since a monkey could not perform such tasks.
Understanding of general categories	Patients can select objects that are related to a pictured item presented to LVF, a task that requires mental processing. For example, if a picture of a wall clock was shown to the right hemisphere (LVF), the left hand will select a toy wrist watch. This shows that the right hemisphere has grasped the general category (timepiece) and is not just searching for a physical match.
Simple arithmetic problems	For example, if numbers are shown to the LVF, the left hand (held out of sight) can signal the correct answer. If two different pairs of numbers were shown to RVF and LVF separately, the right and left hands could signal two separate answers but the patient will only say the answer for the RVF.
Responding to spoken cues	If an object is named outloud, the left hand (right hemisphere) can locate the object because hearing is partially bilateral (about 10% goes to same side and 90% goes to opposite hemisphere).
Sorting	The left hand can sort objects into groups by touch on the basis of shape, size and texture.
Spatial awareness	On some tests the right hemisphere was found to be superior to the left (major) hemisphere – on tests that involve drawing spatial relationships and performing block design tests.
Emotion	If a pinup picture is shown in a series of geometric figures to the LVF there is an emotional reaction (such as a giggle) but the patient usually says he saw nothing or just a flash of light. The patient who saw the picture with his LVF cannot explain why he giggled. Odours to right nostril (right hemisphere) can't be named but can be identified as pleasant or unpleasant – the patient might grunt or turn away. The patient can also identify the correct object with his left hand which shows that the right hemisphere can identify the smell-object. This emotional responsiveness is used to effect by some patients in ordinary testing – if the right hemisphere hears the left hemisphere stating an incorrect answer, the right hemisphere expresses annoyance.

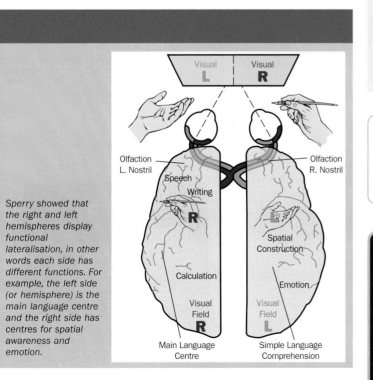

Sperry showed that the right and left hemispheres display functional lateralisation, in other words each side has different functions. For example, the left side (or hemisphere) is the main language centre and the right side has centres for spatial awareness and emotion.

Evaluating the study by Sperry

There are no simple answers. Evaluating a study requires you to think. We have provided some pointers here, linked to the KEY ISSUES covered through this book – see page XIV for a table of these key issues.

The research method
This study can be described as a natural or quasi-experiment because the IV (presence or absence of split brain) varied naturally. The DV is the participant's performance on a variety of tests. However, as each of these people are described in detail it could also be argued that Sperry's work is a series of case studies. *What are the strengths and limitations of these research methods in the context of this study?*

The sample
We do not know to what extent the split-brain patients had brain damage caused by the severe epileptic fits (or the fits may have been caused by brain damage in the first place). *How does this affect the conclusions drawn from the study?*

Ethical issues
It is easy to be confused about ethical issues in this study – the split-brain procedure was not done for the purpose of the study and therefore is not an ethical issue. However, we might question the ethics of using patients for the purpose of scientific study and question their ability to give informed consent. *What ethical issues should have concerned the researchers in this study, and how might they have dealt with these issues?*

Reductionist
What are the strengths and limitations of reductionism in the context of this study?

Qualitative or quantitative?
What kind of data were collected in this study? What are the strengths and limitations of producing this kind of data in the context of this study?

Applications/usefuless
How valuable was this study?

What next?
Describe **one** change to this study, and say how you think this might affect the outcome.

Debate

Was this a 'landmark study'?

Did Sperry produce results of major significance? Divide your class into groups; each group should produce one argument for and one argument against Sperry. You might do some further research first. What does your class conclude?

...Links to other studies and issues...

The most striking connection is to the multiple personality study of **Thigpen and Cleckley**. Both studies look at split consciousness. In the case of Sperry, some of his patients appeared to have two consciousnesses that were not always aware of each other. In the case of Eve, there are more than two consciousnesses, but could this have a biological cause like Sperry's patients? Both studies challenge us to consider what we understand about identity and personality.

More brains

The novel *A Scanner Darkly* by Philip K. Dick (and the film of the same name starring Keanu Reeves) turns around the idea of a split brain and actually quotes the work of Sperry as a central part of the plot. Some of the other legacy of the work is described below.

Hemispherectomy

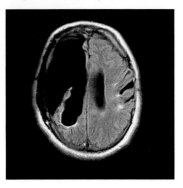

Hemispherectomy involves the surgical removal or disconnection of one of the two halves of the brain. This MRI scan shows a brain after hemispherectomy. Most of the left hemisphere has been removed and the rest has been deconnected from the right hemisphere.

If one part of the brain is damaged perhaps it would be best to remove it. One radical way to do this is the removal of one hemisphere of the brain (i.e. half the brain). Hemispherectomy was first attempted in 1928 by US neurosurgeon **Walter E. Dandy** as a treatment for brain cancer. In the 1950s the technique was first used for epilepsy and it continues to be used today.

It is most commonly used on children and only those with serious conditions that do not respond to other treatments. Sometimes the surgeons remove a large part of the hemisphere but more commonly they just disconnect the damaged part from the rest of the brain.

Children appear to have remarkable powers of recovery and hospital stays are commonly less than a week. The operation is remarkably successful in that patients commonly stop having seizures yet are able to regain the ability to walk.

The modern use of the hemispherectomy was pioneered by **Benjamin Carson** who performed his first operation in 1985 in the USA. He specialises in child brain surgery. Talking about hemispherectomy he said: *'you can't get away with that in an adult, but a child has the ability to actually transfer functions to other parts of the brain. So you can take out half of the brain of a kid, and you'll see the kid walking around, you'll see him using the arm on the opposite side, and in many cases even engaging in sporting activities.'*

'The human brain is the thing that makes you who you are. I never get over my awe of the brain' (Carson, 2002).

Hemispherectomy surgeon Benjamin Carson holding up a model of the skulls of conjoined twins.

Right brain left brain

One of the legacies of Sperry's research was to elevate the role of the right hemisphere from being the 'minor' hemisphere to one with special functions. This has led to the 'cult' of right versus left brained thinking. In 1972 Robert Ornstein suggested that society had placed too much emphasis on left-brained thinking and that we should liberate the creative powers of the right brain. Right-brain education programmes have been developed and tapes sold to develop 'whole-brain learning'. The right side was seen as the more intuitive, feminine side of human nature which was a feather in the cap of feminists. However, Corballis (1999) concludes that the differences between the hemispheres are minor and the right brain left brain movement should be regarded as little more than commercial exploitation.

Sperry at the movies

The novel A Scanner Darkly *by Philip K. Dick (released as a film in 2006) imagines a world where users of mind expanding drugs risk brain damage from taking large doses. The central character is a police agent who's own use of the drug severs the connection between the two hemispheres of his brain. The book quotes the work by Sperry and speculates on what happens to when you have two disconnected brains in the same head. If one half of the brain doesn't know what the other is doing then maybe the police officer can become a secret agent without even knowing about it?*

Here's looking at you kid

'I used to think that the brain was the most interesting part of the body. Then I thought, "What part of my body is telling me that?"' Emo Philips

Think about this. When people carry out research into the brain what is doing the research? A brain looking at a brain?

Sniff your way to success

Can breathing through one nostril affect how well your brain works? Not as silly as it sounds, perhaps. We know that the two hemispheres of the brain control different parts of the body and different cognitive functions. Add to this the nasal cycle in which each nostril takes turns to do the heavy breathing over a two-hour cycle (GP Notebook, 2005) and finish it off with the idea of a mental cycle where the left and right brains take it in turns to do the heavy thinking and you see where we are heading with this. Sniff your way to genius!

In an ingenious set of studies where people performed mental tests with tissue paper stuffed up one nostril Shannahoff-Khalsa *et al.* (1991) were able to show that forced breathing through one nostril had an effect on cognitive performance. For this outstanding finding the scientists were awarded the 1995 IgNobel Prize for Medicine (the same prize as mentioned on page 58 and elsewhere in this book).

Interestingly, the technique of breathing through one nostril at a time is an exercise in yoga called Anuloma Viloma. In this breathing technique, you inhale through one nostril, retain the breath, and exhale through the other nostril in a ratio of 2:8:4. Don't ask!

Multiple choice questions

1 The split-brain operation was performed:
   a To conduct this experiment.
   b For patients with mild epilepsy.
   c For patients with severe epilepsy.
   d Both a and c.

2 Visual stimuli were flashed on the screen for:
   a 1 second.   b 0.1 seconds.
   c 0.01 seconds.   d 0.001 seconds.

3 The right hand and right nostril are connected to the:
   a Right hemisphere.
   b Left hemisphere.
   c Right and left hemisphere respectively.
   d Left and right hemisphere respectively.

4 When a $ sign was flashed to the left visual field, the patient could:
   a Draw the $ sign with his left hand.
   b Draw the $ sign with his right hand.
   c Tell you he saw a $ sign.
   d Both a and c.

5 When the word 'keycase' was flashed so that 'key' is presented in the LVF and 'case' in the RVF, the patient can
   a Spell out the word 'case' with his right hand.
   b Spell out the word 'case' with his left hand.
   c Say the word 'key'.
   d None of the above.

6 When a patient held an object in their left hand, they could:
   a Say what it was.
   b Find a similar object with their right hand.
   c Find a similar object with their left hand.
   d Both a and b.

7 Split-brain patients had:
   a Personality changes.
   b Problems with short-term memory.
   c Short attention spans.
   d Both b and c.

8 The right hemisphere was found to be:
   a The main language centre.
   b Word blind.
   c Able to engage in some verbal functions.
   d Lower in IQ.

9 The patient gave an emotional response (a giggle) if a photograph of a pin-up was displayed to the:
   a Right visual field.
   b Left visual field.
   c Either field.
   d The patients never giggled.

10 Sperry ended his article by highlighting the fact that:
   a His patients were essentially abnormal.
   b The study was unethical.
   c There were important individual differences in what the split brain patients could do.
   d All of the above.

Answers are on page 145.

Exam-style questions

See page XII–XIII for notes on the exam paper and styles of question.

Section A questions

1 Sperry studied the abilities of split-brain patients.
   (a) Describe **one** difference between the ability of split-brain patients and 'normal' people to identify objects by touch alone. [2]
   (b) Give **one** explanation for this difference. [2]

2 (a) From the study by Sperry, explain why the split-brain operation was carried out on the patients in the study. [2]
   (b) Outline the major function of the corpus callosum. [2]

3 The results of Sperry's study of split-brain patients suggest that we effectively have two minds. Outline **two** pieces of evidence from the study that show this. [4]

4 (a) Describe the technique that Sperry used to present information to only one side of the brain? [2]
   (b) Explain why 'normal' people do not have any difficulty with the technique used to test the split-brain patients. [2]

5 From the paper by Sperry on split-brain patients, outline evidence which indicates that language is processed in the left hemisphere of the brain. [4]

6 (a) In Sperry's study, describe **one** problem with generalising from the sample. [2]
   (b) Explain what is meant by the term 'left visual field' as used in the paper by Sperry. [2]

Section B questions

   (a) Identify the aim of the study by Sperry. [2]
   (b) Describe the sample used in the study by Sperry, and give **one** limitation of the sample. [6]
   (c) Describe how behaviour was tested in the study by Sperry. [6]
   (d) Describe **one** of the ethical issues raised in the study by Sperry and suggest how it could be dealt with. [6]
   (e) Outline the conclusions of the study by Sperry. [8]
   (f) Suggest **two** changes to the study by Sperry and outline how these changes might affect the results. [8]

Section C questions

   (a) Outline **one** assumption of reductionism in psychology. [2]
   (b) Describe how the biological approach could explain the abilities of split-brain patients. [4]
   (c) Describe how the approach taken by Sperry is an example of reductionism. [6]
   (d) Discuss the strengths and limitations of reductionism, using examples from the study by Sperry. [12]

Key issue: reductionism

Reductionism is the idea that complex things can always be reduced to (or explained by) simpler things. This is applied to objects, phenomena, explanations and theories.

So if we look at the subject of chemistry we can see that all the chemical elements are made up of the physical particles as described by physicists. If we look at biology we can see that all life is made up of chemical elements, and if we look at psychology we can see that all behaviour is carried out by biological systems. Follow the argument back and we can hope to explain everything in terms of their basic particles and everything then becomes physics. Reductionists believe that psychology can only become a genuine science if it bases itself on biology.

> Reductionism is the idea that the nature of complex things can be reduced to the sum of simpler or more fundamental things. This is believed to be true for objects, phenomena, explanations, theories, and meanings.
>
> Holism is the idea that living matter or reality is made up of organic or unified wholes that are greater than the simple sum of their parts.

Reductionism and the machine metaphor

The idea of reductionism is commonly attributed to the philosopher **René Descartes** (1596–1650). He argued that in order to discover what makes things tick in our world we need to adopt a 'rational analysis' of everything in it. That means we have look for the components of things to understand how they work. This is the reductionist approach. Descartes suggested that the world is like a machine and the best way to figure out how the machine works is to take it apart and look at the bits. Many of us have done this with various household appliances but be warned that stage two (putting the bits back together again) is much trickier than stage one.

Descartes argued that animals are complicated examples of machines. In his view they are just bundles of reflexes, responding automatically to whatever stimuli the world presents. If this is the case then it raises some difficult questions about what life is. If an animal is a biological machine and we think it is alive, then what about your computer? That is also a machine capable of complex activities. Is the computer also alive?

Descartes did not suggest that humans are just machines. He suggested instead that we have the body of a machine but this machine is operated by a soul. This mirrors our experience of life in that we seem to have control over the machine for at least some of the time. But the problem for us to deal with is where is this ghost (or soul) in the machine, where does it come from and where does it go?

There is no doubt that the reductionist approach is very useful in scientific enquiry. It can focus in on a problem and isolate variables that are having an effect. The issue is whether it provides a complete picture of things and events or whether, by identifying the components, it just gives us one part of a much bigger story.

A drawing by Descartes showing his view of the human visual system. It presents a person as a biological machine.

Cracking cheese Gromit

Wallace and Gromit illustrate the problem of reductionism. We know that they are not really alive (sorry to have to tell you this) and in fact their movements are painstakingly created by Aardman Animations who move the models bit by bit. The story can be reduced to a series of simple movements and if you watch a documentary on how the films are made you can see the plasticine models being moulded and moved. The magic of this is that the final result of all these small movements is a film that brings laughter (and a few tears) to millions. The models appear to be alive. On one level we can explain the Wallace and Gromit phenomena in terms of the movements of plasticine characters (the reductionist explanation) but the films have extra ingredients that can't be described in terms of the simple movements. Sometimes people refer to this by saying *'the whole is greater than the sum of the parts'*. Reductionism takes us so far, but it doesn't seem to give us the whole picture.

Baking cakes

Can we explain everything by breaking it down into its constituent parts? Think about a cake (turn this into a practical activity if you like). A cake is made up of a number of ingredients which you can put out on the table. They don't look much, but put together in a particular way they create some new qualities that none of the ingredients has by itself. The whole cake is much more than the ingredients that make it up. Somehow the whole cake gains some extra qualities, so if you just look at the ingredients you could not guess what it will become when it is baked.

Holistic approaches

The alternative to reductionist explanations is to take a holistic approach. Such approaches focus on systems as a whole rather than on the constituent parts. The holistic view is that you can't predict how the whole system will behave from a knowledge of its components; that reductionist explanations can only play a limited role in helping us to understand behaviour and may even prevent us from discovering some useful explanations. However, holistic approaches don't provide simple answers. It is a line of argument that is sometimes useful and sometimes not.

Examples of reductionist explanations in psychology

Behaviourism
Behaviourists attempt to explain all learning in terms of simple associations (see page 60). What looks like clever and thoughtful behaviour in an animal is, according to behaviourists, just a series of responses learnt by trial and error. For example, some hamsters can learn to climb upside down along the top of their cage to make a bold escape attempt. They haven't planned it out, they have learned what is successful and what isn't.

Theory of evolution
The theory of evolution is used to explain human behaviour in terms of adaptiveness and genetics. The theory assumes that everything we do must in some way enhance our reproductive success and hence the survival of our genes. In subsequent generations only the genes for adaptive behaviours will survive.

Medical model of mental disorders
The belief that complex psychological events are caused by simple chemical changes is reductionist. An example of this is the condition known as GPI (general paresis of the insane) in which a person suddenly develops a degenerative mental condition. At the beginning of the twentieth century it was believed to be a mental illness; however, it was eventually found to be the final stage of the sexually transmitted disease, syphilis. GPI is now rare because syphilis can be successfully treated before it attacks the brain. What if all mental disorders can be reduced to a simple answer like this? The reductionist approach says this will happen when we know more about the brain.

Activity

Reductionism is a useful method for answering some problems but not others. For example if we want to find out the cause of an illness then it is a good idea to study each variable individually and eliminate the ones that have no effect. Eventually we might find a single cause for the illness and be able to treat it, though it is fair to say that this approach does not work for every illness. On the other hand if we want to find out what an emotion like love is then it is more difficult to see how we can reduce it to its component parts, though you can have a try if you like.

Make two lists of ideas in psychology, one list of ideas that can be examined with a reductionist approach and one list of ideas that require a more holistic approach.

Reductionism: the explanation of life, the universe and everything?
The argument for reductionism runs as follows, when we look at complex problems like how human society works then we might start with

SOCIOLOGY (the study of groups of people), but if we can reduce our explanations to the components of groups then we get to ...

PSYCHOLOGY (the study of individual people), and if we focus down on the component parts of people we get to ...

BIOLOGY (the study of organic matter), and if we reduce our explanations to the components of living organisms we get to ...

CHEMISTRY (the study of inorganic matter) and if we reduce our explanations to the building blocks of inorganic materials we get to ...

PHYSICS (the study of matter and energy). So if we want to find out why people commonly live in families and decorate their bathrooms with tiles with cute pictures of dolphins we should study physics.

Life, the universe, and everything

Will physics ever be able to explain why human beings cover their bathroom walls with rubbish pictures of dolphins?

Qs

1 Select **one** core study and describe the basic components identified in this study.

2 Briefly discuss **two** advantages and **two** disadvantages of reductionism, using examples from this study.

3 As you work your way through the core studies make a list of the key components in every study. What are they reducing the behaviour to? Is this a useful way to think about the concepts they are studying?

...Links to other studies and issues...

The **reductionist** approach is a very useful tool for scientists because it promises to give simple answers to difficult questions. It is also part of the way we think in everyday life. Think about what you say when you realise you are starting to get a cold, you look for an immediate CAUSE of that cold, like someone sneezing on you yesterday or being caught in the rain. The more likely answer is much more complicated and will involve your general health, your immune system and your state of mind, but what we want to know is a simple cause. Among the core studies, the study on the taxi drivers (**Maguire et al.**) looks to one part of the brain to explain their extraordinary skills of navigation, and the study on autism (**Baron-Cohen et al.**) looks to one central cognitive deficit as an explanation of the condition.

Reductionism also links to some of the other issues, in particular **determinism and free will** because if we can reduce our behaviour to, for example, a series of chemical changes this will challenge the idea that we have control over our lives.

End paper: the biological approach

The biological approach

The biological approach has an underlying assumption that people are biological machines. These biological machines are made up of chemicals and cells which control our thoughts, feelings and behaviour. This approach includes both genetics and physiology. In this chapter our focus has been on biological research, in other words the influence of the physical elements of your body (see page 222 for a discussion of genetics and evolution).

One strength of the biological approach is that there is a lot of evidence concerning the influence of the brain on behaviour. The fact that we can't explain all behaviour in this way is seen by biological psychologists as being because we have yet to discover all the mechanisms of the brain but that one day we will be able to map out the physiology of behaviour in the way that we have mapped out the human genome.

The main problem with this approach is that it does not correspond to our experience of being alive. We experience our lives as if we have choices. If our lives are just the product of chemical reactions then there can be no choice. And if there is no choice then there can be no good or bad, no right from wrong. This problem is explored in the sections on reductionism (page 140) and determinism (page 120).

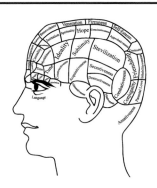

Phrenology is the attempt to identify personal characteristics by 'reading' the bumps of the skull. It is based on the idea that certain functions are located in certain parts of the brain and that these will be visible in the shape of the skull.
You will often find a modern phrenology head on the desks of psychology lecturers. Nobody knows why this is.

Biological machines

If we think of people as biological machines then it suggests certain solutions to everyday problems. Look at the following quote from physiological psychologist Peter Milner:

'I am interested in organisms as pieces of machinery, and I would like to know much the same about them as I once wanted to know about the gadgets I saw around me: first, what happens when the controls or inputs are manipulated and, a little later, how it happens' (Milner, 1970, page 1).

This quote has a strange irony to it. If I went to my doctor and said 'I feel like a machine. I am a gadget. One of my bits is going wrong, could you fix it please', the doctor might regard this statement as a sign of my mental instability and immediately send for the straight-jacket. If, on the other hand, I make this statement to a conference of psychologists, and make it not about myself but about 'people', then I can be hailed as a scientific genius.

The idea that we can regard people as objects in science means that people might be treated as objects in everyday life. When objects break down we fix them by the use of spare parts (brain surgery) or by throwing them away (murder). It is difficult not to be shocked at such a brutal approach to people and to such a pessimistic vision of human behaviour and experience.

The history of biological psychology

Brain science goes back centuries and there is evidence that people were doing simple brain operations thousands of years ago. For example the technique of *trepanation* (making a hole in the head) was carried out in Africa, Europe and South America. There is evidence of South American people doing this using surgical tools made of bronze and sharp-edged volcanic rock 4000 years ago. It is believed that trepanation was used for both spiritual and magical reasons, as well as to treat headaches, epilepsy and mental illness. As techniques became more sophisticated people would have the 'stone of madness' removed from their skulls by the travelling barber.

The story of the biological approach in psychology starts with the French scientist and philosopher **René Descartes** (see page 140). At the time he was writing, a number of scientists were studying the human body as if it were a machine. Descartes suggested that we are made up of two principal components, a body and a soul. He argued that a body without a soul would be an automaton that was completely controlled by external stimuli and its internal chemistry. According to Descartes we are a ghost in a machine, and he set about trying to understand how the machine works.

It was not until the demonstrations of **Franz Josef Gall** (1758–1828) that we realised the brain is the control centre of this machine. Unfortunately, Gall went on to develop the bogus science of phrenology which attempted to read a person's personality through an analysis of the shape of their skull. Phrenology was based on the idea that the shape of the skull exactly matched the shape of the brain, which is sadly not true. Brain research was moved on by French scientist Pierre Flourens who systematically removed parts of animals' brains in order to observe the effects.

The brain and cognition

If there are areas of the brain that control specific movements then maybe there are also areas for cognitive functions. One of the early examples of evidence for this came from the work of Paul Broca (1824–1880) who was able to show that a small area of the brain is responsible for the production of speech. Damage to this area renders a person speechless even though they can still understand the spoken word. This area is still referred to as Broca's area. Some of the work has been surprisingly disappointing, such as the attempt by Karl Lashley (1890–1959) to look for the part of the brain responsible for memory. Despite decades of work with rats in which he systematically removed parts of their brains to observe the effects on their memory, he was unable to find a specific site. He eventually proposed the *Law of Mass Action* which states that the decline in performance of the animal is related to the amount of brain tissue that is removed rather than which bit is removed.

The past hundred years has seen an explosion in brain research and we now know a lot more about how the brain is wired and how it influences our behaviour. Most recently the development of a range of scanning techniques has allowed us to observe the brain while it is actually working. Despite all this research the big questions still remain unanswered. In particular what makes the collection of chemicals and cells in the brain become the reflective, thinking, feeling organism that is aware of itself and able to act and make choices. If there isn't a ghost in the machine then how is this biological machine managing to work itself?

Applications of the biological approach

Serotonin and Prozac

There is currently a widely held theory that depression is caused by lowered levels of the neurochemical serotonin. The basic idea here is that depression is mainly a biological condition and can be alleviated by chemicals that boost the levels of *serotonin*. The most common class of drugs to do this is SSRIs (selective serotonin reuptake inhibitors); the most commonly known is Prozac.

In the UK in 2002 there were over 26 million prescriptions for anti-depressants (costing nearly £400 million) of which around 60% were for SSRIs (DoH statistics). The number of antidepressants taken in the UK has trebled in ten years. There is little difference in the effectiveness of the many different antidepressant drugs though there is a difference in price as the SSRIs are much more expensive, so the cost to the NHS has gone up by 20 times in the same ten years.

Between 60% and 80% of people report improvement in their mood or behaviour when taking antidepressants.

Among the problems with SSRIs are the side effects of which the most worrying is the evidence linking the drug to suicidal thoughts. The UK government recommends that SSRIs are not given to under-18s for this reason.

Descartes did not suggest that humans are just machines. He suggested instead that we have the body of a machine but this machine is operated by a soul. This mirrors our experience of life in that we seem to have control over the machine for at least some of the time. But the problem for us to deal with is where is this ghost (or soul) in the machine, where does it come from and where does it go?

The big issue with taking any drug to change your mood is the idea that a single chemical in a complex structure like the brain will bring about changes in complex emotions like depression. Depression has many causes. Sometimes it is events that overwhelm us like the loss of a job, and sometimes it is an illness that brings about a change in our daily activities. It might also be influenced by internal changes such as our chemical balance. The problem is to see how so many different experiences can be alleviated by one simple action.

Brains are not just for thinking

There is an online museum of Scientifically Accurate Fabric Brain Art (http://harbaugh.uoregon.edu/Brain/). This is the world's largest collection of anatomically correct fabric brain art, including the brain on the right knitted by Karen Norberg. The museum's curator says 'While our artists make every effort to insure accuracy, we cannot accept responsibility for the consequences of using fabric brain art as a guide for functional magnetic resonance imaging, trans-cranial magnetic stimulation, neurosurgery, or single-neuron recording.' There is also a sister site, the Gallery of Wooden Brain Art. And you might take a look at the Brain Handbag (see http://www.mindhacks.com/blog/2007/11/a_handbag_shaped_li.html). It is clear that the idea that we only use 10% of our handbag is a myth.

Animals on Prozac

It has been suggested that Prozac 'makes people more human' but if that is the case what does it do to the many animals it has been given to? Marc Abrahams is the editor of the *Annals of Improbable Research* and he collected a list of examples which included,

- The treatment of bears kept in captivity to reduce their repetitive pacing behaviours.
- Investigating the social behaviour of male and female prairie voles.
- The backward tumbling response of pigeons.
- Ventilatory control of goats (make of that what you will).
- The effect of prozac on stress responses in mice.
- The investigation of aggressive responses in lobsters and their decisions to fight or retreat.

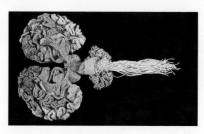

Perhaps the most famous example is the work of Peter Fong, of Gettysburg College in Pennsylvania, who gave Prozac to clams. The effect was that the clams began reproducing at ten times their normal rate. For this work, Professor Fong was awarded the 1998 IgNobel Biology Prize (http://www.improb.com/).

Psychosurgery

Psychosurgery can be dated to a research report given at a talk in London by Jacobsen and Fulton in 1935. They had been training two chimpanzees to carry out a memory task. One of them, called Becky, was particularly temperamental and became very distressed when she failed the task. She would fly into a tantrum and refuse to try again. Fulton and Jacobsen surgically removed part of the frontal lobes of her cerebral hemispheres which have a lot of connections with the *limbic system*. They reported that Becky no longer became distressed during the memory task.

Egas Moniz was at the talk and speculated whether it would be possible to reduce anxiety states in people by a similar operation. Within a year, Moniz had started to carry out *frontal lobotomies* on distressed patients. By 1950 over 20,000 people around the world had been treated in this way, including prisoners and children.

Was the operation effective? As with many forms of treatment, the effectiveness was assessed by the people carrying out the operations. Surprisingly enough, they thought that the operations were very successful. However, it eventually became clear that the benefits of this sort of gross destruction of brain tissue were often very small, and sometimes the consequences were disastrous. Moniz himself, who won the Nobel prize in 1949, was shot in the spine by one of his own lobotomised patients. This operation is relatively rarely used today, but it is worth reflecting on how the report of one chimpanzee's behaviour could lead to so many people having their brains mashed.

Psychosurgery was popularised in the United States by Walter Freeman who invented the brutal technique known as 'ice pick lobotomy', a procedure which literally used an ice pick and a rubber mallet instead of standard surgical equipment to perform a lobotomy. The technique left no visible scars and could be carried out under local anaesthetic. Tens of thousands of people were given this barbaric treatment during the middle period of the last century and often to little positive effect.

Activity

One way of exploring how common the biological approach is in our everyday explanations is to look at the way we describe daily activities. Make a list of the things that we do or explanations that we make that have some biological assumptions behind them. This list can include things you eat or drink, and changes you think happen inside you such as hormones.

Just to get you started, what about having a cup of coffee in the morning to help us get up. It assumes (largely correctly) that the chemicals in coffee will give us a lift.

Biological core study 7: Maguire *et al.* (brain scanning)

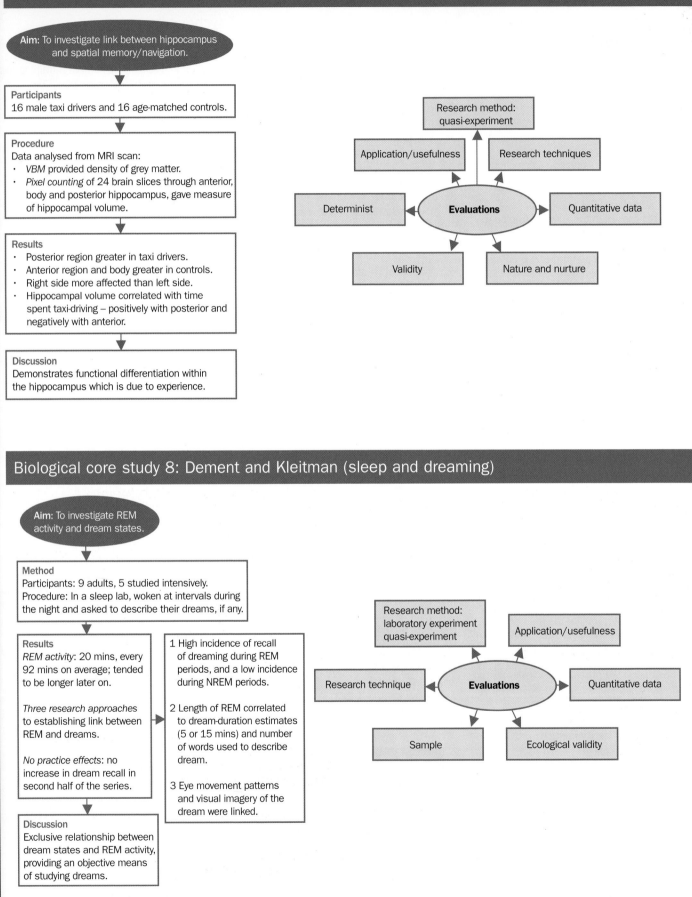

Aim: To investigate link between hippocampus and spatial memory/navigation.

Participants
16 male taxi drivers and 16 age-matched controls.

Procedure
Data analysed from MRI scan:
· *VBM* provided density of grey matter.
· *Pixel counting* of 24 brain slices through anterior, body and posterior hippocampus, gave measure of hippocampal volume.

Results
· Posterior region greater in taxi drivers.
· Anterior region and body greater in controls.
· Right side more affected than left side.
· Hippocampal volume correlated with time spent taxi-driving – positively with posterior and negatively with anterior.

Discussion
Demonstrates functional differentiation within the hippocampus which is due to experience.

Research method: quasi-experiment

Application/usefulness

Research techniques

Determinist

Evaluations

Quantitative data

Validity

Nature and nurture

Biological core study 8: Dement and Kleitman (sleep and dreaming)

Aim: To investigate REM activity and dream states.

Method
Participants: 9 adults, 5 studied intensively.
Procedure: In a sleep lab, woken at intervals during the night and asked to describe their dreams, if any.

Results
REM activity: 20 mins, every 92 mins on average; tended to be longer later on.

Three research approaches to establishing link between REM and dreams.

No practice effects: no increase in dream recall in second half of the series.

1 High incidence of recall of dreaming during REM periods, and a low incidence during NREM periods.

2 Length of REM correlated to dream-duration estimates (5 or 15 mins) and number of words used to describe dream.

3 Eye movement patterns and visual imagery of the dream were linked.

Discussion
Exclusive relationship between dream states and REM activity, providing an objective means of studying dreams.

Research method: laboratory experiment quasi-experiment

Application/usefulness

Research technique

Evaluations

Quantitative data

Sample

Ecological validity

Biological core study 9: Sperry (split brain)

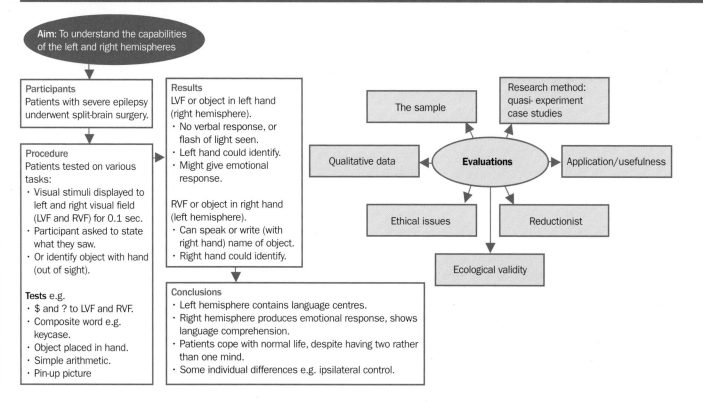

Aim: To understand the capabilities of the left and right hemispheres

Participants
Patients with severe epilepsy underwent split-brain surgery.

Procedure
Patients tested on various tasks:
- Visual stimuli displayed to left and right visual field (LVF and RVF) for 0.1 sec.
- Participant asked to state what they saw.
- Or identify object with hand (out of sight).

Tests e.g.
- $ and ? to LVF and RVF.
- Composite word e.g. keycase.
- Object placed in hand.
- Simple arithmetic.
- Pin-up picture

Results
LVF or object in left hand (right hemisphere).
- No verbal response, or flash of light seen.
- Left hand could identify.
- Might give emotional response.

RVF or object in right hand (left hemisphere).
- Can speak or write (with right hand) name of object.
- Right hand could identify.

Conclusions
- Left hemisphere contains language centres.
- Right hemisphere produces emotional response, shows language comprehension.
- Patients cope with normal life, despite having two rather than one mind.
- Some individual differences e.g. ipsilateral control.

Evaluations
- The sample
- Research method: quasi-experiment case studies
- Qualitative data
- Application/usefulness
- Ethical issues
- Reductionist
- Ecological validity

Further reading and other things

A good place to start is *Tall Tales about the Mind and Brain* (2007) by Sergio Della Sala. The book presents a sweeping survey of common myths about the mind and brain. In a lighthearted and accessible style, it exposes the truth behind these beliefs, how they are perpetuated, why people believe them, and why they might even exist in the first place. There are a number of other excellent texts about the remarkable workings of the brain that explore the ideas by describing case studies of ordinary people. The work of Oliver Sachs (for example, *The Man who Mistook his Wife for a Hat*) or V. S. Ramachandran (for example, *Phantoms in the Brain*) is well worth taking the time to read.

One remarkable science fiction that draws directly on the work of Roger Sperry is *A Scanner Darkly* by Philip K. Dick. The book and the subsequent film with Keanu Reaves explores the consequences of living with a split brain. Another common theme in the movies is of people who lose control of part of their body so, for example, their right hand becomes homicidal and starts killing people even though the owner doesn't want to do it. In the scientific literature this is often referred to as anarchic hand and a Google search will bring up a lot of interesting information on this phenomenon.

Maguire et al.
- Original article (and other related articles) at http://www.fil.ion.ucl.ac.uk/Maguire/a_level.html
- Cabbies' brain power. Some interesting anecdotes and some other links. http://news.bbc.co.uk/1/hi/sci/tech/677202.stm
- Interview with Eleanor Maguire about her research, http://www.abc.net.au/rn/talks/8.30/helthrpt/stories/s345.htm

Dement and Kleitman
- Original article can be obtained from your local library by giving them the full reference and ordering a photocopy.
- Series 'How the body works' on YouTube e.g. http://www.youtube.com/watch?v=M9XVm-ks1ME&mode=related&search=Brain%20waves
- Science of sleep http://www.bbc.co.uk/science/humanbody/sleep/articles/whatissleep.shtml

Sperry
- Original article at http://people.uncw.edu/Puente/sperry/sperrypapers/60s/135–1968.pdf
- YouTube videos of split brain patients e.g. (http://www.youtube.com/watch?v=ZMLzP1VCANo)

MCQ answers

Maguire et al. (MCQs on page 119)	1c 2d 3b 4c 5a 6c 7a 8d 9a 10b
Dement and Kleitman (MCQs on page 129)	1d 2b 3c 4a 5d 6d 7a 8c 9b 10b
Sperry (MCQs on page 139)	1c 2b 3d 4a 5a 6c 7d 8c 9b 10c

1   (a) Briefly describe the experimental group and the control group in the study on brain scanning by Maguire *et al*.   [2]

     (b) Why do psychologists use control groups in experimental research?   [2]

Stig's answer

(a) The experimental group was the taxi drivers. The control group was normal people.

(b) You have to use control groups to act as a comparison, to control for the results.

Chardonnay's answer

(a) The experimental group were 16 male taxi drivers who had a minimum of 1½ years experience. Their mean age was 44 (range 32–62). The control group were a group of normal adult males, age-matched with the taxi drivers.

(b) A control group means you have something to compare the experimental group to. If you found that one participant had a higher activity in the right hemisphere you don't know if this is abnormal or not unless you have something to compare this with.

Examiner's comments

Stig, your part (a) needs a bit more detail (look at Chardonnay's answer) to really show the examiner what you know. Part (b) is fine, but to ensure the full marks you need to communicate the idea of a control group acting as a benchmark or point of reference, i.e. 'comparing against the norm'.

Chardonnay, you are flaunting your knowledge in part (a) with bags of detail, more than sufficient for two marks.

Your part (b) communicates to the examiner a good understanding of the idea of the control group acting as a benchmark for normal brain activity.

Stig (1 + 1 marks) Chardonnay (2 + 2 marks)

---

2   (a) From the study by Maguire *et al*. outline **two** differences between the brain scans of the taxi drivers and the control group.   [2]

     (b) Outline **one** conclusion that can be drawn from these differences.   [2]

Stig's answer

(a) One difference is that the brains of the controls had a larger anterior hippocampus than in the brains of the taxi drivers whereas the posterior hippocampus was larger in the taxi drivers.

(b) These differences show that the brains of taxi drivers and normal people are different which must be due to the fact that they use their spatial memory more than most people.

Chardonnay's answer

(a) In the taxi drivers there was a correlation between time spent driving taxis and the size of their hippocampus. There was a positive correlation for the posterior hippocampus and a negative correlation for the anterior hippocampus.

(b) We can conclude from this that the size of the hippocampus changes as a consequence of learning navigational skills, which suggests that the changes are not innate but due to experience.

Examiner's comments

Not the most elegant phrasing Stig but you have described the two key differences accurately. In part (b) you have failed to give a conclusion – you have just stated the finding (their brains are different) and then offered an explanation which is not the same as a conclusion. A conclusion is an interpretation of the results – what do they show us? It helps to start a conclusion with the phrase 'This suggests that ...'.

Chardonnay has managed to provide a sound conclusion but her answer for part (a) falls short of the mark. She has given a finding but not one which is a difference between the taxi drivers and controls. This means she fails to gain any marks for part (b) because it doesn't relate to differences.

Stig (2 + 0 marks) Chardonnay (0 + 0 marks)

---

3   Dement and Kleitman investigated the relationship between sleep and dreaming.

     (a) Outline **one** finding from this study about the relationship between sleep and dreaming.   [2]

     (b) Give **one** reason why the conclusions of this study might not be valid.   [2]

Stig's answer

(a) They found that dreaming occurred in one particular kind of sleep – REM sleep. Participants reported dreams almost every time they were woken from REM sleep but rarely at other times.

(b) One reason why this conclusion may not be valid is that the study only looked at adults and even then it was only a few adults so we can't be certain that this is representative.

Chardonnay's answer

(a) There was a correlation between the length of REM activity and the number of words a participant used to describe a dream.

(b) One problem with the study was that it lacked ecological validity.

Examiner's comments

Stig, a good answer and I am glad you conveyed the idea that whilst dreaming mostly occurred in REM sleep, it did also occur on a few occasions (11/160 wakings) in NREM.

In part (b) you give a thorough explanation of why the study might lack validity – because of certain unique characteristics of the sample.

Chardonnay, spot on. You have reported a finding related to Dement and Kleitman's second hypothesis and this answers the question well.

Part (b) is too brief. The addition of just a bit of extra information would turn this into 2 marks, for example 'It was conducted in a laboratory'.

Stig (2 + 2 marks) Chardonnay (2 + 1 marks)

4   Dement and Kleitman investigated the link between REM sleep and dreaming. Identify **four** characteristics of REM sleep.   [4]

Stig's answer

They are rapid eye movements, faster brain activity, having dreams and can't remember another.

Chardonnay's answer

The four characteristics are that people have random eye movements. Fast EEG activity which shows that the brain is very active. The research by Dement and Kleitman showed that people very frequently have dreams in REM sleep and it is more likely to occur later in the night.

Examiner's comments

Tough question, but you've had a good stab at it, Stig, identifying three legitimate characteristics but lost out on the final marks because four were required.

Chardonnay, you are on sparkling form! You have correctly identified four characteristics of REM.

Stig (3 marks) Chardonnay (4 marks)

5   Sperry commented on his study of split-brain patients that: 'the second hemisphere does not know what the first hemisphere has been doing'.

   (a) Describe **one** piece of evidence from his study that supports this statement.   [2]
   (b) Explain why split brain patients do not experience problems as a result of this in their everyday lives.   [2]

Stig's answer

(a) When Sperry showed a dollar sign to the right visual field and a question mark to the left visual field, the split brain patient could recognise the dollar sign with his left hand but couldn't say what it was.

(b) In everyday life people don't see things for a split second so they have time for the thing to be seen by both hemispheres.

Chardonnay's answer

(a) Patients who were given two objects to hold in each hand then could recognise the objects but only using the hand that had originally held the object.

(b) This doesn't matter in everyday life because you usually can look at an object using both eyes rather than just touching it.

Examiner's comments

Stig, you have got a bit confused … easily done in this study. Remember, Left Visual Field is processed by the Right Hemisphere (no language) which, in turn, controls the left hand. It helps to find some way of remembering this, such as the diagram on page 135.

But Stig, you have got part (b) right...

...which is more than Chardonnay who has lost her fizz! Your part (a) is fine, but your part (b) is not clear. Be careful in this study not to confuse eyes with visual fields. They are not the same thing!

Stig (0 + 2 marks) Chardonnay (2 + 0 marks)

6   In Sperry's study of split brain patients the capabilities of each brain hemisphere were studied.

   (a) Give **one** result from this study that demonstrates the language limitations of the right hemisphere of the brain.   [2]
   (b) Give **one** result from this study that demonstrates that the right hemisphere is not completely unable to understand words.   [2]

Stig's answer

(a) The right hemisphere doesn't have any language because if something is shown to the left visual field it can't be named.

(b) The right hemisphere is not totally word blind because, in some patients, they could identify an object with their left hand if the word was shown to their right hemisphere.

Chardonnay's answer

(a) In one of the studies that Sperry did, they showed the word 'keycase' to the patient. The patient only reported the word 'case' because this was in the right visual field (left hemisphere).

(b) The right hemisphere isn't completely word blind because it can sometimes respond to words.

Examiner's comments

Stig, you've got the visual field-hemisphere link right this time in part (a) and your part (b) is spot on too.

Chardonnay, your part (a) is on the right track, though really you should have explained why the patients could not report the word 'key', as this relates to the lack of language ability in the right hemisphere. This would have given your answer better focus. In part (b) you would get one mark for the word 'respond', but for the second mark you would need to say how e.g. by pointing/picking up an object with the left hand.

Stig (2 + 2 marks) Chardonnay (1 + 1 marks)

7 (a) Outline **one** assumption of the biological approach in psychology. [2]
  (b) Describe how the biological approach could explain navigation. [4]
  (c) Describe **one** similarity and **one** difference between the study by Maguire *et al*. and any other biological study. [6]
  (d) Discuss the strengths and limitations of the biological approach, using examples from the study by Maguire *et al*. [12]

Total [24]

Chardonnay's answer

(a) One assumption of the biological approach is that behaviour can be explained by biological or physiological occurrences or processes. Thus, genes, brain functioning, hormones are all very important for what we do and how we behave.

(b) The biological approach could explain navigation in terms of a number of things. For example, as a species, we may all be somehow genetically predisposed to be able to find our way around and be able to find our way home as once upon a time our survival would have depended upon it. Also, the biological approach would explain navigation in terms of which parts of the brain are specialised in storing mental maps. In this study, it is the hippocampus.

(c) Maguire is similar to Dement and Kleitman because they both are interested in the brain and use scanning technology. Maguire uses MRI scanning and Dement and Kleitman use EEG.

Maguire is different from Dement and Kleitman because Maguire looks at a particular part of the brain – i.e. the hippocampus – and is interested in its size. Dement and Kleitman were not measuring any particular brain part, but overall brain activity as measured by the EEG. The EEG is used by attaching electrodes to the scalp and gives a live and continuous read out of changes in brain activity. MRI maps the structure of the brain tissue rather than activity. Also, it is a bit like a snapshot photo taken at one moment in time and does not show any changes as they are happening.

(d) One strength of the biological approach is that it is very scientific. It uses scientific equipment and generally the experimental method. It always takes place in controlled conditions. All together, this means that the results are usually valid and have high status. For example, in Maguire, they use some of the latest scanning technology and the study takes place in a laboratory. VBM and pixel counting to measure the volume of the hippocampus is very scientific. The downside to this is that this is quite a dehumanising way to study human beings – as if they were chemicals or lab rats.

Another strength of the biological approach is that it can help develop treatments and therapies for certain illnesses or problems. For example, you can use drugs to treat insomnia or mental illnesses. In rarer cases, brain surgery may be a good treatment. However, all these treatments have side effects which are sometimes quite severe.

One weakness of the biological approach is that it does not always show cause and effect. It might show that being a taxi driver is associated with a larger hippocampus (posterior region), but it doesn't show that this is *because* of being a taxi driver. It may be that the taxi drivers had this already and it helped them to pass The Test – i.e. that the larger hippocampus caused them to become taxi drivers. So, we do not always know the direction of cause and effect. However, Maguire might say that this is not true because she correlated the size of the hippocampus with number of years of taxi driving and found a positive correlation. This supports her idea that the brain has changed (morphed) because of the taxi driving.

Another weakness of the biological approach is that it treats people like nothing more than complex machines or living organisms. This is very determinist and doesn't look at people as a whole. For example, the biological approach ignores other important aspects of navigation such as the cognitive aspects.

Examiner's comments

(a) Spot on Chardonnay – you have identified a range of biological explanations for human behaviour.

(b) This is excellent, Chardonnay, more than enough for full marks here. You show a good understanding of both the biological approach as well as navigation. You use specialist terminology appropriately (genetically predisposed, hippocampus, mental maps etc).

(c) You have provided one similarity and one difference, but these are not in equal depth. The similarity is a good valid point but you could have developed it a bit more. The difference you identify is very good and shows a more than appropriate understanding in the differences between the two technologies and what they can measure in the brain. Therefore, 1 + 3 for this question part.

(d) Some good material here, Chardonnay – your discussion of the scientific nature of the biological approach is sufficiently detailed and well related to the study. You are able to pick out details of the procedure and make them relevant to your point;. Your discussion of the issue of the *direction* of cause and effect is also presented in a well-balanced and even handed way, showing a good analysis of the results and alternative explanations.

However, there are also some little mistakes. One minor one is that the test taken by taxi drivers is called 'The Knowledge'. Perhaps more importantly is that, for your second strength (therapies) you did not manage to relate this to the specified study. Also, in your second weakness, I think you have got mixed up between determinism and reductionism. This weakness could have done with further development – what do you mean by cognitive aspects? (e.g. how we remember landmarks or find some road layouts more difficult to remember than others) and some further discussion (are there any benefits to focusing upon a single feature such as the hippocampus for an experiment?).

All in all, your part (d) is still pretty good. There is a range of strengths and weaknesses, you have structured your answer coherently and you express yourself grammatically and spell well. The quality of your evaluation is generally good. Therefore, you would get top of band 3.

Chardonnay (2 + 4 + 4 + 9 marks = 19/24 marks)

CHAPTER 5

This chapter looks at three core studies in social psychology.

- Milgram's demonstration of obedience in situations requiring destructive behaviour.

- Reicher and Haslam's simulation of a prison environment to investigate the effects of group processes.

- Piliavin, Rodin and Piliavin's field experiment to study the factors that affect willingness to help in an emergency situation.

Social psychology

Introduction

What is Social Psychology?

Social psychology is concerned with social interaction and the phenomena of social behaviour. It looks at the behaviour of the individual within a social context. One of the most influential US psychologists of the twentieth century was Gordon W. Allport who defined social psychology as:

'With few exceptions, social psychologists regard their discipline as an attempt to understand and explain how the thought, feeling and behaviour of individuals is influenced by the actual, imagined or implied presence of others. The term "implied presence" refers to the many activities the individual carries out because of his position (role) in a complex social structure and because of his membership in a cultural group' (1968, p. 3).

This definition suggests that social psychology is mainly concerned with issues of social influence, and through the middle part of the twentieth century that was the case. Modern social psychology, however, has wider interests which we can group under the following headings:

- **Social perception and judgement** is about how we make sense of and judge people and groups.
- **Social interaction** is about how we relate to others and so includes areas such as conflict and cooperation and relationships.
- **Social influence** is concerned with the ways in which our interactions with other people affect the way we think, feel and behave and covers issues such as persuasion, attitude change, obedience and conformity.
- **Self-perception and identity** is concerned with how we make sense of ourselves and how we judge ourselves.

Social psychology attracts a lot of attention because it is about the events and processes that make up our daily lives. It looks at our feelings, our thoughts and our behaviour, and tries to describe and explain aspects of the human condition such as love and hate, happiness and sadness, pride and prejudice, comedy and tragedy. It is the personal science and it is about me and you.

And what makes it even more compelling is that everyone is an amateur social psychologist and if we weren't we would not be able to function in everyday life. Just walking down the street I have to make judgements about other people. At the extreme end of the scale I might judge whether they are potentially dangerous and avoid them if I judge them to be a risk. If I couldn't judge when someone has finished talking I would always be interrupting them in conversation. I make judgements about whether people like me, or find me funny, and I also make judgements about whether someone needs some support or maybe whether they are telling lies. In daily life I am a relatively competent social psychologist. The task of academic social psychology is systematically to investigate these processes.

Some social phenomena defy explanation by psychologists. World record attempts are one such social phenomena – people trying to outdo all other people. For example Colombian beekeeper Marian Tellez, 35, is shown here covered with Africanised bees in an attempt to set a new Guinness world record in Bucaramanga, Colombia, September 15, 2005.

It is remarkable that someone would choose to do this and it is even more remarkable that it is a world record attempt because this means others have done it before and there are rules for completing this task. Oh, by the way, Marian's record is an estimated 500,000 bees, beating the previous record of 350,000.

Social delusions

Published in 1841 and still in print today *Extraordinary Popular Delusions and the Madness of Crowds* by Charles Mackay is a history of popular follies. The book looks at how people come to believe in shared (i.e. social) irrational ideas. In the nineteenth century some people believed in the 'science' of alchemy that aimed to change all metal into gold and create a medicine that would cure all disease and give eternal life. Modern versions of such social delusions might be the beliefs in homeopathy or astrology. MacKay also wrote about economics where the price of a commodity rises beyond any realistic value before suddenly crashing. An example of this was the Dutch tulip mania of the early seventeenth century. During this mania, speculators from all walks of life bought and sold tulip bulbs, some of which briefly became the most expensive objects in the world, until the burst in 1637. Recently, the world stockmarkets saw a similar mania over technology stocks before the dot-com crash in 2002 slashed values and put many companies out of business. If we believe that an object is very valuable then we will pay a lot of money for it but if we stop believing then it becomes worthless.

Self perception

How do we know ourselves? A theory put forward by C.H. Cooley (1902) suggested that self-concept is influenced by an individual's beliefs about what other people think of him/her. We see ourselves reflected in the behaviour of others. If people laugh at my joke then I am funny, if they scowl at me, I am bad, and so on. People are a mirror to show me what I am like.

The mirror is not always accurate because I can misinterpret what people really think of me. Cooley says that we develop a sense of self by:

a   assessing how people see us;

b   assessing how people judge us;

c   putting our own judgement on these assessments.

Sometimes we perceive ourselves as others do and sometimes we get it very wrong. For example Dunning and Kruger (1999) explored the breadth and depth of human incompetence and, in particular, self-delusion. They hypothesised that incompetent people overestimate their own ability, citing the example of McArthur Wheeler, who robbed two banks in broad daylight while making no attempt to disguise himself. He was arrested that night after CCTV footage was shown on the news. When police showed him the surveillance tapes, Mr Wheeler was very surprised. He is reported to have mumbled 'But I wore the juice'. Mr Wheeler had been under the impression that rubbing his face with lemon juice would make it invisible to cameras.

Dunning and Kruger also asked people to rate how funny some jokes were and also to rate how good they were at judging humour. The people who were worst at judging humour (in the jokes) believed they were actually good at it. They got similar results with logic tests and law entrance exams. For this work the authors received the 2000 IgNobel Prize for Psychology.

Social influence: groupthink

An example of social influence is the work of Irving Janis on *groupthink*. Janis first used the term to describe a situation where each member of a group tries to match their opinion to those that they believe are held by the rest of the group. Although this is usually not a problem, in some situations the group might end up agreeing to a decision that each individual thinks is unwise. Sometimes a group of people can talk themselves into a bad decision.

Groupthink tends to occur on committees and in large organisations and Janis originally studied a number of military decisions made by US governments. He suggested some symptoms of groupthink which are shown below.

The Butler Report looked at how the UK arrived at the decision to attack Iraq in 2003. The report commented on the informal meetings that took place between a select group of advisers to Prime Minister Tony Blair. This was referred to as a 'kitchen cabinet' to describe where the discussions and decisions took place. The suggestion is that a small group of largely unelected advisers held meetings without formal rules and were led by the charisma of Tony Blair (*The Times*, 2004). Maybe they developed a groupthink, convincing each other that going to war was the best decision.

Did groupthink play a part in the decision to attack Iraq?

The symptoms of groupthink
1 Illusion of invulnerability
2 Unquestioned belief in the moral purpose of the group
3 Collective rationalisation of group's decisions
4 Shared stereotypes of outgroup, particularly opponents
5 Self-censorship; members withhold criticisms
6 An illusion that everyone agrees with the decision
7 Direct pressure on dissenters to conform
8 Self-appointed 'mindguards' who protect the group from negative information

Social influence   Social interaction

Self perception   Social perception

Social perception

An example of work on social perception is *attribution theory* – the theoretical models of Fritz Heider, Harold Kelley and Edward E. Jones. It is concerned with the ways in which people explain (or attribute) the behaviour of others. For example, it distinguishes between *situational* and *dispositional* explanations. Imagine you arrange to meet someone outside a club and they arrive late. You might well blame them because they didn't leave enough time to get there (dispositional explanation) whereas they might explain it as due to the bus not turning up (situational explanation). We commonly explain our own behaviour in terms of situations while believing that other people are personally in control of theirs. This bias is called the *fundamental attribution error* and is the cause of numerous domestic arguments. There are a number of other errors that we are prone to when we judge social behaviour but it is not fair to suggest that we are more wrong than right. We might have some biases but most of the time we are able to accurately read people's intentions and make intelligent predictions about their behaviour.

Social interaction

The start of social psychology is sometimes dated to 1897 and the experimental work of Norman Triplett into the effects of competition on performance. Triplett observed that racing cyclists achieved better times on a circuit when they had someone pacing them. In a ride of 25 miles the average times per mile were:

Alone:	2 min 29.9
With a pacer:	1 min 55.5
In competition:	1 min 50.4

He went on to observe this improved performance in other tasks and found, for example, that children wound fishing reels faster when there were other children also winding fishing reels in the same room.

...Connections...

If psychology is about human behaviour and experience then maybe all psychology is social psychology. Without other people we cannot survive our early years – it is very rare for an individual to survive and develop as an adult without social contact with other people. In this chapter we have included examples of research from mainstream social psychology, but elsewhere in the text there are many studies that have a social aspect to them. The cognitive study of **Loftus and Palmer** shows the influence of people on perceptual judgements, and the developmental studies of **Freud** and **Bandura et al.** are also about our social behaviour. In the final chapter of this book on individual differences there are papers on identity (**Thigpen and Cleckley**) and our social judgements of abnormality (**Rosenhan**).

MILGRAM: OBEDIENCE

Do as you are told

The big moral question in the middle of the twentieth century was how the horrors of the Second World War (1939–45) could have happened and how they could be prevented in the future. During that war the Nazi government in Germany initiated a policy to exterminate 'worthless' ethnic groups. This led to the deaths of millions of people of Jewish descent, and the killing also extended to the mentally ill, homosexuals, gypsies and people of Slavic descent. It is not easy to kill this number of people and so death camps were set up to increase the killing efficiency. Auschwitz was the most efficient camp established by the Nazi regime, peaking at 12,000 deaths a day. Although the total number of Jewish dead in Auschwitz will never be known for certain, estimates vary between one and two-and-a-half million.

Concentration camp victims

Who could do such a thing?

How could someone go to work each day to kill thousands of people and dispose of the bodies? The first response is to think of these people as monsters. They cannot be like us because we would not do these things. But can we be so sure of our humanity? Perhaps it was not monsters but ordinary people with ordinary lives who did these things. Social psychologists set out to investigate this and find out under what circumstances people will comply with authority.

Milgram was of Jewish descent and the killings of the Second World War had an enduring effect on his life and his work.

'The impact of the Holocaust on my own psyche energised my interest in obedience and shaped the particular form in which it was examined.' *(Milgram, cited in Blass, 2004, page 62)*

Solomon Asch carried out some studies on conformity to group pressure (Asch, 1955). Subjects were recruited to take part in a test of perception. They were asked to say which line from a choice of three matched the target line. Unknown to one subject in each group the rest of the group members were confederates of the experimenter and primed to give certain responses. For most of the trials they gave the obvious and correct answers, but on a few 'critical' trials they all gave the wrong answer. The subject was the last in the group to answer and had to listen to all the others giving their wrong answers. He then had to either give a different answer to the rest of the group or conform to the group pressure by giving a wrong answer. In around 40% of the trials, the subject conformed to the group.

Stanley Milgram worked with Asch while he was a postgraduate student and devised variations of Asch's study. In particular he carried out a cross-cultural version with data gathered in Norway, Paris and the USA (Milgram, 1960). He was interested in national character and devised an elaborate hoax to investigate it. As in the Asch study, subjects had to make a judgement in a group, but in this case they made the judgement in a single cubicle where they could not see the subjects but only hear them. In fact there were no other group members and the subject just heard recorded voices. When he returned to the USA he devised plans for a new study. He wanted to make the Asch study more relevant to everyday behaviour. His moment of inspiration came when he stopped thinking about how to change the level of conformity and asked just how far a person would go under the experimenter's orders. At that moment the obedience study was born.

Vietnamese civilians murdered by US troops during the My Lai massacre.

Atrocities

Atrocities happen in each generation. We commonly like to talk about them as being done by other people; people not like us and not part of our society but the truth is very different. In the history of Western Europe there are many atrocities big and small. One of the biggest was the slave trade that transported millions of Africans around the world with a callous disregard for life or welfare. There was also the incident, in 1937, when the Spanish dictator Franco invited the German airforce to bomb a market town of Guernica the Basque region of Spain killing and injuring many people. The list is endless.

The Milgram study is commonly related to the Second World War but even as he conducted his studies a new horror was unravelling in South East Asia where the USA had started a major conflict with the people of Vietnam. It is often referred to as the Vietnam War, though not if you are Vietnamese. The USA was finally defeated by the peasant army of the Vietnamese in 1973 with a loss of 55,000 American lives. Less commonly reported are the 1.5 million Vietnamese lives lost, many of whom were civilian peasants.

My Lai

Milgram commented on one particular act of savagery by the US Army. On the morning of March 16, 1968 a company of soldiers moved into the peasant village of My Lai looking for armed fighters. They found only women, children and the elderly, but they treated them as insurgents and tortured, raped and finally murdered them. Somewhere between 350 and 500 villagers were slaughtered before the killing frenzy was stopped when a US Army helicopter crew famously landed between the American troops and the remaining Vietnamese hiding in a bunker. The 24-year-old pilot, Warrant Officer Hugh Thompson, Jr., confronted the leaders of the troops and told them he would open fire on them if they continued their attack on civilians. This helicopter crew are still hailed as heroes today in Vietnam (www.cnn.com/WORLD/9803/16/my.lai) but were treated by many as traitors in the USA.

The massacre was covered up and denied for a year but eventually the information became public knowledge. Just one man (William Calley) was charged and eventually served three years under house arrest before being pardoned by President Nixon.

Milgram wanted to know how this event could happen. And there are many other issues to consider, for example:

- Some of the 120 soldiers on that patrol opted out of the killing. How did they do manage to do that while the others felt they had to obey orders?
- What factors led the helicopter crew to decide to intervene against their own colleagues?

The remarkable work of Stanley Milgram

Milgram's obedience study had such an impact that the variety and originality of his other work is often missed. He was one of the most innovative psychologists of the last century. The items on this page are just a selection of his work. If you want to know more then try his book *The Individual in the Social World* (1992).

Six degrees of separation

'It's a small world, isn't it?' we say to each other when we discover a personal connection with someone who lives miles away from us. In one of his many innovative studies, Milgram set out to test this idea in 1967. He asked some people from Kansas (in the Midwest of the USA) to send packages to a stranger in Massachusetts, on the East Coast several thousand miles away. The senders were told the stranger's name, occupation, and roughly where they lived. They were told to send the package to someone they knew on a first-name basis who they thought was most likely, out of all their friends, to know the target personally. That person would do the same, and so on, until the package was personally delivered to its target.

Milgram reported the results enthusiastically but also selectively. One of the packages got through in four days but it was one of the few that did. Most didn't make it but the ones that did were able to get there in about six hops. This led to the famous phrase 'six degrees of separation' which commonly appears in writings on the experience of urban life. It suggests that any two people in the world can be connected by an average of six acquaintances. It is a delightful idea and may well be right but Milgram did not find the clear evidence to support this.

Modern communications allow researchers to look at the small-world hypothesis again. A recent study of over 60,000 email users (Dodds *et al.*, 2003) attempted to reach one of 18 target people in 13 countries (including Estonia, India and Norway) by forwarding email messages to acquaintances. Most of the chain messages were not completed but there are many reasons for this, including apathy on the part of the people who were contacted and also email overload which is a new stress issue for many workers in the West. Using the chains that did reach their destinations the researchers calculated that social searches can reach their target in five to seven steps. So maybe Milgram was right after all.

Familiar strangers

Milgram noticed a strange phenomenon of city life: we regularly see people we recognise but never talk to or interact with. He called these people 'familiar strangers'. They might be the person who always gets on the same bus as you, or you see in the corner shop. Milgram got his students to carry out a novel study on these familiar strangers (Milgram, 1977). They chose a suburban railway platform and one morning photographed the commuters waiting for a train. The students numbered the people on the photograph and then a few weeks later gave out the pictures and a questionnaire. The students got on the train and by the time the train arrived in New York City 119 out of the 139 passengers had completed the survey.

On average the commuters reported seeing four familiar strangers in the picture but only having spoken to an average of 1.5. Other questions revealed that although 47% of the passengers had wondered about the familiar strangers, less than one-third reported feeling even a slight inclination to start a conversation.

Other techniques

Milgram devised too many research techniques to even mention here. We have given two examples but there was also the *dropped letter technique* to measure prejudice and helping behaviour, where he would leave un-posted letters addressed to organisations lying around in public places to see which organisation would attract the most support and get their letter posted.

He also developed techniques to investigate *obedience requests* on the subway trains, the *cyranos* (people saying the words written by someone else) and the *mental maps* of cities (the mental images that people have of the streets in their town). Psychologists can usually retire if they develop one new method; Milgram developed many.

www There is a group on Facebook called 'Six degrees of separation' which has demonstrated an average of 4 or 5 degrees of separation between its members – add your name to the nearly 400,000 members.

'The soldier does not wish to appear a coward, disloyal, or un-American. The situation has been so defined that he can see himself as patriotic, courageous, and manly only through compliance.' Stanley Milgram (www.stanleymilgram.com)

Biographical notes on Stanley Milgram

Stanley Milgram was born in New York City in 1933 to working class Jewish parents who had immigrated to the USA from Europe. Milgram excelled in all subjects at school where his classmate was Philip Zimbardo. His first degree was in political science but after a crash course in psychology he started a doctorate in psychology at Harvard University in 1954.

In 1960 he moved to Yale University and carried out the obedience studies for which he is most famous. The work was acknowledged by psychologists and the public but the controversy it caused affected his career. In 1967 he returned to New York to work at the City University where he stayed for the rest of his life. Milgram preferred to investigate topics that affected ordinary people in their everyday lives. For example, his mother-in-law is reported to have asked why people no longer give up their seats on subway trains so Milgram sent out teams of students to investigate this.

The Milgram family had a history of heart disease and Stanley survived four heart attacks before succumbing to the fifth in 1984. His work stills jumps off the pages of psychology books and magazine articles (see the excellent biography by Blass, 2004).

Stanley Milgram (1933–1984)

...Link to the core study...

Milgram's background as a political scientist and his concern to explain the Holocaust meant that he was drawn to the social psychology of conformity. His initial work looked at national differences in conformity to see whether it was the structure of a society that led people to carry out atrocities. He found that rates in different societies were fairly similar so Milgram came up with another approach. How far would you go in obeying unjust authority? Now read on.

Stanley Milgram (1963) Behavioural study of obedience.
Journal of Abnormal and Social Psychology, 67, pages 371--378.

Abstract

Obedience to legitimate authority was tested by asking subjects ('teachers') to administer increasingly strong electric shocks to another subject (the 'learner') every time he made a mistake on a learning task. The experiment took place in a laboratory at Yale University, where 40 male volunteers were selected.

Method

The naïve subject was deceived about the true aims of the experiment (he thought it was about learning) and deceived about the identity of the learner who was in fact a confederate.

When the shock level reached 300 volts the confederate banged on the wall and stopped responding. The experimenter delivered a standard set of 'prods' if the teacher suggested he should stop.

Subjects were debriefed after the experiment.

Results

Prior to the study psychology students estimated that less than 3% would go to the maximum shock level. In fact 65% of the subjects continued to the maximum voltage; only five participants (12.5%) stopped at 300 volts.

Discussion

The extent of destructive obedience and the tension shown were unexpected. Possible explanations include prestige of institution, sense of obligation to continue with the experiment, and the subject's lack of opportunity to think about or discuss what he was doing.

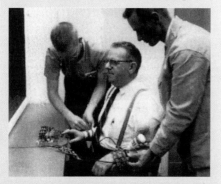

The learner is strapped into an 'electric chair apparatus' and an electrode attached to his wrist so he can receive shocks if he makes a mistake on the learning task.

Aim

Obedience is an indispensable part of social life. In order to live in communities some system of authority is required. The issue of obedience was particularly relevant in the 1960s, when explanations were sought for the inhumane obedience of Germans who systematically slaughtered millions of innocent people during the Second World War.

Obedience may be deeply ingrained in the human character and may be thought to be destructive, but we should also remember that it serves productive functions as well, such as acts of charity and kindness.

The aim of this study was to investigate the process of obedience, to demonstrate the power of a legitimate authority even when the command requires destructive behaviour.

The aims of this study are often described as the 'Germans are different hypothesis'. Milgram describes this in a film he made (but this aim is not given in the actual article published in 1963). He believed that the inhumane obedience of Nazi Germans could be explained by the fact that Germans are by disposition much more obedient than people from other cultures/countries; it is in their national character. Milgram intended to conduct this study with Germans but first wanted to run a pilot study, to see if his procedure worked. He did not expect high levels of obedience from Americans. As you will see, in reading this article, he actually found that Americans were highly obedient, evidence that obedience is due to situational rather than dispositional (personality) factors. The issue of situation versus personality is examined on page 160.

Note – you can obtain the film where Milgram describes his aims from Uniview.

Method

Participants

Milgram advertised for 500 New Haven men to take part in a scientific study of memory and learning at Yale University (see newspaper ad on right). Everyone was to be paid $4.50 (a reasonable sum of money in those days) simply for coming to the laboratory. The payment did not depend on remaining in the study.

The final group of subjects was selected from all those who volunteered, consisting of 40 men aged between 20 and 50, from various occupational and educational backgrounds (postal clerks, salesmen, engineers and labourers).

The part of the experimenter was played by a biology teacher, dressed in a technician's coat. The learner (or victim) was played by a 47-year-old accountant, trained for the role. Both of these men were accomplices of Milgram (confederates).

Procedure

Each subject was told that the experiment aimed to see how punishment affected learning. Each study would involve one teacher and one learner. The naïve subject was introduced to the other 'subject' (the accountant); lots were drawn for the parts of teacher and learner. The naïve subject always got the part of teacher.

Learner and teacher were taken to the experimental room where the learner was strapped into an 'electric chair apparatus' in order to prevent excessive movement when the electric shocks were delivered (see photograph on left). An electrode was attached to the learner's wrist and also attached to a shock generator in the next room. The experimenter advised them that, *'Although the shocks can be extremely painful, they cause no permanent tissue damage'* (page 373).

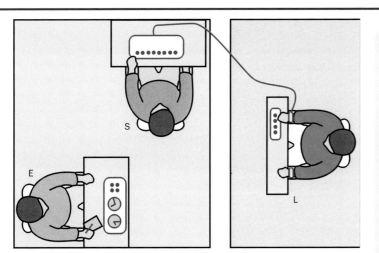

The study in a nutshell: experimenter (E) persuades subject (S) to give painful electric shocks to a 'learner' (L), seated in a separate room. The learner is strapped into his chair and an electrode placed on his wrist which is connected to the generator in order to administer the shocks. The learner provides answers using a four-way panel in front of him.

Qs

1 Why was it necessary to conduct a 'preliminary run' for the teacher and learner?

2 Identify five aspects of the method which were designed to increase the concern felt by the naïve subject.

3 If you felt uneasy about the experiment would you have felt able to take your money and go? Explain your answer.

4 Why do you think that it was important for the participants to be debriefed (Milgram used the term 'dehoaxed')?

5 Why do you think it was important to have a standardised set of responses for the experimenter?

6 Orne and Holland (1968) argued that the subjects didn't really believe the shocks were real because such things don't happen in a psychology experiment. What evidence is there that the subjects did believe the shocks were real?

Learning task

The teacher was asked to read a series of word pairs to the learner, and then read the first word of the pair along with four terms. The learner had to indicate which of the four terms was originally paired with the first word.

Shock generator

This machine had 30 switches each labelled with a number from 15 to 450 volts, in increments of 15 (see right). There were also labels to describe the intensity.

In order to convince the naïve subject that the shocks were genuine, they were given a sample shock of 45 volts, on their wrist.

The teacher was told to give a shock for a wrong response and, each time, to move one level higher on the shock generator. The teacher also had to announce the voltage each time, thus reminding him of the increasing intensity.

Preliminary and regular run

A pilot run of the experiment showed that it takes some time before subjects can get the procedure right so each subject (teacher) was given 10 words to read to the learner. The learner made 7 errors on this practice run and so received 7 shocks, reaching the moderate level of 105 volts.

Feedback from the victim

The learner had a predetermined set of responses, giving approximately three wrong answers to every correct answer. The learner made no sign of protest or any other comment until a shock level of 300 volts was reached. At this point he pounded on the wall but thereafter ceased to provide any further response to questions; the subject usually turned to the experimenter for advice and was told

The shock generator (in photograph above) had labels for every group of 4 switches:

Slight shock	15	30	45	60
Moderate shock	75	90	105	120
Strong shock	135	150	165	180
Very strong shock	195	210	225	240
Intense shock	255	270	285	300
Extremely intense shock	315	330	345	360
Danger: Severe shock	375	390	405	420
XXX			435	450

to wait 5–10 seconds before treating the lack of response as a wrong answer. He was to continue increasing the shock levels with each wrong answer. After the 315 volt shock the learner pounded on the wall again but after that there was no further response from the learner.

Experimenter feedback

If the subject turned to the experimenter for advice about whether to continue giving shocks, the experimenter was trained to give a series of standard 'prods' (see right) which were always made in sequence. Prod 2 was only used if prod 1 was unsuccessful. If the subject refused to obey prod 4 then the experiment was terminated. The sequence was begun anew on each hesitation.

Dependent measures

Each subject was scored between 0 and 30 depending on when they terminated the experiment. An obedient subject was one who administered all the shock levels i.e. scored 30.

Further records

Most sessions were taped and some photographs taken through one-way mirrors. Notes were kept on any unusual behaviour and observers wrote descriptions of subjects' behaviour.

Interview and dehoax

All subjects were interviewed after the experiment and were asked various open-ended questions. They were also given some psychological tests. After this, procedures were undertaken to ensure that the subject would leave the laboratory in a state of well-being. A friendly reconciliation with the learner was arranged.

Standard prods used by experimenter if 'teacher' wished to stop.

Prod 1	'Please continue', or 'Please go on'
Prod 2	'The experiment requires that you continue.'
Prod 3	'It is absolutely essential that you continue.'
Prod 4	'You have no other choice, you must go on.'
Special prods	If the teacher asked whether the learner might suffer permanent physical injury, the experimenter said: 'Although the shocks may be painful, there is no permanent tissue damage, so please go on.'
	If the teacher said that the learner clearly wanted to stop, the experimenter said: 'Whether the learner likes it or not, you must go on until he has learned all the word pairs correctly. So please go on'.

Milgram: the core study *continued*

Results

Preliminary Notions

Milgram described the experimental situation to 14 psychology undergraduates and asked them to predict how 100 hypothetical subjects would behave. Their answers were in close agreement, expecting that no more than 3% of subjects would continue to 450 volts.

Experimental results

Subjects accept situation
With few exceptions the subjects were convinced of the reality of the experimental situation. In the post-experimental briefing they were asked to indicate how painful the shocks had been for the learner. The modal response was 'extremely painful'.

Signs of extreme tension
Many subjects showed nervousness and a large number showed extreme tension, *'subjects were observed to sweat, tremble, stutter, bite their lips, groan and dig their finger-nails into their flesh'.* Fourteen displayed nervous laughter which seemed bizarre and three had *'full-blown uncontrollable seizures'.*

Distribution of scores
The quantitative results are shown in the graph below.

Distribution of breakoff points

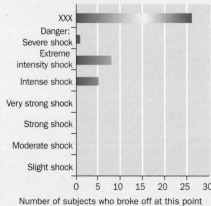

Number of subjects who broke off at this point

The two key findings are:
- Over half of the subjects (26/40 or 65%) went all the way with the electric shocks.
- Only nine (22.5%) stopped at 300 volts (intense shock).

In addition Milgram provided comments from the subjects, to illustrate the findings, see right.

Discussion

Two findings emerged which were surprising:

Finding 1
The sheer strength of the obedient tendencies that were displayed, despite the fact that
- People are taught from childhood that it is wrong to hurt another person.
- The experimenter had no special powers to enforce his commands.
- Disobedience would bring no material loss to the subject.

This behaviour was not expected by the students in the pre-experiment survey, nor by the persons who observed the experiment through one-way mirrors who expressed complete disbelief at the subjects' behaviour.

Finding 2
The extraordinary tension generated by the procedures. One observer related:
'I observed a mature and initially poised businessman enter the laboratory smiling and confident. Within 20 minutes he was reduced to a twitching, stuttering wreck, who was rapidly approaching a point of nervous collapse. He constantly pulled on his earlobe, and twisted his hands. At one point he pushed his fist into his forehead and muttered "Oh God, let's stop it." And yet he continued to respond to every word of the experimenter, and obeyed to the end.' (page 377)

Activity

Before conducting this study, Milgram asked various people (psychiatrists, undergraduates and some ordinary people) to predict how the subjects would behave in this study.

Try conducting a survey yourself – briefly outline the experimental procedure and ask people to predict how 100 hypothetical participants would behave (i.e. predict how many will stop before or at 300 volts and how many would continue to the maximum voltage).

Experiment or investigation?

There is some debate about whether this study is an experiment or not. We can be certain that it was conducted in a laboratory (a place specially designed for conducting research; a controlled environment). This leads many people to assume it was an experiment but to be classed as an experiment there must be an IV and DV.

Some people say it was simply an investigation to see how willing subjects were to obey unjust authority.

However, it could be argued that the shock levels were the IV and the DV was willingness to obey. Milgram himself described it as an experiment.

Qs

1. Milgram included comments from two of the subjects (see below). What do these comments tell us?
2. Identify at least **three** features of this study that made it more likely that subjects would behave more obediently than they would normally? (Note: in a sense these features are 'demand characteristics'.)
3. What were the two findings that surprised Milgram?
4. Milgram says that obedience is 'an indispensable feature of social life'. Do you agree? Why or why not?
5. Give **one** example of some quantitative data collected in this study and **one** example of qualitative data collected in this study.

Comments from subjects
Qualitative data was also presented in this report, such as comments from some subjects:
'I think he's trying to communicate, he's knocking ... Well it's not fair to shock the guy ... these are terrific volts. I don't think this is very humane ... Oh, I can't go on with this.
'He's banging in there. I'm gonna chicken out. I'd like to continue, but I can't do that to a man ... I'm sorry I can't do that to a man. I'll hurt his heart. You take your [money].'
Some subjects simply got up and left, without saying anything.

Those who continued to the end often heaved a sigh of relief, mopped their brows, some shook their heads apparently in regret, some remained calm throughout.

Further details of the study were provided by Milgram in his book Obedience to Authority *(1974). These may be useful when considering your evaluations. For example,*

- *The subjects were sent a follow-up questionnaire, which showed that 84% felt glad to have participated, and 74% felt they had learned something of personal importance.*

- *Milgram did think about abandoning the study when it became clear that some subjects were quite stressed. However he decided that* 'momentary excitement is not the same as harm' *(1974, page 212).*

- *Milgram questioned whether the reason so many people were shocked by the experiment might be more to do with the unanticipated findings rather than the methods used.*

- *Milgram also conducted more than 20 variations of his original study, for example in a more run-down location, with shocks delivered face-to-face with the learner or with a second 'teacher' who disobeyed. In these conditions obedience dropped.*

Why did they obey?

Milgram offered the following 13 explanations for why the subjects (teachers) obeyed:

1 The location of the study at a prestigious university provided authority.

2 Subjects assume that the experimenter knows what he is doing and has a worthy purpose, so should be followed.

3 Subjects assume that the learner has voluntarily consented to take part.

4 The subject doesn't wish to disrupt the experiment because he feels under obligation to the experimenter due to his voluntary consent to take part.

5 This sense of obligation is reinforced because the subject has been paid (though he was told he could leave).

6 Subjects believe that the role of learner was determined by chance; therefore the learner can't really complain.

7 It is a novel situation for the subject who therefore doesn't know how to behave. If it was possible to discuss the situation with others the subject might have behaved differently.

8 The subject assumes that the discomfort caused is minimal and temporary, and that the scientific gains are important.

9 Since the learner has 'played the game' up to shock level 20 (300 volts) the subject assumes the learner is willing to continue with the experiment.

10 The subject is torn between meeting the demands of the victim and those of the experimenter.

11 The two demands are not equally pressing and legitimate.

12 The subject has very little time to resolve this conflict and he doesn't know that the victim will remain silent for the rest of the experiment.

13 The conflict is between two deeply ingrained tendencies: not to harm someone and to obey those whom we perceive to be legitimate authorities.

Evaluating the study by Milgram

The research method
This study was conducted in a controlled laboratory environment. *What are the strengths and weaknesses of using a controlled environment in the context of this study?*

Milgram described the study as an experiment. *What are the strengths and weaknesses of using this research method in the context of this study?*

There are no simple answers. Evaluating a study requires you to think. We have provided some pointers here, linked to the KEY ISSUES covered through this book – see page XIV for a table of these key issues.

The sample
The subjects were US males and volunteers. *In what way are the participants in this sample unique?*

How might this affect the conclusions drawn from the study?

Quantitative and qualitative data
Some of the results can be described as quantitative data and other findings are qualitative. *Give examples of both kinds of data in this study.*

What are the strengths of quantitative data in the context of this study?

What are the strengths of qualitative data in the context of this study?

Ecological validity
Psychological research aims to find out about how real people behave in the real world. *To what extent do you think the subjects in this study behaved as they would have done in everyday life when faced with a command from an authority figure?*

Personality versus situation
Some psychological explanations propose that behaviour is determined by your personality. Other explanations suggest that situational factors have a major influence. *What does this study tell us about the relative effects of personality and situation on behaviour?*

Ethical issues
What ethical issues should have concerned Milgram in this study? To what extent do you think he dealt with these ethical issues successfully? What else might he have done?

Applications/usefulness
Psychologists aim to conduct research which will help make people's lives better. *From your point of view, how valuable was this study?*

What next?
Describe **one** change to this study, and say how you think this might affect the outcome.

Debate

Do the ends justify the means?

You might work in groups and prepare two lists: one list of all the plus points of this study and one list of all the minus points. On balance do you think that Milgram was justified in conducting this study?

You could conduct the debate as a trial and have a jury decide on the verdict.

...Links to other studies and issues...

Milgram's conclusion is that we are made by the situations we are in. This idea is explored further in the section on **situations and personality** . The issue of situations and opportunity are also dealt with in the studies by **Griffiths** and also **Piliavin** *et al.* Both these studies share another characteristic with Milgram in that they attempted to explore human behaviour in real-life settings.

Still following orders?

The Milgram study is probably the most well known and most powerful piece of social psychology. It was a mixed blessing for Milgram's career, however, because its controversial nature meant that the most prestigious universities were not keen to employ him. The ethical issues mean that it has been difficult to replicate the study until now when the development of technology allows us to carry out the study in a virtual world (see Slater *et al.*, 2006).

Is evil banal?

One of the conclusions that is commonly drawn from Milgram's study is that evil acts can be done by ordinary people. But is this the best explanation?

At the time of Milgram's studies a trial was taking place in Jerusalem of one of the Nazi leaders involved in *Endlosung der Judenfrage* (the final solution to the Jewish question). Adolf Eichmann had been part of this project from the beginning and in 1942 he was given the job of Transportation Administrator which put him in charge of all the trains that carried Jews to the death camps in Poland. In 1960, some time after the war, he was captured and put on trial.

The question that Milgram was asking, and that also became the centre of Eichmann's trial, concerned what sort of person could carry out such evil actions. Eichmann's defence was that he was just following orders, but this was not accepted by the court which heard evidence of how he had gone beyond his orders to devise more efficient ways of working and to continue the slaughter even after he was ordered to stop. He was found guilty and hanged.

The analysis of the trial that interested Milgram was in a book by Hannah Arendt (*Eichmann in Jerusalem*, 1963) where she describes how ordinary Eichmann appeared to be. This observation led her to refer to the '*banality of evil*' suggesting that evil acts are carried out unthinkingly by people who are not aware of the consequences and not committed to what is going on. Milgram saw this as an explanation of his own work.

Recent reviews of the evidence, however, tell a very different story (see Haslam and Reicher, 2008). For a start, Arendt only attended the start of the trial when Eichmann was trying to portray himself as someone who was blindly following orders. Later in the trial he was to show how closely he identified with the Nazi ideology and how aware and proud he was of his role in the mass murder of the Jews.

Milgram's view that it is ordinary people who do these things does not square with the evidence. As Haslam and Reicher (2008) point out, '*people do great wrong, not because they are unaware of what they are doing but because they consider it to be right.*' Haslam and Reicher offer an alternative explanation in terms of social identity theory (see page 164).

William Shatner boldly obeys.

Popular culture

Milgram's experiment and the subsequent replications have entered popular culture and are still commonly referred to outside the world of psychology. During his life Milgram made a number of scientific films on his work and advised on a made-for-TV movie about the obedience experiment called *The Tenth Level* starring William Shatner and John Travolta. Unfortunately, it is not thought to be masterpiece.

There are numerous other references to the work in film including a scene in *Ghostbusters* where Bill Murray's character is shown as a sly professor administering electrical shocks to a college student while flirting with an attractive female. One of the film-writers, Harold Ramis, has said this parody was inspired by the Milgram study (Blass, 2004).

A film called *The Milgram Experiment* by Maxwell Addae has recently been produced that follows the story of a pair of career con artists who have mastered the art of portraying authoritative figures (check it out on YouTube).

Peter Gabriel's 1986 album *So* has a track that was inspired by the Milgram experiment – *We do as we're told* (*Milgram's* 37). The '37' refer to the 37 out of 40 participants who showed complete obedience in one particular experiment.

Check out YouTube for videos of this and other Milgram related activities.

Milgram and ethics

Many text books use the obedience study as an example of lack of ethical sensitivity. We would argue that they are wrong to do so. It is true that after the study was carried out there was an ethical storm about them. For example Diana Baumrind (1964) wrote a damning critique, arguing that just because someone volunteers for a study this does not take away the researcher's responsibilities towards them. She used direct quotes from Milgram's study to illustrate the lack of regard she believed was given to the subjects. For example:

'*In a large number of cases the degree of tension [in the subjects] reached extremes that are rarely seen in sociopsychological laboratory studies. Subjects were observed to sweat, tremble, stutter, bite their lips, groan, and dig their fingernails into their flesh. These were characteristic rather than exceptional responses to the experiment.*' (page 375)

Baumrind accepted that some harm to subjects is a necessary part of research, for example testing out new medical procedures, because the results could not be achieved in any other way. Social psychology, however, is not in the same game as medicine and is unlikely to produce life-saving results, thus does not justify harming subjects.

The case for the prosecution was very powerful. Milgram's application to join the American Psychological Association (APA) was put on hold while they investigated the study, and he was not given the post he hoped for at Yale.

The case for the defence, however, is overwhelming. At the time of study psychologists were less sensitive about ethical issues than today, however there were ethical guidelines in place. In fact Milgram took more care than his colleagues about such issues. His obedience study contains the first reference to *debriefing* in a psychological report and he kept in contact with his subjects after the study to check their progress.

His work was eventually endorsed by the APA and he was awarded the Prize for Behavioral Science Research of the American Association for the Advancement of Science in 1964.

Finally, the obedience study has created a mirror for the world to see itself in. We can't look on at atrocity and comfort ourselves that we would never do it. We have to confront the fact that ordinary people can do despicable things. The Milgram study still dominates social psychology as arguably its greatest piece of work.

Multiple choice questions

1   Identify the sampling method used:
  a   Volunteer sample.
  b   Opportunity sample.
  c   Random sample.
  d   Male sample.

2   Which ethical issue was not really a problem in this study?
  a   Right to withdraw.
  b   Deception.
  c   Debriefing.
  d   Psychological harm.

3   At what shock level did the learner start banging on the wall?
  a   200 volts.   b   250 volts.
  c   300 volts.   d   350 volts.

4   How many prods did the experimenter use?
  a   2   b   4
  c   6   d   8

5   After the experiment, the subject was:
  a   Introduced to the learner.
  b   Dehoaxed.
  c   Given psychological tests.
  d   All of the above.

6   Students predicted that:
  a   1% would obey fully.
  b   3% would obey fully.
  c   5% would obey fully.
  d   10% would obey fully.

7   What percentage of participants stopped at 300 volts?
  a   12.5%   b   17.5%
  c   22.5%   d   27.5%

8   What percentage of participants stopped at 450 volts?
  a   50%   b   55%
  c   60%   d   65%

9   Milgram offered explanations for why the subjects obeyed. Which of the following was not one of his reasons?
  a   Sense of obligation.
  b   The setting was prestigious.
  c   They were paid.
  d   They didn't take the task seriously.

10   Does Milgram suggest that obedience is:
  a   A bad thing?
  b   A good thing?
  c   Both bad and good.
  d   Unusual.

Answers are on page 185.

Exam-style questions

See page XII–XIII for notes on the exam paper and styles of question.

Section A questions

1   Milgram's study has been criticised for being low in ecological validity.
  (a)   Outline **one** argument demonstrating that it was low in ecological validity.   [2]
  (b)   Outline **one** argument demonstrating that it was high in ecological validity.   [2]

2   Identify **four** aspects of Milgram's study that encouraged the participants to behave in a highly obedient way.   [4]

3   (a)   Describe **one** ethical issue raised in Milgram's study.   [2]
  (b)   Describe what steps Milgram took to deal with this ethical issue.   [2]

4   In Milgram's study the participants showed signs of stress.
  (a)   Give **one** example of the stress shown by subjects.   [2]
  (b)   Explain why the participants may have been stressed.   [2]

5   (a)   Describe how Milgram measured obedience.   [2]
  (b)   Suggest **two** factors that would explain why subjects were so obedient in Milgram's study.   [2]

6   Outline **two** pieces of evidence from Milgram's study that showed that the participants believed the shocks were real.   [4]

7   Some people regard Milgram's study as being controversial.
  (a)   Give **one** reason why the results of Milgram's study might be judged to be controversial.   [2]
  (b)   Outline Milgram's reason for doing this research.   [2]

Section B questions

(a)   Identify the aim of the study by Milgram.   [2]
(b)   Describe the sample used in the study by Milgram, and give **one** limitation of the sample.   [6]
(c)   Describe how behaviour was measured in the study by Milgram.   [6]
(d)   Outline the results of the study by Milgram.   [6]
(e)   Outline the conclusions of the study by Milgram.   [8]
(f)   Suggest **two** changes to the study by Milgram and outline how these changes might affect the results.   [8]

Section C questions

(a)   Outline **one** assumption of the social approach in psychology.   [2]
(b)   Describe how the social approach could explain obedience.   [4]
(c)   Describe **two** differences between the Milgram study and any other study using the social approach.   [6]
(d)   Discuss the strengths and limitations of the social approach, using examples from the study by Milgram.   [12]

Key issue: personality and situation

Why do we do the things we do? Is it because we are the sort of person who does those things (our personality) or because of the situation we are in at the time? The obvious answer is that it is a bit of both but which is the most important factor? Psychologists take different views on this. Look at the information on this page and see what you think. In some of the core studies the behaviour of people is explained by personality and in others by the situation people are in. Do you think the explanations have got the balance right?

Not my fault

When we make a judgement about someone's behaviour we have to decide how responsible they are for it. It's the difference between saying 'it was an accident' and 'it was your fault'. If we think they are responsible then we make dispositional (personality) explanations (for example, she's late because she doesn't think it matters to get here on time) and if we think they are not responsible we make situational explanations (for example, she's late because the bus didn't turn up).

We have a tendency to overestimate how much control someone has, and we tend to make dispositional explanations when a situational one would be more appropriate. When we judge our own behaviour, however, we are more likely to see ourselves as a victim of circumstances and not so responsible.

The issue of assigning responsibility for behaviour is an important question in social psychology. Why are we obedient? Why do we choose to help? Why do we behave differently when we are given power? The studies in this chapter all look at such questions and seem to point to the answer being more to do with the situation we are in rather than the personality we have.

The Milgram study

The Milgram study illustrates the two sides of this question. One of the initial aims of the study was to test whether there was something in the character of some nations that made them more prone to extreme obedience or, alternatively, whether anyone can be made to behave obediently in the 'right circumstances'. On first analysis of the Milgram study we might well take the situational approach and suggest that people obeyed because certain features of the situation led them to suspend their sense of autonomy (acting independently) and become an agent of the authority figure. The situational factors that lead to such obedience include the proximity of the authority figure and the distance from the victim. This would suggest that it is not evil people who commit evil crimes but ordinary people who are just obeying orders.

It is not that simple, however, and when you look further into the study you find individual differences of behaviour that are due to personal choice. To start with, not all the participants obeyed, and 35% stopped before the highest shock. For example one participant, Gretchen Brandt, was a 31-year-old medical technician involved in a later Milgram obedience study with only female participants. When the shock level reached 210 volts she said '*Well, I'm sorry, I don't think we should continue*'. In response to the various prods she said, '*I think we are here of our own free will*' and refused to go further. It transpired that she had spent her youth in Germany before the Second World War (1939–45) and said '*Perhaps we have seen too much pain*' (Milgram, 1974).

One person or many?

The situation we are in influences our behaviour but does it change us as a person? Do we become someone else? It sometimes seems like that and maybe if we play a role long enough we start to take on the characteristics of that role and become that person. For example, many doctors appear to be patronising and arrogant when they deal with the general public. Were they always like that or is that something that has developed through playing the role of 'doctor' for many years? The US author Kurt Vonnegut captured this idea in his book *Mother Night* when he wrote '*We are what we pretend to be, so we must be careful what we pretend to be.*'

A **situational factor** is anything in the environment, including the behaviour of other people.

A **dispositional factor** is an enduring aspect of an individual's behaviour – their disposition or personality.

In a nutshell

'The social psychology of this century reveals a major lesson: often, it is not so much the kind of person a man is as the kind of situation in which he finds himself that determines how he will act.' *(Milgram, cited in Blass, 2004, page 101)*

Some situations make strange behaviours look ordinary.

"Would you sit in a vat of baked beans please?"

"You must be kidding."

"It's for charity."

"When do I start?"

Kurt Lewin's Equation

$B = f(P,E)$

To put this into words, behaviour (B) is a function (f) of a person's personality (P) and the environment they are in (E).

Kurt Lewin (1890–1947) was one of the most important psychologists in the development of applied psychology. He is often referred to as the founder of social psychology and is most famous for his work on the behaviour of groups. He created a psychological equation of behaviour that is probably the most well known formula in the subject. It seems odd to try and write human behaviour in a mathematical formula and Lewin's Equation looks very simple but it has a lot of meaning. Behavior (B) is a function (f) of personality (P) and environment (E).

When we look at someone else's behaviour we usually judge them to be in control of it. So if we see someone doing a kind act we think they are a kind person. In other words the kind act is because that is the sort of person they are rather than because they are in a situation that provokes kindness.

Think about another example. Most of us think we are honest and don't cheat, but if you had the opportunity to see your exam questions before you sat the paper and you knew that nobody would know you had seen them, what would you do? The situations we are in and the opportunities we have will affect our behaviour. It's not part of our personality to cheat all the time but, just this once, in this situation, with this much at stake...

Activity

Design your own investigation into demand characteristics (see top right for discussion of demand characteristics). First you need to decide on a task for people to do, like help you colour in a picture or sign your petition. Then you need to decide on two conditions to compare how responsive they are. One possibility is to vary the reason for the task (for example, doing it as a favour, for a psychology study, or for charity) or you could vary where you ask them (for example at home or in the classroom) or how you appear (for example, smart or scruffy).

Demand characteristics

One way that situations affect us is by giving us cues on how we should behave. Depending on where we are we will behave differently. For example if someone bumps into you in a shop you might feel offended and say something, but at a football match you probably won't think anything of it. Different situations *demand* different behaviours, so as a student you sit relatively quietly and listen, but as a member of the public outside the Big Brother house you jump up and down and shout nonsense at the top of your voice. You are the same person but behaving as the situation *demands*.

Orne (1962) described these cues to behaviour as *demand characteristics* and showed how powerful they can be in a number of studies. One of these involved a psychologist asking a few friends for a favour. When they agreed they were asked to do five press-ups. Their reaction tended to be to ask 'why?', with a degree of puzzlement. Another group of friends were asked if they would take part in an experiment. When they agreed they were asked to do five press-ups. Their reaction tended to be to ask 'where?'. This suggests that people are prepared to do things as research participants that they would not normally be prepared to do in other social contexts.

The implication for psychology is that the laboratory and the experience of being a participant creates demand characteristics. If this is so then the behaviour we observe might be due to the participant being in a psychology study rather than solely due to the variable being tested.

Orne describes how demand characteristics can affect research into sensory deprivation and hypnosis (Orne and Scheibe, 1964). One group of participants were told they were in a sensory deprivation study. They undertook a series of tasks, signed release forms and were left on their own for four hours in a room which had some visible trappings of sensory deprivation including a red 'panic' button. However, the experimenters had not created any sensory deprivation at all. Another group of subjects were told they were control subjects in a sensory deprivation study. They did the same series of tasks and sat in the same room for four hours (only with the panic button removed). Both sets of subjects then repeated the original tasks. The performance of the subjects who thought they had undergone sensory deprivation had deteriorated significantly on a number of the measures in comparison with the control group.

The participants in the sensory deprivation condition appeared to have a very good idea, at least subconsciously, of the way they were expected to behave. Their behaviour promptly confirmed these expectations. Does this sort of thing also happen with stage demonstrations of hypnosis? The people who go up on the stage know how they are supposed to behave. Are they really in a different mental state (hypnotised) or are they just responding to the social demands of the situation?

(Demand characteristics are also discussed on page 17).

Uniforms

Putting on a uniform requires people to behave in certain ways. For example if you wear the uniform of a police officer you have to intervene when you see trouble happening and give directions to people when they ask the way. You behave differently and people treat you differently. The police officer might not behave like that on the days when he (or she) is off duty and not wearing the uniform. Or what about putting on a nurse's uniform (a real one)? You will be required to listen to people when they tell you about their aches and pains and you will generally have to behave like an angel. Of course once you take the uniform off you can be as uncaring and callous as you like. The behaviour of the nurse is a feature of the uniform, and probably not the personality of the person wearing it. Take this a step further and put on a comedy nurse's uniform and your behaviour will change again but I think we'll leave it there.

Does wearing the nurse uniform make you behave in a more caring way? Does it make people treat you differently?

Qs

1 Select **one** appropriate core study and explain what it tells us about how situations affect behaviour.

2 How could the same behaviour be explained in terms of personality?

   Select another core study and say how demand characteristics may have affected the results.

3 How could the research have dealt with this problem?

   Why do people behave differently in the light room and the dark room (see above)?

4 How do you think the people in the dark room would have behaved if they knew each other?

5 How do you think you would behave in the dark room?

...Links to other studies and issues...

The debate about how much behaviour is due to personality or situation runs through many of the core studies. The text on this spread looks at the Milgram study, and some of the other studies you might think about are:

• **Samuel and Bryant's** description of Piaget's work on child judgements. In the original study he asked the same question twice. If someone asks us the same question twice we think that they require a different answer to the first one. The behaviour is therefore a response to the demand characteristics of the situation.

• The **Rosenhan** study shows how people's behaviour can change in different situations and also how the interpretation of this behaviour can change as well.

This issue is especially relevant to all the studies in social and developmental psychology as we try to explain the extent to which our behaviour comes from our own choices or whether it is framed by the environment we live in. This also relates to the debate about **determinism** and **free will** as we try and judge how responsible an individual is for their actions.

REICHER AND HASLAM: BBC PRISON STUDY

Tyranny and terror

The big question of the Milgram study concerned the development of tyranny and our response to it. The social psychologists of the time focused their explanations on the events of the Second World War. This war is still used as a cultural reference point and it is common to hear politicians and commentators referring to Nazi Germany or to Hitler. These references are usually very simplistic and tap into a basic understanding that something very wrong happened there and it shouldn't be allowed to happen again. The problem with these references are that the world is a different place in the twenty-first century and looking back 50 years will not necessarily help us to understand the present and deal with our modern crises.

In today's world we want to understand about how terror and tyranny develop and we need to go beyond seeing it as being divided into the good guys (obviously us) and the bad guys (anyone who gets in our way or challenges us). The work of European social psychologists such as Steve Reicher and Alex Haslam is important in exploring the natures of tyranny and terror so that we can improve our understanding and respond in positive ways.

Social identity (SIT)

Social identity theory was developed by **Henri Tajfel**. It states that the social groups and categories to which we belong are an important part of our self-concept, and therefore a person will sometimes interact with other people, not as a single individual, but as a representative of a whole group or category of people. A simple example of this is the common experience of doing something to make your family proud of you and you feel as if you are representing your family and don't want to let them down. Sometimes you act as an individual and sometimes as a group member and during one conversation you might change between these two identities. In business meetings people sometimes suggest that they are wearing 'a different hat' to convey the idea that they are adopting a social identity.

There are three basic psychological processes underlying social identification. The first of these is *categorisation* which is a basic tendency to classify things into groups. This commonly leads to an exaggeration of the similarities of those items in the same group, and an exaggeration of the differences between those in different groups. This means that when we categorise people, we accentuate the similarities to ourselves of people in the same group, and exaggerate the differences from ourselves of people in other groups.

The second psychological process is that of *social comparison*. Social groups do not exist in isolation, but in a social context in which some groups have more prestige, power or status than others. Once a social categorisation has been made, the process of social comparison means that the group is compared with other social groups, and its relative status is determined. This comparison has an inbuilt bias in favour of groups like ourselves because we know more about them.

The third psychological mechanism underlying social identity concerns the way that *membership* of a social group affects our self-concept. According to Tajfel and Turner (1979), people want to belong to groups which will reflect positively on their self-esteem. If the group does not compare favourably with others, and membership of it brings about lowered self-esteem, people will try to leave the group, or to distance themselves from it. If leaving the group is impossible, then they may look for ways that group membership may provide a positive source of self-esteem.

Prisons

This core study is about prisoners and prisons. If putting people into prisons makes their behaviour worse and the behaviour of their guards brutal then we need to look again at our criminal justice policy. Over 9 million people are held in prisons worldwide (Home Office, 2003) with about half of them being detained in just three countries (USA, Russia, China). In England and Wales in January 2008, 79,724 people were being held in prison (75,383 men and 4,321 women) (NOMS, 2008). The table on the right shows rates of people being imprisoned in selected countries. You might wonder why some countries lock up many more people than others.

Country	Prisoners per 100,000 population
Nigeria	32
Japan	53
France	93
Germany	98
China	117
England and Wales	141
South Africa	402
Thailand	404
USA	701

From **International Centre for Prison Studies (2008).**

Terrorists or freedom fighters? Some people see the Palestinian group Hamas as terrorists but others see them as fighters for the legitimate rights of the Palestinian people.

War on Terror

Terrorism was not invented on September 11, 2001 though the destruction of the World Trade Centre in New York on that date changed the way the West viewed the world. The attack on the twin towers was the first attack by an outside force on the USA and suddenly people didn't feel safe. It is perhaps worth noting 'the other September 11th' when on September 11, 1973 a USA-backed military coup in Chile overthrew the democratic government of Salvador Allende. In the aftermath of the coup the loss of life was similar to that at the World Trade Centre. Terrorism has a complex history.

After the World Trade Centre attacks, US President George W. Bush used the phrase 'War on Terror' to describe the USA's response to this act. Some would argue, however, (Merrin, 2005) that the war was already over and the USA had lost. In one day the terrorists has destroyed the World Trade Centre, created a global media explosion that still reverberates today and destroyed the sense of safety held by citizens of the USA. Terror was created on a huge scale on one day and nothing that has happened since has reduced that. In modern history it is hard to think of an event that has created such a sense of shock and awe. It was The One Day War.

The most visible consequences of the War on Terror have been the invasions of Iraq and Afghanistan. One of the confusing things about these missions is the idea that you can fight a perception (a sense of terror) by sending in a terrifying army. It is not clear whether a sense of terror has been reduced by any of these actions.

The Stanford Prison Simulation – a mock prison

The Stanford Prison Experiment (SPE) is one of the most famous of all psychology experiments. At the height of the American War in Vietnam, when opposition to the war was very strong on university campuses and students were involved in violent protests, the US Navy funded a study to investigate the effects of prison life on guards and prisoners. Philip Zimbardo was the lead psychologist in the team that created a mock prisoner in the basement of the Stanford University psychology department. Their work was dramatic and surprising, and the results are still commonly cited today.

The study

In brief, 24 subjects were selected from an initial pool of 75 respondents to a newspaper advertisement which had asked for male volunteers to participate in a psychological study of prison life. The volunteers were interviewed and completed a questionnaire designed to screen subjects, and the selected people were described as 'normal', healthy, male college students who were predominantly middle class and white.

Zimbardo took the role of Warden and his other researchers took on roles of day to day management of the prison. He also recruited an ex-convict for advice about the prison and also to intimidate the prisoners when they asked to leave. The subjects were randomly assigned their roles of either 'prisoner' or 'guard', and signed contracts on that basis. The contract offered $15 a day and guaranteed basic living needs, though it was made explicit to the prisoners that some basic civil rights (for example, privacy) would be suspended. The prisoners were given no information about what to expect and no instructions on how to behave. The guards were told to maintain a reasonable degree of order within the prison necessary for its effective functioning, though they were explicitly prohibited from using physical aggression.

Both sets of subjects were given uniforms to promote feelings of anonymity. The guards' uniform (plain khaki shirt and trousers, whistle, baton, and reflecting sunglasses) was intended to convey a military attitude and impression of power. The prisoners' uniform (loose-fitting smock, number on front and back, no underwear, light chain and lock around ankle, rubber sandals and a cap made from nylon stocking) was intended to be uncomfortable, humiliating and to create a sense of subservience and dependence.

Results

The role play soon took an ugly turn and following an attempted revolt by the prisoners, the guards became more and more extreme in their behaviour. Things that were originally rights for the prisoners soon became privileges. The prisoners were subjected to sustained intimidation and humiliation by the guards as the psychologists looked on.

Things deteriorated very quickly with some of the prisoners showing severe signs of distress. Eventually a combination of a lawyer appearing from one of the families of the prisoners and a confrontation between Zimbardo and his then girlfriend (and later wife) persuaded Zimbardo to bring the study to an end after six days instead of the planned 14.

Afters

Zimbardo has never published an account of the study in a refereed journal (i.e. where academic peers review the research before publication) and he has still not released all of the data. This control of the data means that Zimbardo has also been able to control the story that is told about the events. The main lesson that Zimbardo draws from the study is that the roles we are asked to play will structure our behaviour. The guards became brutal and cruel because they had been assigned to the role of guard. There are other explanations for what happened here, however, but the restriction on access to the data and the lack of scrutiny by other scientists limits the confidence we can have in the conclusions that Zimbardo makes.

In the mock prison the guards humiliate the prisoners in a line-up.

Biographical notes on Philip Zimbardo

Philip George Zimbardo was born into poverty in New York City, the grandchild of Sicilian immigrants. The family were constantly on the move (31 times to be exact) because they couldn't pay the rent. Zimbardo was often ill as a child, including one spell of spending six months in a hospital aged five which he describes as a formative experience in his development, leading him to recognise the importance of making and sustaining human relationships.

Zimbardo went to secondary school in the Bronx with Stanley Milgram. When asked if it was a coincidence that both of them developed an interest in social influence his response was *'We were both interested in situational influences because growing up poor, one sees failure and evil in your midst and you don't want to believe it is the dispositions of your family and friends, but rather in situational forces imposed on them.'* (Zimbardo personal communication).

Professor Zimbardo has conducted research in many other areas of psychology, such as shyness, persuasion, hypnosis and most recently terrorism. He helped to create the US Public TV programme *Discovering Psychology* and acts as series host. Zimbardo has received numerous awards for his distinguished teaching, creative research, dedicated social action, and career-long contributions to psychology. He was recently president of the American Psychological Association.

www You can read about the SPE at http://www.prisonexp.org/

...Link to the core study...

Reicher and Haslam's study stands alone as an observation on the way that terror and tyranny develop but it also acts as a re-evaluation of the social psychology of the last century. In particular it gives us a new understanding of the issues raised by Milgram (see pages 154) and Zimbardo's SPE (see above).

In one sense the study is about prisons but in another it is a more general investigation of how groups of people negotiate power and responsibility.

Reicher and Haslam: the core study

Stephen Reicher and S. Alexander Haslam (2006) Rethinking the psychology of tyranny: The BBC prison study. *British Journal of Social Psychology*, 45, pages 1–40.

Abstract

To study the way people respond to a system of inequality (tyranny), do they accept it or do they resist it?

Method

A mock prison was created and filmed by the BBC. Male volunteers were sought and then selected through screening. The final 15 were matched in groups of 3 and then randomly allocated as guards (5) and prisoners (10). Ethical issues were carefully monitored. This was an experimental case study with planned interventions (IVs) to create: permeability, legitimacy (security) and cognitive alternatives. Dependant variables (DVs) were measured using observation (qualitative) and psychometric measures (quantitative self-rating scales) related to social, organisational and clinical variables.

Results

Phase 1 was 'rejecting inequality'. Social identification in prisoners only started once the groups became impermeable. The guards showed little social identification which led to ineffective leadership and ultimately conflict because the prisoners no longer perceived the inequalities as legitimate (the guards did not deserve their privileges).

Phase 2 was 'embracing inequality'. Participants set up an egalitarian social system which soon failed. The suggested replacement was a tyrannical regime which was judged unethical and therefore the study was stopped after eight days.

Discussion

There are four possible critiques that can be made of this study: the role of television (were participants play-acting?), the role of personality (were there important individual differences?), the reality of the set-up (were participants really engaged?), and the impact of interventions (did the IV cause the DV?).

The findings cannot be explained in terms of a 'natural' tendency to assume roles and assert power (as proposed by Zimbardo). Social identification provides a better account for both this study and Zimbardo's Stanford Prison Experiment (SPE – see previous page). But more importantly this study provides a new framework for understanding tyranny – the failure of groups renders members powerless and willing to accept alternatives that run against personal values and norms, thus making tyranny psychologically acceptable.

Introduction

The shadow of events of the Second World War continues to hang over academic psychology. The central question is 'how do we come to condone the tyranny of others or else act tyrannically ourselves'? Tyranny is defined as *'an unequal social system involving the arbitrary or oppressive use of power by one group or its agents over another'* (page 2).

At one time anti-social behaviours such as prejudice, discrimination and genocide were explained in terms of individual characteristics i.e. such behaviours were due to the personality of the perpetrators. Then there was a shift in psychology towards explanations that focused on group processes and explanations which suggested that group behaviour tends to be extremely anti-social. This equating of tyranny with groups has a long history, for example Gustave LeBon (1841–1931) argued that individuals lose their sense of personal identity and responsibility when in a crowd and thus become capable of barbaric acts. Philip Zimbardo suggested that this process of *de-individuation* is an *'ageless life force, the cycle of nature, the blood ties, the tribe'* (Zimbardo, 1969, page 249).

Tyranny as role and power

Zimbardo's most famous research was the Stanford Prison Experiment (SPE) which was critical in cementing the shift from individual to group explanations for extreme behaviours. This study showed that immersion in a group undermines the constraints that normally prevent anti-social behaviour. In addition, when a group also has power this seems to encourage extreme anti-social behaviour.

The impact of the SPE was important ethically as well as theoretically, as the subjects in the experiment experienced considerable stress. This meant that subsequent research was increasingly limited to lab experiments with minimal or no interaction between participants. The ultimate result has been that research on important social topics such as oppression and genocide has become remote from the social realities of such phenomena, focusing on individual-level rather than group processes.

Such ethical issues have also meant that the conclusions from the SPE have never been challenged because the study could not be replicated. Such a replication is long overdue for two reasons:

1   The conclusions that were drawn are questionable. Zimbardo and his team concluded that the behaviour of the SPE guards and prisoners was due to a natural acceptance of their roles. However, their behaviour may have been more to do with the instructions given to them by the experimenters. When Zimbardo briefed the guards he told them to create fear and give the prisoners a sense of powerlessness. In another study (Lovibond et al., 1979) guards were trained to respect prisoners and include them in decision-making processes. In this case both prisoners and guards were much less aggressive. It is also worth noting that, in the Zimbardo study, some of the guards were tough but fair, and others even sided with the prisoners. These individual differences challenge the idea that behaviour in the SPE is simply due to role acceptance.

2   These conclusions have been generalised to a wide range of real-life situations from prisons to terrorism, and thus the traditional analysis of the SPE has had profound and troubling social implications. The implications are that people have little choice in what they do – they simply behave according to assigned roles. This implies they have little responsibility for their actions and thus tyrants cannot be held responsible for what they do. The conclusions also discourage the oppressed from challenging tyranny because tyrants are not responsible for their behaviour – their behaviour is an inevitable product of the situation.

An alternative analysis: The social identity approach

Social identity theory (described on page 162) proposes that people only act in terms of group membership if they identify with the group (self-categorisation). Individuals who belong to a group behave in relation to the norms and values of the group, which may be pro- or anti-social, thus resulting in pro- or anti-social behaviour. There are various predictions that arise from SIT:

*   *Permeability* – if group members believe that it is possible to move out of the group/category they will not categorise themselves as group members.

*   *Security* affects the extent to which individuals are aware of cognitive alternatives to the status quo, and thus will challenge inequalities.

Aim

The aim of the study was to create an institution that resembled a variety of hierarchical institutions such as a prison or school, office, barracks etc; specifically an environment which would enable the study of inequalities between groups in terms of power, status and resources. Thus the study was not a replication of the SPE but set up so that certain conceptual issues raised by the SPE could be revisited. The main question is whether the concepts of social identity and social categorisation provide a more satisfactory account of group behaviour than the view of role acceptance.

The main predictions are that

- Dominant group members will identify with their group.
- Subordinate group members will only identify with their group and challenge intergroup inequalities *if* relations between the groups are seen as impermeable and insecure.

Qs

1 Give **one** criticism of the conclusions drawn from the SPE.
2 Give a brief outline of social identity theory.
3 In what way was this study an experimental case study?
4 Why were the researchers so concerned about the ethics of this study and what did they do to ensure the study was carried out in an ethically acceptable manner?
5 Describe **two** of the dependent measures in this study.
6 What was the purpose of the planned interventions?
7 Explain what is meant by 'permeability'?

www Website for The Experiment
http://www.psychology.ex.ac.uk/projects/theexp/intro.shtml

Biographical notes on Steve Reicher and Alex Haslam

The picture shows **Professors Steve Reicher** (on right) and **Alex Haslam** who head psychology departments at opposite ends of the country – St. Andrews and Exeter respectively. How did they come to work together? Alex explains, *'Steve and I have known each other (and been friends) for about 20 years. We have always worked on similar issues (leadership, group dynamics) and always from a similar perspective (the social identity perspective), due in large part to the fact that we had the same PhD supervisor, John Turner' (personal communication).*

Method

Method

The study was conducted in December 2001 in conjunction with the BBC. The role of the BBC was to (a) create the prison environment according to the researcher's design, (b) film the study over a period of up to 10 days at Elstree Studios in London and (c) prepare the film for broadcast (four × 1 hour programmes screened in May 2002). This programme is distinct from reality TV – reality TV programmes are designed for entertainment and academics are invited to comment afterwards.

The method used was an experimental case study:

- It is experimental because interventions (IVs) were introduced at specific points in the study to observe the effects.
- It is a case study because the behaviour of only one group was observed.

Ethics

The study was considered by various ethical committees and was monitored throughout by independent psychologists and another ethics committee. Participants signed a comprehensive consent form which informed them of the potential psychological and physical risks (e.g. discomfort, confinement, constant surveillance and stress).

Participants

Male volunteers were sought through national newspapers and leaflets. An initial pool of 332 applicants was reduced to 27 through screening which involved psychometric tests (assessing e.g. authoritarianism, depression, self-esteem), assessment by clinical psychologists, and medical and character references. The final 15 were chosen to ensure a diversity of age, social class and ethnic background. These 15 were divided into five groups of three people matched as closely as possible on personality variables that might be significant i.e. racism, authoritarianism (social control by individuals) and social dominance. From each group of three one person was randomly selected to be a guard and the other two were prisoners. One prisoner was not involved at the beginning of the filming.

Procedure

Prisoners were allocated to lockable 3-person cells off a central atrium. This was separated from the guards' quarters by a lockable steel mesh fence. There were facilities throughout for video and audio recording. Various measures (dependent variables, DVs) were taken (not all measures were taken on every day because this would have overwhelmed the participants):

- *Social variables* e.g. social identification.
- *Organisational variables* e.g. compliance with rules.
- *Clinical variables* e.g. depression.

The guards were briefed the night before the study began. They were told that they were responsible for the smooth running of the institution and that they must respect the basic rights of the prisoners. The guards were allowed to lock prisoners up, see into prisoners' cells, and use rewards and punishments (such as a bread and water diet). The guards had far better living conditions than the prisoners.

There were three planned interventions (independent variables):

1 **Permeability** (the expectation of movement between groups)
   Participants were told that the guards were selected because of certain personality characteristics (e.g. reliability, initiative), and also told that if prisoners showed these traits they might be promoted to being guards. This created 'permeability'. One guard was promoted but after that participants were told no further promotions (or demotions) would be possible.

2 **Legitimacy** (when decisions are based on real differences)
   After three days participants were to be told there were actually no differences between guards and prisoners but it would be impractical to re-assign participants. This meant that the group division was, afterall, not legitimate.

3 **Cognitive alternatives** (being able to think about possible alternatives)
   On day 4 prisoner 10 was to be introduced. He was chosen because of his background as a trade union official and therefore it was thought he might provide the skills to negotiate and organise collective action.

Results

Phase 1: Rejecting inequality

Social identification

Social identification was measured every day with rating scales (e.g. 'I feel strong ties with prisoners/guards') and also was assessed through observation. As expected the prisoners showed little group identification until the group boundaries became impermeable (after the promotion), when they started to discuss how they could work together to improve conditions. Contrary to expectations the guards did not identify with their group.

Graph showing changes in social identification.

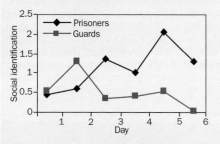

Security of intergroup relations

Low group identity amongst guards led to ineffective leadership. This meant that the prisoners did not regard the guards' authority as legitimate (there was no evidence of the qualities by which their selection had been justified), leading to conflict and insecurity. This meant there was no need for the legitimacy intervention which had been intended to create insecurity and trigger the search for cognitive alternatives.

Prisoner 10 ($DM_p - p$ for prisoner) joined on Day 5 and established a negotiating structure. Quantitative measures showed that participants became increasingly aware of cognitive alternatives (e.g. 'I think the relationship between prisoners and guards is likely to change').

Further measures

(a) Willingness to comply with authority

(b) Willingness to engage in acts of organisational citizenship (i.e. actions to make the prison system work). Measures of both a and b dropped significantly on Day 5 when the prisoners started to work against the guards' regime.

(c) Self-efficacy (a person's belief in their own ability to do things e.g. 'When my group is confronted with a problem, we can usually find several solutions).

(d) Depression
The unity of the prisoners led to increased self-efficacy scores and decreased depression scores, whereas the opposite was true for the guards who became more disorganised and mutually recriminatory.

Combined impact

The outcome was that, late on the evening of Day 6, some prisoners broke out of their cell and occupied the guards' quarters, making the guards' regime unworkable.

Phase 2: Embracing inequality

The participants met with the experimenters to draw up terms of a new commune. Within a day, however, this new social structure was in crisis because two ex-prisoners violated communal rules. A new group (one ex-guard and three ex-prisoners) formulated a plan for a new and harsher prisoner-guard hierarchy. The supporters of the commune were largely passive in response to the new proposals. Publicly they may not have wished to show support but privately, when later debriefed, some had warmed to the idea of a strong social order. This was reflected in psychometric measures of right-wing authoritarianism (e.g. 'People should always keep to the rules', 'There are two kinds of people – strong and weak').

Over the course of the study prisoners and guards showed an increase in right-wing authoritarianism. However, a fascinating pattern emerged if the data were analysed as a function of the new guards/prisoners – the new plan meant a re-assignment of participants to roles, those participants who sought to be guards actually showed a slight *decrease* in authoritarianism whereas this increased in participants who chose to be prisoners (see graph below). At the end the scores for guards and prisoners were nearly the same.

The new regime could not be imposed due to ethical constraints and the existing regime was not working so the study was stopped on Day 8.

Graph showing the reverse pattern which emerged when guards and prisoners selected their own roles.

(Note that measures were taken on every day but only some are shown here).

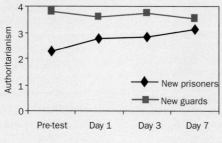

Discussion

Four critiques of the study

1. The role of television

Were the participants simply play-acting because of the cameras? If so, why did the participants' behaviour change at the times predicted e.g. before and after permeability? In any case 'being watched' is not such an usual situation as we are all watched by surveillance cameras.

2. The role of personality

Were the 'prisoners' especially strong characters? The fact that participants' 'character' on relevant dimensions (e.g. authoritarianism) changed over time suggests that personality cannot explain the course of events. In addition, dominance only occurred through shared identity rather than forcefulness of personality. For example FC_p was a mild character who became a leading figure through shared identity. Without support even the most forceful of characters failed. This is not to deny the importance of individual differences (different participants may have created different outcomes) but to emphasise the interdependence between individuals and groups.

3. The reality of inequality and power

Did the participants really become engaged with the role play and thus act in a meaningful way? The prisoners expressed dislike of being locked up and being deprived of, for example, cigarettes; the guards' conversations reflected the seriousness they felt about the role, for example, the disparity between prisoners and guards. All of this points to engagement with the situation.

If the guards were engaged, why didn't they use their power? The answer is that they chose not to because they didn't want to be authoritarian.

4. The impact of interventions and key variables

Did the interventions (IVs) have the intended effect? It could be argued that something else affected the DV – for example the introduction of DM_p made prisoners feel uncertain about what would happen next. This is unlikely because there is no theoretical basis for this chain of events whereas there is theoretical justification for the suggested impact of the interventions.

It also could be that the observed effect (DV) was accidental. However qualitative and quantitative measures were in agreement, establishing a clear effect.

A social identity account of tyranny

The conditions of social identification

The findings show that people do not automatically assume roles. Instead their behaviour relates to social identification which shifts with contextual factors such as permeability, security and legitimacy. This study demonstrated how such factors moderate the relationship between identity and role.

The study also demonstrates how extreme behaviours can be restrained by making actors visible and hence accountable. TQ$_g$ was a successful businessman which may explain his reluctance to play the part of a brutal guard. This shows that behaviour is not always dominated by the present context; past and future contexts matter.

The consequences of social identification

The study demonstrated the interrelationships between social, organisational and clinical variables. Shared social identity led to effective organisation (mutual support and trust) and positive mental states (lack of depression, anxiety and burnout).

Reactions to group failure

There were two instances of group failure (1) failure of the guards to control the prisoners, (2) failure of the commune. In both instances group members were prepared to relinquish their existing norms and values and adopt new ones in order for a viable social order to be established.

Conclusions

1 The results support the SPE conclusions that collective conflict and tyranny cannot be understood by looking at individuals; any account must look at group processes.

2 The results contradict the traditional view that group processes are toxic i.e. inevitably lead to uncontrolled, mindless and anti-social behaviour.

3 The results show that it is the breakdown of groups that creates the conditions under which tyranny can flourish.

4 This analysis can be applied to the SPE – tyranny flourished when the prisoners were told they could not leave and thus the group became disoriented and broke down.

5 This study shows it is possible to run ethical field studies into social processes rather than conducting sterile experiments.

Evaluating the study by Reicher and Haslam

The research method

This study was conducted in a controlled laboratory environment. *What are the strengths and weaknesses of using a controlled environment in the context of this study?*

The study was also described as a case study. *Explain in what way this was a case study, and describe the strengths and weaknesses of using this research method in the context of this study.*

There are no simple answers. Evaluating a study requires you to think. We have provided some pointers here, linked to the KEY ISSUES covered through this book – see page XIV for a table of these key issues.

The sample

The subjects were British males and volunteers. *In what way are the participants in this sample unique? How might this affect the conclusions drawn from the study?*

Quantitative and qualitative data

Some of the results can be described as quantitative data and other findings are qualitative. *Give examples of both kinds of data in this study.*

What are the strengths of quantitative data in the context of this study?

What are the strengths of qualitative data in the context of this study?

Ecological validity

Reicher and Haslam suggest that the behaviour in this study had parallels with real life. For example, we are constantly filmed in our everyday lives. They also suggest that the participants took the task seriously. *To what extent do you think the participants in this study behaved as they would have done in everyday life? Is being filmed the same as everyday life? Did they take the task seriously? Are there other explanations for their behaviour?*

Personality versus situation

Some psychological explanations propose that behaviour is determined by your personality. Other explanations suggest that situational factors have a major influence. *What does this study tell us about the relative effects of personality and situation on behaviour?*

Ethical issues

Do you think this study was ethically acceptable? Outline reasons for and against.

Applications/usefulness

Psychologists aim to conduct research which will help make people's lives better. *From your point of view, how valuable was this study?*

What next?

Describe **one** change to this study, and say how you think this might affect the outcome.

Debate

Which environment was more like a real prison?

The SPE or the BBC Prison? Who is right – Reicher and Haslam or Zimbardo? In which study were the set-up and the interventions more 'realistic'?

Activity

Choose one of the topics to debate in class, or if you prefer – pretend to be Philip Zimbardo and write a letter to Reicher and Haslam stating what you think of their study!

...Links to other studies and issues...

This study is about real people in real situations. Although the prison is contrived it is clear the participants were not just acting out a part. This study falls in the tradition of social psychology studies such as **Milgram** and **Piliavin *et al.*** that observe the complexities of behaviour in real life settings. Having said that, the study has a wide range of controls that we associate with experimentations (for example the **Loftus and Palmer** study) and a wide range of measures to capture biological, emotional and cognitive changes.

Reicher and Haslam: afters

More tyranny

Since the publication of Reicher and Haslam's work, Zimbardo has challenged the conclusions that have been drawn from their study and has launched a new account of his Stanford Prison Experiment in his book *The Lucifer Effect* (2007). This book contains many new details about the original study that had previously been unpublished. In this section we look at the two studies to see how they can used to explain more recent examples of tyranny.

Abu Ghraib

In 2004 accounts started appearing in the world media of abuse of Iraqi prisoners at the Abu Ghraib prison in Baghdad. These reports were accompanied by a number of photographs taken by the soldiers. These images were the driving force behind Zimbardo deciding to write his book *The Lucifer Effect*. In the book Zimbardo revisits the Stanford Prison Experiment and uses it to explain the behaviour of the guards at Abu Ghraib. The message that Zimbardo draws from the SPE is that there are no bad apples, only bad barrels. He argues that in the SPE ordinary members of the public found themselves in a far from ordinary situation and behaved in cruel and brutal ways to other people. It could have been you, says Zimbardo. The factors that facilitated this, according to Zimbardo, included the uniforms that the participants wore and the roles they were assigned.

Zimbardo suggests that when we look at Abu Ghraib we should see not the actions of the guards but the actions of the system that created them. He describes how in his role as expert witness for one of the guards, Staff Sergeant Ivan 'Chip' Frederick, he made this point to the military court, though with little success.

A different interpretation of Abu Ghraib, however, does not see the guards as

Iconic image of US troops abusing Iraqi prisoners at the Abu Ghraib prison.

victims of the US government but as the agents of their much closer Machiavellian masters. In this reading of events the uncomfortable truth for us is that the guards were responding to what they perceived to be the requests of PsyOps units (Psychological Operations). One of those charged, Private Lynndie England, who featured prominently in the first batch of photographs and was subsequently jailed, insisted she was acting on orders from '*persons in my chain of command*'. '*I was instructed by persons in higher rank to "stand there, hold this leash, look at the camera", and they took pictures for PsyOps*' (see for example, Ronson, 2004).

An issue for psychologists (and us all) to confront is why some people will decide to take their own lives along with random members of the public in the name of a holy cause. The picture above shows London suicide bomber Mohammad Sidique Khan, from Dewsbury in West Yorkshire, relaying a message before claiming the lives of six people and injuring 120 in the Edgware Road Circle Line attack in London. How is this related to tyranny?

Zimbardo on 'The Experiment'

The following is Zimbardo's response to Reicher and Haslam's study. Is he raising legitimate concerns or just protecting his own research? You decide.

'*It was unfortunate that this "Made for TV Experiment" was ever conducted. The SPE is now judged to be unethical, so BBC-TV had no right to try to replicate it.*'

'*I cannot go into all the ways that this alleged replication should never be considered as an 'experiment' or even as serious social science, which I have done at great length in my review that recommended rejecting its publication.*'

'*It is sad for me to see these researchers not content to take their hired gun big salary for this job and go back to their labs and do some real serious research instead of using that mockery of research to challenge the value of my mock prison study.*'

The ethics of torture

If you can use psychological techniques to prevent acts of tyranny taking place what would you do? Is it OK to use psychological torture to interrogate suspected terrorists? The debate over this has split opinion in the American Psychological Association (APA). Most controversial is the role of psychologists at detention facilities such as Guantanamo Bay. Following growing concerns about this, the then APA President Ronald Levant visited Guantanamo Bay in 2005 saying '*I accepted this invitation to visit Guantanamo because I saw it as an important opportunity for the Association to provide input on the question of how psychologists can play an appropriate and ethical role in national security investigations.*' (Levant, 2007 page 2).

He was accompanied on the trip by Steven Sharfstein, President of the American Psychiatric Association who was so alarmed by what he encountered that he called for all psychiatrists to have nothing more to do with military interrogations. No such clear statement has come from the APA and the involvement of psychologists continues at military interrogation facilities.

It should be remembered that Guantanamo is outside international law and even US law. The inmates have not been arrested and charged, they have been kidnapped and tortured. They are not prisoners of war according to the US, and so are not covered by the Geneva Conventions. They have no legal representation and no obvious chance of release.

Most revealing in Levant's description of what he encountered at Guantanamo is the following,

'*We next visited the brand new psychiatric wing, which has both inpatient and outpatient services. I had a very unusual experience as we were standing at the nursing station, receiving a briefing from the psychiatrist. Behind me a voice asked "Dean Levant? Is that you?" That was the last thing I expected to hear at GTMO! I turned to see a former doctoral student in clinical psychology from Nova Southeastern University (NSU), who is now a military psychologist. I thought to myself, "NSU's graduates sure have done a good job of getting out into the world!"*' (ibid, page 5)

Study psychology, see the world and use sensory deprivation techniques on kidnap victims. It could catch on.

Multiple choice questions

1   The study was:
    a   Case study.   b   Experiment.
    c   Observation.   d   All of the above.

2   At the start of filming there were:
    a   5 prisoners   b   7 prisoners
    c   9 prisoners   d   10 prisoners

3   The conclusion drawn from the SPE was
    that:
    a   Individual characteristics determine
        behaviour in groups.
    b   Groups are likely to behave pro-socially.
    c   Groups create social identification.
    d   The behaviour was due to role
        acceptance.

4   The study was planned to run for:
    a   8 days.   b   9 days.
    c   10 days.   d   14 days.

5   Which of the following was not a planned
    intervention in the study?
    a   Permeability.   b   Security.
    c   Legitimacy   d   Cognitive
                               alternatives

6   How did Reicher and Haslam intend to
    trigger the search for cognitive
    alternatives?
    a   The introduction of prisoner 10.
    b   Telling prisoners there was no
        difference between prisoners and
        guards.
    c   Increasing sense of security.
    d   Removing permeability.

7   Which of the following was true?
    a   The prisoners showed a high level of
        identification when permeability was
        high.
    b   The prisoners showed a high level of
        identification when permeability was
        low.
    c   The guards showed a high level of
        group identification.
    d   Both b and c.

8   At the end of the study right-wing
    authoritarianism in the 'new' guards:
    a   Increased.
    b   Decreased.
    c   Was nearly the same as prisoners.
    d   Both b and c.

9   What evidence suggested that the
    participants were not play-acting?
    a   Their behaviour changed as predicted.
    b   They said they weren't play-acting.
    c   They appeared to be very distressed.
    d   None of them were actors.

10 The group failed when:
    a   The guards failed to control the
        prisoners.
    b   The commune collapsed.
    c   The 10th prisoner was introduced.
    d   Both a and b.

Answers are on page 185.

Exam-style questions

See page XII–XIII for notes on the exam paper and styles of question.

Section A questions

1   In Reicher and Haslam's study one of the interventions was
    intended to increase 'permeability'.
    (a) Describe how 'permeability' was created.   [2]
    (b) Describe how the situation was changed so the groups
         became impermeable.   [2]

2   In the Reicher and Haslam study one of the interventions
    did not have to be used.
    (a) Describe this intervention.   [2]
    (b) Explain why it was not necessary to implement it.   [2]

3   The BBC Prison study was an attempt to re-examine the
    conclusions of an earlier prison simulation – the Stanford
    Prison Experiment (SPE).
    (a) State **one** conclusion that was the same in both studies.   [2]
    (b) State **one** conclusion that was the different.   [2]

4   Psychologists sometimes make the distinction between
    situational and individual explanations of behaviour. Consider
    the Reicher and Haslam study and:
    (a) Give a situational explanation for the behaviour of the
         prisoners.   [2]
    (b) Give an individual explanation for the behaviour of the
         prisoners.   [2]

5   Reicher and Haslam identified various potential criticisms
    of their prison study.
    (a) Outline **one** of these criticisms.   [2]
    (b) Outline their answer to this criticism.   [2]

6   From the prison study by Reicher and Haslam identify
    four self-rating scales that were used.   [4]

Section B questions

(a) Identify the aim of the study by Reicher and Haslam.   [2]

(b) Describe the sample used in the study by Reicher and Haslam,
     and give **one** strength of the sample.   [6]

(c) Describe the independent variables in the study by Reicher and
     Haslam.   [6]

(d) Outline ethical issues that were raised in the study by Reicher
     and Haslam.   [6]

(e) Outline the conclusions of the study by Reicher and Haslam.   [8]

(f) Suggest **two** changes to the study by Reicher and Haslam and
     outline how these changes might affect the results.   [8]

Section C questions

(a) Explain what quantitative and qualitative data are.   [2]

(b) Describe how qualitative data was collected in the study by
     Reicher and Haslam.   [4]

(c) Describe **one** similarity and **one** difference between the Reicher and
     Haslam study and one other social core study.   [6]

(d) Discuss the strengths and limitations of the qualitative approach,
     using examples from the study by Reicher and Haslam.   [12]

Key issue: promoting human welfare

Why do we do psychology? The most obvious answer is 'to find out stuff'. The issue to consider is what sort of stuff are we finding out and what will we do with this stuff. Psychology tries to find out about how people think, feel and behave, and this seems to be interesting and helpful stuff to find out. But what if someone uses this information for their own benefit regardless of its effects on others?

The aim of science is to **understand** the world we live in, **predict** it and, if possible, **control** it. This is fine when we think about the weather. If we know how weather events happen then we can predict them and know when to take out our umbrellas or snow-shoes. One day we might even be able to control the weather so that Skegness can at last become the sun-kissed beach resort it has always dreamed of being.

If we apply these principles to psychology then we also want to understand behaviour and, if possible predict it, but when it comes to controlling it there are a number of extra issues that we have to consider. In particular, who should control whom, and what should the controllers get people to do? Will this make the world a better place for the individuals, the community or the controllers?

The basic issue is this: if psychologists can do even a fraction of what they claim to do in changing the ways people think, feel and behave, then they ought to be pretty sure that the changes they are making are able to bring some benefit to the world in which we all live.

Giving Psychology away

In 1969 George Miller gave his presidential address to the American Psychological Association and made a plea for the development of psychology. He entitled his address '*Psychology as a means of promoting human welfare*', and suggested that we should '*give psychology away*'. Rather than trying to develop a psychological technology to control people, Miller believes that psychology should present '*a new and different conception of what is humanly possible and humanly desirable*'. He goes on to say that we should think '*...not in terms of coercion by a powerful elite, but in terms of the diagnosis of problems and the development of programs that can enrich the lives of every citizen*'.

Miller argues that psychology has the potential to be one of the most revolutionary activities ever developed by people. He suggests that '*if we were ever to achieve substantial progress toward our stated aim – toward the understanding, prediction and control of mental and behavioural phenomena – the implications for every aspect of society would make brave men tremble*' (p. 1065). This is frighteningly true, of course, because if powerful people had the means to control our feelings, thoughts and behaviour they would surely do it. Don't get too worried about this though because psychology rarely lives up to the hype and nothing that it has done so far is very revolutionary. It is remarkable how little we know about people, and even how little we know about our own behaviour. Psychologists might have developed models of memory, theories of attachment, behaviour therapies and intelligence tests but these hardly match up to the developments in other sciences such as gunpowder, the steam engine, computers, atom bombs, the mapping of the human genome, the microwavable chip and so on.

Miller suggests that we are looking in the wrong direction if we are waiting for the great discoveries and applications of psychology to appear. Maybe the greatest benefit of psychology will come from how we think of ourselves:

'*I believe that the real impact of psychology will be felt, not through the technological products it places in the hands of powerful men, but through its effects on the public at large, through a new and different public conception of what is humanly possible and humanly desirable.*' (p. 1066)

If psychology can tell us more about how I think, feel and behave then maybe I can be more in control of myself and more aware of what I can become. If I have that information then I can make more choices about my life.

So the challenge for psychology is how to help everyone to become their own psychologist, able to reflect on and change their own behaviour rather than relying on 'experts' to tell them what to do. Miller finished his paper by saying:

'*I can imagine nothing that we could do that would be more relevant to human welfare, and nothing that could pose a greater challenge to the next generation of psychologists than to discover how best to give psychology away.*' (p. 1074)

Control The state that exists when one person or group has power over another.

Sensory deprivation The cutting out of all incoming sensory information, or at least as much of it as possible. Sometimes used as a method of torture.

Insignia of military PsyOps units.

Psychology and war

Psychologists have been active in military actions for over a century. Some of their interventions have been to help soldiers deal with the traumas of combat and get them ready to go back into action, some interventions have been in propaganda to increase the confidence of our troops or undermine the morale of the enemy, and they have also developed interrogation techniques. If you believe a prisoner has information that could save the lives of others how far should you go to get that information from them? These are not easy questions for anyone but it is worth considering that the involvement of PsyOps (Psychological Operations) at Abu Ghraib prison in Iraq and at Guantanamo Bay has moved these techniques outside the internationally agreed rules for the treatment of prisoners.

Qs

1. Select **one** core study and explain how this study makes a useful contribution to our understanding of behaviour and experience.

2. Select another core study that you think has information that could be used to change someone's behaviour. Think of **one** situation where it is a good thing to use this technique to change behaviour and **one** situation when it is wrong.

3. Try to think of psychology's great findings. What do you think are its greatest discoveries and inventions? If your list is a bit short then ask your teacher or, better still, a professional psychologist. Give them a list of successes in the other sciences like the human genome, the micro-chip, the moon landing, the mobile phone and then ask for psychology's equivalent. It never fails to wind them up.

4. If you were going to give psychology away, what do you think would be the most useful things for people to be given?

Controlling behaviour: You decide

George Miller suggests that psychology should try and tell us about *'what is humanly possible and humanly desirable.'* (page 1067). It is clear that some psychology lives up to this ambition and that some falls short. We leave you to judge where to put the line.

When we try and change behaviour we have an effect on the individual we are changing, the community they are in and there might also be some benefit or cost for the person who is bringing about the change.

Look at the examples in the box below and think about (a) and (b):

(a) Who benefits most, the individual, the community, or the controller?

(b) Whether you think this example of psychology is promoting human welfare.

---

1 A therapist helps an individual get over their fear of people so that they can get out of their house without having a panic attack.

2 A consumer psychologist creates a shop design that encourages people to stay in it longer and spend more money.

3 A business psychologist designs an anti-stress programme that reduces the workers stress levels and reduces the number of days off sick.

4 A clinical psychologist diagnoses someone as having a personality disorder. The patient hasn't done anything wrong yet but they might in the future so they are sent to a psychiatric hospital.

5 A military psychologist is asked to use psychological techniques to interrogate someone who it is believed has valuable information about terrorism.

6 A brain scientist claims that she can use brain scans to spot the difference between murderers and non-murderers, and as a result suggests that brain surgery can be used on potential murderers to prevent crime.

Psychological research might be used to help design shopping centres which are just right for people who use them. Here's an example of a shopping centre design that gives a sense of space when we're inside the building but gives us very few cues for getting out.

Therapists can help you across the psychological road to a better place, but what if that is not the road you wanted to cross and the other side does not turn out to better than where you were?

Psychobabble

Media psychologists popularise the subject and bring basic ideas to public attention. On the sofa with Richard and Judy, or commenting on the Big Brother House, media psychologists tell us about what someone's behaviour means and what their intentions are. They seem to be giving psychology away because they are telling us about ourselves but not everyone agrees with this. The accusation against them is that they simplify and distort what we know and on occasions actually tell lies. Psychologists can't read minds, intentions or body language any better than members of the general public. These tricks belong with other attempts to bluff people with phoney insights such as clairvoyance and fortune telling.

Therapy

Psychologists have devised many therapies over the last hundred years which have had some success. The therapies range from the lengthy psychoanalysis of Freud to the more focused cognitive therapies such as Rational Emotive and Behaviour Therapy (REBT). Therapy seems to be a generally good thing but there are two main concerns, (i) the power relationship between the powerful therapist who seems in control of things and the relatively powerless client, and (ii) the categorisation of common behaviours as psychological problems. This second point has seen a massive growth in the use of therapy and medication to change people's behaviour. Of course, if we were happy with ourselves in the first place then we wouldn't have to pay a therapist or take loads of damaging tablets to change our behaviour and sense of self.

Changing the world

Psychological research has not developed any weapons of mass destruction but it does throw up some difficult moral questions, so it is important to consider what we want to achieve from our studies. J.B. Watson (see page 61) set the agenda for modern psychology when he wrote the following:

'The interest of the behaviourist in man's [sic] doings is more than the interest of the spectator – he wants to control man's reactions as physical scientists want to control and manipulate other natural phenomena. It is the business of behaviouristic psychology to be able to predict and to control human activity.' (Watson, 1930, page 11)

If we follow Watson's suggestion we can use psychology to change the world. This is fantastic as long as (a) it needs changing in the first place, and (b) we change it for the better rather than for the worse. There is also the issue of who is going to do the changing, who gets changed and who decides what change is 'for the better'. You can see the problem here, especially if those being changed are quite happy as they are.

...Links to other studies and issues...

Several of the studies in this text have made positive contributions to human welfare. For example the **Milgram** study holds up a mirror on our behaviour for us to look at and become aware of what we are capable of. The **Rosenhan** study highlighted the poor way that psychiatric patients were being treated in mental hospitals and had the effect of improving that treatment. There are two core studies that describe the use of therapy to bring about changes in behaviour – one is **Freud's** account of Little Hans and the other is the *Three Faces of Eve* (**Thigpen and Cleckley**). Interestingly these two studies are written by the therapists themselves and in the case of Eve there is considerable dispute about whether this account is accurate and whether the therapy had a beneficial effect on the patient.

This issue also links to the ideas around **behaviourism** and **determinism** and **free will**. The behaviourists believed that people do not have free will but instead just respond to rewards and punishments in the environment. If this is the case then the logical solution is to take control of the environment and train people with rewards and punishments to behave in a way to be well and be happy.

Good, and not so good, Samaritans

At first sight the city is a lonely and alien place. Buildings hover over the streets and cast long shadows over the faceless and nameless people who scurry beneath them. Many people only experience the city when they commute into work or to shop. To them it can be a dangerous and unfriendly place.

Every so often a news story captures the public imagination and turns into a modern parable of city life. The case of James Bulger in Liverpool is one of these stories (see page 178) and so was the case of Kitty Genovese (below), a young woman murdered in a New York street in 1964. This murder made the news because of the reported behaviour of the residents of the neighbourhood in which the attack took place.

Social psychologists including Stanley Milgram became interested in the newspaper accounts of the murder. John Darley and Bibb Latané devised a number of laboratory studies that demonstrated the bystander effect.

Kitty Genovese

The assault

Kitty Genovese drove home from her bar job arriving at 3.15 a.m. When she got out of the car she was approached by Winston Moseley who stabbed her. She screamed and her cries were heard by several neighbours but on a cold night with the windows closed only a few of them recognised the sound as a cry for help. When one of the neighbours shouted at the attacker, Moseley ran away, and Genovese made her way towards her own apartment around the end of the building. She was seriously injured but now out of view of those few who may have had reason to believe she was in need of help.

Other witnesses observed Moseley enter his car and drive away, only to return five minutes later. He searched the apartment complex, following the trail of blood to Genovese, who was lying in a hallway at the back of the building. Out of view of the street and of those who may have heard or seen any sign of the original attack, he proceeded to rape her, rob her, and finally murder her. The time from the first assault until her death was about half an hour.

Later investigation revealed that at least 38 individuals nearby had heard or observed portions of the attack, though none could have seen or been aware of the entire

incident. Many were entirely unaware that an assault or homicide was in progress; some thought that what they saw or heard was a lovers' quarrel or a group of friends leaving the bar outside which Moseley first approached Genovese.

The New York Times ran the story under the headline *'Thirty-Eight Who Saw Murder Didn't Call the Police'* which was not exactly true. The article began, *'For more than half an hour thirty-eight respectable, law-abiding citizens in Queens watched a killer stalk and stab a woman in three separate attacks in Kew Gardens'*. It is from this semi-correct article that the murder became famous and the local residents were damned.

The Genovese family

It was a difficult call for us to know whether to describe the case of Kitty Genovese in this book. It appears in many psychology articles and most introductory texts and, remarkably, she is probably more famous with psychology students than most of the psychologists they study. She is famous, however, for the way she died and we doubt this is how she would have wanted to be remembered. She had family and friends and a full and interesting life. She was much more than a gruesome headline.

Doorway where Kitty Genovese died.

Explanations of the bystander ef

The *bystander effect* (also known as bystander apathy) is a phenomenon where persons are less likely to intervene in an emergency situation when others are present than when they are alone.

There have been numerous attempts to explain this effect by psychologists and some of them are outlined here.

Pluralistic ignorance

Imagine this, you are walking down the street and you see some smoke coming out of a building. You are not sure it's smoke, it might be steam. It could be a fire but it might not be. How can you tell? The most obvious thing to do is to look at the reaction of other people. As you look around they seem to be relaxed about it and just walking on. It must be steam you think, so you walk on too. But maybe those other people were also unsure and they walked on because they saw you looking relaxed. Between all of you, and without saying a word, you have negotiated that the situation is not an emergency. This effect is called *pluralistic ignorance*.

In a laboratory study, participants were directed to a room to fill in questionnaires. They were either alone or with two other people. While they were in the room steam started to come through a vent in the wall.

Then there is her family. There can be no closure for the families of murder victims, especially for the Genovese family. The story still surfaces from time to time and still appears in psychology texts like this one. About 40 years after the murder yet another television programme was made. Kitty's brother Bill said *'I was consulted in a project for the History Channel not long ago. See, they're going to do the story anyway, so we may as well cooperate. At least we have some measure of control if we cooperate'* (Gado, 2005).

Calling the police

Although the residents are always given the blame in the Kitty Genovese story, their perception of the local police contributed to the social climate. At the time of the attack one local resident commented, *'Shortly after moving in I heard screaming on the street several times, called the police and was politely told to mind my own business'* (Rosenthal, 1964, page 46).

Another resident wrote to the New York Times saying, *'Have you ever reported anything to the police? If you did, you would know that you are subjected to insults and abuse from annoyed undutiful police such as "why don't you move out of the area" or "why bother us, this is a bad area" or "you will have a call answered 45 min"'* (Rosenthal, 1999 page 46).

The question was how many people would report this. Seventy-five per cent of people left on their own reported the steam but only 38% of people in a group did so (Latané and Darley, 1968).

Diffusion of responsibility

It's such a relief when someone else sorts out an emergency. The more people there are in a group the less chance that it will be you, you hope. Experimental studies show that adding people to a group reduces the chance of an individual stepping up to help in an emergency (Darley and Latané, 1968).

In another experiment students were recruited to take part in some discussions via an intercom. Each student had to talk for two minutes, then comment on what the others said, though in fact there was only one real person taking part. The other 'students' were pre-recorded. As the student listened to one of the other voices the person appeared to have an epileptic seizure and started choking before lapsing into silence. If the student believed they were the only person to hear this emergency then 85% tried to help, but if they thought that the other people could also hear it the intervention rate dropped as low as 30% (Darley and Latané, 1968).

Stimulus overload

People living in cities are bombarded every day with stimuli and with social interactions. Some days it is just too much. Strangers approach you with clipboards trying to sell you something. Traffic is continuous, noisy and unpredictable, and then there are the thousand text messages that demand your attention. Milgram (1970) suggested that people have stimulus overload and so restrict their attention to the events that they believe are most important. These are likely to be things that are personally relevant or connected to people they know. The lives of strangers will inevitably come way down the list.

When do you help and when do you walk by? Not an easy decision.

The tradition with firing squads is to load all of the guns with blanks except for one but not say which one has the bullet. This allows everyone in the firing squad to believe they did not shoot at the victim. This helps to diffuse their responsibility for the execution.

The somebody else's problem (SEP) field

In an ironic take on the bystander effect The Hitchhiker's Guide to the Galaxy (by Douglas Adams) describes the somebody else's problem field (SEP field). This fictional technology is a cheaper and more practical alternative to an invisibility field. A SEP field can be created around a bizarre and unbelievable scene so that the unconscious mind of an observer defines it as 'somebody else's problem', and therefore doesn't see it at all.

An example of this was given in Adam's third book Life, the Universe and Everything, when a UFO landed in the middle of a cricket ground during a match, and the crowd didn't notice it. The SEP field requires much less energy than a normal invisibility field and a single flashlight battery can run it for over a hundred years.

The idea of the SEP field has some grounding in real life, in that people may not notice things that don't fit their view of the world: when people look at branded goods they see attractive design and not the sweat shop conditions in which many of them are made.

Parables

A parable is a story that is told to illustrate a religious, moral or philosophical idea. It is possible to see some psychology studies, such as the Milgram experiment and the Stanford Prison Simulation, as parables.

The good Samaritan is a famous Christian parable (Luke: 10: 25–37), told by Jesus to illustrate the idea that it is important to show compassion for all people regardless of race. The parable tells of a man attacked, robbed and left for dead at the side of the road. He is ignored by two passers-by, both religious men. A third man, however, stops and helps. He is a Samaritan (i.e. from Samaria) and therefore of a different race from the man who was robbed. He would have less reason to stop than the first two men but his compassion was such that he could not pass by and do nothing. This story produces the term 'good Samaritan' to describe someone who helps a stranger. The charity group 'the Samaritans' in this country provides free support to people contemplating suicide.

The good Samaritan study

Students at a theological college were asked to present a sermon on helping; on their way to the sermon, they passed a man slumped and groaning in a doorway. If the students thought they were late 10% helped, compared with 63% who thought they were early. Some of those who didn't help said they didn't notice the victim (Darley and Batson, 1973).

...Link to the core study...

The moral panic that arose in the 1960s about the alienation of people in cities stimulated a lot of laboratory experiments related to helping behaviour. There will always be questions over how far these studies can be applied to everyday life. A small number of brave researchers took their studies out into the city. This is one example.

One of the issues to consider as you read the study is the view that is taken of people in the city. In particular they are seen as relatively passive with the most important variable being the number of other people near to them.

Piliavin *et al.*: the core study

Irving M. Piliavin, Judith Rodin and Jane Allyn Piliavin (1969) Good samaritanism: an underground phenomenon? *Journal of Personality and Social Psychology*, 13 (4), pages 289–299.

Abstract

A field experiment was conducted to observe the effect of several variables on helping behaviour.

Method

The experiment was staged on the New York subway during the middle of the day (11 a.m. to 3 p.m.) and the 4,500 participants were the passengers on the train.

Four teams of students, each team consisting of a victim, model and two observers, staged a standard collapse on the subway.

In each team the victims were always male, 3 of whom were white and 1 was black. The observers were always female. Each team boarded a train and after 70 seconds the victim collapsed.

The IVs for this study were:

- Victim drunk or ill (carried a cane).
- Victim black or white.
- Model intervened either after 70 or 150 seconds, or no model.
- Group size.

Main results

The frequency of helping was considerably higher than found in previous lab experiments. The main findings were:

1. An apparently ill person is more likely to receive help than one who appears drunk, and help is forthcoming more quickly.

2. The race of the victim has little effect except when the victim is drunk and then they are more likely to be helped by someone of the same race.

3. The longer the emergency continues without help being forthcoming, the more likely that someone will leave the critical area near the victim.

4. The 'diffusion of responsibility' effect was not found in this study, in fact helping was greater in seven-person groups than in three-person groups.

Conclusion

The results can be explained in terms of a cost–reward model.

Introduction

Since the murder of Kitty Genovese psychologists have conducted many studies in order to find explanations for bystander behaviour, such as a study by Latané and Rodin (1969) which showed that assistance was more likely if bystanders were acquaintances rather than strangers. Much of this work has been conducted in laboratories which is not a problem if some research is also conducted in the field to provide confirmation from a more natural setting.

Aim

The main aims of this study are outlined in points 1 and 2.

1. **Type of victim (drunk or ill)** People who are seen as partly responsible for their plight receive less help (Schopler and Matthews, 1965). In addition, bystanders might be reluctant to help a drunk because he/she may behave embarrassingly and/or become violent.

2. **Race of victim (black or white)** Research suggests that people would be more likely to help someone of their own race.

3. **Impact of modelling** Past research (Bryan and Test, 1967) shows that people are more likely to help in an emergency situation if they have seen someone else displaying the behaviour.

4. **Group size** Darley and Latané (1968) found that increased group size led to decreases in frequency of responding and an increase in latency (how long it takes to offer help).

Method

Participants

About 4,500 men and women who were travelling on the 8th Avenue express subway train in New York City weekdays between 11 a.m. and 3 p.m. over a two-month period. There were slightly more white people than blacks, and on average there were 43 people in a compartment on any one trial and, on average, 8.5 people in the 'critical area'.

Procedure

On each trial, a team of four General Studies students boarded the train separately. There were four different teams. Two girls acted as observers and took seats outside the critical area. The male model and victim remained standing. After approximately 70 seconds the victim staggered forward and collapsed, and remained lying on his back staring at the ceiling until receiving help. The express train does not stop for 7½ minutes between 59th and 125th Street, the start and stopping points for this study. If no help was forthcoming when the train stopped the model helped the victim to his feet.

New York subway train

Victim

The four victims (one in each team) were aged 26–35, one was black. All were male and were dressed identically. Each victim participated in both cane and drunk trials.

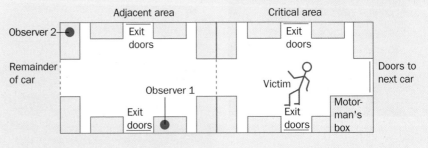

Layout of subway carriage showing the critical area and position of the victim.

Activity

Try role-playing this experiment. Arrange your classroom to look like the subway carriage. Make a list of all the different conditions and have a go trying them out while the observers keep a record of all data.

Qs

1   Was the sample a random, volunteer or opportunity sample?
2   Why was a subway train a good place to conduct the experiment?
3   State **two** hypotheses for this study.
4   Why do you think the results differ from those of Latané and Darley? (You should think of at least two explanations).

On 38 trials the victim was drunk and 65 trials the victim was sober.

- *The 'drunk' condition* The victim smelled of alcohol and carried a bottle wrapped in a brown paper bag (as they do in New York).
- *The cane condition* The victim appeared sober and had a black cane.

Model
Four white males aged between 24 and 29 played the models. There were three possibilities:

- *No model* The model didn't help at all.
- *Early model* helped after 70 seconds.
- *Late model* helped after 150 seconds.

The point of this was to see if a 'model' (someone offering help) affected the behaviour of other passengers.

Measures
On each trial one observer noted:

- Race, sex and location of every person seated or standing in the critical area.
- Total number of persons in the carriage.
- Total number who helped the victim.
- Race, sex and location of every helper.

The second observer noted:

- Race, sex and location of every person in the adjacent area.
- Time when help was first offered.

Both observers noted any comments made by nearby passengers and also tried to elicit comments from a passenger sitting next to them.

Biographical notes

Irving and Jane Piliavin are both retired professors of sociology at the University of Wisconsin at Madison. Irving is a keen poker player and they both like watching American football. Jane tells the story of how the Samaritan study came about: *'[Irv] was working with Bibb Latané on a post-doc designed to give people in other fields (his is social work) the opportunity to retrain. He was riding on the subway himself ... when a drunk rolled off his seat and fell to the floor. Nobody did anything for a long time (until he did). By the time he got [home] a few hours later he had designed the study'* (personal communication).

Judith Rodin worked with the Piliavins on the Samaritan study but has since moved on to the more administrative side of academia, and was the first woman to become a President of an Ivy League University in America, the University of Pennsylvania.

Results

The frequency of helping was impressive compared with previous lab experiments.

Amount of help offered
Piliavin *et al.* report that the cane victim received spontaneous help 95% of the time (62/65 trials) whereas the drunk victim was spontaneously helped 50% of the time (19/38 trials).

- On 49 of the 81 (60%) trials when the victim was given help, the help was given by two or more helpers.
- On 21 out of the full 103 (20%) trials (with and without a model) 34 people left the critical area after the victim collapsed.

Time taken to help
Results are shown in the graph. Help was slower to be forthcoming in the drunk condition. Only 17% of the drunk victims were helped before the model stepped in and 'encouraged' others to help, whereas 87% of the cane victims were helped before the model stepped in. The median latency for cane trials (nonmodel condition only) was 5 seconds whereas it was 109 seconds for drunk trials.

Time taken for help to be offered

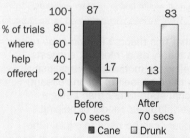

% of trials where help offered

Gender
90% of the first helpers were males.

Race
Black victims received less help less quickly especially in the drunk condition. Also in the drunk condition there was a slight 'same race' effect – whites were slightly more likely to help whites than to help blacks.

Comments
More comments from subway passengers were obtained in the drunk condition than in the cane condition. Similarly most of the comments were made on the trials where no help was given within the first 70 seconds. Many women made comments such as '*It's for men to help him*' or '*You feel so bad when you don't know what to do*' (p. 295).

Group size
The more passengers who were in the immediate vicinity of the victim the more likely help was to be given. This appears to be the reverse of Darley and Latané's 'diffusion of responsibility' effect. This may be because the original effect was produced in lab experiments where all helpers bar one were confederates. In a field experiment the greater number of potential helpers may have counteracted any diffusion effect. Second, the fact that potential helpers could see the victim may have reduced the tendency to diffuse responsibility.

Deciding to help

The main message from early studies on bystanders was that people are reluctant help in emergencies but is this really the case?

James Bulger

The event in the UK that provoked a similar moral panic to the murder of Kitty Genovese (see page 172) was the murder of two-and-a-half-year-old James Bulger in 1993. The boy was abducted from his mother in a shopping centre by two ten-year-old boys. The three boys walked around Liverpool for over two hours before James was tortured and murdered next to a railway line. The haunting image of the time (see picture below) was from cctv cameras in the shopping centre that captured the moment of abduction.

MOTHERCARE
15:42:32 12/02/93 3HR

In a strange coincidence with the Genovese murder, 38 witnesses appeared at the trial of the two ten-year-olds. These people had seen or, in some cases, had contact with the boys during their journey across the city. None of them had intervened decisively enough to save the toddler despite the fact that there were signs that something was wrong (for example an injury to the child's head and apparent distress).

Were these witnesses an example of the bystander effect? Such an interpretation is probably neither helpful nor accurate. Another view (for example, Levine, 1999) suggests they can be seen in terms of the sense they made of an ambiguous situation and the social categories they used to interpret it. In particular they assumed the boys were brothers and this category of 'family' prohibited any intervention. We don't interfere in 'domestics' and we don't tell other people how to treat their children.

The following witness quotes come from the trial (cited in Levine, 1999): '*I saw a little boy apparently two and a half to three years of age ... [...]. He was holding, it looked to be a teenager's hand, which I presumed was his older brother.*'

One witness reported this exchange with one of the boys, '"*I'm fed up of having my little brother." He says, "It's always the same from school" and he said, "I'm going to tell me mum, I'm not going to have him no more."*'

Group membership and bystanders

The studies that followed the Kitty Genovese attack dealt with bystanders as if they were isolated individuals. Recent research has looked at the social identity of bystanders and the groups they have allegiance to. For example, Dovidio *et al.* (1997) found evidence that people were more likely to help members of their own social group (the 'ingroup'). In their study, students were asked to volunteer to help a student distribute questionnaires for their research project. They were more likely to offer help if they thought the student was an ingroup member. This work connects to the Reicher and Haslam study concerning group behaviour.

Levine *et al.* (2002) reworked one of the early bystander studies (the 'good Samaritan' experiment on page 173) and looked at the effect of group identity. They advertised for fans of Premier League football teams to take part in a study. Some Manchester United fans were selected and put together to create a sense of group identity. The fans were directed as a group across the college campus to another room. On the way they witnessed a runner having an accident where he fell over and appeared to hurt himself. In one condition he was wearing neutral clothes and in the other two conditions he wore either a Manchester United shirt (their own team) or a Liverpool (despised rivals) shirt. The injured runner was usually helped when he wore a Manchester United shirt, but he was rarely helped when he wore the other shirts.

Football fans might look like muppets but they'll help their fellow fans.

The London bombs, July 2005

What happens in a real emergency? Do people help or do they look the other way? The London bomb attack produced numerous cases of personal heroism that challenge the view of the uncaring city. If you look, for example, at the pictures of the No. 30 bus that was bombed you can see almost as many people going to help as there are running away. We have remarkable first-hand footage of the events taken by people on their camera phones. In fact the news made the internet blog sites before it was broken on the BBC, which is a new way that people can communicate and help each other.

What follows are some accounts of people involved in the London bombs. Although we selected the quotes we have not tried to put our own explanation on the events. We think they show the remarkable variation of human behaviour and the complexity of human experience.

A woman who was seriously injured in one of the trains commented, '*There was nobody around. There were people talking across from me – people trying to calm each other – but I felt that my experience was quite lonely. It feels like there were lots of lonely individuals in one setting.*'

A man on one of the other trains describes the horror in the carriage, then says, '*Your humanity strikes in, you think is there anyone you can save here or take out with me? A right hand came out and held onto my leg and I tried to see where they were and you couldn't see anything. It was just a mass of bodies and I thought instinctively I've got to get that person out.*'

A former firefighter was widely pictured shepherding a bomb victim to safety as she clutched a surgical mask to her burnt face. He was hailed a hero in the press but he commented, '*I was filled with a certain level of guilt that I was made out to be a hero – the real heroes were the people who lost their lives.*'

And a woman on the Piccadilly line train said '*... people so often comment on the arrogance of Londoners and how unfriendly we are – yesterday there was none of that. We all rallied together helping one another get through it – holding hands, sharing water, calming those who were panicked.*'

(BBC, 2005; Yahoo news, 2005)

The evidence seems to show that people will help each other even in extreme situations especially if they feel connected to each other.

Multiple choice questions

1 Which of the following was an IV that was *not* manipulated by the experimenters?
 a Race of victim.   b Drunk or not.
 c Group size.   d Model present.

2 The subjects were:
 a Psychology students.
 b General studies students.
 c Passengers on the subway.
 d Both b and c.

3 The victims were:
 a All male and white.
 b All male, black and white.
 c All white, some men and some women.
 d Black and white, men and women.

4 The model intervened:
 a 70 secs. after the victim collapsed.
 b 70 secs after the train left the station.
 c 140 secs. after the victim collapsed.
 d Both a and c.

5 Which of the following is a DV in this experiment?
 a Willingness to help.
 b Race of helper.
 c Time taken to offer help.
 d All of the above.

6 Passengers were more willing to help:
 a Women.
 b Drunks.
 c Victims with a cane.
 d Black victims.

7 Passengers in the critical area who did not help dealt with their arousal by:
 a Asking someone to help the victim.
 b Turning away from the victim.
 c Making a comment about why they weren't helping.
 d Leaving the critical area.

8 The diffusion of responsibility effect predicts that:
 a Helping increases when group size increases.
 b Helping decreases when group size increases.
 c Helping decreases when group size decreases.
 d Group size has no effect on rates of helping.

9 The results of this study showed that the diffusion of responsibility effect:
 a Occurred.
 b Didn't occur.
 c May have occurred but was counteracted by the number of potential helpers.
 d The study did not consider this effect.

10 Piliavin *et al.* proposed that the first thing that happens in an emergency situation is:
 a Rewards.
 b Costs.
 c Arousal.
 d Both a and b.

Answers are on page 185.

Exam-style questions

Section A questions

1 Previous psychological research found that people didn't help in emergency situations due to diffusion of responsibility.
 (a) What is meant by the term diffusion of responsibility? [2]
 (b) Explain why this effect was not observed in the study by Piliavin *et al.* [2]

2 Piliavin *et al.* proposed a model of response to emergencies on the basis of the results from their study.
 (a) Identify the **two** factors that influence a person's decision to help or not. [2]
 (b) Use these two factors to explain **one** of the results from the study. [2]

3 (a) Describe **one** ethical issue that was a problem in this study by Piliavin *et al.* [2]
 (b) Describe how Piliavin *et al.* might have dealt with this ethical issue. [2]

4 Piliavin *et al.* designed a study where some of the researchers acted as 'models'.
 (a) Identify **two** of the model conditions. [2]
 (b) Outline **one** conclusion that was drawn from these. [2]

5 Piliavin *et al.* (subway Samaritan study) suggested that helping behaviour can be explained using an arousal/cost reward model. Using this model suggest **two** ways of reducing arousal in the subway emergency. [4]

6 Outline **two** practical problems that occurred in conducting the subway Samaritan study by Piliavin *et al.* [4]

See page XII–XIII for notes on the exam paper and styles of question.

Section B questions

(a) Describe the aim of the study by Piliavin *et al.* [2]

(b) Describe how data was collected in the study by Piliavin *et al.* [6]

(c) Give **one** advantage and **one** disadvantage of the method used to collect data in the study by Piliavin *et al.* [6]

(d) Explain how the reliability of these measurements could be assessed. [6]

(e) Outline the findings of the study by Piliavin *et al.* [8]

(f) Suggest **two** changes to the study by Piliavin *et al.* and outline how these changes might affect the results. [8]

Section C questions

(a) Outline **one** assumption of the social approach in psychology. [2]

(b) Describe how the social approach could explain the development of how people behave in emergencies. [4]

(c) Describe **one** similarity and **one** difference between the study by Piliavin *et al.* and any other social study. [6]

(d) Discuss the strengths and limitations of the social approach, using examples from the study by Piliavin *et al.* [12]

Key issue: ethics

Ethics are the values and customs of a person or a group. They deal with issues such as right and wrong, good and bad, and what it means to be responsible for our actions. Every group has a code of behaviour that gives some guidance on how to behave. Sometimes this code is written down and our laws are an example of this. If you break the law and get caught you will be given a punishment. Not all parts of the good behaviour code are written down and we have to pick them up from the people we mix with. You often only find out about the code when you accidentally break it, so for example if you turn up to a party in fancy dress then people will laugh but if you turn up to a wedding in the same costume there will be less laughter.

What are ethics?

The ethics of a behaviour can be judged using four categories (Daeg de Mott, 2001): consequences, actions, character and motive. When we look at *consequences*, we judge whether a behaviour is right or wrong by looking at the result of the behaviour. If it leads to a result that brings about an improvement for someone's life, we might think it is a good thing. When we look at the *actions*, however, we look at the act itself, and consider what it is that the person is doing. The category of *character* is concerned with whether the person is a good (or virtuous) person who is generally ethical. When we look at *motives*, we are concerned with the intentions of the person carrying out the behaviour, and we consider whether they were trying to do something good.

Nothing is clear cut in the study of ethics and these categories sometimes give us different assessments. The puzzle is to decide whether you think the behaviour is ethical or not. Look at the following two examples and see what you think.

Example one: therapy

Rapoff *et al.* (1980) used an ammonia spray to punish a deaf–blind five-year-old boy who was engaging in serious self-injurious behaviour (self mutilation), and in so doing reduced the amount of self-harmful behaviour.

This sounds a shocking thing to do and many of you will immediately decide that this treatment is unethical but we are going to argue the opposite. The *consequence* of this action, if it is successful, is that the boy will have a better quality of life. The *act* does not look to be a good thing, but we might well judge the *motives* of the therapist to be sound because they want to help the child. Depending on what we believe about therapists in general or what we know about Rapoff in particular we can make an assessment of *character* and decide whether we trust them to do the right thing. Considering that there are no easy solutions when dealing with very challenging children and that this solution at least avoids the use of medication, you might be inclined to judge this as an ethical treatment. Feel free to disagree.

Example two: the Milgram study

Milgram's study is commonly cited in psychology texts as an example of research that broke ethical guidelines. However, the *consequences* of the study were that we have a much sharper insight into human behaviour. The *act*, again, does not look good but Milgram's *motives* were to find out about human behaviour and, in particular, why people are able to commit atrocities. We would also argue that Milgram's *character* was sound as shown by the way that he tried to deal with ethical issues before and after the study.

Activity

The ethical question is: if you believe someone has information that you want, how far can you go to get that information? Think about this for the following situations,

(a) A kidnapper telling you where the victim is.

(b) Your brother telling you where he has hidden the remote.

Activity

1 Before you read this page consider what is ethically acceptable in psychological research. Draw up your own list of ethical guidelines.

2 In a small group rank the ethical issues in order of importance.

Ethics are judgements about what is right and wrong, and good and bad.

Ethical guidelines (also called ethical principles or code of conduct) are instructions to guide professional conduct and practice. They aim to resolve ethical issues.

Ethical committee A group of people within a research institution who must approve a study before it begins.

Debriefing A post-research interview conducted for ethical and practical reasons: (1) to inform participants of the true nature of the study and ensure their well-being, (2) may be used to gain important feedback about procedures used in the study.

Clay Bennett / © The Christian Science Monitor (www.csmonitor.com). All rights reserved.

Ethics and psychology

In psychology we are interested in the moral and ethical codes that people develop and live by, but that is not the concern on this page. What we are interested in here is the ethical code that psychologists develop for their own behaviour. Psychologists deal with people in a number of ways including doing research with them and offering them therapy or advice. In order to ensure the safety of the people who come into contact with psychologists, psychologists have developed some guidelines of good practice which are commonly referred to as ethics.

Many studies are criticised for their lack of ethics. It is not acceptable for participants to be harmed during the course of any study. However, what constitutes 'harm'? Is it harmful for a person to experience mild discomfort or mild stress? Is it acceptable to lie to participants about what an experiment is about? Such deception may be necessary so that participants' behaviour is not affected by knowing what the aim of the experiment is.

Ethics is a topic which has no straightforward answers. Psychologists have to weigh up various factors when deciding whether a study is ethically acceptable. Professional organisations such as the British Psychological Society (BPS) produce ethical guidelines or 'codes of conduct' to help do this.

Ethical guidelines for psychological research

We have listed below the guidelines that are commonly agreed by psychologists. Of course, nothing is ever simple and judgements about ethics depend on more than just a set of guidelines, including how useful the research will be. For example, if a study might create a life saving drug then a certain amount of risk might be acceptable but if the study is for a beauty product then the risk is not necessary or acceptable.

Consent – Have the participants of the study given their informed consent to take part? In other words did they know what they were letting themselves in for? Have the parents of child participants given informed consent to the research procedures? Have payments been used to induce risk taking behaviour, thus enticing people to give their consent?

Deception – Have the participants been deceived? Was there any other way to carry out the study other than by using deception? Have the procedures been approved by other psychologists?

Debriefing – Have the participants been effectively debriefed? In other words, when the study is over have the participants been told what was happening and asked if they have any concerns? Has any stress caused by the procedures been removed?

Withdrawal from the investigation – Do the participants know they can withdraw from the study at any time without penalty or scorn? This guideline is sometimes interpreted to mean that participants can withdraw their data from the study long after the work has been completed.

Confidentiality – Participants in psychological research have the right to expect that information they provide will be treated confidentially and not passed on to other people or sold to national newspapers.

Protection of participants – Investigators must protect participants from physical, emotional and mental harm during the investigation.

Observational research – Unless the participants give their consent to being observed, observational research must only take place where those observed could normally be expected to be observed by strangers.

Giving advice – Psychological advice must only be given if the psychologist is qualified in the area that the advice is requested in.

Colleagues – Psychologists should take action if they believe that any of the above principles are being violated by a colleague.

Missing guidelines

The principles in the list on the left offer a framework for the conduct of research. It is debateable whether they are a full list of the things that psychologists ought to be concerned about. There are some omissions from the list that we might like to add as extra guidelines of good practice. For example, what about:

The use of the research: We can ask our psychologists to try and ensure that their findings are used to help people rather than to harm them. So if, for example, psychologists found out what features of a casino encourage people to gamble more than they want, they should tell the punters but not the casino. If they tell the casino then that organisation will most probably use that information to persuade punters into losing more money at the gaming tables.

Including all people: It is known that in the USA and the UK the practice of psychology has relatively few people from ethnic minorities and the focus of the research is on majority communities rather than the diversity of modern life. It is difficult to see how individual research projects could be designed to always deal with diversity issues but universities could ensure a balance in their research programmes.

You might think of some other issues of right/wrong, good/bad that psychologists should consider. The discussion isn't closed.

Some decisions are easier than others

What do you with a child with severe learning difficulties who self-injures themself? These self-injuries can be so severe that it is felt necessary to use physical restraint such as a straight jacket to prevent them. In these circumstances what do you do to try and change the behaviour of the child so that they could live a life without physical restraint?

If someone is able to make an informed choice then it is clearly unethical to use noxious sprays such as ammonia in an attempt to change their behaviour. The decision is not so easy with the child described above. Rapoff et al. (1980) used a range of aversive stimuli such as an ammonia spray and managed to stop the child from self-injuring. Some readers will be uncomfortable with this and think it unethical while others will see it as a practical answer to a very difficult problem.

Qs

1 Select **one** core study that illustrates each issue below and suggest how the researchers might have dealt with this issue.
- Deception
- Psychological harm
- Invasion of privacy

2 A psychologist wishes to conduct a study observing the behaviour of children going to and from school. Outline how you might conduct such a study in an ethical manner.

3 Do you think there are any new ethical issues for psychologists, for example if they collect information from people online through Facebook or MSN?

...Links to other studies and issues...

The study of ethics is concerned with judgements about right and wrong. All psychological research can be judged against an ethical code. It is important to realise, however, that ethical codes change over time and so it is not helpful to judge behaviour from a hundred or even fifty years ago against the ethics of the twenty-first century.

If you select any of the core studies it is possible to find at least one of the ethical guidelines that has been infringed. For example, **Milgram's** participants experienced a stressful situation that stayed with some of them for the rest of their lives (see Blass, 2004). In the Bobo study (**Bandura et al.**), some of the children were left in a room with a violent adult and most of them ended up in tears. The issue to consider along with the guidelines is the value of the research, or in other words, was it worth breaking the ethical guidelines?

Ethics are also linked to some of the other key issues, for example,

Case studies: there have been many examples in psychology where the subject of the case study has been harmed by their involvement with the psychologists, or at least not benefited as much as they might.

Promoting human welfare: the decision to promote human welfare is an ethical one because there are alternatives such as just looking after yourself or choosing to ignore the needs of other people.

Social core study 10: Milgram (obedience)

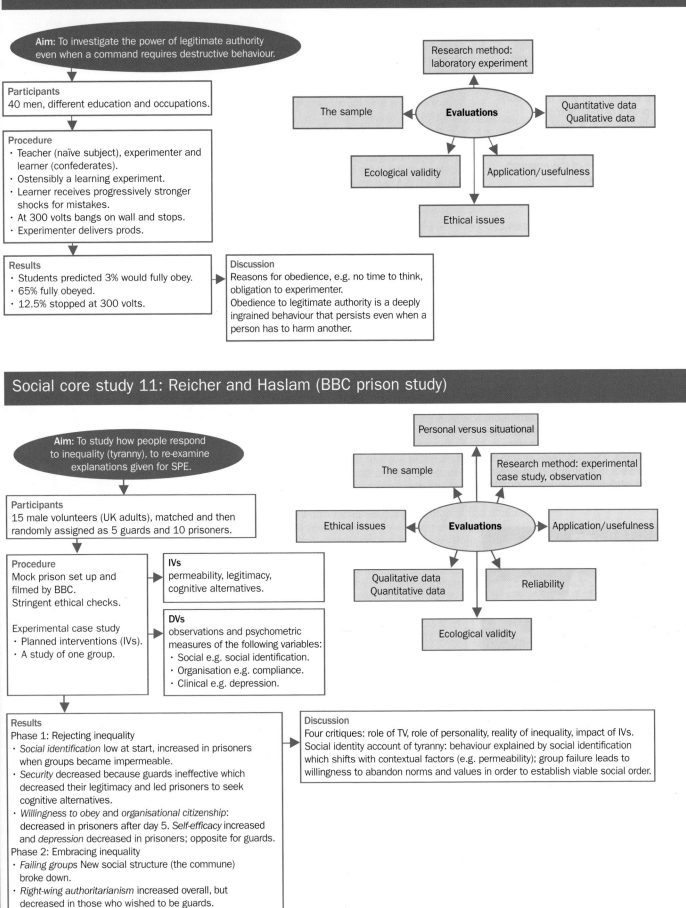

Aim: To investigate the power of legitimate authority even when a command requires destructive behaviour.

Participants
40 men, different education and occupations.

Procedure
- Teacher (naïve subject), experimenter and learner (confederates).
- Ostensibly a learning experiment.
- Learner receives progressively stronger shocks for mistakes.
- At 300 volts bangs on wall and stops.
- Experimenter delivers prods.

Results
- Students predicted 3% would fully obey.
- 65% fully obeyed.
- 12.5% stopped at 300 volts.

Discussion
Reasons for obedience, e.g. no time to think, obligation to experimenter.
Obedience to legitimate authority is a deeply ingrained behaviour that persists even when a person has to harm another.

Evaluations
- Research method: laboratory experiment
- The sample
- Quantitative data / Qualitative data
- Ecological validity
- Application/usefulness
- Ethical issues

Social core study 11: Reicher and Haslam (BBC prison study)

Aim: To study how people respond to inequality (tyranny), to re-examine explanations given for SPE.

Participants
15 male volunteers (UK adults), matched and then randomly assigned as 5 guards and 10 prisoners.

Procedure
Mock prison set up and filmed by BBC.
Stringent ethical checks.

Experimental case study
- Planned interventions (IVs).
- A study of one group.

IVs
permeability, legitimacy, cognitive alternatives.

DVs
observations and psychometric measures of the following variables:
- Social e.g. social identification.
- Organisation e.g. compliance.
- Clinical e.g. depression.

Results
Phase 1: Rejecting inequality
- *Social identification* low at start, increased in prisoners when groups became impermeable.
- *Security* decreased because guards ineffective which decreased their legitimacy and led prisoners to seek cognitive alternatives.
- *Willingness to obey* and *organisational citizenship*: decreased in prisoners after day 5. *Self-efficacy* increased and *depression* decreased in prisoners; opposite for guards.
Phase 2: Embracing inequality
- *Failing groups* New social structure (the commune) broke down.
- *Right-wing authoritarianism* increased overall, but decreased in those who wished to be guards.

Discussion
Four critiques: role of TV, role of personality, reality of inequality, impact of IVs.
Social identity account of tyranny: behaviour explained by social identification which shifts with contextual factors (e.g. permeability); group failure leads to willingness to abandon norms and values in order to establish viable social order.

Evaluations
- Personal versus situational
- The sample
- Research method: experimental case study, observation
- Ethical issues
- Application/usefulness
- Qualitative data / Quantitative data
- Reliability
- Ecological validity

Social core study 12: Piliavin, Rodin and Piliavin (subway Samaritan)

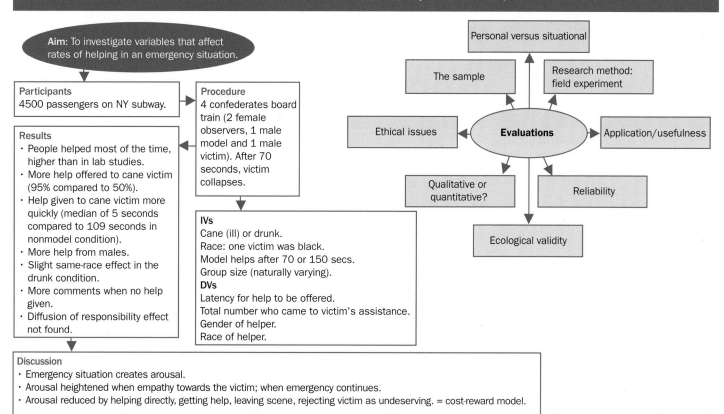

Aim: To investigate variables that affect rates of helping in an emergency situation.

Participants
4500 passengers on NY subway.

Procedure
4 confederates board train (2 female observers, 1 male model and 1 male victim). After 70 seconds, victim collapses.

Results
· People helped most of the time, higher than in lab studies.
· More help offered to cane victim (95% compared to 50%).
· Help given to cane victim more quickly (median of 5 seconds compared to 109 seconds in nonmodel condition).
· More help from males.
· Slight same-race effect in the drunk condition.
· More comments when no help given.
· Diffusion of responsibility effect not found.

IVs
Cane (ill) or drunk.
Race: one victim was black.
Model helps after 70 or 150 secs.
Group size (naturally varying).
DVs
Latency for help to be offered.
Total number who came to victim's assistance.
Gender of helper.
Race of helper.

Evaluations
- Personal versus situational
- The sample
- Research method: field experiment
- Ethical issues
- Application/usefulness
- Qualitative or quantitative?
- Reliability
- Ecological validity

Discussion
· Emergency situation creates arousal.
· Arousal heightened when empathy towards the victim; when emergency continues.
· Arousal reduced by helping directly, getting help, leaving scene, rejecting victim as undeserving. = cost-reward model.

Further reading and other things

Books worth looking at include *Groupthink* by Irving Janis (1982, Houghton Mifflin) which describes how groups can sometimes talk themselves into very bad decisions. Another classic text worth getting hold of is *When Prophesy Fails* by Leon Festinger (1964, Harper and Row) which tells the remarkable story of how some social psychologists joined a cult that believed the end of the world was approaching.

In fiction there are many films and books that explore human relationships and tell us something about who we are and why we behave in the ways that we do. Personal favourites to pick up would be *Coming Through Slaughter* by Michael Ondaatje (1984, Picador) which is a vivid account of Black musicians in New Orleans. Or what about *The Sorrow of War* by Bao Ninh (1991, Minerva) which gives a unique account of how people respond to extreme circumstances.

Milgram
* Original article can be seen at http://www.garfield.library.upenn.edu/classics1981/A1981LC33300001.pdf
* Milgram published the results from all of his obedience studies in a book *Obedience to Authority* (1974). This includes interviews with many of the participants.
* The excellent biography of Stanley Milgram by Thomas Blass, *The Man Who Shocked the World* (2004, Perseus Books).

* Research by Milgram is discussed in a chapter of *Skinner's Box* by Lauren Slater, a book which contains the background to a number of key studies in Psychology.
* Derren Brown's fascinating recreation of the Milgram experiment ('The Heist'), see http://www.youtube.com/watch?v=y6GxIuljT3w

Reicher and Haslam
* Original article can be obtained from the authors, see http://www.psychology.ex.ac.uk/projects/theexp/intro.shtml
* Article in *The Guardian* http://www.guardian.co.uk/uk_news/story/0,3604,638243,00.html
* Book: Haslam, S. A. and Reicher, S. D. (2002). *A user's guide to 'The Experiment': Exploring the psychology of groups and power.* London: BBC Learning.

Piliavin *et al.*
* Original article http://www.garysturt.free-online.co.uk/pil.htm
* A real life bystander account http://www.guardian.co.uk/crime/article/0,2763,1542032,00.html and see Wikipedia for other links http://en.wikipedia.org/wiki/Bystander_effect
* See 'Bystander Phenomenon revisited' for some recent research http://bps-research-digest.blogspot.com/2005/12/bystander-phenomenon-revisited.html

MCQ answers

1   In Milgram's study the experimenter encouraged participants to continue giving electric shocks using a series of 'prods'.

   (a) Outline **two** of the 'prods' that were used.   [2]
   (b) Describe **one** way that the results of Milgram's study can be applied to everyday life.   [2]

Stig's answer

(a) He told them 'The experiment demands that you continue'. And also 'You have no other choice'.

(b) You could use this to help training soldiers to obey officers especially in the heat of battle when it is important to obey. This study shows that small steps lead people to obey.

Chardonnay's answer

(a) The participants were encouraged to continue by certain statements given by the experimenter, such as 'Go on'.

(b) You could use the findings to help train policemen in how to effectively tell people what to do for their own safety.

Examiner's comments

Stig, in part (a) you have identified two prods, the second one is not exactly right but is close enough for full marks. Your answer in part (b) identifies a real-life situation and also explains how the insights from this study could be used ('small steps' is the way to get people to obey).

Chardonnay, you have identified one of the prods but not in enough detail to gain any credit – looks like you might have just been guessing. In part (b), you identify an appropriate everyday situations but have not made the all-important link to the study – in what way can Milgram's results be used in this situation?

Stig (2+2 marks) Chardonnay (0+1 marks)

2   In Milgram's study on obedience 40 subjects took part.

   (a) Outline how Milgram obtained this sample?   [2]
   (b) Outline **one** advantage of using this method to obtain a sample for a study.   [2]

Stig's answer

(a) The subjects answered an ad that was placed in a newspaper.

(b) One advantage of this is you get people who are very willing.

Chardonnay's answer

(a) The subjects were recruited by volunteering because they read an advertisement in the newspaper and volunteered to take part.

(b) This is a good way to get subjects because you can get access to a wide range of different people so you get a more varied sample than, for example, an opportunity sample.

Examiner's comments

Stig, a bit more detail required for two marks in part (a), for example, you might have included something about the contents of the advert. Again, in part (b) you need to slightly expand your point, perhaps by saying that volunteers are more likely to engage with the experiment.

Chardonnay, part (a) is fine as you have got advert + volunteering; so 2 marks here. In part (b) you make a nice comparison with a standard opportunity sample. This is always a useful way of adding detail to a question on advantages or disadvantages – make a comparison with an alternative method.

Stig (1+1 marks) Chardonnay (2+2 marks)

3   In the BBC Prison Study by Reicher and Haslam, participants were given the task of being a prisoner or guard. Describe **two** behaviours that showed the participants were sufficiently engaged with their task.   [4]

Stig's answer

One behaviour was that they seemed very involved in what they were doing and got quite upset with the other group (prisoners or guards).

Another behaviour was that they were being filmed so they had to take it seriously.

Chardonnay's answer

The prisoners were clearly unhappy and minded being deprived of things like cigarettes and being locked in their cells. If they weren't really involved they wouldn't have minded so much.

The guards' conversations showed how seriously they took their roles because they discussed it all the time.

Examiner's comments

I think you're guessing here Stig. Your first answer makes some sense but you need to provide evidence to support what you are saying to get the full two marks (what evidence is there that they got upset?). Your second answer isn't really an answer to this question – just because we know they were being filmed that doesn't mean they would have to be engaged with the task.

Chardonnay's answer clearly show she's read the article because she provides answers along the lines as those given in the report, and provides sufficient detail for full marks.

Stig (1+0 marks) Chardonnay (2+2 marks)

4   Reicher and Haslam sought to explain how inequality in groups may lead to tyranny.

    (a) Explain what is meant by 'tyranny'.   [2]

    (b) Outline the explanation they provided at the end of their study about how tyranny becomes possible.   [2]

Stig's answer

(a) Tyranny is when there is an unequal social system and this means one group has power over another group.

(b) Reicher and Haslam suggested that tyranny becomes possible when groups are failing. The members are then willing to abandon their preferred norms and values in preference for establishing a viable social order.

Chardonnay's answer

(a) Tyranny is like having power over some other people.

(b) The explanation given at the end of the article was that groups aren't necessarily anti-social and toxic, nor does group membership mean that people automatically accept roles.

Examiner's comments

This time it is Stig who knows his stuff. He has given an excellent definition of tyranny (taken from the article) and also provides a very clear conclusion about the factors that create tyranny. Well done.

Chardonnay's definition is a bit thin. She deserves one mark for mentioning power but that's about it. Her answer to part (b) shows her familiarity with the study but she hasn't really answered the question. She has described some of the conclusions but not addressed the issue of the factors that lead to tyranny, so no marks even though it shows knowledge of the study.

Stig (2+2 marks) Chardonnay (1+0 marks)

---

5   The study by Piliavin *et al.* on subway Samaritans could be described as a field study. Describe **one** strength and **one** weakness of conducting field studies in the context of this study.   [4]

Stig's answer

One strength of doing a field study is it is a more natural environment and this was a natural environment.

One weakness is that you can't ask for informed consent.

Chardonnay's answer

Strength of a field study: this study looked at helping behaviour in a natural environment where people might have to help someone.

Weakness: you can't control variables as clearly so it is more difficult to be sure that the DV was changed due to the IV, e.g. in this study that helping was due to crowd size.

Examiner's comments

Both your points are true, Stig, but you have forgotten to relate them to the Piliavin study. Don't forget to read the question carefully to make sure you haven't left anything out.

Chardonnay, you have successfully described both a strength and a weakness and linked them to the Piliavin study. Well done.

Stig (1+1 marks) Chardonnay (2+2 marks)

---

6   Piliavin *et al.* conducted a study on subway Samaritans.

    (a) Identify **two** of the independent variables in this study.   [2]

    (b) Describe the effects of **one** of these variables on the behaviour of people in the study.   [2]

Stig's answer

(a) Race of the victim and whether he was drunk or had a cane.

(b) They didn't find much effect for race.

Chardonnay's answer

(a) One condition was whether the victim was drunk and the other condition was whether he was ill (holding a cane).

(b) They found that people on the subway were less willing to offer help to a drunk victim than one holding a cane, and if they did offer help they were much slower.

Examiner's comments

Yep, spot on for part (a), Stig. The part (b) needs more information to get the two marks.

Hmmm, Chardonnay. This is a common mistake. Whether the victim was drunk or ill is just one variable, i.e. the 'type of victim' (though two conditions).

Nice detail in part (b) referring to frequency and latency of helping.

Stig (2+1 marks) Chardonnay (1+2 marks)

7 (a) Describe the aim of the study by Piliavin *et al*.   [2]
   (b) Describe how data was collected in the study by Piliavin *et al*.   [6]
   (c) Give **one** advantage and **one** disadvantage of the method used to collect data in the study by Piliavin *et al*. [6]
   (d) Explain how the reliability of these measurements could be assessed.   [6]
   (e) Outline the findings of the study by Piliavin *et al*.   [8]
   (f) Suggest **two** changes to the study by Piliavin *et al*. and outline how these changes might affect the results.   [8]

Total [36]

Chardonnay's answer

(a) The aim of the study was to see whether or not people will be helpful.

(b) The data was collected when a group of four students got on a New York subway train. One of them played the 'victim' (collapses) and another the 'model' (the person who goes to help the victim if no-one else does). The other two were females and they were the observers. Seventy seconds into the journey, the victim would collapse and lie on the floor until one of the passengers came to help them. If a passenger didn't help them, the model would step in either 70 seconds or 150 seconds after the collapse. The observers noted down things like how long it took before someone helped.

(c) One advantage of the method was that it was standardised and the victim always wore the same clothes and always travelled on the same subway line and always collapsed at exactly the same time and so on. This means it was highly controlled and so we can be more certain that the results are valid (i.e. changes in helping behaviour are due to the manipulation of the IV).

One disadvantage is that there were not enough drunk conditions. The students did not like playing the drunk and so out of all the trials, only about a third of them used the drunk model.

(d) One way to check on the reliability of measurements could be by checking the inter-rater or inter-observer reliability. This would involve matching, for each trial, the two observers records for e.g. time taken to help. For high reliability, they should agree upon the time taken. These two sets of recordings could be correlated with each other and there should be a high positive correlation.

(e) There were lots of findings in this study. First of all, there was a high rate of helping overall. In particular, the white ill person was helped the most. The ill victim was helped very quickly and spontaneously (62/65 conditions). However, the drunk victim was helped less often and less quickly. Males were more likely to be first helpers than females. Also, more comments were made in the drunk condition. Finally, there was no diffusion of responsibility effect.

(f) One change to the study could be to change the setting. For example, instead of doing the study in a subway where everyone can see the victim, it could be in a shopping centre or a park. This might change the results.

Another change could be to have female victim. Again, this might change the results because women might feel safer to help a female victim even if they wouldn't help a male victim. So more women would help.

Examiner's comments

(a) A bit brief/vague Chardonnay – you could have mentioned that their aims included whether type of victim and race of victim had any impact upon helping behaviour, or whether diffusion of responsibility occurs in a real life setting. Really you have only just scraped 1 mark out of 2 here.

(b) This is a fairly standard sort of mistake. It's a question of emphasis on what you decide to include and what you decide to omit. What you have written is perfectly accurate. It's just that you have spent too long describing the procedure and not enough time talking about what data was collected (gender and race of first helper, number of people in the carriage, time taken to help, comments passengers made, any other responses to the emergency such as leaving the carriage). You have also omitted that the data was collected against the different victim conditions (white versus black, and cane versus drunk). What you have written is still creditworthy – but will prevent you from getting top marks.

(c) I particularly like your explanation of validity. Often students say 'that would make it more valid' without giving an example of what it means. So, nice touch, Chardonnay.

For the disadvantage you give, you need to explain further why this is a disadvantage and how this might limit the results and conclusions which we can draw, so 3+2 marks here.

(d) This is really excellent, Chardonnay. Questions about reliability can be quite tough so you have done well to explain it clearly and put it in the context of this study. A full 6 marks for this question part.

(e) This is all accurate stuff, Chardonnay. And you report a range of the results and you have managed to get in a bit of 'fine detail' (62/65 conditions). You should try and remember a few more fine details (difficult, I know) e.g. median speed of helping is 5 seconds for ill but a whopping 109 seconds for drunk. Or you could even include one of the quotes of one of the bystanders ('It's for the men to help'). The reason why remembering these fine details is so helpful is that they really help you get into that top mark band. Your use of psychological terminology is secure and you obviously understand the results. Therefore, top of middle band for you, 6 out of 8 marks.

(f) Two valid and potentially interesting suggestions. How would moving the study to a shopping centre change the results? Would there be more or less helping? You need to try to predict what would happen and explain why. You have done this, to some extent, for your second change. Overall, both aspects (description of the changes and how this might affect the results) could do with more description and explanation. So 2+2 here, giving you 4 marks for this question part.

Chardonnay (1 + 4 + 5 + 6 + 6 + 4 mark = 26/36 marks)

CHAPTER 6

This chapter looks at three core studies in individual differences.

- Rosenhan's astonishing demonstration of the unreliability of psychiatric diagnosis.

- Thigpen and Cleckley's case study of a woman with three different personalities.

- Griffith's investigation into gambling on fruit machines.

Individual differences

What are individual differences?

Much of psychology is concerned with how groups of people behave and their typical or 'average' behaviour. For example if we were looking at the effectiveness of a new happiness drug we could give the drug to one group of people and a sugar pill to another group, and then consider the average score for each group to see if the drug had any effect on happiness. Most psychologists are interested in these average or mean scores. In contrast, the study of *individual differences* focuses on the differences within each group, how individual people differ in their behaviour and personal qualities, and what this tells us about human behaviour.

One strand of work on individual differences tries to measure the differences between individuals in qualities such as personality, intelligence and creativity. These qualities are very difficult to define. We have an everyday understanding of them but when you try to create a precise definition and precise measures the situation becomes a little complicated.

The study of individual differences has always attracted a lot of controversy because it seems to create divisions between people – we are telling people that they have more or less of a human quality than another person. The reason this results in controversy is because of the arguments about why we have individual differences; for example, if one person scores more on an IQ test than another person is that because they are genetically different or because they have been educated differently? The questions become even more controversial when the average scores of groups of people are considered.

Other areas of work that are sometimes included under the general heading of individual differences is the work on people with mental health issues, and also the work on individual identity and group identity.

Is it mad to be happy?

In a gentle parody of psychiatric diagnosis Richard Bentall (1992) proposed that happiness should be classed as a mental disorder and referred to under the new name of 'major affective disorder, pleasant type'. He suggested that the relevant literature shows that happiness is statistically abnormal, is made up of a discrete cluster of symptoms, is associated with a range of cognitive abnormalities, and probably reflects the abnormal functioning of the central nervous system. You would think that an article like this would contribute to the sum of human happiness but sadly some people took it seriously and it made them sad. Humour is a serious business.

Personality

A major area of individual differences is the study of personality. Personality is a collection of emotional, cognitive and behavioural patterns that are unique to a person. It is an interesting observation that we easily recognise an individual's personality but have great difficulty in describing it. One way that psychologists have attempted to describe personality is to define common traits that we all share and then measure individuals on these dimensions. So, for example, if we say that sociability is a trait then we would devise a sociability test and give everyone a score on that scale. In this way we can build up a picture of an individual (and their individual differences).

According to trait theory, a sociable person is likely to be sociable in any situation because of the traits in their personality. The counter argument is that people behave as the situation demands and it is *where* someone is rather than *who* someone is that best predicts how they will behave (see the social psychology studies and also the notes on demand characteristics on page 161).

Psychologists have proposed several models of personality traits and the one most commonly cited at the moment is Costa and McCrae's (1992) *Five Factor Model*, which proposes five key dimensions of personality: extraversion, agreeableness, conscientiousness, neuroticism, and openness to new experiences.

Personality types

'Let me have men about me that are fat, sleek-headed men and, such as sleep o'nights. Yond Cassius has a lean and hungry look. He thinks too much, such men are dangerous.' William Shakespeare, Julius Caesar, Act I, scene ii.

Caesar is making judgements about individual differences in personality from observations of body shape. This approach was also used by Sheldon in his twentieth-century descriptions of three major body types and matching personalities: the endomorph is physically quite round, and is typified as the 'barrel of fun' person. By contrast, the ectomorph is lean and hungry with little body fat. He/she is intense, thoughtful and private. The mesomorph has a more athletic body and tends to be assertive, adventurous and courageous.

Although this typology is intuitively appealing there is very little evidence to support the connection between body shape and personality.

Measuring personality

Most psychological tests ask direct questions in similar multi-choice format. These questionnaires will usually give you a personal score and you can compare yourself against the scores of others. In this way you can find out whether you are more or less shy, for example, than the average person. These tests are easy to use, easy to answer and require little interpretation (see the section on **psychometrics** later in this chapter). In contrast *projective tests* require a lot of interpretation. In such tests a neutral stimulus is used; it is presumed that an individual will project their thoughts and feelings onto

Rorschach type image

this stimulus when describing it. Sometimes these thoughts and feelings will have been hidden from the individual themselves.

The most famous of these tests is the *Rorschach inkblot test* which is named after Hermann Rorschach (1884–1922) who developed the inkblots, though he did not use them for personality analysis. The individual is shown ten standard abstract designs, and responses are analysed to give a measure of emotional and intellectual functioning and integration.

The rationale for the test sounds very plausible (and they are used in the **Thigpen and Cleckley** study) but there is little evidence to support the analyses derived from these tests. One fundamental problem is that analysis has to be carried out by another person whose own inner thoughts and feelings may be projected onto their interpretations.

Differences between people

Self and identity

Who am I? is a question we all face sometimes. One way of exploring this sense of self is to ask people to give 20 answers to this seemingly simple question. We might put down our family associations and the groups we belong to or even the things we own. Some people will put down their religion or their ethnicity or their nationality. They will also put down some personal qualities.

But how do we know who or what we are? One source of evidence is the reaction of other people to us. If people laugh at me then I am funny (or ridiculous) and if people smile at me then I am friendly. These reactions act as a mirror to my personality telling me what other people think of me.

These reactions might also affect how much I value myself. My self-image describes how I see myself and my self-esteem refers to how much we approve of or like ourselves. A number of techniques have been used to get information on self concept and self esteem such as asking people to draw self portraits. These drawings inevitably disclose something of what we think about ourselves.

Try it yourself. Sketch out a self-portrait. It doesn't have to be a great work of art, but think about what you'd put in to show people who you are.

Self-portrait

Red hair

Some surprising variables predict differences in individual experience. For example, people with red hair are more sensitive to pain (New Scientist 15.10.02). A group of red-haired and dark-haired women were given an anaesthetic and then subjected to an electric shock. The process was repeated until the women said they felt no pain. The researchers found that red heads required 20 per cent more anaesthetic to dull the pain.

Benjamin Zephaniah captures a sense of identity through his poetry.

Multiple identities

Nobody can be defined by one quality. We all have a unique mix of personal qualities and social affiliations that help to define who we are.

For many, a key affiliation that contributes to their identity is their football team. The Birmingham poet Benjamin Zephania has been a lifelong supporter of Aston Villa (he has our sympathy – ed.) though his support on the terraces has been well tested in the past.

He says, '*When I was a teenager, I used to come here every other week. It was a lot different then – 25,000 people stood here on the famous Holte End, I was almost the only black face.*'

'*I always remember one game when I came here with my uncle and Villa were winning 2–0 and everybody was happy. And then the other team, I forget who they were, started to come back and beating Villa. The mood changed and suddenly the crowd noticed I was the only black kid and they took it out on me. It was terrible.*' (BBC website)

Despite these experiences Zephaniah is now patron of Aston Villa Supporters' Club. In his poem 'Knowing Me', he expresses his passion for the club and shows how it is part of his wider sense of identity.

With my Jamaican hand on my Ethiopian heart

The African heart deep in my Brummie chest,

And I chant, Aston Villa, Aston Villa, Aston Villa,

Believe me I know my stuff.

'*Race is an important part of my identity, but I wish it wasn't. I'd like to identify myself as a martial artist, an Aston Villa supporter, or a hip-hop reggae person; but when a policeman stops me on the street it has nothing to do with that.*' (The Guardian, 21.03.05)

Online identities

One showcase for our identity can be found on the social networking sites on the internet such as Facebook. Most people who join Facebook post up at least one picture of themselves, and commonly many pictures of themselves and their friends. The choice of image is informative about the person's sense of social identity and how they want to project it.

On Facebook you can be whoever you want and you can control your image much more than you can in everyday life. A novel aspect of Facebook is that is allows anyone to broadcast details of their identity and existence to all of the other 75 million users of Facebook worldwide. You can be an international star instantaneously with a campaign on Facebook or a video on YouTube. The differences between your identity in real life and your identity in cyberspace is an interesting question for psychology to consider.

One line of research has looked at the identities that people create for themselves in online games. These games, such as *World of Warcraft*, attract thousands of players worldwide who develop friendships and cooperative groups with other gamers. For some people these friendships are more constant than their relationships in real space. One difference between these cyber identities and 'real' life is that the gamer can choose how to present themselves and it is estimated that over half of gamers sometimes use identities with a different gender to their own (Hussain and Griffiths, 2008). Interestingly, it is females who swap gender more than males.

Rosenhan: starters

Madness and schizophrenia

The concept of madness has been around for a long time, but the diagnosis of specific mental disorders only dates back around 100 years. The way a society deals with people who are different tells you a lot about that society. Sometimes people are revered for their differentness and sometimes they are persecuted. In the Western world, people who have been categorised as mad have been subjected to an unimaginably wide range of brutal and cruel treatments. They have been feared, ignored, beaten, chained, locked up and tranquilised. In the twenty-first century when we have discovered so much about health, the causes of mental disorders remain largely unknown and the treatments are still very controversial.

Schizophrenia is perhaps one of the most misunderstood and feared conditions. A literal translation of the term is 'shattered mind' which gives rise to the common misconception that it refers to a split personality. The condition was first described by Kraepelin in 1887 and further defined and named by Bleuler in 1911.

Symptoms

Schizophrenia is a serious mental disorder in which the person has persistent problems in perception or reality testing. The symptoms are divided into positive symptoms (those that are additional to normal experience and behaviour) and negative symptoms (reduction in normal experiences or behaviour). The positive symptoms include delusions, hallucinations and thought disorder. The negative symptoms include unusual emotional responses and lack of motivation.

Diagnosis is inevitably based on self-reports from the patient and observations from expert witnesses such as a psychiatrist. There is no biological test for schizophrenia, so the judgement depends on the expertise of the diagnostician. This makes the condition very different from medical conditions such as measles or meningitis and is one reason why it is difficult to see schizophrenia as a disease.

Louis Wane

Louis Wane (1860–1939) was a popular artist who was most famous for his unusual and sometimes disturbing paintings of cats. The cats had many human features and would be placed in scenes to parody the fads of modern life. He is often referred to in psychology texts because some of the pictures were very vivid and abstract and seemed to indicate an different perception of the everyday world. Wane experienced a number of psychological problems in his life and some commentators suggest that you can see his growing mental distress in the paintings. His behaviour became florid and unpredictable and he is sometimes described as having schizophrenia though this diagnosis was not made at the time. One of his pictures is shown below.

Categorising people

People find it easy to make judgements of 'oddness' in other people. 'He's never been quite right, you know' they might nudge someone and say, but we find it hard to say what it is that is so odd about the person. Psychological diagnosis is an attempt to classify oddness in people.

Diagnosis

The psychological diagnosis of personality has a long history. The Greeks, for example, recognised diagnoses such as senility, alcoholism, melancholia and paranoia. The first comprehensive system of psychological disorders was created in 1896 by Emil Kraepelin. He believed that mental disorders have the same basis as physical ones, and that the same diagnostic principles should be applied – the careful observation of symptoms. The advantages of introducing a diagnostic system include:

- diagnosis is a communication shorthand;
- it suggests which treatments are likely to be successful;
- it may point out the cause;
- it aids scientific investigation by collecting together people with similar symptoms.

In 1952, the Diagnostic and Statistical Manual of Mental Disorders (DSM) was developed by the American Psychiatric Association. DSM IV is widely used today in the USA. In the UK and the rest of the world it is more common to use the International Statistical Classification of Diseases and Related Health Problems (ICD), published by the World Health Organisation.

A diagnosis is arrived at using 'family' (i.e. group) resemblances. If you think of a big family that you know, then you will notice that most of the family members have some similar physical features, yet each member of the family is different from the others. It is a similar recognition process with mental disorders. Each person who has a particular condition has some similar features in their behaviour to other people with the same condition.

MAD *We use the term madness in a number of ways.*

- *Feelings of anger: 'she makes me so mad!' we snarl between gritted teeth.*
- *Senseless or laughable behaviours: we might say 'that was a mad idea'.*
- *Showing enthusiasm: 'I'm mad for it'.*
- *Showing irrational behaviour or being mentally unsound.*

All these definitions overlap each other but they are all very distinct as well. The madness we are talking about in this chapter is the fourth definition. Perhaps because we fear this condition we have many different words we use other than mad, for example, crazy, daft, demented, distraught, insane, lunatic, bonkers, cracked, daffy, gag, fruitcake, nuts, wacky. These words have very flexible meanings and can refer to the other definitions mentioned above. This shows how we tend to blur the boundaries between acceptable and unacceptable behaviours.

'The cause of lunacy?' The term lunatic (also loony, lunacy) comes from the Latin word 'luna' meaning moon. It highlights the commonly believed link between madness and the phases of the moon. Modern science has not established a link between the moon and madness but the connection might have arisen from the increased level of light at the full moon. This might have kept people awake and so made them susceptible to sleep deprivation symptoms.

Activity

Make a list of five people who you think are 'odd' and a list of five people who you think are 'normal'. Now try and make two more lists. First, what are the qualities that the 'odd' people have that the 'normal' people don't? Secondly, what are the behaviours that the 'odd' people do that the 'normal' people don't?

This task should give you some insight into the problems of devising a diagnostic system for mental illness.

Visual and auditory hallucinations

Drugs

People have been aware of hallucinations for centuries. Some have seen them as a gift that provides special visions of life. One way of inducing hallucinations is to take certain drugs, for example LSD or mescaline. These have sometimes been referred to as mind-expanding drugs because of the feeling that the user has of seeing new things that they were not previously aware of. Mescaline is made from South American cacti such as the peyote cactus. It has been used in religious rituals for centuries. Users typically experience visual hallucinations and altered mental states which are often described as pleasurable and illuminating but occasionally there are feelings of anxiety or revulsion.

The dangers with hallucinogens come from the dramatic effect they have on the chemistry of the brain. The unwanted effects can include dizziness, sickness, anxiety, feelings of dying or not being able to return to normal consciousness. None of these are pleasant but the major concern is hallucinogen persisting perception disorder (HPPD) which occurs with a number of drugs and leaves the user experiencing hallucinations even when the drug has left their system.

Could it be that people with schizophrenia are having similar altered states?

What is it like to hear voices?

Hearing voices is a relatively common experience. Many people can have internal conversations with their family and friends even when they are alone. People who have recently been bereaved often report hearing the voice of the deceased person. Sometimes, however, the voices appear to be more distanced and often more troubling. The voices might be present all day and have the effect of preventing the voice-hearer from doing things in their daily life. The experience of hearing voices is very varied and difficult to describe.

Joan of Arc was a French heroine of the 100 Years War who inspired the French to many victories over the English. From the age of 12 she heard voices which initially encouraged her in her religious observance, and later told her to do battle with the English. She was eventually captured, tried and burnt by the English who believed her voices came from the Devil. The French, however, believed the voices came from God and after her death she was made a Catholic saint.

Are voices a symptom of illness?

People who hear voices often find it disturbing, and dealing with someone who is hearing voices can also be quite disturbing. In recent times hearing voices has been seen as a symptom of mental disturbance and treated with major tranquillisers. Not everyone responds to this treatment and some people can learn to live with their voices without serious medication. In fact some people regard their voices as positive and there are numerous accounts of people finding their voices inspirational or comforting. Perhaps hearing voices should not always been seen as a symptom of mental disturbance but merely as a variation in human experience.

Mental health in the UK

There is still a lot of stigma attached to mental distress which means that it is often hidden. In its broadest definition, mental distress touches most people during their lives.

- It is estimated that as many as one in six adults in the UK are affected by mental distress at any one time.
- The most common conditions are mixed anxiety and depression which affect about 9% of adults every year.
- Up to 670,000 people in the UK have some form of dementia – 5% of people over 65 and 10–20% of people over 80.
- One in four consultations with a GP concern mental health issues. Up to 630,000 people are in contact with specialised mental health services at any one time.

Schizophrenia

The rate of schizophrenia is declining in this country but it is estimated that around 1% of the population will experience episodes during their lifetime and the prevalence of the disorder in any one year is between 2 and 4 in 1000. The prevalence rates are similar for men and women but it tends to show earlier in men with the prevalence in men aged 15–24 twice that of women.

Chemical treatments

The most common treatment for schizophrenia in the UK for the last 50 years has been anti-psychotic medication which is relatively successful in reducing symptoms (WHO, 2001) but has damaging side effects, such as:

- Parkinson-like symptoms characterised by muscle rigidity and tremor.
- Tardive dyskinesia (TD) which involves abnormal facial movements, smacking lips, chewing, sucking, and twisting the tongue. TD often persists after the treatment has stopped and cannot be treated.

Sources: ONS 2000, MIND website, Sainsbury Centre for Mental Health website.

ABNORMALITY

Rosenhan and Seligman (1989) suggest that there are seven properties that we can use to help us decide whether a person or a behaviour is abnormal.

1. *Suffering is a common feature of abnormality though it is not always present.*

2. *Maladaptiveness is when a behaviour neither helps the individual nor the groups to which they belong.*

3. *Irrationality and Incomprehensibility refers to behaviour that seems to have no rational meaning.*

4. *Unpredictability and Loss of Control: we expect people to be consistent, predictable and in control of themselves.*

5. *Vividness and Unconventionality refers to behaviours that stand out and shock us.*

6. *Observer Discomfort refers to behaviour that makes us feel uncomfortable maybe because it breaks some unwritten rules about how we should behave.*

7. *Violation of Moral and Ideal Standards: refers to the rules that we think people should live by.*

...Link to the core study...

What do we mean by the terms 'sane' and 'insane'? Does insanity exist in the individual or the society that judges them? These are the questions that **Rosenhan** is looking at in this study. At the time of the study there was growing unease with the medical approach to mental disorders and growing scepticism at the claims of psychiatrists to be able to diagnose and treat these disorders.

David L. Rosenhan (1973) On being sane in insane places.
Science, 179, pages 250–258.

Abstract

Is abnormality a characteristic of certain individuals or is it something that is perceived because of the context they are seen in?

Study 1

Rosenhan arranged for eight pseudopatients (men and women) to present themselves to 12 different US psychiatric hospitals. Their only symptom was hearing voices, all other details of their life history were honest except their name. All were admitted to the hospital and all bar one were diagnosed as schizophrenic. They endeavoured to behave normally and recorded their observations in a notebook. The average stay was 19 days (range 7–52 days).

It may be that psychiatrists are more inclined to call a healthy person sick (a false positive, type 2 error) than a sick person healthy (a false negative, type 1).

Study 2

A further study was conducted to see if this error would persist. Staff at a psychiatric hospital were told the results of this study and warned that pseudopatients would present themselves over the next three months. No pseudopatients sought admission yet 41 (out of 193) real patients were suspected by at least one staff member and 23 by at least one psychiatrist. This is a type 1 error.

The results from these studies suggest that psychiatric diagnosis is highly unreliable.

Other results

- The label 'schizophrenia' is sticky – on discharge the pseudopatients were labelled 'schizophrenia in remission'.
- The label of abnormality changes the way the individual is perceived – 'normal' behaviours in an abnormal setting are seen as abnormal.
- Patients are depersonalised – staff ignored direct questions and avoided eye contact (study 3).
- Patients are powerless – many human rights were taken away, e.g. privacy.

Conclusion

It is not possible to distinguish the sane from the insane when they are labelled 'abnormal' because this creates expectations. One solution would be to place abnormal individuals in community health care to avoid the institutional context and/or focus on behavioural diagnoses rather than global labels such as 'schizrenia'.

As touch, taste, sight, smell and hearing boarded the charter flight for Havana, Professor Nicholson knew in his heart that he had lost more than just good friends. In fact, he had finally lost his senses.

Cartoon © Nick D. Kim, nearingzero.net. Used by permission.

Introduction

'If sanity and insanity exist, how shall we know them?' This was the question posed by Rosenhan.

We may be convinced that we can tell the normal from the abnormal, but the evidence for this ability is not compelling:

- It is common to read about murder trials where the prosecution and defence each call their own psychiatrists who disagree on the defendant's sanity.
- There is much disagreement about the meaning of terms such as 'sanity', 'insanity', 'mental illness' and 'schizophrenia'.
- Conceptions of normality and abnormality are not universal; what is considered normal in one culture may be seen as quite aberrant in another.

This is not to suggest that there is no such thing as deviant or odd behaviours, nor that 'mental illness' is not associated with personal anguish. Murder and hallucinations are deviant. Depression is linked to psychological suffering.

Is the diagnosis of insanity based on characteristics of the patients themselves or the context in which the patient is seen? Many distinguished researchers have presented the view that the diagnosis of mental illness is *useless at best and downright harmful, misleading, and pejorative at worst*' (page 251).

The question of personality versus situation can be investigated by getting 'normal' people (that is people who do not have, and have never had serious psychiatric symptoms) to seek to be admitted to a psychiatric hospital. If such 'pseudopatients' were diagnosed as sane this would show that the sane individual can be distinguished from the insane context in which he is found.

On the other hand, if such pseudopatients were diagnosed as insane then this suggests that it is the context rather than the individual's characteristics that determine the diagnosis, that the psychiatric diagnosis of 'insanity' has less to do with the patient and more about the (insane) environment in which they are found.

Biographical notes

David Rosenhan is Emeritus Professor of Law and Psychology at Stanford University, a post he has held since 1970 – thus his interest in the legal definition of abnormality discussed at the start of this core study. Slater (2005) informs us that Rosenhan recruited his pseudopatients by ringing friends up and asking if they were doing anything in October. This included his friend Martin Seligman with whom he wrote one of the classic textbooks for Abnormal Psychology. Slater also reports that Rosenhan recently has been afflicted by a paralysing condition as yet undiagnosed: *'this renegade researcher, one who devoted the better part of his career to the dismantling of psychiatric diagnosis. Now here he was, a diagnostic question himself.'* (page 65)

Study 1

Aim
To see if sane individuals who presented themselves to a psychiatric hospital would be diagnosed as insane.

Method

Pseudopatients
The 'pseudopatients' were five men and three women of various ages and occupations (graduate student, psychologist, pediatrician, psychiatrist, painter and housewife). Rosenhan was one of the pseudopatients.

Setting
Twelve different hospitals were used, located in five states across America. The hospitals represented a range of different kinds of psychiatric institutions – modern and old, well-staffed and poorly staffed. Only one was a private hospital.

Procedure
Each pseudopatient called a hospital and asked for an appointment. On arrival (s)he told the admissions officer that (s)he had been hearing voices which included the words 'empty', 'hollow', and 'thud' spoken in an unknown voice. These symptoms were chosen because they indicated an existential crisis ('Who am I?'), a symptom not previously reported for schizophrenia.

Beyond the description of auditory hallucinations, each pseudopatient stated the facts of their lives as they actually were. None of their life histories were pathological (i.e. abnormal).

Pseudopatients, once they were admitted to the psychiatric ward, ceased to show any symptoms of abnormality. There was some nervousness because of the shock of being admitted so easily, and also because they were afraid of being detected as a fraud, and afraid of being on a psychiatric ward.

The pseudopatients secretly did not take their medication but otherwise followed the ward routine. They spent their time making notes about their environment. The reports from the nurses showed that the patients were friendly, cooperative and 'exhibited no abnormal indications'.

They did not know when they would be discharged; one of the conditions of taking part in the study was that they had to get out by their own devices.

Results

All pseudopatients were admitted and, bar one, diagnosed as schizophrenic; each was eventually discharged with a diagnosis of schizophrenia 'in remission'.

Once you become a patient in a psychiatric hospital, do you start to fit the description of 'insane'?

This diagnosis shows the 'stickiness' of the label – once a schizophrenic always a schizophrenic albeit in remission (i.e. symptoms not present at the moment). Length of hospitalisation varied from 7 to 52 days, with an average of 19 days.

Explanation

The failure to detect the pseudopatients' sanity cannot be due to:

- The quality of the hospitals – several were considered to be excellent.
- The time available to observe them – they were in hospital for a reasonable time.
- Their behaviour – which was sane (many of the real patients recognised this, saying 'You're not crazy. You're a journalist or a professor.').

The failure to detect sanity may be because doctors have a strong bias towards the 'type 2 error' – they are more inclined to call a healthy person sick (a false positive, type 2 error) than a sick person healthy (a false negative, type 1 error). It is clearly more dangerous to misdiagnose illness than health, and err on the side of caution.

However, what holds for medicine may not hold for psychiatry, especially because psychiatric diagnoses carry personal, legal and social stigmas.

Study 2

Aim
To see if the tendency towards diagnosing the sane as insane could be reversed.

Method
The staff in one psychiatric hospital were informed of the results of the first study (which they found hard to believe) and told that at some time during the next three months, one or more pseudopatients would try to be admitted to the hospital. Each member of staff was asked to rate all patients who sought admission using a 10-point scale where 1 reflected high confidence that the patient was a pseudopatient.

Results
Over the three months 193 patients were admitted for treatment. None of them were actually pseudopatients but:

- 41 were judged to be pseudopatients by at least one staff member.
- 23 were suspected by at least one psychiatrist.
- 19 were suspected by a psychiatrist and one other staff member.

Explanation
The hospital staff were now making more type 1 errors (calling a sick person healthy) because they were trying to avoid making type 2 errors. *'One thing is certain: any diagnostic process that lends itself so readily to massive errors cannot be a very reliable one'* (page 252).

Note that the actual participants in this study were the doctors and nurses. The pseudopatients were the confederates of the researcher, i.e. part of the research team.

Qs

1. What hypothesis was Rosenhan testing?
2. Describe what the pseudopatients did to make it appear they were insane.
3. Why did Rosenhan choose to use 'existential' symptoms?
4. Briefly state what was demonstrated in studies 1 and 2?
5. Explain the term 'schizophrenia in remission' in your own words.
6. Describe a situation where the label 'schizophrenia in remission' might be a handicap to an individual.
7. Doctors prefer to err on the side of caution. Rosenhan gave the example that it is better to call a healthy person sick – but some people might think it was more cautious to call a sick person healthy. Which view do you prefer and why?
8. Rosenhan points out that it may be OK to make a type 2 error when diagnosing physical illness but the same is not true for mental illness. Why?
9. Explain whether you would have agreed to be a pseudopatient. Why or why not?

Study 3

Aim

To investigate patient–staff contact.

Method

In four of the hospitals pseudopatients approached a staff member with the following question 'Pardon me, Mr/Mrs/Dr X, could you tell me when I will be eligible for grounds privileges?' (or '... when will I be presented at the staff meeting?' or '... when am I likely to be discharged?'). The pseudopatient did this as normally as possible and avoided asking any particular person more than once in a day.

Results and conclusion

The most common response was a brief reply as the member of staff continued without pausing and making no eye contact. Only 4% of the psychiatrists and 0.5% of the nurses stopped; 2% in each group actually paused and chatted.

In contrast, as a control, a young lady approached staff members on the Stanford University campus, and asked them six questions. All of the staff members stopped and answered all questions, maintaining eye contact.

The avoidance of contact between staff and patients serves to depersonalise the patients.

Depersonalisation *can be defined as a sense of being cut off or detached from one's self. This feeling may be experienced as viewing one's own mental processes or behavior from the outside; some patients feel as if they are in a dream.*

Discussion

Stickiness of psychodiagnostic labels

The results show the profound effect of a 'label' on our perceptions of people. Many studies in psychology have demonstrated the same thing. For example, Asch (1946) showed that central personality traits (such as 'warm' and 'cold') have a powerful effect on how we perceive someone's total personality. In the same way, once a person is labelled 'abnormal', this means that all subsequent data about them are interpreted in that light. For example, one pseudopatient who described a warm relationship with his mother but distant one with his father, and good relationships with his wife and children apart from occasional angry exchanges, was described by a psychiatrist:

'39-year-old male ... manifests a long history of considerable ambivalence in close relationships, which begins in early childhood ... Affective stability is absent. His attempts to control emotionality with his wife and children are punctuated by angry outbursts ... And while he says he has several good friends, one senses considerable ambivalence ...' (page 253).

In another example a psychiatrist suggested that a group of patients sitting outside the cafeteria before lunch were exhibiting the oral-acquisitive nature of their illness – in reality they didn't have much else to do except turn up for lunch early.

Labels are self-fulfilling for psychiatrists and for the patients themselves. There is a considerable overlap between sane and insane – the sane are not 'sane' all of the time, nor are the insane insane all of the time. It makes no sense to label oneself permanently depressed on the basis of occasional depression. It seems more useful to focus on behaviours.

The experience of psychiatric hospitalisation

The term 'mental illness' is of recent origin. It was coined to promote more humane behaviour towards those who were psychologically disturbed; instead of diagnosing such individuals as witches they were seen to be suffering from a physical illness. However, it is doubtful that people really regard mental illness in the same way as they regard physical illness. You can recover from a broken leg but not from schizophrenia (you remain 'in remission').

The mentally ill are society's lepers. That such attitudes are held by the general population is not surprising; what is surprising is that the professionals (nurses, doctors, psychologists, social workers) hold similar attitudes. Or perhaps it is not surprising given the very limited contact between staff and patients that was observed in this study. For example, the average amount of time that attendants spent 'out of the cage' (the glassed quarters where professional staff had their offices) was 11.3% of their total time at work and much of this was spent on chores rather than mingling with patients. This 'out of the cage' measure was not an ideal way to assess nurse–patient interaction because some of the time out of the cage was not spent mingling with patients, for example attendants might emerge to watch TV or to fold sheets. However, it was really the only reliable way to measure interaction. On average the nurses emerged from the cage 11.5 times per shift.

The physicians, especially psychiatrists, were even less available and were rarely seen on the wards. On average the physicians appeared on the ward 6.7 times per day.

The general quality of staff–patient contact was demonstrated in study 3.

Qs

1 In what way is a diagnosis a 'self-fulfilling prophecy'?

2 In what way is the label 'schizophrenia' a 'central trait'?

3 How did one psychiatrist interpret a pseudopatient's report that he had occasional fights with his wife?

4 Rosenhan suggests that some mental health professionals have negative attitudes towards the mentally ill. Identify **two** pieces of evidence for this view.

5 Why was 'out of the cage' used to assess nurse-patient interaction?

6 Explain what the term 'mortification' means.

Powerlessness and depersonalisation

The staff treated the patients with little respect: punishing them for small incidents, beating them and swearing at them. Such treatment is depersonalising and creates an overwhelming sense of powerlessness. This was further exacerbated by the living conditions in a psychiatric hospital: patients cannot initiate contact with staff, personal privacy is minimal (e.g. staff can enter private rooms with no permission, no doors on toilets), anyone can read patients' files (e.g. volunteers on the wards), and physical examinations are conducted in semipublic rooms. In general activity around the patient is conducted as if he was invisible.

The sources of depersonalisation

The first source is the attitudes held by all of us towards the mentally ill, attitudes characterised by fear, distrust and also benevolence. Our ambivalence leads to avoidance.

Second, the hierarchical structure of the hospital leads to depersonalisation. Those at the top have least to do with patients, and their behaviour inspires the rest of the staff.

There are other sources of depersonalisation, such as lack of money, staff shortages and also the use of psychotropic drugs. Drugs convince staff that treatment is being conducted and therefore further patient contact is not necessary.

The consequences of labelling and depersonalisation

We prefer to invent knowledge (e.g. labelling someone as 'schizophrenic') rather than admit we don't know. This is not merely depressing but frightening. How many people, one wonders, are sane but not recognised as such in our psychiatric institutions? Once hospitalised the patient is socialised by the bizarre setting, a process Goffman (1961) called 'mortification'.

Summary and conclusion

It is clear that we cannot distinguish the sane from the insane. Hospitalisation for the mentally ill results in powerlessness, depersonalisation, segregation, mortification and self-labelling – all counter-therapeutic.

One solution might be to use other approaches to the treatment of mental illness: community mental health facilities to avoid the effects of the institutional setting, or to use behaviour therapies which avoid psychiatric labels.

A second solution is to increase the sensitivity of mental health workers and recognise that their behaviour is also controlled by the situation.

Debate

'There is nothing to be gained by a diagnosis of schizophrenia.'

Divide your class into groups and prepare a case for the prosecution or defence and then conduct a class debate. Whichever view you support, make sure you are also prepared to answer the claims of the opposition.

Evaluating the study by Rosenhan

The research method
The studies were controlled participant observations. Only study 3 was an experiment (a field experiment) – in the other studies various independent variables were tested but there was only one condition for each so cause-and-effect conclusions can't be drawn.

There are no simple answers. Evaluating a study requires you to think. We have provided some pointers here, linked to the KEY ISSUES covered through this book – see page XIV for a table of these key issues.

What are the strengths and limitations of these research methods in the context of this study?

The sample
There were two samples: pseudopatients and hospitals. *In what way are the samples unique? How does this affect the conclusions drawn from the study?*

Quantitative or qualitative?
Both quantitative and qualitative data were collected in this study. *Give examples of each kind of data. What are the strengths and limitations of each kind of data in the context of this study?*

Ethical issues
All the pseudopatients were volunteers but the hospitals did not agree to take part in the first study and professionals were deceived in all of the studies. *What ethical issues should have concerned the researchers in this study, and how might they have dealt with these issues?*

Personality versus situation
What does this study tell us about the relative effects of personality and situation on behaviour?

Ecological validity
Observations may lack objectivity which would affect the validity. You might also consider the effect of demand characteristics. The willingness to commit a patient on flimsy evidence may be because the psychiatrist wouldn't suspect for a minute that someone might be pretending and therefore assumes that anyone seeking admission must have a good reason to do so. This may challenge some of the conclusions.

To what extent can we generalise the findings from this study to real life?

Applications/usefulness
How valuable was this study? What influence do you think it has had on the treatment of abnormality?

What next?
Describe **one** change to this study, and say how you think this might affect the outcome.

...Links to other studies and issues...

This study is one of a select group that had a dramatic effect on public perceptions and continues to have a lasting influence. Other studies in this text to have such an effect include, **Milgram** and **Bandura** *et al.* These studies are all still cited many years after the research was conducted and provide moral stories for the understanding of human behaviour. By looking at unusual (or abnormal) behaviour we gain some clues as to what we mean by normality. Other studies that give us insights about this include **Baron-Cohen** *et al.* and **Freud.**

Rosenhan: afters

Still crazy after all these years

Each generation develops its stories to explain the altered states we call madness. We seem to be fascinated and fearful of these states in equal measure and we constantly explore these ideas in fiction.

Reaction to Rosenhan's study

Rosenhan's article created a major storm when it was published. On the one hand there was a barrage of criticism about psychiatrists and their diagnoses; on the other hand the psychiatric profession fought back against Rosenhan, arguing that since psychiatric diagnosis mainly relies on self-reports from patients, the study no more demonstrates problems with psychiatric diagnosis than lying about other medical symptoms. Psychiatrist Robert Spitzer (1975) claimed:

'If I were to drink a quart of blood and, concealing what I had done, come to the emergency room of any hospital vomiting blood, the behaviour of the staff would be quite predictable. If they labelled and treated me as having a peptic ulcer, I doubt I could argue convincingly that medical science does not know how to diagnose that condition.'

Spitzer had a key role in the development of the DSM (below) and hence increased the number of people defined as mentally disordered.

Making us crazy

One of the biggest controversies about psychiatric diagnosis is whether disorders are real. The current version of the Diagnostic and Statistical Manual (DSM) runs to 900 pages, describing more than 300 mental disorders. The DSM defines many sorts of behaviour as mental disorders, some of which do not seem to deserve the label. For example, you or I might call Oppositional Defiant Disorder 'being awkward'.

A diagnosis can be worth a lot of money: it may enable a patient to sue an employer for causing illness; it allows the pharmaceutical industry to produce medication for each one. You might not be surprised that some of the main funders of DSM development are pharmaceutical companies. The world thinks it is going mad because the drug companies tell it so, and psychologists collude in this nonsense because it is good for our business as well (Kutchins and Kirk, 1997). An example of the level of psychiatric diagnosis can be seen in the figures for medication prescribed in the UK. In 2003, doctors made out 27,700,000 prescriptions for anti-depressants. That's an awful lot of pills.

Madness at the movies

For most people their only direct observation of people with serious mental disturbance is at the movies. Sometimes these films can give us a meaningful insight into these altered mental states and films like *The Madness of King George* and *A Beautiful Mind* show the pain in a compassionate way. Other films play on our stereotypes of madness to make great drama. The classic Psycho taps into our fears of madness to create one of the most iconic horror films. The risk of violence from people with mental disorders is, however, very low, but many people derive their fears from fictional stories.

One flew over the cuckoo's nest

Ken Kesey's 1962 cult book of life in a mental hospital in the USA was turned into a film in 1975 starring Jack Nicholson. The film was awarded all five major Oscars and has recently been cited as 'culturally significant' by the US Library of Congress. In the film, Randle P. McMurphy, a serial petty criminal who has been sentenced to a fairly short prison term decides to have himself declared insane so he'll be transferred to a mental institution which he thinks will be more comfortable than prison. In the asylum McMurphy's ward is run by the tyrannical Nurse Ratched, who has crushed the patients into submission.

Jack Nicholson as McMurphy.

As McMurphy takes on Nurse Ratched in a series of power games he becomes a hero to the patients and starts to empower them. All the time the viewer is challenged to question just how sane or insane the inmates are.

McMurphy destabilises the culture of the asylum and he is eventually pacified by a lobotomy after he responds violently to one of Nurse Ratched's psychological power games.

The myth of mental illness

What is the difference between a medical and mental disorder? We go to see medical doctors for both conditions and they use similar treatments (e.g. drugs) but is this the best approach? In his critique of the medical model Thomas Szasz (1960) raised some general points about the problems of diagnosis. Szasz argued that the medical model is unhelpful to our understanding of psychiatric conditions. The medical model suggests that all psychiatric problems will eventually be understood in terms of simple chemical reactions, and that 'mental illnesses' are basically no different to other diseases. Szasz argued that there are two errors in this view:

1. A disease of the brain is a neurological defect and not a problem of living. For example, a defect in a person's vision may be explained by correlating it with certain lesions in the nervous system. On the other hand, a person's belief, whether this is a belief in Christianity, or Communism, or that their internal organs are rotting, cannot be explained by a defect of the nervous system. Some beliefs are perfectly acceptable and some are thought to be a sign of mental disorder, but they are all beliefs.

2. In medicine when we speak of physical disturbances we mean either signs (for example, fever which is measurable) or symptoms (for example, pain which is reported). When we speak about mental symptoms, however, we refer to how patients describe themselves and the world around them. They might say that they are Napoleon or that they are being persecuted by aliens. These are symptoms only if the observer believes that the patient was not Napoleon, or not being persecuted by aliens. So to see a statement as a mental symptom we have to make a judgement based on own (and our society's) beliefs.

Szasz suggests that the idea of mental *illness* is used to obscure the difficulties we have in everyday living. Not long ago it was witches and devils that were held responsible for problems in social living. The belief in mental illness is no more sophisticated than a belief in demonology. Mental illness, according to Szasz, is 'real' in exactly the same way as witches were 'real'.

The simple point to draw from Szasz's complex argument is that if you are feeling stressed or down because of things that are happening to you are work or at home then it is unlikely that the problem will be solved by (a) calling it mental illness and (b) dealing with it by taking medication.

Multiple choice questions

1 Which of the following symptoms of schizophrenia did the pseudopatients describe?
   a Having visual hallucinations.
   b Being controlled by outside forces.
   c Hearing voices.
   d Having two minds.

2 How many patients were admitted with a diagnosis of schizophrenia?
   a 8   b 7
   c 6   d 5

3 The average number of days the pseudopatients spent in hospital was:
   a 7   b 12
   c 19   d 26

4 A type 2 error is calling a:
   a Healthy person sick.
   b Healthy person healthy.
   c Sick person sick.
   d Sick person healthy.

5 The pseudopatients were discharged with a diagnosis of:
   a Schizophrenia in reverse.
   b Lapsed schizophrenia.
   c Schizophrenia existential.
   d Schizophrenia in remission.

6 In the second study, how many real patients were wrongly identified as pseudopatients by at least one psychiatrist?
   a 19   b 23
   c 41   d 63

7 When the pseudopatients approached a staff member with a question, the psychiatrists stopped and answered the question:
   a 0.5% of the time.   b 1.5% of the time.
   c 2% of the time.   d 4% of the time.

8 Who recognised that the pseudopatients were not real patients?
   a Some nurses.   b Some doctors.
   c Some patients.   d All of the above.

9 Which of the following is not true about the label 'schizophrenic'?
   a It creates expectations.
   b It is 'sticky'.
   c It may not be accurate.
   d It is Russian.

10 Behaviour therapies might be preferable to hospitalisation because:
   a They don't involve labels.
   b The patient is not viewed as normal or abnormal.
   c They focus on behaviours.
   d All of the above.

Answers are on page 225.

Exam-style questions

Section A questions

1 In Rosenhan's study 'sane in insane places' the terms 'type 1' and 'type 2' errors were used.
   (a) Explain what a 'type 2 error is'. [2]
   (b) Suggest why health professionals made type 2 errors in the original diagnosis of the pseudopatients. [2]

2 In the study by Rosenhan pseudopatients were admitted to mental hospitals.
   (a) Name **two** of the pseudopatients' behaviours which were taken as evidence of abnormality. [2]
   (b) Outline **one** reason why it is difficult to define abnormality and normality. [2]

3 Rosenhan (sane in insane places) suggested mental patients experienced powerlessness and depersonalisation.
   (a) Give **two** examples to support this. [2]
   (b) Outline **one** possible explanation for the behaviour of staff in this study. [2]

4 Rosenhan used the phrase 'stickiness of psychodiagnostic labels'?
   (a) What did he mean by this phrase? [2]
   (b) Give **one** example how the label 'schizophrenic' affected the way pseudopatient's behaviour was interpreted by staff. [2]

5 In the study by Rosenhan, the pseudopatients were incorrectly diagnosed as schizophrenic. Give **two** possible explanations why the hospital made this mistake. [4]

6 Describe **two** independent variables that were tested in Rosenhan's study of 'sane in insane places' and the effects of each of these variables. [4]

See page XII–XIII for notes on the exam paper and styles of question.

Section B question

(a) What was the aim of the Rosenhan study? [2]

(b) Describe the sample used in the Rosenhan study and give **one** limitation of it. [6]

(c) Describe how data was gathered in the Rosenhan study. [6]

(d) Give **one** advantage and **one** disadvantage of observational studies. [6]

(e) Suggest **two** changes to the Rosenhan study and outline any methodological implications these changes may have. [8]

(f) Outline the results of the Rosenhan study. [8]

Section C question

(a) Outline **one** assumption of the individual differences approach in psychology. [2]

(b) Describe how the individual differences approach could explain abnormality. [4]

(c) Describe **one** similarity and **one** difference between the Rosenhan study and any other individual differences study. [6]

(d) Discuss the strengths and limitations of the individual differences approach using examples from the Rosenhan study. [12]

Key issue: ethnocentrism

Psychology is the study of people carried out by people. Inevitably, the problems psychologists investigate also form part of their own experience. Psychologists study prejudice but they also have to struggle to deal with it. Early research in the first part of the twentieth century was based on US and European theories of racial superiority. As ever, the person who carries out the studies finds that the group they belong to is the bestest. For example a review of 73 studies on race and intelligence in 1925 came to the conclusion that the *studies taken all together seem to indicate the mental superiority of the white race* (Garth, 1925, p. 359). This work would not stand up to any scientific scrutiny today (or then to be fair) but it reflected the views of some psychologists at that time.

What is ethnocentrism?

Ethnocentrism is the bias that we have to see things from the point of view of ourselves and people like us. When we talk about **ego**centrism we mean that someone is only seeing the world from their own point of view. With **ethno**centrism the viewpoint is a little wider but is still restricted – to the group the person belongs to.

Why are we ethnocentric? It seems like it is a bad thing and something that we ought to be able to avoid but the thing to consider here is that ethnocentrism has some positive as well as negative effects. Ethnocentrism can be defined as the following syndrome of behaviours (LeVine and Campbell, 1972):

- A tendency to under-value the outgroup's products.
- An increased rejection and hostility towards outgroup members.
- A tendency to over-value the ingroup's products.
- An increased liking for ingroup members (accompanied by pressures for conformity and group cohesion).

This definition is helpful because we can see both sides of the coin. The first two points are what we commonly refer to as as prejudice but the last two are best described in terms of group loyalty or cohesion. The more we like our own group, the more we dislike the other group, and vice versa. Group membership is part of ordinary life and ethnocentrism is something we experience every day. Sometimes this is quite harmless such as when you go to the pantomime and the performers set up a singing competition between the right and left sides of the theatre. Sometimes it has a slight edge such as the rivalry between football teams and their supporters, and sometimes it is the source of extreme hostility between different ethnic groups, for example.

Support the team

With an ethnocentric standpoint we tend to see our own team as the best. Also, we underestimate the failings of our own team and exaggerate those of the opposing team. There are a number of reasons for this, including our access to evidence. We are likely to know far more about the behaviour and opinions of ingroup members. Also, if we support similar people, we are likely to receive reciprocal support back from them. We expect our friends to support us and not to do us down, particularly in the company of strangers. It is all to do with social cohesion and a sense of belonging. The teams (or groups) we belong to include ones we choose like, for example, being the fan of a football club and also ones that we are given like our families and communities. People will often support their family members regardless of what they do or what they say.

Discrimination is the behavioural expression of prejudice.

Ethnocentricity is being unable to conceptualise or imagine ideas, social beliefs, or the world from any viewpoint other than that of one's own particular culture or social group. The belief that one's own ethnic group, nation, religion, scout troop or football team is superior to all others.

Ingroup: Any social group to which you belong, as distinct from the outgroup.

Prejudice is a fixed, pre-set attitude, usually negative and hostile, and usually applied to members of a particular social category.

Racism is using the pervasive power imbalance between races/people to oppress dominated peoples by devaluing their experience, behaviour and aspirations.

Activity

Below there are some examples of ethnocentric thinking. Spot the bias (answers on facing page).

- Europeans drive on the wrong side of the road.
- Japanese people read their books back to front.
- America lost the Vietnam War.
- Portuguese is a difficult language to learn.

Can you think of your own examples?

Ethnocentrism and psychology

Who does psychology study? Most psychology is about Europeans and North Americans. An analysis of introductory text books (Smith and Bond, 1993) found that they mainly cited work by researchers from America. In a fairly standard American text by Baron and Byrne (1991) 94% of the 1,700 studies mentioned were in fact from America. In a British text (Hewstone et al., 1988), about 66% of the studies were American, 32% were European and under 2% came from the rest of the world.

Ethnocentrism creates two possible sources of bias:

- Researchers mainly study their own culture; many of the studies in this text are about young Western white people.
- Researchers find it difficult to interpret the behaviour and experience of people from other cultures.

Scientific racism

Psychology has a history of not challenging race science. There might well be questions to consider about the differences between groups of people but a reasonable enquiry is difficult to make because of scientific racism, which we can define as the attempt to justify racial politics through the use of bogus scientific arguments. One of the problems with studies of racial difference is that it is very difficult to define race, and the idea that there are biologically different races of people is controversial to say the least. There are other problems (Jones, 1991) including:

- Social movement has meant that many people have ancestors from many parts of the world.
- The differences between people of the same race are much greater than the differences between people of different races.
- It is near impossible to get reliable comparisons between people from different ethnic groups because you can't use the same measures.

The greatest footballer (Stuart Pearce) at the greatest football club (Nottingham Forest). No sign of ethnocentrism here.

Even the rat was white

In 1955, when Robert Guthrie enrolled in a master's program at the University of Kentucky, he was the only black face in a sea of white.

'I remember one of my white professors eyeing me as if I were an anthropological specimen and remarking, "You are from one of our Negro schools,"' Guthrie recalls (APA website).

After serving in the US army Guthrie returned to psychology and wrote the classic text *Even the Rat Was White*. In the book he describes the role of racial bias in the history of psychology, in the development of divisive theories and also in the failure to value the work of black psychologists. The book describes the biographies of early African-American psychologists and their scientific contributions, as well as their problems, views, and concerns towards the field of social psychology. He uses research documents that are not often found in the mainstream by referring to journals and magazines such as the *Journal of Black Psychology*, the *Journal of Negro Education,* and *Crisis*.

The second edition of his book, published in 1998, reviews the progress of the last 25 years and discusses the new challenges for black psychologists. Guthrie argues that the 'myth of mental measurement' and eugenicist philosophy continue to exist and create negative stereotypes of oppressed peoples.

Ethnocentric bias, how to spot it and what to do about it

As you read through psychology books and look at the core studies you can ask yourself the following questions;

- *Who is writing this study?*
- *What biases might they have?*
- *Who are they writing about?*
- *Who is included in the findings and who is not?*
- *How would the results be different if the study was carried out on a different group of people? Why?*

It is an interesting thought that the populations of the UK and USA combined make up less than 8% of the people in the world yet they are the subjects of most of the psychology we read. If we carried out these studies in the most populous countries of the world, India and China, would we collect different data? For example, is the phenomenon of multiple personality something that occurs in every culture? And are people in other cultures as obedient as the people in the Milgram study?

Qs

1   Select **one** core study that provides insights into ethnocentrism and outline what it shows us about ethnocentrism.

2   Select **one** core study that has a narrow group of participants and suggest how the results would be different if you selected a group of people from a different part of the world.

3   What psychological variables do think are most likely to be affected by the cultural group to which the participants belong?

Activity answers

- It's the right side actually.
- It's not back to front to them.
- Two errors here, it's not 'the Vietnam War' to the Vietnamese, and the USA is only a small part of America.
- Probably not. In Portugal children as young as four are fluent in it.

Not all people are the same, but is the diversity of human experience included in psychology?

Ethnocentric bias and psychiatric diagnosis

The diagnosis of mental disorders

There has been a historical tendency to view black people as 'sick' (Sayal, 1990). Sometimes they were seen to have a physical sickness, for example, black skin was said to be a form of leprosy, and sometimes they were seen to have a mental sickness, for example runaway slaves were diagnosed as having a mental disease ('drapetomania' – an incurable urge to run away).

In Britain, the proportion of black people in the population is 5%, yet 25% of patients on psychiatric wards are black. Black patients in psychiatric hospital are more likely than white patients to see a junior rather than a senior doctor, they are more likely to receive major tranquillisers, and more likely to receive electro-convulsive therapy (Littlewood and Lipsedge, 1989). There are two possible answers to this puzzle, first, that people from ethnic minorities show more psychiatric symptoms than the general population, and second, that the behaviour of people from ethnic minorities is more likely to be interpreted as being disordered by psychiatrists.

Playing dominoes

One explanation for the high incidence of schizophrenia diagnoses for black people is that the people who make the diagnoses have little experience of black people and so do not understand their behaviour and conversation. Horsford (1990) discussed how a white middle-class psychiatrist can often misinterpret behaviour which is perfectly ordinary within an African-Caribbean culture, as being abnormal, simply because it is not the sort of behaviour shown by white professional people. An example of this is the way Caribbean men play dominoes. If you are used to the sedate way that white people play bridge, for example, then watching the dominoes game might be quite startling, and you may think that it is aggressive and threatening.

Ethnocentric bias will usually work against people in minority groups. In this case it need not be because of racism in psychiatrists but because it is more difficult to interpret and understand the behaviour of people who come from different social groups to yourself.

...Links to other studies and issues...

The question of ethnocentric bias runs through all psychology. This doesn't mean to say that we should discard all psychological research but that we have to recognise that our findings might not apply to all people. Some psychologists have tried to take their studies outside of their own cultures. Other researchers have taken **Milgram's** obedience studies to other countries, for example, and found some support but also some differences. The response to unusual behaviours varies from culture to culture and so the **Rosenhan** study would probably get different results if it was transported to other countries. The work of **Freud** also seems to be very located in European and US cultures and it would be interesting to see how relevant the ideas were for people in other parts of the world.

This issue is an example of how bias can creep into our scientific research. We can guard against this if we follow the **Sceptical Toolbox** described on page 40 as this should help us to see alternative explanations to the findings that are presented to us. The bottom line is to remember that individuals are very different one from another, and also cultures have massive variations. The possibilities for human behaviour and experience are almost limitless.

Multiple personality disorder (MPD)

Multiple personality disorder (MPD) is a psychiatric condition characterised by having at least one 'alter' personality that controls behaviour. The 'alters' are said to occur spontaneously and involuntarily, and function more or less independently of each other. In the USA the condition is referred to as Dissociative Identity Disorder (DID).

MPD is defined as the occurrence of two or more personalities within the same individual, each of which is able to take control sometime in the person's life. In the popular imagination it is commonly confused with schizophrenia because of the split personality aspect of it (see page 192). There are very striking differences between the two conditions, most critical of which is the reality testing of the individual (i.e. checking that one's perceptions actually represent reality). People with schizophrenia commonly have problems testing reality and do not see things in the same way as people without the condition. In everyday speech they are experiencing a period of insanity. In the case of multiple personality, none of the personalities have difficulty with reality testing.

The symptoms are:

- The patient has at least two distinct identities or personality states. Each of these has its own, relatively lasting pattern of sensing, thinking about and relating to self and environment.

- At least two of these personalities repeatedly assume control of the patient's behaviour.

- Common forgetfulness cannot explain the patient's extensive inability to remember important personal information.

- This behaviour is not directly caused by substance abuse or by a general medical condition.

What is the cause of MPD?
It is commonly believed that MPD is a response to extremely traumatic situations from which there is no physical means of escape. The traumatic situations might involve physical or emotional pain or anticipation of that pain. If the person 'goes away in their own head' they can remove themselves from the pain and function as if it had not occurred.

MPD: not a new explanation
References to multiple personality go back a long way and appear in the Bible, for example in the Gospel of St Mark 5: 8–10: 'He ... said to him, "Come out of the man, you unclean spirit!" And Jesus asked him, "What is your name?" He replied, "My name is Legion; for we are many." And he begged him not to send them out ....'

The controversy: does MPD exist?
One view suggests that MPD is real and commonly a response to childhood sexual abuse. The other view suggests that MPD is created in the therapist's office by the use of hypnotism and guided imagery. Look at the information here and come to your own opinion though it is only fair to say that we (the authors) remain divided about the existence of MPD. It is clear that a small number of people have some powerful experiences where they feel they are not really there and that they are watching what is happening rather than taking part in it. The controversy is about whether the best way to describe this is to call it multiple personality.

What is dissociation?
Your perception of yourself and your experience of the world depend on a number of factors including feelings, thoughts, memories and sensations. You make sense of these inputs to create your view of reality. If some of these information sources become disconnected then it can change your sense of identity or your perceptions of the world. This is what happens in dissociation.

Dissociation is common enough in everyday life. Maybe you are driving somewhere on a familiar route and when you arrive at your destination you realise you can't recall the entire journey. It is almost as if you went into automatic pilot mode. Or maybe you have to give a talk or a performance to a large group of people. You are nervous about it but you keep control of yourself and almost watch yourself doing the performance as if you are in the audience. It almost feels as if someone else is doing it. 'Is that really me?' you ask yourself. In this way we can use dissociation to help us deal with stressful events. Dissociation can be a useful coping strategy to deal with events that are embarrassing, stressful or painful.

Dissociation is also sometimes experienced as a side effect of drugs or alcohol.

Types of dissociation
Amnesia: A loss of memories of specific events or experiences, or sometimes not remembering personal information.

Depersonalisation: This can include out-of-body experiences like seeing yourself as part of a movie, or feeling that your body is not real.

Derealisation: Things around you appear unreal so that objects might appear to change shape or other people seem to be robots.

Identity confusion: A sense of uncertainty about who you are and maybe a struggle inside to define who you are.

Identity alteration: This refers to a dramatic shift in your identity that changes your behaviour in noticeable ways.

Iraqis carry the body of a man in a Baghdad street following airstrikes. People in extreme situations like war zones often experience dissociation. It is seen as a symptom of post traumatic stress disorder which is a diagnosis that was invented to describe the experience of US veterans of the war in Vietnam.

Dissociation as a response to trauma
The following survivor account of the July 2005 bombs in London shows how one person used dissociation to deal with the initial crisis. She experiences the event as surreal and like a movie.

'It was about three minutes after we left King's Cross when there was a massive bang and there was smoke and glass everywhere. The lights went out, and with the smoke, we couldn't breathe. We sort of cushioned each other during the impact because the compartment was so full. It felt like a dream, it was surreal. The screaming from the front carriage was terrible. It was just horrendous, it was like a disaster movie, you can't imagine being somewhere like that. You just want to get out. I kept closing my eyes and thinking of outside.' (*Guardian*, 2005)

Readers beware
Whenever you come across symptoms, either medical or psychiatric, there is a tendency to think they describe something about you. This is because they do. In this case we all experience some forms of dissociation in our daily lives. We are all a bit different in different situations. You behave in one way with your friends and another way with your parents; believe me, they are grateful for this. (See also the Barnum Effect on page 221).

Altered states and popular delusions

Mesmerism

In the eighteenth century Viennese doctor and showman Anton Mesmer developed a technique that eventually took his name – mesmerism. Mesmer discovered that if he could create the right atmosphere he could influence the behaviour of suggestible people. In a theatrical performance he would wear brightly coloured clothes and move around people, waving a magnetised stick and playing the part of a healer. He was able to induce people to dance or fall asleep. The act was similar to the modern day stage hypnotist and circus tent evangelist. Opinion was divided as to whether Mesmer was a conman or whether he had invented something quite remarkable. With royal patronage from Louis XVI, Mesmer set up a Magnetic Institute in Paris but a scientific investigation of his work concluded that the effects experienced by people during mesmerism were due to their imaginations.

Another popular delusion is that we can contact the dead by joining hands and wearing gothic clothes.

Hypnosis

'When using hypnosis, one person (the subject) is guided by another (the hypnotist) to respond to suggestions for changes in subjective experience, alterations in perception, sensation, emotion, thought or behaviour' (APA, 2005).

Hypnosis commonly involves (a) intense concentration, (b) extreme relaxation, and (c) high suggestibility. It can be used for entertainment, personal development and therapy. The patients of hypnotherapists are usually people looking for such things as pain relief or a way of giving up smoking. More controversially, some therapists use hypnosis to recover repressed memories of sexual abuse or memories of past lives. Freud started the work into repressed memories (see page 93) and he initially used hypnosis, though wisely moved away from it quite quickly.

Altered states?

Hypnosis is commonly believed to be a trance-like altered state of consciousness. This view sees hypnosis as a route to hidden parts of the mind. An alternative and more plausible view sees hypnosis as a response to social demands where people who are especially suggestible respond to cues from the hypnotist (Wagstaff, 1981). In other words, hypnosis is an extreme example of social conformity where the person behaves as they think they are expected to. Connections are made between hypnotism and mesmerism, and also with a belief in demonic possession and exorcism.

Demonic possession

There are different ways of explaining similar phenomena. The idea of demonic possession sees the victim as having other entities, in this case demons, inside them. The way to remove the demons is through exorcism. This has been carried out in ceremonies such as those caricatured in movies such as *The Exorcist* and more commonly in the USA today at mass religious meetings where the preacher will cast out demons in a dramatic show. Maybe the phenomenon of multiple personality is a different way of explaining a similar experience.

Interpreting unusual experiences

Many unusual experiences have been reported by people. It appears to be a feature of humankind that we try and make the best sense we can of our world. Sometimes this means we have to go beyond the evidence and trust our senses. Not everyone will agree with the way you interpret your world and there are many phenomena that have believers and non-believers.

There is a common belief in near death experiences where people describe the sensation of going down a tunnel of light, presumably towards the next world. Then there is the issue of alien abduction where people believe they have been abducted and experimented on by beings from other planets (check the internet to see just how common this belief is).

So when we look at the accounts of multiple personality do we judge them as flawed attempts to explain unusual experiences or as the description of a human phenomenon?

Repressed memory therapy (RMT)

The assumption behind RMT is that psychological problems such as eating disorders, depression and extreme anxiety are caused by repressed memories. Repressed memories are not in conscious awareness and cannot be recalled without help from a therapist, but is the therapist helping the patient recall something they have forgotten or are they helping them to invent a memory? The repressed memories are often of shocking childhood experiences such as sexual abuse. RMT therapists believe that psychological health can only be restored by recalling and dealing with the repressed memories.

RMT is so controversial that in the UK The Royal College of Psychiatrists has banned members from using therapies designed to recover repressed memories of childhood abuse. In the USA a report for The American Psychological Association in 1996 noted that *'there is a consensus among memory researchers and clinicians that most people who were sexually abused as children remember all or part of what happened to them although they may not fully understand or disclose it. At this point it is impossible, without other corroborative evidence, to distinguish a true memory from a false one.'* (http://www.apa.org/pubinfo/mem.html)

...Link to the core study...

We take it for granted that we have one personality that is relatively consistent and predictable. We ask someone 'How are you today?' and not 'Who are you today?'. The revelation of this study was that, for at least one person, this second question was more appropriate. The therapists described an unusual phenomenon and set a pattern for how we would describe this type of experience. They wrote up their case study in medical journals and also presented it to the wider public. Today we are used to seeing personal issues discussed openly (and endlessly) on television but this case was reported at the start of the celebrity psychiatrist circus where psychological problems are given a public airing not only for information but also for entertainment.

The therapists became very famous for the study in contrast to the subject of the case study who was effectively kept hidden for 25 years. Even today there are a lot of unanswered questions about this story. Read the study and decide for yourself whether MPD is real or a creation of therapists.

Corbett H. Thigpen and Hervey Cleckley (1954) A case of multiple personality. *Journal of Abnormal and Social Psychology*, 49, pages 135–151.

THIGPEN AND CLECKLEY: MULTIPLE PERSONALITY DISORDER

Abstract

Eve White (EW) was referred to a psychiatrist, Dr Thigpen, because she experienced severe headaches and blackouts that had no physical cause. Therapy revealed some fairly unexceptional emotional problems.

The ordinariness of this case changed when the therapist received a letter from EW, with some strange handwriting at the bottom. At her next visit a new 'person' emerged – Eve Black (EB), a very different physical presence, flirtatious and confident whereas EW was demure and retiring.

EB was aware of all EW did but the same was not true in reverse. When EB was 'out' she often behaved mischievously and would leave EW to be punished. This explained events in EW's past where she could not account for things she did. This was substantiated by her husband and parents.

Psychometric and projective personality tests were used to show a difference between the two Eves. EW had a higher IQ and memory function but EB was psychologically healthier – regressed rather than repressed. In some ways they were one personality at two stages of life. EB's role was to embody all the angry feelings thus enabling EW to maintain a nice, loving persona.

After eight months of therapy a third personality, Jane, emerged, who was superficially a compromise between EW and EB. An EEG showed that EB was different to EW and Jane. The solution lay in some integration of the three personalities but the therapists recognised that it would be morally wrong for them to 'kill off' any one personality.

Thumbnail sketches

Eve White

Demure, retiring, in some respects almost 'saintly', face often looks sad, reads and composes poetry, steadfast, lacking boldness and spontaneity, industrious worker, competent housekeeper, not self-righteous but seldom playful, soft voice, dresses in a simple way, devoted to her daughter.

Eve Black

Party girl, childishly vain, egocentric, enjoys taunting and mocking, does things 'on a whim', immediately amusing and likeable, voice a little 'coarse', uses slang, dresses a little provocatively, posture and gait light-hearted, developed a skin rash when wearing nylon stockings, could never be hypnotised.

Introduction

Multiple personality disorder was rare but reasonably well known in the 1950s, based on a few detailed case histories which were viewed with some suspicion.

The patients

Eve White

Dr Thigpen had treated a 25-year-old married woman, 'Eve White', for several months. Eve White (EW) was referred to the psychiatrist because of 'severe and blinding headaches', and said that 'blackouts' often followed the headaches. During early interviews EW discussed her emotional difficulties and personal conflicts. Thigpen regarded the case as relatively normal but was puzzled by a recent trip for which she had no memory. Hypnotism enabled them to clear up this amnesia (i.e. her failure to recall the trip).

Several days later a letter was received. The letter was unsigned but clearly from EW because of the handwriting. The final paragraph was puzzling. Had EW inserted this paragraph as a prank? It was hard to imagine the *'matter-of-fact ... meticulously truthful and consistently sober'* EW becoming playful. She denied sending the letter at her next visit though she remembered beginning such a letter.

At this time she started to become rather agitated and asked if hearing voices was a sign of insanity. At that moment a strange look came over her face and she put her hands to her head as if seized by a sudden pain. After a tense moment of silence, her hands dropped and with a quick smile and bright voice said *'Hi there, Doc!'*.

Appearance of Eve Black

EW was transformed from a retiring and conventional figure, lacking attractiveness, into a novel feminine apparition.

'The newcomer [had] a childishly daredevil air, an erotically mischievous glance, a face marvellously free from the habitual signs of care, seriousness and underlying distress, so long familiar in her predecessor. This new and apparently carefree girl spoke casually of Eve White and her problems, always using "she" or "her" in every reference, always respecting the strict bounds of separate identity. When asked her own name she immediately replied, "Oh, I'm Eve Black"' (page 137).

The therapist (Dr. Thigpen) thought of the following lines at this moment *'The devil entered the prompter's box, and the play was ready to start.'*

The film The Three Faces of Eve *staring Joanne Woodward (who won an Oscar for her performance of Eve) was based on a book of the same name by Thigpen and Cleckley, both released in 1957.*

Part of the letter received by Dr Thigpen, showing the different handwriting used in the final paragraph.

The case study

Thigpen and Cleckley spent the next 14 months (approximately 100 hours) interviewing Eve White (EW) and Eve Black (EB), collecting material about their behaviour and inner lives.

Initially, in order to interview EB, EW had to be hypnotised. Soon it became possible to simply ask to speak to EB and she would come forth. This complicated EW's life because it meant that EB was able to pop out more easily at other times too.

Eve Black's life history

It appeared that EB had enjoyed an independent life since EW's early childhood. EW had no knowledge of her existence until some time after EB emerged unbidden in the psychiatrists' office. When EB was 'out' EW was completely oblivious of what EB did and was apparently unconscious. In contrast EB had some awareness of what EW did when EB was not out. She could report what the other did and thought but didn't participate in these thoughts and actions. EB regarded EW's distress about her failing marriage as silly. EB was not cruel but like a 'bright-feathered parakeet who chirps undisturbed while watching a child strangle to death' (page 138).

EB claimed that during childhood she often emerged to play pranks, though she also lied easily so that it was difficult to take her account as reliable evidence. However, EW provided indirect support for EB's reports because she could remember punishments and accusations for things she didn't know she had done but which were described by EB. EW's parents and husband also confirmed EB's stories. For example, EW was punished when, aged six, she wandered off through the woods to play with some other children. Her denials were not believed at the time and she was severely punished. EB had separately reported this incident, saying that she enjoyed the adventure and enjoyed being able to withdraw and leave EW to be punished.

Another incident was reported by EW's husband who lost his temper with EW when he found she'd spent a lot of money on new clothes and hidden them away. EB confessed to being the culprit in this shopping spree.

EB denied any association with EW's child or the husband, whom she despised. She had never made herself known to them nor EW's parents. There would be no reason for them to suspect that EW was really two people and, in any case, EB was able to pass herself off as EW, imitating her tone of voice and gestures. However EW's parents were aware of unexplained changes in her, which they described as her 'strange little habits'.

Therapy

It was difficult to proceed with the therapy because EB was unwilling be involved. However a bargain was struck where she would be allowed more time 'out' if she cooperated more and avoided serious misbehaviour – otherwise the psychiatrists suggested they would limit the extent to which EB was 'allowed out'.

EB reported that she had caused the severe headaches and imaginary voices. She also claimed to be able to wipe EW's memory if she thought very hard about it. One example of this was a report (from a distant relative) that a previous marriage had occurred. EB eventually confessed that when EW was working away from home for a while EB had gone to a dance and ended up marrying a man she scarcely knew. She lived with this man for several months though EW had no recollection of this.

The aim of therapy was to achieve reintegration of the two personalities. They tried to call out both personalities at once but EW experienced a violent headache and became very distressed; EB tried once and said it gave her 'such a funny, queer, mixed-up feeling that I ain't gonna put up with it no more' (page 122).

During the course of therapy EW decided to leave her husband and, at that time, her daughter went to live with EW's parents. The headaches, blackouts and voices disappeared and she managed to do well at her job and achieve some stability. EB had been causing less trouble and seldom 'came out', though she did occasionally go on dates with 'bad company'. Fortunately EW was spared the knowledge of this.

Psychological consultation report

Psychological tests were conducted on the two Eves by a clinical psychologist, who reported that the basic behaviour pattern was similar in both personalities.

	EW	EB
Psychometric tests:		
IQ test	110	104
Memory scale	Above IQ.	On a par with her IQ.
Projective personality tests:	Rigid and not capable of dealing with	Able to conform to the environment;
Rorschach testand drawings	her hostility. Conflict in role as wife and	a healthier profile than EW. Result
of human figures	mother, resulting in anxiety.	indicates **regression** – a wish to
	Result indicates **repression**.	return to an earlier period of life.

The projective tests (see page 190) suggested that the existence of dual personalities was due to a wish to return to an earlier stage of life (EB in fact used EW's maiden name). EW's hostility towards her roles as wife and mother made her feel guilty which activated the defence mechanism of repression, removing the conflict from her conscious awareness. Playing the role of EB permits her to discharge her feelings of hostility towards EW and others. The problem started earlier in life. EW felt rejected by her parents when her twin sisters were born; EW loved them dearly, EB despised them. In a sense EB's role was to embody all the angry feelings thus enabling EW to maintain a nice, loving persona.

Qs

1. Identify **three** differences between EW and EB.
2. Describe **one** example of something EB did which got EW into trouble.
3. Thigpen and Cleckley reported that they tested EB's claim that she could erase items from EW's memory. How do you think that they have done this?
4. What are 'psychometric and projective tests'?
5. What did the psychometric tests show about the two selves?
6. Describe what you think may have caused EW's problem?
7. What do you think EW felt about her mother and her marriage?
8. How did the therapists 'contact' EB?
9. How did the therapists manage to get EB to take part in the therapy?

The case study *continued*

Eight months into therapy

After eight months the situation changed for the worse again. EW's headaches and blackouts returned. EB was questioned but denied any part in this new development and said she too was experiencing blackouts. During one session of hypnosis EW stopped talking, her eyes shut and her head dropped. After a silence of two minutes, she blinked, looked around the room as if to work out where she was and, in a husky poised voice, said to the therapist 'Who are you?'. It was immediately apparent that this was neither EW nor EB. This new person, Jane, was more mature and bold than EW but not difficult like EB. In a superficial way she could be described as a compromise between the two Eves.

EEG test

A study was done of the brain waves of the three patients using an electroencephalogram (EEG). Tenseness was most pronounced in EB, next EW and then Jane. EW and Jane had a fairly similar alpha rhythm whereas EB's was a little bit faster, on the borderline between normal and abnormally fast. This difference was significant. Slightly fast records are sometimes associated with psychopathic personality (i.e. a personality disorder characterised by a lack of social conscience). There was also evidence of restlessness and generalised muscle tension in EB's tracings but not in the others.

The three personalities

Jane was aware of everything the other two did but could not fully access their memories prior to her emergence. Jane was able to report when EB was lying. She felt free from EW's responsibilities and didn't identify with her role as wife and mother, though she felt compassion towards the child. Jane gradually took over more and more from EW, though she only emerged through EW and had not found a way to displace EB. The therapists felt that Jane might be able to solve the deepest problems that EW sought treatment for, whereas EB would never provide a solution as she *would indeed be a travesty of a woman*. EW's sense of duty and willingness for self-sacrifice would repeatedly bring her back to a marital situation which she did not have the emotional vigour to deal with. Therefore Jane seemed the only solution. EW admitted, during hypnosis, that the best solution for her child, might be for Jane to take over as mother, a role she had not been successful at. Jane, however, was reluctant to come between a distressed mother and her child.

EW was not a physically bold person yet a recent event demonstrated another side to herself. It was a momentous event which moved Jane deeply. Jane showed her compassion for EW in a letter to the therapists: *Today [EW] did something that made me know and appreciate her as I had not been able to do before. I wish I could tell her what I feel but I can't reach her. She must not die yet … She saved the life of a little boy today … she darted out in front of a car to pick him up … but instead of putting him down again, the moment his baby arms went round her neck, he became her baby – and she continued to walk down the street carrying him in her arms … There seemed only one solution to prevent her possible arrest for kidnapping. That was for me to come out and find the child's mother. In the end I had to give up and find a policeman. Later tonight when she had come back out, she was searching for her own baby. She had her baby again for a short while this afternoon; and I'm so happy for that … I feel inexpressibly humble.* (page 147).

The psychotherapist's responsibility

The therapists recognised their role in 'creating' Jane since her emergence was really due to the process of therapy. They may not have 'caused' her existence but certainly played a part in it. The therapists were also faced with the decision of how much to encourage her to 'take over' from the others. The therapists did not think themselves wise enough to make such a decision nor did they think the responsibility was theirs; *Would any physician order euthanasia for the heedlessly merry and amoral but nevertheless unique Eve Black* (page 146). They believed that they had some choice about which personality to reinforce but ultimately the choice lay with the patient.

Activity

Try a role play with two actors – one the therapist, the other the patient who switches between the different personalities.

Biographical notes

Corbett Thigpen and **Hervey Cleckley** and their patient were from Augusta, Georgia in the southern USA. Dr Cleckley was chief of psychiatry and neurology at University Hospital of Georgia. His book, *The Mask of Sanity*, can be read at www.cassiopaea.com/cassiopaea/psychopath.htm

Dr Thigpen retired as a clinical professor of psychiatry at the Medical College of Georgia in 1987. He treated Margaret Mitchell, the author of *Gone with the Wind* (another Georgian), in hospital and became a close friend. He was a life-long amateur magician, but some say this case was probably his best 'trick'.

Qs

1 How do you think the psychiatrists' personal involvement in the case may have affected their ability to report the facts?

2 Much of the data was recalled retrospectively. How do you think this might have affected the reliability of the data?

3 This study was a longitudinal study. Why was it desirable to conduct this study over a long period of time?

4 Thigpen and Cleckley wondered about the ethics of deciding which personality could be 'killed'. Do you think this issue was a problem? (Explain why or why not.)

5 Suggest **two** pieces of evidence which support the claim that this patient did have MPD and **two** pieces of evidence which suggest that this patient did not have MPD.

6 Why did the psychiatrists think that schizophrenia was an unlikely diagnosis?

7 Which of Freud's concepts of id, ego, and superego goes with each of the three personalities?

8 In what way was Jane more similar to Eve White?

9 In what way was Jane not similar to Eve White, but more of a compromise between the two Eves?

10 How might a behaviourist explain the development of Multiple Personality Disorder?

11 How would Freud explain why people develop Multiple Personality Disorder?

Discussion

Discussion

Some possible explanations for Eve's behaviour were:

- She was a skilful actress, though this seems unlikely because it would be hard to see how she could have maintained this act over such a long period of time.
- It could be that Eve was suffering from a hysterical disorder or schizophrenia, though many of the appropriate symptoms were absent.
- The therapists' observations were not objective.

How does disintegration occur?

Identical twins start as one cell but divide at the very outset. The same could be true of a multiple personality. Can it be reintegrated? Jane appeared to be some sort of fusion of the other personalities, not a mere addition of different traits. Like the fusion of hydrogen and oxygen to make water, Jane was a product genuinely different from both ingredients from which it was formed.

What is personality?

In order to understand multiple personality, we need to understand 'personality'. We hear people say things like 'John Doe has become a new man since he stopped drinking' or 'a friend was not himself the other night' or that 'a Δ208 woman's absorption in her home resulted in her losing her entire personality'. In psychiatry the term implies a unified total. Dictionaries define it as 'individuality', 'personal existence or identity'. Bearing this in mind Thigpen and Cleckley felt it was appropriate to speak of Eve White, Eve Black and Jane as three 'personalities'.

However, the physical evidence for this was weak. The differences in EEGs and in psychometric and projective tests were not particularly impressive. A handwriting expert concluded that, even though the handwriting of each personality superficially appeared to be by a different person, they all were clearly written by the same individual.

Final word

Thigpen and Cleckley finished their article with a plea for psychiatry to avoid explanations which offer little real insight. They recognised that they had not been able to propose any new explanation for multiple personalities but found the case very thought-provoking and suggest that further research may yield understanding of this disorder.

Evaluating the study by Thigpen and Cleckley

The research method

This was a case study. *What are the strengths and limitations of this research method in the context of this study?*

> *There are no simple answers. Evaluating a study requires you to think. We have provided some pointers here, linked to the KEY ISSUES covered through this book – see page XIV for a table of these key issues.*

The research techniques

A number of different techniques were used in this study to collect data about the three Eves. *List the different techniques and for each give strengths and limitations.*

The sample

In what way is the participant in this study unique? How does this affect the conclusions drawn from the study?

Qualitative and quantitative

Give examples of both quantitative and qualitative data from this study. What are the strengths and limitations of each kind of data in the context of this study?

Ethical issues

What ethical issues should have concerned the researchers in this study, and how might they have dealt with these issues?

Nature or nurture?

Was Eve born with Multiple Personality Disorder? Were there aspects of her personality that predisposed her to developing a mental illness? Or can we explain her personality changes entirely in terms of events in her life (i.e. nurture)? *What evidence is there from this study to support the nature or nurture side of the debate?*

Ecological validity

The therapists may have 'encouraged' some of Eve's behaviours. *To what extent can we generalise the findings from this study?*

Applications/usefulness

How valuable was this study – for people in general and/or for people dealing with mental illness/Multiple Personality Disorder?

What next?

Describe **one** change to this study, and say how you think this might affect the outcome.

Debate

Was Eve suffering from Multiple Personality Disorder?

Or was it something else? After this case Thigpen and Cleckley saw lots more people supposedly with MPD but they felt that almost all the cases were the result of therapists' suggestions. When a disorder is not 'real' but is caused by a therapist planting ideas in a patient's head it is called 'iatrogenic'. Have a look at the next page for some further discussion of this.

...Links to other studies and issues...

This study has direct links to **Rosenhan's** question about how we can distinguish sanity from insanity. It also links with **Sperry's** account of split-brain surgery. In this work he talks about split consciousness and two people in the same body. There is also a strong link to the work of Elizabeth **Loftus** on memory. She has been prominent in the recovered memory/false memory debate which is central to any evaluation of multiple personality. Finally, there is a link to **Freud** in the use of hypnosis and also the belief in repressed memories of childhood sexual abuse.

---

www You might look at various websites to collect evidence about the nature of MPD – also known as dissociative identity disorder (DID) e.g. www.dissociation.com

The growing controversy

Since the account of Eve by Thigpen and Cleckley the story has grown and becomes progressively more controversial. Most striking is Eve's own account of her experience and the differences between this account and that of her therapists.

The real Eve

Christine Sizemore (Eve's real name) always wanted to tell her own story. She was discouraged from doing this by Thigpen because of the possible harm it would do her if she revealed herself to the world. A less charitable interpretation would be that he was also protecting his control over the story. According to Sizemore she agreed to Thigpen and Cleckley preparing academic reports about her for discussion in scientific seminars, but she was not aware they were writing a book for publication to the general public. She was also not aware that Thigpen filmed some of the filmed therapy sessions. The resulting film *Case Study in Multiple Personality* was made available from his university library. When she found out about this, after 20 years, she took legal action to ban its use.

The battle for control of her story was lost before it started as Thigpen and Cleckley published their book and then sold the rights to Hollywood. When *The Three Faces of Eve,* starring Joanne Woodward, was premiered, Thigpen and Cleckley were the stars of the event, but Sizemore was advised to leave town to avoid distress and not to see the film. Joanne Woodward got an Oscar for playing Chris Sizemore, who got nothing, not even any recognition of her existence. The book and the film told of a successful therapy and a happy ending, but this bore little relationship to the truth. Some time later when she tried to write her own account she

The real Eve – Chris Sizemore pictured at the 50th Anniversary of the World Premiere of Three Faces of Eve *at the Miller Theatre in Augusta Georgia*

discovered that Thigpen claimed to have a document signed by her giving him full rights over her story. In an ironic twist, Christine Sizemore's identity and life story had been taken over by her psychiatrists.

Eventually in 1977 she collaborated with her cousin Elen Pitillo to reveal her identity(ies) to the world with the book *I'm Eve.* This text tells a very different story to that told by Thigpen and Cleckley, a story which starts much earlier in her life, has many more identities and goes on much longer. By the time the book was published she describes herself as being adjusted to her problems and able to live a full and rewarding life.

Sybil

The public view of MPD has been heavily influenced by films such as *The Three Faces of Eve* and *Sybil.* The story of Sybil (Schreiber, 1973) tells of a woman with 16 personalities, created as a response to childhood sexual abuse. Before the publication of the book and the subsequent movie of the same name there were only 75 reported cases of MPD. Since then the diagnosis rate in the USA has gone through the roof as has the number of personalities believed to exist in the patients.

Sybil was eventually identified as Shirley Mason, who died in 1998 at the age of 75. Her therapist was Cornelia Wilbur, who died in 1992. It is now known that Mason had no symptoms of MPD before she began having therapy with Wilbur. The magazine *Newsweek* (January 25, 1999) reported that, according to historian Peter M. Swales (who first identified Mason as Sybil), *'there is strong evidence that [the worst abuse in the book] could not have happened.'*

During her therapy that included hypnosis and mind-altering drugs, Mason read the literature on MPD including the book *The Three Faces of Eve.* It is commonly believed that the case of Sybil is an example of an *iatrogenic* disorder (that is, one caused by the doctor). A different view is put forward by Philip M. Coons who supports the MPD diagnosis and points out that *'the relationship of multiple personality to child abuse was not generally recognised until the publication of Sybil'*.

(http://www.healthyplace.com/commun ities/personality_disorders/wermany/re ading_room/abuse.htm)

A cautionary tale of psychiatric treatment

Bennett Braun was a leading researcher and therapist in MPD in the USA. In 1980 Braun helped establish an MPD facility at the hospital he worked at and by 1984 he was president of the International Society for the Study of Multiple Personality and Dissociation. Within 20 years he had been expelled from the American Psychiatric Association and can no longer treat anyone for MPD, the condition for which he was considered an expert. How did it get to this?

The best way to answer this is to look at just one of his patients, Patricia Burgus. After a difficult birth of her second child in 1982, Burgus began to experience depression and received conventional therapy. After a while she came in contact with Braun who suggested she and her son should be hospitalised. He suggested that she had MPD and had therefore almost certainly survived some childhood trauma.

In hospital she had a range of therapies including hypnosis and mind altering drugs, sometimes being woken up in the middle of

the night to have her treatment. During the sessions Braun helped her 'discover' her multiple personalities and in particular her involvement with a satanic cult dating back to the seventeenth century, that she had experienced sexual abuse as a child and that she had given birth to several children who had been sacrificed by the cult. Eventually she described herself as a high priestess who ran the affairs of the cult without her husband or her everyday self knowing anything about it. The lack of any corroborating evidence for these activities or pregnancies did not deter the therapist. Other patients started to incorporate Burgus into their stories and her role of high priestess became established in the collective fantasy of the psychiatric facility.

Burgus' condition got worse and she was transferred to a regular psychiatric ward where she was taken off the medication and started to recover. The multiple personalities quickly disappeared and the satanic cult was shown to be a sham. Several lawsuits were brought against Bennett Braun and his colleagues. Patricia Burgus and her family eventually accepted a settlement of $10.6 million.

Multiple choice questions

1 Which of the following was not one of Eve White's symptoms?
   a   Hearing voices.
   b   Headaches.
   c   Trouble sleeping.
   d   Blackouts.

2 Approximately how many hours were spent interviewing the patients?
   a   100
   b   120
   c   150
   d   200

3 Which of the following is true?
   a   EB had access to EW's memories.
   b   EW had access to EB's memories.
   c   Neither a nor b.
   d   Both a and b.

4 Eve Black was described as:
   a   Reversed.
   b   Repressive.
   c   Regressive.
   d   Reintegrated.

5 Which of the following is a projective personality test?
   a   Wechsler–Bellevue.
   b   Rorschach.
   c   Cattell.
   d   Snoopy Scale.

6 What score did Eve White get on the IQ test?
   a   102   b   104
   c   106   d   110

7 Who was Jane most similar to?
   a   EB.
   b   EW.
   c   Neither EB or EW.
   d   Tarzan.

8 The EEG test showed that the alpha rhythms were similar in:
   a   EW and Jane.
   b   EW and EB.
   c   EB and Jane.
   d   EW, EB and Jane.

9 Why is it unlikely that the patients were simply acting?
   a   They said they couldn't act.
   b   The therapy took place over a long period of time.
   c   They didn't change their story when hypnotised.
   d   All of the above.

10 What other diagnosis, aside from Multiple Personality Disorder, might have been possible?
   a   Schizophrenia.
   b   Split personality.
   c   Depression.
   d   Obsessive–compulsive disorder.

Answers are on page 225.

Exam-style questions

See page XII–XIII for notes on the exam paper and styles of question.

Section A questions

1   Thigpen and Cleckley were therapists who studied a case of Multiple Personality Disorder.
    (a)   Outline **one** problem with the evidence that they collected in this study.   [2]
    (b)   Suggest how they might have dealt with this problem.   [2]

2   Thigpen and Cleckley diagnosed their patient as suffering from Multiple Personality Disorder. Describe **two** pieces of evidence from the case study that suggest that the patient did have the disorder.   [4]

3   In the study by Thigpen and Cleckley on multiple personality the therapist described the first time Eve Black 'appeared'. He noted that Eve White was transformed from a retiring figure into a feminine apparition.
    (a)   How did the therapist interpret this observation?   [2]
    (b)   Give **one** other interpretation of this observation.   [2]

4   In the study by Thigpen and Cleckley it might be suggested that the patient had several personalities. Describe **one** piece of evidence that might suggest she did have several personalities and **one** piece of evidence that suggests she didn't have several personalities.   [4]

5   Thigpen and Cleckley say that they may have been in part responsible for the appearance of Jane.
    (a)   Explain how they might be responsible.   [2]
    (b)   Outline what they decide to do to resolve the multiple personalities.   [2]

6   Outline **one** strength and **one** weakness of the case study method as it was used by Thigpen and Cleckley.   [4]

Section B question

(a)   What was the aim of the Thigpen and Cleckley study?   [2]

(b)   Describe the sample used in the Thigpen and Cleckley study and give **one** limitation of it.   [6]

(c)   Describe how data were gathered in the Thigpen and Cleckley study.   [6]

(d)   Give **one** advantage and **one** disadvantage of psychometric tests.   [6]

(e)   Suggest **two** changes to the Thigpen and Cleckley study and outline any impact these would have on the results.   [8]

(f)   Outline the conclusions of the Thigpen and Cleckley study.   [8]

Section C question

(a)   Outline **one** assumption of the nurture approach in psychology.   [2]

(b)   Describe how the nurture approach could explain Multiple Personality Disorder.   [4]

(c)   Describe the ethical issues raised by the Thigpen and Cleckley study.   [6]

(d)   Discuss the strengths and limitations of the nurture approach using examples from the Thigpen and Cleckley study.   [12]

Key issue: case studies

Case studies provide some of psychology's best stories. In this text we have looked at a number including the story of **Little Hans** by Freud who used detailed case studies as the main evidence for his theories, the multiple personalities of **Eve** described by Thigpen and Cleckley, and the development of language in Washoe recorded by Gardner and Gardner page 62 and **Kanzi** by Savage-Rumbaugh. These case studies give us detailed information on Hans, Eve and Washoe and they provide some unique insights into behaviour and experience. Freud uses the story of Hans to support the existence of the Oedipus complex in boys, and Thigpen and Cleckley used Eve's story to support their view of multiple personality. The study of the signing chimps provides evidence that animals can use abstract signs to communicate.

All the stories are engaging and have stood the test of time. There is still considerable interest in all of them and they commonly appear in introductory psychology textbooks. Their appeal goes beyond the boundaries of psychology and several case studies have become well known to the general public. There is no doubt that they have contributed to our understanding of ourselves and others but it is also important to look at the scientific value and personal consequences of these studies.

> A **case study** is a research investigation that involves the detailed study of a single individual, institution or event. It uses information from a range of sources, such as interviews and observations to obtain data. These findings are then selected and organised, for instance to represent the individual's thoughts and emotions.
>
> A **biography** is an account of a person's life written, composed, or produced by another.
>
> **Professional ethics** are the rules or standards governing the conduct of a person or the members of a profession, in particular how they deal with members of the general public.
>
> **Serendipity** is the effect by which one accidentally discovers something fortunate, especially while looking for something else entirely different.

'There is no psychology; there is only biography and autobiography.' American Psychiatrist Thomas Szasz.

Biography and autobiography

Case studies are scientific biographies. They try to tell the story of someone and use key details to illustrate psychological theories. Some of the problems that authors have when they attempt to write a biography also come up with case studies.

For example the entertainer Cilla Black wrote her own biography (an autobiography) and said '*I had to do the book because there was an unauthorised biography which didn't tell it like it was.*' How could someone else tell the story of your life? Only you have seen it from the inside. But, if we left the story of your life just to you, then we would also have some problems. The story I would tell about myself is bound to be different to the stories that other people would tell about me. Autobiographies are very different to biographies; this is not to say that we tell lies about ourselves or others but just that seeing a story from the inside is very different to seeing it from afar. Case studies are most commonly biography rather than autobiography and so have that outsider view of the events.

The British author Rebecca West identified the problem for biographers and case study authors when she wrote, '*Just how difficult it is to write biography can be reckoned by anybody who sits down and considers just how many people know the real truth about his or her love affairs. Nobody can know the real truth, perhaps not even yourself.*'

The US author Mark Twain highlights the weakness of biographies when he wrote, '*Biographies are but the clothes and buttons of the man. The biography of the man himself cannot be written.*' The words on the page can only capture the performances that we give everyday and not the internal world of our thoughts and feelings.

Biographies and case studies commonly seem to be about exceptional people doing exceptional things. It is perhaps not surprising that we are drawn towards people who have different experiences to ourselves. This concentration on differentness can give a false impression about ordinary people living regular lives. As Mark Twain wrote, '*There was never yet an uninteresting life. Such a thing is an impossibility. Inside of the dullest exterior there is a drama, a comedy, and a tragedy.*' Your mother was right – you are very special. In fact, you are unique, and your experience of life and your life story is all your own.

Biographies give us interesting insights into the lives of others, they help us to reflect positively on our own lives and they can reassure us that we are not so odd as we sometimes think we are. They also provide us with moral studies that we can use to discuss what we think is right and wrong in human behaviour.

Whose story is it anyway?

One of the issues concerns authorship. If my life story was going be told in a book or a scientific paper then I would like to have some say in it. Apart from anything else it is my story and I ought to be able to tell it. This is the position Eve (Christine Sizemore) was in but her attempts to tell her own story were impeded and discouraged by her therapists who had authored papers and a book about her (see page 208). And if you were Hans wouldn't you like to contribute to the story? (see page 96). The therapists took control of their patients' life stories and in some cases made money out of it. We don't know what the 'talking' chimps like Washoe and Kanzi think about it.

A number of studies are based on the experiences of chimpanzees (see page 52). Such subjects are never given the opportunity to tell their side of the story. Such animals are often wild before being trained to speak. We think they aren't just wild, they are furious.

Activity

Try and write **two** case studies / biographies. For the first one choose a family member and get them to tell you something about themselves, maybe an interesting event or the way they feel about something. Write it down and show it to them to see if they agree with what you have written.

For the second one, write a story of a something you have done. It could be something exciting like your backward pogo stick journey down Everest or something everyday like babysitting for an evening.

For both case study stories look at what was left out and how difficult it is to create a full and accurate record.

KEY ISSUE: CASE STUDIES

Examples of case studies in psychology

Phantom limbs

The neurologist V.S. Ramachrandran uses case studies to explore ideas about how the brain works. In his Reith Lectures for the BBC in 2003, Ramachandran described one patient who has a phantom left arm (which means they feel the presence of the arm even though it had been amputated). He blindfolded the patient and then touched him around his body using a cotton bud and asked him what he felt. Everything was as you'd expect until he touched the left side of the patient's face. Ramachandran reports that *'when I touched his cheek he said oh my god doctor, you're touching my left thumb, my missing phantom thumb and he seemed as surprised as I was. Then I touched him on the upper lip and he said oh my god you're touching my phantom index finger.'*

Only by exploring a person's first-hand unique account do we get this level of insight into the problem. And if you want to know why the patient had those sensations then check out http://www.bbc.co.uk/radio4/reith2003/lectures.shtml.

Genie

Genie was brought up in terrible conditions for the first 13 years of her life, during which she was continually restrained by her father, often strapped to a chair, and never spoken to. When she was discovered she was unable to speak. She seemed to be an ideal case to use to answer a number of scientific questions about the development of language.

Her subsequent care and exploitation by psychologists is a matter of some dispute (Rymer, 1993). For years she lived with the family of one of the psychologists who was studying her and she was well cared for. But when the research money ran out, Genie was abandoned back into abusive environments. Genie's mother successfully sued some of the psychologists involved for *'extreme, unreasonable, and outrageously intensive testing, experimentation, and observation'*. It is argued that concern for psychological research was placed before compassion for the child.

The boy brought up as a girl

The heading for this case study sounds like the subject of a daytime TV show. It is much more than that, however, it is the story of a personal and scientific tragedy.

David Reimer was born in rural USA in 1965 along with his twin brother Brian. When they were eight months they had a minor operation on their penis for medical reasons. The doctor made a mistake and burnt off David's penis. The parents were referred to Dr John Money, who believed that it was possible to bring a child up as a girl even if he had been born a boy. This was his own view, and a rather controversial one, so the case of David Reimer provided him with an opportunity to get evidence to support his theory.

In brief, John Money advised the parents to bring David up as a girl and to keep his true identity from him. The parents accepted Money's advice and David became Brenda. As far as the world knew the change was a success and Money published reports saying that the child was well adjusted in his/her new identity. Nothing could have been further from the truth, however, and although Brenda was strongly encouraged to be feminine she never adjusted to life as girl and at the age of 14, when she/he discovered the truth, decided to live as a male.

Some years later biologist Milton Diamond (1997) made contact with David who was shocked to hear that his story had been presented as a successful example of gender reassignment. He spoke extensively to Diamond and later to journalist Jon Colapinto (2000) who published David's story. He also appeared in television documentaries.

In 2002 Reimer's twin brother Brian took his own life with an overdose of anti-depressants and David's life became more troubled after this. During the next two years he was made redundant and his explosive anger and periods of depression created tensions in his marriage. On 4th May 2004 he took his own life.

Evaluating case studies in Psychology

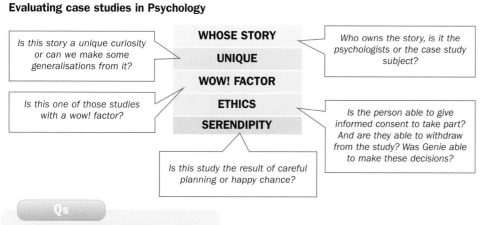

Is this story a unique curiosity or can we make some generalisations from it?

WHOSE STORY

UNIQUE

Who owns the story, is it the psychologists or the case study subject?

WOW! FACTOR

Is this one of those studies with a wow! factor?

ETHICS

SERENDIPITY

Is the person able to give informed consent to take part? And are they able to withdraw from the study? Was Genie able to make these decisions?

Is this study the result of careful planning or happy chance?

Qs

1. Select **one** core study that has used a case study and describe how the data were gathered in this study.

2. Outline **two** strengths and **two** weaknesses of the case study method in the context of your chosen study.

3. Suggest **one** other way a similar research aim could have been investigated without using the case study approach and suggest how this might have affected the results.

4. What are the special ethical issues for psychologists carrying out case studies, and how can they deal with them?

...Links to other studies and issues...

Case studies provide the starting point for a lot of work in psychology. An unusual experience or behaviour is observed and studied and it can give some general insight into human experience and some personal insight into one special life. The study of multiple personality has developed from records of case studies like that of Eve (**Thigpen and Cleckley**). Sigmund **Freud** developed his theories from detailed analysis of a small number of cases studies of which Little Hans is one example. You might well argue that the chimp research of **Savage-Rumbaugh et al**. is also based on case studies as is the work of **Sperry** on split brains.

The are links to other issues in that a lot, but by no means all, of case study evidence is collected as **qualitative** data rather than as **quantitative** data. Much of it has a **longitudinal** element as well as the authors try and give a rich picture of the subject of their study. It is also worth underlining the need to retain a **sceptical** eye on this evidence because our access to the evidence is often fiercely controlled by the authors of the studies.

Griffiths: starters

Addiction

What are addictive behaviours and how do we explain them? Explanations commonly start with biological (or medical) approaches to addiction that concentrate on the abuse of substances such as alcohol or heroin. These explanations only take us so far because it is clear that people develop a range of addictive behaviours that have nothing to do with chemical substances.

Biological explanations of addiction

Biological explanations of addiction focus on *neurotransmitter* substances in the brain, and on genetic differences between people with addictions and people without addictions.

Neurotransmitters

Without going into a full biology lesson, a neurotransmitter is a chemical which moves in the gaps between nerve cells to transmit messages from one nerve cell to another. If you can change the amount of transmitter substance that is available you will have an effect on the transmission of messages in the nervous system. Say, for example, there is a system or nerves that create a feeling of pleasure, and you can increase the available transmitter substance then you might increase the sense pleasure. However, this approach to addiction only takes us so far because it does not take account of the pleasures that are enhanced or restricted by the social situation we are in at the time (Orford, 2001).

Genetics

Studies that analyse the genetic structure of addicted individuals tend to emphasise the role of genetics rather than the environment in addictive behaviours. Some genes have attracted particular attention and have been shown to appear more frequently in people with addictive behaviours than in people without. The problem is that these genes do not occur in all people with the addictive behaviour and they do appear in some people without it. For example, a gene referred to as DRD2 (no, he didn't appear in *Star Wars*) has been found in 42% of people with alcoholism. It has also been found in 45% of people with Tourette's syndrome and 55% of people with autism. It has also been found in 25% of the general population. This means that DRD2 appears more frequently in people with identifiable 'abnormal' behavioural syndromes, but it can not be the sole explanation for the behaviour (Comings, 1998).

Addictive behaviours

One way to think about addiction is to see it in terms of addictive behaviours. This view will include a much wider range of activities than substance addiction. In our everyday speech the term 'addiction' is used as a metaphor for other activities, for example the song *'Addicted to Love'* by Robert Palmer. But can we be addicted to love in the same way as we can be addicted to alcohol? Yes we can, says the psychological approach to addictive behaviours put forward by, for example, Orford (2001) who suggests the following definition,

'Addiction: an attachment to an appetitive activity, so strong that a person finds it difficult to moderate the activity despite the fact that it is causing harm.' (Orford, 2001, page 18)

This approach suggests that people can develop addictive behaviours for a wide range of activities including, drug use, alcohol use, gambling, game playing, eating and sex. Although these behaviours appear to be very different, they all involve a number of similar components. Griffiths (1995) suggests that addictive behaviours have six components, which are described on the right. This psychological approach to addictive behaviours highlights the many similarities in a wide range of damaging behaviour patterns, and indicates that the biological (disease) model of addiction is quite limited.

A further similarity between a number of addictive behaviours can be found in the groups that support people who want to change their behaviour, such as Alcoholics Anonymous, or Gamblers Anonymous, and even Weight Watchers. Orford (1985) suggests that when people change their addictive behaviour it often involves them re-inventing themselves, which means they take on a new identity and change their attitudes and values on a wide range of issues. The organisations that support such change often have an almost 'religious approach' to the problem. They frequently require the person to give personal testimony ('I was a sinner', 'I was a drunk', 'I was a gambler') and accept the authority of the group or a 'higher power'. They usually emphasise that the person should change from being self-centred (egocentric) and pleasure seeking (hedonistic), to being humble and ascetic. All this suggests that the person is undertaking a moral (or spiritual) change rather than a medical change.

Do you feel lucky punk?

Components of addictive behaviours (Griffiths, 1995)

1. Salience: this refers to how important the behaviour becomes to the individual. Addictive behaviours become the most important activity for a person so that even when they are not doing it, they are thinking about it.

2. Euphoria: this is the experience people report when carrying out their addictive behaviour. People with addictive behaviour patterns commonly report a 'rush', or a 'buzz' or a 'high' when they are taking their drugs or when they are gambling, for example.

3. Tolerance: this refers to the increasing amount of activity that is required to achieve the same effect. A drug addict might have to increase the intake of drugs and a gambler might have to increase the stakes.

4. Withdrawal symptoms: these are the unpleasant feelings and physical effects which occur when the addictive behaviour is suddenly discontinued or reduced. This can include 'the shakes', moodiness and irritability. These symptoms are commonly believed to be a response to the removal of a chemical that the person has developed a tolerance to. However, they can also be experienced by gamblers (see Orford, 1985), so the effects might be due to withdrawal from the behaviour as well as the substance.

5. Conflict: people with addictive behaviours develop conflicts with the people around them, often causing great social misery, and also develop conflicts within themselves.

6. Relapse: although people sometimes manage to shake off their addictive behaviour, the chances of relapse are very high. Even when the person has been 'dry' for a considerable time, they can quickly develop the same high levels of addictive behaviour.

What is gambling?

Gambling is commonly defined as the activity of wagering money (or something valuable) on an event where you do not know the outcome. The aim of the wager is to win more money (or valuable things). You usually get the result quite quickly.

There are three key components to gambling

1. The stake: how much is being wagered.

2. The predictability of the event: for some gambling the event is determined mechanically and randomly. The lottery is an example of this and some would argue that so are fruit machines (though gamblers would say this is not so). On the other hand some events have some predictability to the outcome and a little bit of skilled knowledge can be used to enhance your chances of winning the bet. For example if Nottingham Forest were playing Manchester United in a game of football then you could reasonably predict that even if half the United team fell into a hole that suddenly appeared in the middle of the pitch their remaining team mates should still be able to win 6–0. However, this would not prevent many Forest fans betting on their team to win.

Calculating the odds at a race track.

3. The odds: these are agreed between the two people who are gambling prior to the event. They are a ratio of the two possible outcomes and are used to encourage a bet. So, for example, if I am offered odds of 100–1 on Nottingham Forest beating Manchester United then I might well have a flutter because these odds mean that if I bet £1 and by some remarkable turn of events my team wins then I will also win 100 times my stake which will be £100.

It's all in the name

Sometimes things can be dressed up with words to appear to be something they are not. Western military refer to civilian deaths caused by their actions as 'collateral damage'. Somehow that doesn't seem so bad as mass murder. In a similar, though less dramatic, way the gambling industry tries to soften our perception of gambling. For example they refer to the National Lottery as a 'game' and suggest that we 'play the lottery'. But is this really 'playing' and is the lottery a 'game'? Play is often described as an activity where you occupy yourself in amusement, sport, or other recreation. Buying a ticket and scratching out six silver circles (max time 10 seconds) is not much of a game. It's not a game and it's not playing – it's gambling.

Gambling facts and figures

There were 138 casinos operating in Great Britain in 2004–05 and players exchanged £4.16 billion for gaming chips.

The money staked in bingo amounted to £1.78 billion, and £156 million was paid in duty to the Exchequer by the gaming machine industry.

There are approximately 3,600 bookmakers' permits and 8,800 betting office licences presently in force in Great Britain.

The Grand National, traditionally horse racing's biggest event, attracts over 10 million UK viewers and another 600 million worldwide.

6 million people attended racecourses in 2004.

The UK gambling industry employed 96,000 people in 2003–4.

Stakes

The following stakes were placed in 2005 in the UK:

- Betting £47,700 million
- Bingo £1,800 million
- National Lottery £4.900 million

In 2005 Total Duties collected on gambling in the UK were £1,400 million, including:

- Betting £400 million
- Machine Licences £150 million
- Bingo £80 million
- National Lottery £580 million

Sixty-four per cent of English adults say they have taken part in at least one form of gambling in the previous 12 months.

Results from the British Gambling Prevalence Study published in 2000 estimated that 0.6% of adults in the UK are problem gamblers.

These figures do not include all the online gambling that takes place with off-shore companies.

Source: UK government: Department for Culture, Media and Sport www.culture.gov.uk

In gambling space, no one can hear you lose.

One of the features that gambling companies use to encourage you to stake money is to make you more aware of winning than losing. When you lose on a fruit machine (which is most of the time) you don't hear anything. But when you win the machine makes enough noise to wake the dead. The machine clatters – the sound that signifies WINNER and everyone knows it.

Fruit machines are designed to magnify wins and minimise the sense of losing.

...Link to the core study...

Traditional views of addiction saw it as a medical condition but is this so? **Griffiths** is exploring the idea that we develop addictive behaviours for a whole range of activities of which addiction to chemical substances is just one example. The strength of the addiction therefore lies not in the substance but in the habits that develop around it. In truth we can become addicted to almost anything, eating, drinking, gambling, sex, exercise, internet gaming, and may more. One of the many difficulties in exploring these behaviours is to distinguish between people who are enthusiastic about something and so do it a lot, and those who are addicted. It's a fine line and not everyone agrees where that line should be drawn.

Griffiths: the core study

Mark D. Griffiths (1994) The role of cognitive bias and skill in fruit machine gambling. *British Journal of Psychology*, 85, pages 351-369.

GRIFFITHS: GAMBLING

Abstract

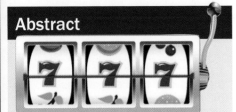

Gambling may best be explained by irrational cognitive processes – heuristics which produce cognitive biases. The hypotheses investigated were whether regular fruit machine gamblers (RGs):

1 were no different from non-regular gamblers (NRGs) in terms of measures of skill,

2 would produce more irrational rationalisations,

3 would be subjectively more skill-oriented than NRGs.

4 Additionally it was suggested that participants in the thinking aloud condition would take longer.

Method

Sixty participants (30 RGs and 30 NRGs) were recruited through advertisements and, for some of the RGs, by personal contact. There was a gender imbalance in the RG group.

Participants played a fruit machine in a local arcade starting with a £3 stake (=30 free plays). They were asked to try to stay on for 60 gambles, after that (when they would have won back their original stake plus £3) they could take the money or continue playing.

Half the participants in both conditions were asked to verbalise all their thoughts while playing the machine (thinking aloud method) to gain insight into their cognitive processes.

Results and discussion

All four hypotheses were supported, suggesting that cognitive distortions may underlie gambling behaviour and further suggesting that pathological gambling might be treated using a cognitive approach such as audio playback therapy.

Introduction

A number of psychologists have been interested in the cognitive psychology of gambling, in other words what is going on in the minds of gamblers. Two approaches have been used: 'normative decision theory' and 'heuristics and biases'.

Normative decision theory

Normative decision theory is concerned with rational decision making. The theory claims it can predict the decisions a gambler will make. However research has not found support as it appears that choices are often irrational. In fact the theory would not predict that people would gamble in the first place because the odds are against them!

Heuristics and biases

Wagenaar (1988) proposed that heuristics are the best way to understand cognitive processes in relation to gambling. The problem for gamblers is that the heuristics they choose produce distortions because they are selected on the wrong occasions. Wagenaar identified 16 such distortions, the six most important ones being:

> A **heuristic** is a strategy used to work something out or solve a problem – it may be a set of rules (such as a recipe for a cake), an educated guess or just common sense. You may have some general heuristics for solving problems, such as 'if it doesn't work try reading the instructions'. Heuristics don't guarantee a solution (whereas algorithms do) and they may lead to **cognitive biases** which skew the way a person perceives the world.

1 **Illusion of control** i.e. behaviours which give you the illusion you are in control, such as choosing your own lottery ticket or having a favourite fruit machine. Such control makes the player think there is skill involved.

2 **Flexible attributions** – gamblers' self-esteem is bolstered by attributing success to their own skill and failure to some external influence. Similarly they put a spin on events so that a loss becomes described as a 'near win' or something that could have been predicted in advance (called hindsight bias).

3 **Representativeness** – a belief that random events have a pattern, e.g. if you toss a coin nine times and keep getting heads it must be increasingly likely that tails will come up next time. Observed events do not represent true odds exactly (try the activity below).

4 **Availability bias** – people's judgements reflect the frequency of relevant instances. For example you hear about lots of people who have won the pools (increased 'availability' of information), which makes you think it is more common than it is.

5 **Illusory correlations** – people (mistakenly) believe that some events are correlated with success, for example rolling dice softly to get low numbers.

6 **Fixation on absolute frequency** – measuring success in terms of absolute rather than relative frequency. Gamblers may win a lot but relative to the number of times they gamble their successes are small.

All of these heuristics lead to biases in cognitive processing, that is distortions in a person's thinking.

The cognitive psychology of fruit machine players

In previous research Griffiths (1990 a, b, c) found that regular fruit machine gamblers used a variety of heuristics during gambling, especially to explain big losses or for bad gambling. Gamblers believed their actions to be, at least in part, skilful and also gained a sense of control through the familiarity with a particular machine.

Qs

1 In what way is this study an experiment? What are the **two** conditions of the IV?

2 Identify (a) a one-tailed hypothesis and (b) a null hypothesis from this study.

3 Identify **three** key aspects of the 'thinking aloud method'.

4 Why do you think participants might have behaved differently if the study had been conducted in a laboratory rather than a natural setting.

Activity

You can investigate the representative heuristic by placing 50 pieces of red paper and 50 pieces of blue paper in a hat. Draw out 10 slips of paper – did you get 5 of each colour?

You can also try asking people to 'mimic' the rolling of a dice. They should write down (or say) 100 digits between 1 and 6. Were there any repeated digits? People avoid this because it doesn't 'feel' random. Try rolling a dice 100 times and see what happens.

Aim and hypotheses

The aim of this study was to compare the behaviour of regular and non-regular fruit machine gamblers – RGs and NRGs. The hypotheses were

1 There would be no differences between RGs and NRGs on objective measures of skill (i.e. on the seven behavioural dependent variables that were monitored – see table on right).

2 RGs would produce more irrational verbalisations than NRGs (assessed using the 'thinking aloud method').

3 RGs would be more skill oriented (i.e. focused on skills involved in gambling) than NRGs on subjective measures of skill (assessed by self-reports in post-experimental semi-structured interviews).

For the purposes of this experiment,

- Fruit machine skill was defined as *'the ability of the individual to affect the outcome of gambling positively (e.g. more gambles with initial money staked and/or more winnings with initial money staked)'.*

- Irrational verbalisations were those which were *'contrary to reason (e.g. personification of the machine or use of heuristics)'.*

Biographical notes

Professor **Mark Griffiths** is Europe's only Professor of Gambling Studies (Nottingham Trent University). He is Director of the International Gaming Research Unit and has won numerous awards for his research (e.g. *John Rosecrance Research Prize, CELEJ Prize, Joseph Lister Prize*, etc.). He has published a vast array of articles in refereed journals, books, book chapters and also does some freelance journalism and has appeared on over 1500 radio/television programmes!

Jamie Davies interviewed Mark, asking him about his own gambling *'Yes I do [gamble], roulette is the game that I play – but when I'm playing roulette I'm actually buying entertainment rather than trying to win money. When I am playing on slot machines though I call it "research!"'* (see www.psychblog.co.uk/interview-the-gambling-man-prof-mark-griffiths-119.html).

Behavioural dependent variables used to assess skill of RGs and NRGs.

Dependent variable	Operational definition
Total plays	Total number of plays during play session
Total time	Total time in minutes of play during one play session
Play rate	Total number of plays per minute during a play session
End stake	Total winnings in number of 10p pieces after a play session was over
Wins	Total number of wins during a play session
Win rate (time)	Total number of minutes between each win during a play session
Win rate (plays)	Total number of plays between each win during a play session

Method

Participants

Sixty participants took part (mean age 23.4 years), half were RGs (29 males and 1 female) and half were NRGs (15 males and 15 females). RGs gambled at least once a week, NRGs gambled once a month or less (but had used fruit machines at least once in their lives).

The participants were recruited through poster advertisements around local university and college campuses. A number of the RGs were recruited via a gambler known to the author.

The gender imbalance was unfortunate but fruit machine gambling is dominated by males.

Design

Each participant was given £3 to gamble on a fruit machine (equal to 30 free plays) in a local arcade. The game selected was FRUITSKILL though some players moved on to other games. They were asked to try to stay on their machine for at least 60 gambles (i.e. break even and win back £3). At that point they were allowed to either keep the £3 or carrying on gambling.

When designing the study there were two considerations which relate to the ecological validity of the study:

- *The setting*: the experiment took place outside the laboratory because some researchers have questioned whether participants in a lab study of fruit machine gambling behave as they would in other more natural settings.

- *Money*: using someone else's money may reduce the excitement and risk taking involved in gambling. However, allowing participants to keep their winnings may compensate for this.

Thinking aloud

Half the participants in each group were randomly assigned to the thinking aloud condition. The thinking aloud method was chosen because it is considered probably to be the best method for evaluating cognitive processes (i.e. what a person is thinking). Not all participants were required to do this in case it had some effect on their behaviour. Previous research has found no effect except a slight slowing down of performance.

Thus an additional hypothesis to be tested was that *'thinking aloud participants would take longer to complete the task than non-thinking aloud participants'.*

The following instructions were given to the 'thinking aloud' participants:

'The thinking aloud method consists of verbalising every thought that passes through your mind while you are playing. It is important to remember the following points:

(1) Say everything that goes through your mind. Do not censor any of your thoughts even if they seem irrelevant to you;

(2) Keep talking as continuously as possible, even if your ideas are not clearly structured;

(3) Speak in complete sentences;

(4) Do not hesitate to use fragmented sentences if necessary. Do not worry about speaking in complete sentences;

(5) Do not try to justify your thoughts.'

The verbalisations were tape recorded using a lapel microphone and later transcribed.

Results

Analysis of behavioural data

A number of differences between the RGs and NRGs were noted but only two significant differences were found:

- RGs had a significantly higher playing rate (8 gambles per minute as compared to 6 per minute for NRGs).
- RGs who thought aloud had a significantly lower win rate in number of gambles (i.e. the number of gambles between each win was significantly lower than for NRGs).

Analysis of verbalisations

The verbalisations were analysed by performing a content analysis (see page 7) on the transcriptions. In order to do this the author first of all produced a coding system by looking through the transcriptions and identifying 30 *utterance categorisations*. Some examples of the coding system can be seen on the right. The author then categorised the statements made by each participant using this coding system. The number of utterances in each category for each participant was adjusted as a percentage of the total for that participant. Finally totals were calculated for RGs versus NRGs.

Attempts were made to establish the reliability of the categorisations made by the author. This was done using two other raters. Inter-rater reliability (see page 6) was low because one rater knew very little about fruit machine gambling and therefore couldn't understand the terminology; the second rater had not been present during the recording of the utterances and therefore had no context and could not make as much sense of the utterances as the author.

The table at the top of the page includes some of the significant findings:

- RGs made significantly more percentage verbalisations in categories 1 and 21.
- NRGs made significantly more percentage verbalisations in categories 14, 15 and 31.
- RGs also referred to their mind going blank and feeling frustrated, topics rarely mentioned by NRGs.
- RGs produced significantly more irrational verbalisations (14%) than did NRGs (2.5%).
- Overall both groups used more rational than irrational verbalisations.

RGs used a variety of heuristics, for example gamblers used hindsight bias to explain their loses: *'I had a feeling it wasn't going to pay very much after it*

Utterance categorisations used in the content analysis with mean scores for NRGs and RGs, and significance values.

		NRGs	RGs	Sig*
Irrational verbalisations				
1	Personification of the fruit machine, e.g. *The machine likes me.*	1.14	7.54	0.0004
2	Explaining away loses, e.g. *I lost because I wasn't concentrating.*	0.41	3.12	0.026
4	Swearing at the machine, e.g. *You bastard.*	0.08	0.60	0.042
Rational verbalisations				
7	Reference to winning, e.g. *I won forty pence I think.*	6.77	9.79	0.042
14	Questions relating to confusion / non-understanding, e.g. *What's going on here?*	13.24	1.56	0.000
15	Statements relating to confusion / non-understanding, e.g. *I don't understand this.*	4.81	1.72	0.008
16	Reference to skill, e.g. *I only won because I was so quick.*	1.47	5.34	0.024
17	Humour, e.g. *Two melons – I like it when I get my hands on two melons.*	0.89	0.41	0.40
21	Reference to the 'number system', e.g. *I got a '2' there.*	1.45	9.49	0.003
25	Hoping/needing a certain feature to appear in the win line, e.g. *I need an orange to win.*	0.77	3.28	0.014
28	Reference to luck, e.g. *My luck's in today.*	0.69	0.52	0.76
31	Miscellaneous utterances, e.g. *I think I'll get a bag of chips after playing this.*	25.53	11.73	0.000

*Sig = significance, the lower the number the more significant (or 'real') the difference. The acceptable level for significance was the 1% level or 0.01.

www.CartoonStock.com

Activity

Try the thinking aloud method (on previous page) yourself. You can do it while engaged in any activity, such as noughts and crosses or you too can play a fruit machine – there are a number of free online sites such as http://web.cyberslotz.co.uk/GameZone/gameZone.htm

You might tape record yourself or a partner and try to analyse your thoughts using the coding system produced by Griffiths. The full system can be found on our website at www.a-levelpsychology.co.uk/ocr

had just given me a "feature"' and there were many flexible attributions, such as '...two nudges, gotta be ...oh, you son of a bitch, you (the machine) changed them'. Some gamblers had completely erroneous perceptions: 'I'm only going to put one quid in to start with because psychologically I think it's very important ...it bluffs the machine'. Note that many of the comments above contain personification, for example stating that the machine 'is in a bad mood' or 'doesn't like me'.

Analysis of skill variables

The post-experimental semi-structured interviews yielded answers to the following questions:

- *Is there any skill involved in playing the fruit machine?* Most NRGs said 'mostly chance' whereas most RGs said 'equal chance and skill'.
- *How skilful do you think you are compared to the average person?* NRGs viewed themselves as below average whereas RGs said 'above average' or 'totally skilled'.
- *What skill (if any) is involved in playing fruit machines?* RGs rated knowledge of 'feature skills', knowledge of when the machine will pay out and knowledge of not playing when it has just paid out.

There were also some indirect skill factors. For example RGs objected to gambling on a particular machine because they weren't familiar with it.

It is interesting to note that of the 14 RGs who broke even after 60 gambles, 10 (i.e. 71%) carried on gambling until they had lost everything, whereas only 2 out of 7 (29%) NRGs did – a highly significant difference.

Discussion

The behavioural data show that, on the whole, there were no differences between RGs and NRGs (supporting hypothesis 1). It was found that RGs gambled more times than NRGs using the same amount of money which might imply RGs have greater skill. However, it may be that the skill of RGs is little more than being able to 'gamble up' small wins into larger ones using 'nudge' and 'hold' buttons.

It is possible that gamblers spend time on fruit machines not to win but because it is intrinsically rewarding in itself and choose machines to maximise their playing time.

The analysis of verbalisations shows that RGs did make more irrational verbalisations than NRGs (supporting hypothesis 2) but made far less than the 80% previously reported by Ladouceur et al. (1988). The rate of irrational verbalisations supports the general notion of cognitive bias in RGs.

It was not surprising that NRGs produced more statements of confusion/non-understanding than RGs as many aspects of the game were new to them. Such differences were important as 'manipulation checks' and show that the assessment procedures did distinguish between NRGs and RGs.

Another key difference was that NRGs rarely reported 'my mind has gone blank' whereas a number of RGs stopped speaking for up to 30 seconds. This was probably because they were on 'automatic pilot', a characteristic of experienced players in any game (e.g. chess) where thought processes are not controlled by conscious cognitive processes. It also could be that RGs go into 'escape mode' because they play to escape real-life problems (e.g. broken home).

The 'thinking aloud method' produced descriptions of behaviour rather than explanations. In order to explain behaviour (i.e. predict when a particular heuristic will be used) rigged fruit machines might be used where sequences of wins and losses are manipulated to reveal the heuristics in the thoughts reported.

Skill orientation differed between RGs and NRGs (supporting hypothesis 3). RGs were more skill oriented in their self-comparison ratings and in questions related to skill factors. Fisher (1993) identified three major skills:

1   *Choosing which machine* to play, including knowing how much has been put in to a machine and how much it has paid out. These skills were listed in this study.

2   *Knowing the reels*, i.e. knowing the order of the symbols (unique to each machine) which enables the 'nudge' feature to be used effectively. Knowledge of reels and of nudges were reported as separate skills in this study.

3   *Gambling*, i.e. using the gamble button. Players believe this increases winnings but machine manufacturers report it is entirely random, therefore it is a 'pseudo-skill'.

Other genuine skills were reported in this study including light oscillation (pressing a button when particular symbols are lit up) and knowing the number system.

The real difference between RGs and NRGs is probably cognitive; RGs think more skill is involved than there actually is. There are also cognitive differences in the way RGs react towards the machine itself, such as personification – though this may be a general tendency to personify something which one is in regular contact with.

The results of this study may be used to rehabilitate gamblers. If cognitive biases stimulate gambling then cognitive therapies may be appropriate. 'Audio playback therapy' might involve taping a player's thoughts (as captured by 'thinking aloud') and playing this back to highlight the irrational verbalisations. This was tried with four of the RGs in this study who said they were surprised by what they said and thought.

Evaluating the study by Griffiths

> There are no simple answers. Evaluating a study requires you to think. We have provided some pointers here, linked to the KEY ISSUES covered through this book – see page XIV for a table of these key issues.

The research method
The study is described as an experiment but also used self-report and content analysis. *What are the strengths and limitations of these research methods in the context of this study?*

The sample
There were various significant characteristics of the sample: some were volunteers, they were recruited from college campuses and almost all of the RGs were male. *In what way do such characteristics affect the representativeness of this sample? How does this affect the conclusions drawn from the study?*

Quantitative or qualitative?
Both quantitative and qualitative data were collected in this study. *Select one kind of behaviour and give an example of how it was measured quantitatively and qualitatively. What are the strengths and limitations of each kind of data in the context of this study?*

Ethical issues
Gambling is not generally approved of and it has the potential to become addictive. *What ethical issues should have concerned the researchers in this study, and how might they have dealt with these issues?*

Reliability
Content analysis was done using a coding system developed and applied by Griffiths. There was low agreement with other raters. *How does this affect the conclusions drawn from this study?*

Ecological validity
Griffiths considered issues relating to ecological validity – the setting where gambling took place and the fact that participants were not using their own money. *To what extent can we generalise the findings from this study to real life?*

Applications/usefulness
How valuable was this study? What influence do you think it has had on the treatment of abnormality?

What next?
Describe **one** change to this study, and say how you think this might affect the outcome.

Debate

How would you explain gambling behaviour?

Divide your class into groups and let each group present an explanation of gambling to consider which one is best.

...Links to other studies and issues...

Addiction is often portrayed as a medical condition. If this is the case and the behaviour is due to brain chemicals or brain structures then this study would fit into the chapter on **biological psychology**. Or it may be due to faulty thinking by the gambler and in which case it could be in the **cognitive psychology** chapter. You could also make a case for this study being in the **social psychology** chapters as well (because social psychology embraces explanations of behaviour in the real world). The study also tells us something about the rewards of gambling and we can explain the development of these using a **behaviourist approach** (**developmental psychology**). The study of addictive behaviours in this book, however, is put in the context of individual differences.

I feel lucky

Gambling is a growing industry in this country and people are being given more opportunities to make bets all the time. Will gambling become the new crack?

Things that increase addictive behaviours

Availability

There are a number of environmental factors that affect the incidence of addictive behaviours in a society. One factor that affects the level of alcoholism is the availability of alcohol and the average consumption of alcohol by the general population. Comparison studies have found near perfect correlations between the number of deaths through liver cirrhosis (generally attributed to alcohol abuse) and the average consumption of alcohol in different countries (Orford, 1985). The availability factor also affects the consumption of cigarettes as shown in the study below.

If we examine the pattern of cigarette consumption compared with the retail price of cigarettes in this country we can observe a remarkable relationship. The chart below shows how the curve for consumption is the mirror image of the curve for retail price (Townsend et al., 1994). Since 1970 any increase in price has brought about a decrease in smoking. At the time of the study there was a slight decrease in the price of cigarettes (figures adjusted to take account of inflation) and a corresponding rise in smoking. This rise in smoking was particularly noticeable in young people, and according to Townsend et al. regular smoking by 15 year old boys increased from 20% to 25% and by 16–19-year-old girls from 28% to 32%. This connection between price and consumption suggests an obvious policy for governments who want to reduce smoking.

Social cues: tobacco advertising

In their response to the Health of the Nation strategy (published by DoH, 1992), the British Psychological Society (1993) called for a ban on the advertising of all tobacco products. This call was backed up by the government's own research (DoH, 1993) which suggested a relationship between advertising and sales. Also, in four countries that have banned tobacco advertising (New Zealand, Canada, Finland and Norway) there has been a significant drop in consumption.

Tobacco advertising has now been banned in the UK and in Europe and smoking has been banned in all public buildings in the UK. This is still quite a recent event so the effect on levels of smoking is not yet known. One clear effect though is that more smokers are experiencing hypothermia after huddling in alleys outside bars and restaurants as they try and find somewhere to have a smoke.

Gambling

If social cues and availability are two key features that encourage addictive behaviours then it is likely that the UK will see an explosion in problem gambling in the next few years. Gambling companies are very visible with their sponsorship of sporting events and on prime time televisions (Lotto). People are also shown positive images of gambling through sports shows and game shows. On top of this the internet offers more and easier opportunities to burn your money.

Just-world effect

The just-world effect (Lerner, 1980), refers to the tendency of some people to believe the world is 'just' and so therefore people 'get what they deserve'. They believe that good things do (or should) happen to good people and bad things should happen to bad people. The National Lottery in the UK is a good example of this in that who gets to win is a complete lottery (the clue is in the name) but the press seem to think that the prizes should go to the 'deserving poor'. There are a lot of negative comments when someone with a criminal record wins the big prize. For example, Michael Carroll from Norfolk has been relentlessly vilified in the press since his big win in 2002.

Psychological studies have found that people who believe in a just world are more likely to believe that rape victims contributed to the assault by their behaviour, that sick people caused their illness and the poor deserve to have no money. The big problem with this type of thinking is the world is not just and the bad guys sometimes win and sometimes bad things happen to good people.

Rather surprisingly it has been shown that belief in a just world has some benefits for the believers. They are likely to have less depression, less stress and greater life satisfaction (Bègue, 2005). I guess it just goes to show that self-delusion is good for you.

Michael Carroll, self-styled 'King of the Chavs', still standing despite being vilified by the press.

The relationship between the price of cigarettes and consumption 1971–1990.

Chart: Consumption (£ billion) and Price index plotted against Year from 1972 to 92. Legend: Consumption, Prices.

The gambler's fallacy

'I'm going to win today. I can feel it in my bones.' Gamblers (and casual punters) often develop irrational beliefs about their ability to control or predict events.

Among the many irrational beliefs is the idea that a random event can be affected or predicted by other random events. This is known as the *gambler's fallacy*. So when watching a roulette wheel, if the little ball hasn't fallen in the number 18 hole for a long while you might believe that 'law of averages' will mean that it must turn up soon. The trouble is that there is no such thing as the 'law of averages' and the chances of the ball dropping into number 18 on the next turn of the wheel are exactly the same as they were on the last one and the one before that.

This faulty thinking can take a number of forms as gamblers might risk their money in the belief that they are having a 'run of luck' or that their 'run of bad luck' will end soon.

An interesting version of this can be seen in people's choices of numbers for the National Lottery. A sequence of related numbers is just as likely to turn up as a series of not related numbers. So the chances of winning on 1, 2, 3, 4, 5, 6 are the same as 8, 12, 17, 34, 36, 42, but who would pick the first sequence? It just seems impossible that such a combination could win.

Multiple choice questions

1 Normative decision theory suggests that gambling is:
   a Rational.
   b Irrational.
   c Both rational and irrational.
   d Neither rational or irrational.

2 Wagenaar suggested that certain heuristics may explain gambling. Which of the following was NOT one of them?
   a Illusion of control.
   b Temperamental bias.
   c Availability bias.
   d Representativeness.

3 Griffiths predicted that regular gamblers would be:
   a Better than NRGs on objective measures of skill.
   b The same as NRGs on objective measure of skill.
   c Less skilful than NRGs on objective measures of skill.
   d This was not one of his predictions.

4 In the study there were:
   a More males.   b More females.
   c Equal numbers. d They were all males.

5 The method used to assess what participants were thinking was called:
   a Thinking aloud.
   b Private thinking.
   c Audio thinking.
   d Thinking bias.

6 RGs were found to be:
   a More irrational than NRGs.
   b Less irrational than NRGs.
   c There was no significant difference between the two groups in terms of irrationality.
   d They were mad, bad and dangerous to know.

7 How many hypotheses were supported by the results?
   a 1   b 2
   c 3   d 4

8 When asked to speak their thoughts, some of the RGs stopped speaking for short spells. The explanation given was:
   a They were losing money.
   b They were on automatic pilot.
   b They went into escape mode.
   d Both b and c.

9 In the discussion Griffiths suggests that fruit machine gamblers play because:
   a They want to win money.
   b They are stupid.
   c The game is intrinsically rewarding.
   d All of the above.

10 A possible therapy that could be developed is called:
   a Thinking aloud therapy.
   b Audio thinking therapy.
   c Audio playback therapy.
   d Auditory therapy.

Answers are on page 225.

Exam-style questions

See page XII–XIII for notes on the exam paper and styles of question.

Section A questions

1   In the study on gambling by Griffiths there are four hypotheses.
    (a) State **one** of these hypotheses.   [2]
    (b) Explain how evidence was collected to support this hypothesis.   [2]

2   Griffiths refers to heuristics in his study on gambling.
    (a) Explain what a heuristic is.   [2]
    (b) Describe **one** of the heuristics that might explain gambling behaviour. [2]

3   In Griffiths' study of gambling describe **one** similarity and **one** difference that were found between regular and non-regular gamblers. [4]

4   Griffiths used a method called 'thinking aloud' to gain insight into gamblers' behaviour.
    (a) Briefly outline what this method involved.   [2]
    (b) Give **one** weakness of using this method to assess gambling.   [2]

5   From the study by Griffiths,
    (a) Give **one** example of a rational verbalisation.   [2]
    (b) Give **one** example of an irrational verbalisation.   [2]

6   In the study by Griffiths on gambling,
    (a) Identify **two** dependent variables used to objectively measure skill. [2]
    (b) For one of these variables state the associated finding.   [2]

Section B question

(a) What was the aim of the Griffiths study?   [2]

(b) Describe the sample used in the Griffiths study and give **one** limitation of it. [6]

(c) Describe how data were gathered in the Griffiths study.   [6]

(d) Give **one** advantage and **one** disadvantage of experimental studies. [6]

(e) Suggest **two** changes to the Griffiths study and outline any methodological implications these changes may have. [8]

(f) Outline the results of the Griffiths study.   [8]

Section C question

(a) Outline **one** assumption of the individual differences approach in psychology. [2]

(b) Describe how the individual differences approach could explain gambling. [4]

(c) Describe **one** similarity and **one** difference between the Griffiths study and any other individual differences study. [6]

(d) Discuss the strengths and limitations of the individual differences approach using examples from the Griffiths study. [12]

Key issue: psychometrics

The term psychometric means 'measuring the mind', though many psychometricians would be very uncomfortable with a term such as 'mind'. A psychological test is a task or set of tasks that can be given in a standard format to an individual or group of people, and which produces a score that can be represented as a number (or a category). It can involve almost any activity though most commonly it involves filling in a questionnaire.

Tests are used to measure a range of qualities including:

- cognitive functions (e.g. IQ tests);
- personality (e.g. Five Factor Personality Inventory, Costa and MaCrae);
- mood (e.g. The Beck Depression Inventory);
- attitudes (e.g. political opinion polls);
- aptitude for various jobs (e.g. The Comprehensive Ability Battery);
- illness behaviour (e.g. the McGill Pain Inventory).

Psychometric methods produce quantitative data which are straightforward to analyse but not always as easy to interpret. The issue with such numerical data is that they may not to capture the richness of experience and ability because some things have to be seen, touched and tasted (see the key issue on **quantitative and qualitative data**.

Psychometric tests are instruments which have been developed for measuring mental characteristics.

The **reliability** of a psychological measuring device (such as a test or a scale) is the extent to which it gives consistent measurements. The greater the consistency of measurement, the greater the tool's reliability.

Validity is the question of whether a psychometric test or psychological measure is really measuring what it is supposed to.

Psychometric tests

Psychometric tests are extensively used in everyday life and you are likely to come into contact with them on a fairly regular basis. They are big business in psychology and the best way to get either famous or rich in the subject is to devise your own psychometric test. Despite being so popular the tests remain very controversial.

Psychometric testing produces some of the greatest differences of opinion and some of the strongest arguments to be found in psychology. The arguments often get confused because of the mixture of scientific and political issues that come into play. There are arguments about,

(a) *Practical issues*: do the tests give accurate and consistent results? Do the complex statistical procedures illuminate or disguise what is going on? Just because you can give someone a score on an IQ test or an extraversion test it doesn't mean that this is an accurate description of them or their behaviour.

(b) *Theoretical issues*: do the tests measure underlying psychological qualities? For example, is there such a quality as 'intelligence' and is it measured by an IQ test? In the end an IQ test tells us how well a person can do at IQ tests. There is clearly more to our intellectual abilities than the features that can be measured on a pencil and paper test.

(c) *Political issues*: can the tests be used to look at differences between groups of people, for example different social classes, or different ethnic groups, or the differences between men and women? What are the social and political consequences of using tests to categorise people?

Sometimes you don't need to give someone an IQ test to find out how intelligent they are.

Qs

1 Choose **one** appropriate core study and describe the way in which the psychometric test was used to collect data in this study.

2 Outline **two** strengths of using these tests in your chosen study and give **two** limitations of using these tests in your chosen study.

3 Suggest **one** way in which data could have been gathered for your chosen study without the use of these tests and say how you think this might affect the results.

4 Why are psychometric tests used so much and why are they so popular?

5 What psychological variables do you think can NOT be measured by a psychometric test?

Performance and ability

One of the key issues to consider is the distinction between performance and ability. Performance is what you actually do, and ability is what you are capable of. It is a common experience of students that their teachers say 'you have the ability, but you are not doing the work'. The teachers mean that the reason you got a Grade E in your homework was due to poor performance and not poor ability (and obviously not the teacher's fault either). Any test we give to someone can only measure their performance on that test, and not their ability. So when we are measuring intelligence, we are, in fact, measuring *performance* on the particular test and not the underlying *intellectual ability*. And when we measure personality we are only measuring a person's responses to those questions in that room at that particular time.

Some of the many factors that affect performance include;

(a) Language of the test: words mean different things to different people.

(b) Test situation: some people work well in quiet environments with few distractions, whereas others can only concentrate if the television is on in the background.

(c) Expectations: if you expect that you will not be able to answer the questions you will be more likely to give up easily.

(d) Motivation: if you are competitive and want to win everything then you will try harder to do well (if its an IQ test, for example).

The Barnum Effect

Are psychometric tests able to give us some unique insights into personality or are they just an example of the Barnum Effect?

We love to hear information about ourselves. It is maybe our top topic of conversation and we pay good money for people to tell us things about ourselves. Unfortunately we are not good at distinguishing sense from nonsense in this information. The *Barnum Effect* (named after P. T. Barnum, the famous North American hoaxer and showman) refers to a powerful tendency to believe information given to us about our personal qualities. This is used to good effect by fortune tellers, astrologers, handwriting 'experts' and various other contemporary shamans. If the 'expert' can say what people are prepared to accept, and can phrase it in such a way that it implies some intimate insight, then there is a good, if dishonourable, living to be made.

Our gullibility to personality statements was tested by Forer (1949). This is an excellent example of scientific enquiry and it also gives us some insight into the appeal of the pseudosciences. Some of Forer's students filled in a personality questionnaire and agreed to give their opinion of the results when they received their personal profile. When each student received their profile they believed it was a unique description of their personality. Most of the students endorsed most of the statements as being true about them. All in all they were very impressed with the description about them.

In fact the students all received the same 13 statements shown on the right. When you look at them, try to imagine that you are being told this about you in a sincere voice by someone who claims to have knowledge of these matters. Better still, try saying these statements to someone else after reading their tea leaves.

Barnum statements

1 *You have a great need for other people to like and admire you.*

2 *You have a tendency to be critical of yourself.*

3 *You have a great deal of unused capacity which you have not turned to your advantage.*

4 *While you have some personality weaknesses, you are generally able to compensate for them.*

5 *Your sexual adjustment has presented problems for you.*

6 *Disciplined and self-controlled outside, you tend to be worrisome and insecure inside.*

7 *At times you have serious doubts as to whether you have made the right decision or done the right thing.*

8 *You prefer a certain amount of change and variety and become dissatisfied when hemmed in by restrictions and limitations.*

9 *You pride yourself as an independent thinker and do not accept others' statements without satisfactory proof.*

10 *You have found it unwise to be too frank in revealing yourself to others.*

11 *At times you are extroverted, affable, sociable, while at other times you are introverted, wary, reserved.*

12 *Some of your aspirations tend to be pretty unrealistic.*

13 *Security is one of your major goals in life.*

Issues with psychometric tests

- **Acquiescence**: people have a tendency to agree with items on a test.
- **Social desirability**: people have a tendency to respond in a way that makes them look good.
- **Middle categories**: many questionnaires ask people to respond on a five-point scale, and there is a tendency for people to use the middle value (Kline, 1993).
- **Coaching**: people can be coached to do well and so mask their true score.
- **Cultural differences**: most tests are designed in one culture and tested on people from that culture to establish standards. These tests, and standards, are then used in different cultural settings assuming that the same standards apply (an example of ethnocentricism).

Measuring people

To measure something you have to compare it against something else. If we are measuring a table, it is easy because we can use a ruler, but if we are measuring people what can we use?

1 **Direct measurement** e.g. using a physical measure such as grip strength or reaction time. We can measure how fast people respond to something or where their eyes fixate on a scene they are looking at. These are relatively rare measures however.

2 **Criterion-referenced measurement** e.g. comparing the performance of an individual against an ideal performance.

3 **Norm-referenced measurement** e.g. comparing the performance of an individual against performance of other people, most commonly the peer group. This is far and away the most common way of using psychological (and educational) measurement.

...Links to other studies and issues...

Psychometric tests are a major feature of modern psychology and they appear in a number of the core studies. For example the case study of Eve (**Thigpen and Cleckley**) tried to show the difference between the two personalities by administering some tests to each one of them in turn. The patients in the split-brain studies (**Sperry**) were given cognitive tests to estimate changes in their thoughts and behaviour. The prison study by **Reicher and Haslam** also uses a range of psychometric measures to track changes in the participants over the course of the study.

A number of the issues around psychometric testing are also dealt with elsewhere. Most important in the development of tests are the issues of **reliability** and **validity** and many of the techniques for measuring these qualities have been designed specifically for psychometric testing. The issue of **promoting human welfare** is also connected because psychometric testing has sometimes been used to promote divisions in society (see the text on eugenics, page 223).

Activity

Design a psychometric test to measure either (a) stupidity (not necessarily the opposite of intelligence) or (b) charmingness.

- Identify five items for your test.
- How will you check its reliability?
- How will you assess its validity?

(Read more about reliability and validity on pages 6, 12, 18 and 130–131).

The individual differences approach

The individual differences approach commonly looks to measure and rank people and categorise us by the small differences that distinguish one person from another. In some ways the remarkable thing about people is how much they share. People are able to communicate, they seek out other people and they have warm attachments to other people that endure over time. There are remarkable similarities in the ways that people make sense of the world but at this point in our history we seem most concerned by what distinguishes one person from another rather than what unites us. Hence the rise in importance of individual differences in psychology.

The most influential development in individual differences has been psychometric tests (see previous spread) which aim to provide simple and reliable ways to measure attitudes, cognitions, abilities and aptitudes of people.

The history of individual differences

Francis Galton (1822–1911)

The study of individual differences can be traced back to the work of **Francis Galton**. He invented and defined the field. In 1884 Galton created a mental testing laboratory – the anthropometric lab for testing data about people, such as visual acuity, strength of grip, colour vision, hearing acuity, hand preference, etc. He hoped to use these measures to estimate people's hereditary intelligence.

Before Galton, psychology had been looking for general principles of experience. By contrast, Galton's anthropometric laboratory looked for individual differences and operated within his cousin Darwin's ideas of individual variability and selection. Although we would not recognise Galton's tests as measures of mental abilities today they do mark the beginning of mental testing.

Galton is also credited with developing a staggering range of techniques and concepts that define the field even today (see Fancher, 1996).

- *Self-report questionnaires*: in 1873 Galton wrote to all the Fellows of the Royal Society (eminent scientists) with a lengthy questionnaire to discover the common features of people who are successful in science.
- *Nature and nurture*: he invented this term to describe the difference between environmental and inherited influences.
- *Twin studies*: he devised the first of these, as well as carrying out the first comparisons of natural and adopted children to their parents.
- *Scatterplots*: Galton wanted to find ways to present his data on family resemblances and he devised the scatterplot (scattergraph).
- *Statistics*: Galton developed regression lines and the correlation coefficient.

The above is a phenomenal list but it is only a selection of his output and you can add word association to it. Galton devised a word association technique; his paper on this was read by Freud and contributed to the development of one of the major techniques of psychoanalysis. And if you're still not impressed then he also invented the weather map, and hence weather forecasting.

Hope for us all: Charles Darwin (1809–1882) did not do very well at school, and in his autobiography he said of his education that 'Nothing could have been worse for the development of my mind ...' *(Darwin, 1969, page 27).*

Evolution

If you had to pick one scientific idea that had the greatest effect on modern thought then you might well pick the theory of evolution. This theory has transformed the way we look at ourselves and continues to exert an influence on psychology particularly with the growing interest in genetic explanations of behaviour. Darwin argued that human beings were descended from animal ancestors and demonstrated the similarities in the physical structures of people and animals, even down to the structure of the brain.

Natural selection

The two key ideas of Darwin's theory are

- *genetic variation*: all individuals are genetically unique (an example of individual differences – if all members of a species were entirely uniform there would be no evolution), and
- *selection*: the individuals who breed are the ones who are better adapted to the environment they are living in.

The features that make some individuals survive and reproduce are likely to be passed on to the next generation. This is a process of selective breeding where the selection is done by the environment (i.e. *natural* selection). The issue this raises for humans is that we are able to tamper with natural selection by the development of medicine that keeps people alive, and by the development of laws that prevent murderous disputes, or regulate fertility through the conventions of marriage. Maybe this will have an effect on how the species develops. If so then what should we do about it?

Not so intelligent?

'*It is an important and popular fact that things are not always what they seem. For instance, on the planet Earth, man had always assumed that he was more intelligent than dolphins because he had achieved so much – the wheel, New York, wars and so on – whilst all the dolphins had ever done was muck about in the water having a good time. But conversely, the dolphins had always believed that they were far more intelligent than man – for precisely the same reasons.*'

Douglas Adams, *The Hitch-hiker's Guide to the Galaxy*

Testing intelligence

In 1884 Francis Galton set up a stall at the International Health Exhibition in London and tested visitors' mental abilities for the sum of 3 pence. This is often seen as the start of mental testing. As many as 9,000 people took the tests which included measures of reaction times to sounds, lights and touch, and other easily measurable motor activities and sensory judgements.

Binet's pioneering tests

The first tests that we can recognise as IQ tests were developed in France by **Alfred Binet** who started his scientific studies by examining the relationship between head size and intelligence. He discovered that there was little connection between size of head and intelligence. He was later commissioned by the minister of public education to develop a technique to identify children in need of special education, and from this the intelligence test was born. The test was used to give an estimate of a child's mental age by comparing the child's performance on various tasks with the performance of children of various ages. It was later suggested that the mental age of the child should be divided by the chronological age to give an index of intelligence and so the notion of IQ was developed (the formula is given below). This is an example of norm referencing.

$$\text{Intelligence Quotient (IQ)} = \frac{\text{Mental Age}}{\text{Chronological Age}} \times 100$$

Binet believed that children who were in need of extra help could be identified by these tests, but he vigorously argued against the idea that intelligence is a fixed quantity that cannot be improved by further help. This approach got sadly lost in the translation of tests into English and in their transportation to America. In contrast to the approach of Binet, the fiercest supporters of intelligence testing in the English speaking world were scientists who believed that individual differences are mainly due to genetic factors, and who proposed eugenic solutions to the perceived problems of society. For example, Lewis Terman who introduced the IQ test to America, wrote,

'If we would preserve our state for a class of people worthy to possess it, we must prevent, as far as possible, the propagation of mental degenerates' (Lewis Terman, 1921, cited in Kamin, 1977).

The big words disguise the sentiments of the quote. To paraphrase Terman, he is saying we must stop poor and uneducated people from having children. All this would seem unpleasant but unimportant were it not for that fact that over half of the states in the USA brought in sterilisation laws for the 'feeble minded' and carried out tens of thousands of operations (Kamin, 1977).

IQ and controversy

The testing of intelligence is probably the most controversial issue in psychology. It attracts extreme opinions, for example,

'The measurement of intelligence is psychology's most telling accomplishment to date.' (Herrnstein, 1973)

'The IQ test has served as an instrument of oppression against the poor.' (Kamin, 1977)

Intelligence testing is so controversial because in our society we value intelligence above almost all other qualities or skills. The IQ test has a particularly narrow definition of intelligence and concentrates on a few cognitive skills and ignores skills such as common sense and problem solving. On top of this problem is the underlying belief that our personal level of intelligence is something we are born with rather than something we develop. If intelligence can be shown to be due mainly to genetic factors then it suggests something about who we should encourage to have children and who we should discourage. This argument has been central to all discussion about intelligence from Francis Galton right up to today.

Eugenics

Eugenics refers to the attempt to improve the quality of human beings through selective breeding, so for example, if we wanted to improve the general level of intelligence in the country we would encourage intelligent people to have lots of children and unintelligent people to have none. Of course this only works if the factors that lead to differences in intellectual performance can be inherited.

There are many problems with the eugenics approach to intelligence including the controversial assumptions that

- There is a single human quality that we can call intelligence rather than many different types of intelligent behaviour.
- Intelligence can be reliably and validly measured.
- Intelligence is a fixed quantity and cannot be improved.
- The differences in intelligence between people are mainly due to genetic factors.

Despite all these issues, the idea of eugenics keeps reappearing and each generation has to figure out the best way forward.

Other intelligences

Musical intelligence

Some people can develop advanced musical intelligence if it is adaptive in their community. Lord (1960) studied how singers of oral verse in a rural Balkan community became singers of epic songs. This requires a high level of linguistic and musical intelligence because the singer has to learn musical and linguistic formulae that allow them to construct appropriate songs. This is no mean feat as each song lasts throughout a whole evening, and a different song is sung on each of the forty days of the holy month of Ramadan. The singer has to learn the skill by observation of these events for many years, practice in private and then perform in front of a critical audience.

Micronesia navigator showing expert intelligence.

Navigational intelligence

Many of us are capable of getting lost in a shop so the idea that some people can navigate across thousands of miles is almost unimaginable. This is an essential skill, however, in island communities like Micronesia where islands can be thousands of miles apart. Gladwin (1970) studied how men in the Puluwat Islands of Micronesia train to become master navigators. This position is achieved by very few individuals because it demands an extremely high aptitude, involving a combination of different kinds of intelligence. The master navigators must memorise vast amounts of factual information such as the identities and locations of all the islands to which anyone might travel to, the names and paths of all of the stars which a navigator can use to spot their course, and the techniques for using this information to devise a route. They also have to develop exceptional practical skills involved with sea travel such as reading currents, the weather and the waves.

Intelligent behaviours like the above are being lost in the modern world where technology takes over the tasks, though it sometimes does them as well as the intelligent human experts.

Individual differences core study 13: Rosenhan (sane in insane places)

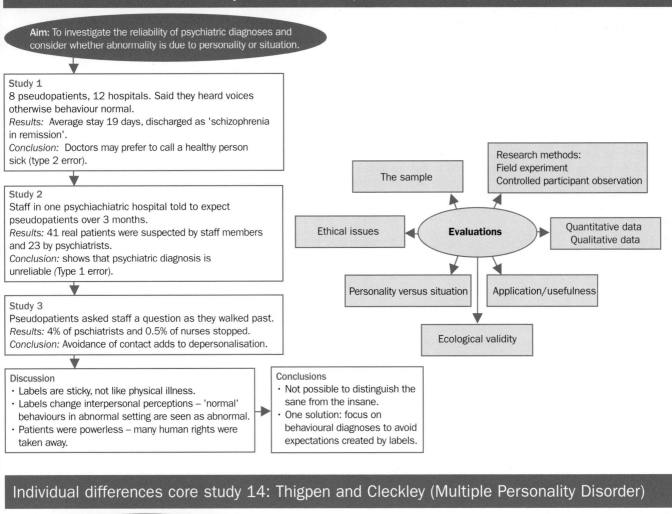

Aim: To investigate the reliability of psychiatric diagnoses and consider whether abnormality is due to personality or situation.

Study 1
8 pseudopatients, 12 hospitals. Said they heard voices otherwise behaviour normal.
Results: Average stay 19 days, discharged as 'schizophrenia in remission'.
Conclusion: Doctors may prefer to call a healthy person sick (type 2 error).

Study 2
Staff in one psychiachiatric hospital told to expect pseudopatients over 3 months.
Results: 41 real patients were suspected by staff members and 23 by psychiatrists.
Conclusion: shows that psychiatric diagnosis is unreliable (Type 1 error).

Study 3
Pseudopatients asked staff a question as they walked past.
Results: 4% of pschiatrists and 0.5% of nurses stopped.
Conclusion: Avoidance of contact adds to depersonalisation.

Discussion
· Labels are sticky, not like physical illness.
· Labels change interpersonal perceptions – 'normal' behaviours in abnormal setting are seen as abnormal.
· Patients were powerless – many human rights were taken away.

Conclusions
· Not possible to distinguish the sane from the insane.
· One solution: focus on behavioural diagnoses to avoid expectations created by labels.

The sample

Research methods:
Field experiment
Controlled participant observation

Ethical issues

Evaluations

Quantitative data
Qualitative data

Personality versus situation

Application/usefulness

Ecological validity

Individual differences core study 14: Thigpen and Cleckley (Multiple Personality Disorder)

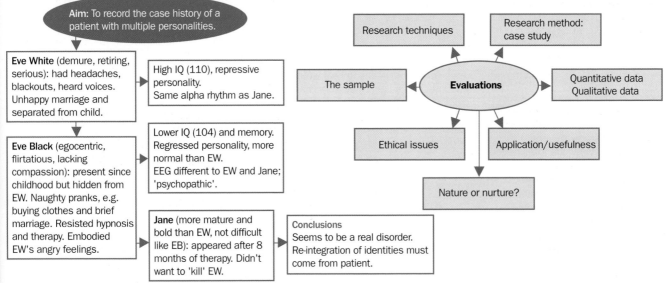

Aim: To record the case history of a patient with multiple personalities.

Eve White (demure, retiring, serious): had headaches, blackouts, heard voices. Unhappy marriage and separated from child.

High IQ (110), repressive personality.
Same alpha rhythm as Jane.

Eve Black (egocentric, flirtatious, lacking compassion): present since childhood but hidden from EW. Naughty pranks, e.g. buying clothes and brief marriage. Resisted hypnosis and therapy. Embodied EW's angry feelings.

Lower IQ (104) and memory. Regressed personality, more normal than EW. EEG different to EW and Jane; 'psychopathic'.

Jane (more mature and bold than EW, not difficult like EB): appeared after 8 months of therapy. Didn't want to 'kill' EW.

Conclusions
Seems to be a real disorder. Re-integration of identities must come from patient.

Research techniques

Research method: case study

The sample

Evaluations

Quantitative data
Qualitative data

Ethical issues

Application/usefulness

Nature or nurture?

Individual differences core study 15: Griffiths (gambling)

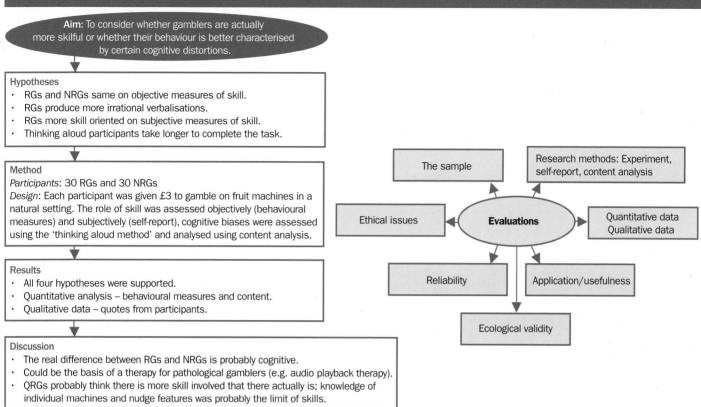

Aim: To consider whether gamblers are actually more skilful or whether their behaviour is better characterised by certain cognitive distortions.

Hypotheses
- RGs and NRGs same on objective measures of skill.
- RGs produce more irrational verbalisations.
- RGs more skill oriented on subjective measures of skill.
- Thinking aloud participants take longer to complete the task.

Method
Participants: 30 RGs and 30 NRGs
Design: Each participant was given £3 to gamble on fruit machines in a natural setting. The role of skill was assessed objectively (behavioural measures) and subjectively (self-report), cognitive biases were assessed using the 'thinking aloud method' and analysed using content analysis.

Results
- All four hypotheses were supported.
- Quantitative analysis – behavioural measures and content.
- Qualitative data – quotes from participants.

Discussion
- The real difference between RGs and NRGs is probably cognitive.
- Could be the basis of a therapy for pathological gamblers (e.g. audio playback therapy).
- QRGs probably think there is more skill involved that there actually is; knowledge of individual machines and nudge features was probably the limit of skills.

Evaluations
- The sample
- Research methods: Experiment, self-report, content analysis
- Ethical issues
- Quantitative data / Qualitative data
- Reliability
- Application/usefulness
- Ecological validity

Further reading and other things

A starting point for your further exploration of individual differences and diversity would be *The Mismeasure of Man* (1984, Pelican) by Stephen Jay Gould. This gives a readable account of the development of intelligence testing over the last 100 years. With regard to the altered states we commonly refer to as madness there is a bookshop full of texts. Most recommended are *One Flew over the Cuckoo's Nest* by Ken Kesey (first published in 1962 – available now from Picador), which tells a (fictional) story of life in a US mental hospital in the late 1950s. A more recent and more immediate UK version is *Buster Fired a Wobbler* (1989, Penguin) by Geoff Burrell, which is based on his own experiences as a psychiatric nurse. Two books that define the argument about mental disorder and challenge the illness model that is still so powerful are *The Divided Self* by R. D. Laing (1990, Penguin) and *The Myth of Mental Illness* by Thomas Szasz (1984, Harper and Row).

The uniqueness of individuals is a common theme in the movies. It is portrayed as if this uniqueness is a shock as if we should really all be the same and anyone who deviates from this is odd (or abnormal). But who is to say what is normal and what isn't? This is explored in *One Flew Over the Cuckoo's Nest* and, more charmingly in the excellent James Stewart film, *Harvey*. In fact there is a website dedicated to psychopathology in films http://home.epix.net/~tcannon1/psychmovies/welcome.html.

Rosenhan
- Original article http://courses.ucsd.edu/fall2003/ps163f/Rosenhan.htm#_ftn.
- Research by Rosenhan is discussed in a chapter of *Skinner's Box* by Lauren Slater, a book which contains the background to a number of key studies in Psychology.
- Episode of the Simpson's 'Stark raving Dad' which covers many of the points in the article, see http://www.holah.karoo.net/rosenhan.htm for link – and if you haven't discovered Holah.co.uk, look now.

Thigpen and Cleckley
- Original article can be obtained from your local library by giving them the full reference and ordering a photocopy.
- Video of the real Eve talking as all three personalities http://www.youtube.com/watch?v=RpJxZaaFv9U
- Read about a murderer with Multiple Personality Disorder, and also about Eve and Sybil in the Crime Library at http://www.crimelibrary.com/criminal_mind/psychology/multiples/index.html.

Griffiths
- Link to original article at http://blogcast.psychblog.co.uk/dr-mark-griffiths-the-gambling-man.htm and also link to interview with Mark Griffiths.

MCQ answers

Rosenhan (MCQs on page 199)	1c 2a 3c 4a 5d 6b 7d 8c 9d 10d
Thigpen and Cleckley (MCQs on page 209)	1c 2a 3a 4c 5b 6d 7c 8a 9b 10a
Griffiths (MCQs on page 219)	1a 2b 3b 4a 5a 6a 7c 8d 9c 10c

1 Rosenhan conducted a study where pseudopatients sought treatment in mental hospitals.

    (a) Outline **one** way in which the hospital staff were treated unethically. [2]

    (b) Suggest what might have been done to deal with this unethical treatment, and what effect this might have had on the results. [2]

Stig's answer

(a) The staff didn't know they were part of a study.

(b) If the staff knew the truth the study would have been pointless.

Chardonnay's answer

(a) The staff were deceived – not aware that pseudopatients would be presenting themselves and, in the second study, didn't know that really there weren't any pseudopatients.

(b) One way would be to debrief all staff afterwards and offer them the opportunity to withdraw their data. However then the results would be biased because of attrition.

Examiner's comments

Stig, you're right in part (a) but it would be a good idea to identify the ethical guideline. Similarly in part (b) you are probably right in speculating that the study would have been pointless – but why? More specifically, to answer the question you need to refer to the actual results of the study!

Chardonnay, you have given a very clear answer in part (a), over and above the requirements of the question. Your part (b) is an excellent answer showing quite a sophisticated understanding of ethical issues.

Stig (1 + 0 marks) Chardonnay (2 + 2 marks)

---

2 In the study by Rosenhan (sane in insane places)

    (a) Describe **one** example of how the hospital staff dealt with requests for information from the pseudopatients. [2]

    (b) Outline **two** effects this had on the pseudopatients. [2]

Stig's answer

(a) Most of them gave a brief answer without eye contact and just walked on.

(b) It depersonalised them.

Chardonnay's answer

(a) The staff largely ignored the patients.

(b) The effects were that the patients didn't feel they counted and were not real people. They were depersonalised and it lowered their self-esteem.

Examiner's comments

Stig, to the point and spot on in part (a). This is a good example of getting full credit without waffling. In part (b) the question asks for two effects, so only one mark awarded – a mark carelessly thrown away.

Chardonnay, your answer is a bit too brief in part (a), it just doesn't display a sufficiently detailed knowledge of the study. You might have added 'and walked away when spoken to'. In part (b), you have given two effects – depersonalisation and reduction in self-esteem so fine for 2 marks.

Stig (2 + 1 marks) Chardonnay (1 + 2 marks)

---

3 In the study on Multiple Personality Disorder Thigpen and Cleckley used psychometric tests:

    (a) Identify two tests completed by Eve. [2]

    (b) Explain why it was necessary for an independent tester to analyse the results of the tests carried out on Eve. [2]

Stig's answer

(a) Eve did an IQ test and a personality test.

(b) It was better to have an independent tester so that he wouldn't affect how she performed.

Chardonnay's answer

(a) Eve did an IQ test and a projective personality test (the Rorschach test).

(b) They employed an independent tester so that the tester was not biased in how they interpreted Eve's responses or that she didn't act up to him how she might have done with Thigpen and Cleckley who she knew quite well.

Examiner's comments

Stig, 1 mark for IQ test, but your second answer ('personality test') is a bit too vague to gain credit. For part (b) your answer is again lacking in detail; you need a bit more by way of explanation – so just 1 mark again.

Chardonnay shows you how it's done. Both of her answers are spot on. She has described the personality test in more detail in part (a). In part (b) she provides plenty of detail giving a full explanation – over and above what is required for 2 marks.

Stig (1 + 1 marks) Chardonnay (2 + 2 marks)

4   Thigpen and Cleckley's study of Multiple Personality Disorder focused on one individual, Eve. This is a case study.
Give **one** advantage and **one** disadvantage of the case study method in the context of this study.   [4]

Stig's answer

One advantage of the case study method is that it allows you to study one individual case of multiple personality or other abnormal disorder. Such cases are very rare so it is really the main way to study the disorder while giving sufficient detail.

A disadvantage is that any individual is unique, there were special things about Eve's case which are unique and therefore the conclusions drawn from this may not apply to other cases.

Chardonnay's answer

Advantage: Case studies allow us to gain rich detail about one individual case.

Disadvantage: The problem is that the individual is likely to be unique in some way and we can't generalise from this case.

Examiner's comments

This time Stig you are the one who provided bucket loads of detail and get full marks – but not just because of the detail. You have carefully read the question and realised that you also had to include the context, i.e. effectively relate your answer to Thigpen and Cleckley's study.

Chardonnay, you are right about the advantage and disadvantage of a case study but you haven't connected each of these to the Thigpen and Cleckley study.

Stig (2 + 2 marks) Chardonnay (1 + 1 marks)

5   Griffiths suggested that regular fruit machine gamblers would be more irrational than non-regular gamblers.

(a) Explain why he expected to find this difference.   [2]

(b) Identify **one** piece of evidence from the study that shows that regular gamblers are more irrational than non-regular gamblers.   [2]

Stig's answer

(a) Griffiths expected to find that regular gamblers would be more irrational than non-regular gamblers because they can't be thinking rationally or they wouldn't be gambling.

(b) The regular gamblers said more irrational statements than the non-regulars (14% versus 2.5%).

Chardonnay's answer

(a) Griffiths expected this difference because another psychologist proposed that gamblers use heuristics which distort cognitive processes and this leads to irrational behaviour.

(b) The regular gamblers made more percentage verbalisations which were irrational whereas the non-regular gamblers made more percentage verbalisations which were rational.

Examiner's comments

Stig, there is no need to repeat the question in your answer; your somewhat lengthy answer doesn't actually say very much. However there is a glimmer of knowledge here – one argument against normative decision theory is that it predicts people would not gamble at all, as you say. In part (b) you have given a briefer answer and the inclusion of the percentages gives you full marks.

Chardonnay as usual you have given a careful and well-informed answer for part (a) but in part (b) it's your turn to write a lot of words but say very little – really all you have said is that there was a difference. You did say 'percentage verbalisations' which is the key point about where the evidence comes from, but not sufficient for 2 marks.

Stig (1 + 2 marks) Chardonnay (2 + 1 marks)

6   In his study on gambling Griffiths endeavoured to ensure that the design was ecologically valid.

(a) Describe **one** aspect of the design that aimed to achieve this.   [2]

(b) Explain how this would have made the study more ecologically valid.   [2]

Stig's answer

(a) Using real fruit machines was one way to do this.

(b) This would mean the participants played the machines like they would normally in everyday life.

Chardonnay's answer

(a) The study was conducted in a fruit machine arcade.

(b) If the study was in a lab then they might have been less relaxed but in an everyday natural setting people are likely to behave more like they do in real life.

Examiner's comments

You need to read what you have written Stig; of course they are real fruit machines but Griffiths could have used real fruit machines in a lab. It's more natural than playing a fruit machine on the internet though, so one mark. Chardonnay's got the key factor – real machines in a *natural* setting.

In part (b) Stig you've thrown away another mark by not spelling out the detail – why would they behave differently in the real arcade than in the lab. Chardonnay has included this detail for the full 2 marks.

Stig (1 + 1 marks) Chardonnay (2 + 2 marks)

7   (a) What was the aim of the Rosenhan study?   [2]
    (b) Describe the sample used in the Rosenhan study and give **one** limitation of it.   [6]
    (c) Describe how data was gathered in the Rosenhan study.   [6]
    (d) Give **one** advantage and **one** disadvantage of observational studies.   [6]
    (e) Suggest **two** changes to the Rosenhan study and outline any methodological implications these changes may have.   [8]
    (f) Outline the results of the Rosenhan study.   [8]

Total [36]

Chardonnay's answer

(a) The aim of the Rosenhan study was to see whether diagnosis of abnormality (schizophrenia) is really valid and reliable. In particular, is abnormality just a feature of the situation that people are in, rather than a characteristic of the person?

(b) The main sample was the hospitals that were visited by the pseudopatients and the staff (nurses, doctors, orderlies) who were in these hospitals. Altogether, there were 12 hospitals and Rosenhan says that they were varied in terms of whether they were state run or private run, and whether they were old or modern. One limitation of this sample is that it is still quite a small proportion of the mental hospitals in America – probably there were several hundred of them at the time.

(c) A lot of data was gathered in this study – both qualitative and quantitative. In the main study, the pseudopatients were hospitalised (mostly diagnosed with schizophrenia) and they observed mainly the staff while they were there. The data was also how long they had to stay in hospital before they were discharged. In the second study, the data was gathered from doctors and nurses according to whether they thought there were pseudopatients when in fact there were none.

(d) One advantage of an observational study is that it is looking at behaviour which really happens (rather than what people say happened). This should mean that the study has some validity.

One disadvantage of observational studies is that even though you can see what is going on, you do not necessarily know why people behaved in that way – why they did things. It might be that observational studies actually give a limited understanding of behaviour because we don't know the reasons why.

(e) One change (if the study were done today) could be to use CCTV on the wards as well as the pseudopatients to collect data. This would mean that the pseudopatients would not have to take notes so much (and might not be thought of as so obsessive); and that more data could be collected, from places even when the pseudopatient wasn't present, e.g. things that might be said about him or her in the cage. This change would give more data and could be quite revealing. Also, it might actually be more objective as the data doesn't just rely upon the collection of a participant observer who might be over-involved and over-emotional about what is going on.

A second change would be to interview the doctors and nurses afterwards so that you could get a better idea about why they made the mistake.

(f) The results of the Rosenhan study were that all the pseudopatients were admitted and that they remained in hospital for an average of 19 days (range of 7 to 52 days). While they were in the hospital, in general, there was a lot of powerlessness and depersonalisation. Patients were generally ignored by staff who spent most of their time in 'the cage' (their office). There was a tendency to interpret their behaviour as abnormal, e.g. when waiting for the canteen, it was said patients had 'oral acquisitive nature' rather than they were just waiting there because they were bored. The diagnosis was 'sticky' as even when they were discharged, they were signed off with 'schizophrenia in remission' rather than absolutely fine. This study showed that psychiatrists made a Type II error (calling a sick person healthy); but the second study showed that doctors also could make a Type I error (calling a healthy person sick) as doctors and nurses thought that real patients were pseudopatients.

Examiner's comments

Overall, Chardonnay, your answer is about the right length and you have devoted proportionate time to each of the six question parts.

(a) This is spot on Chardonnay. Lots of people forget about the situation versus disposition aspect of Rosenhan's aim, so well done.

(b) Again, candidates often trip up here and say that the sample were the pseudopatients; you're right, the main sample was the hospitals and staff. There is some detail here (the variety etc.) though you didn't remember that the hospitals represented five different states; still it is good enough for the full 3 marks. The limitation part is marked separately and you have made a valid point here, but could have developed your point by talking about the possible lack of representativeness of US mental hospitals, for instance, so 1 out of 3 marks for this limitation.

(c) In a way this is quite a tricky question to answer because there could be a huge amount to say – but only 6 marks are available. Therefore, you do have to be quite shrewd. Your answer is a mid-band answer. For the top band you needed just a few more details such as, the sort of behaviours recorded by the pseudopatients in the main study.

(d) Valid points here, Chardonnay. However you haven't elaborated the advantage as much as would be appropriate for full marks and so this only just qualifies for 2 out of 3 marks. Your disadvantage is described more fully and so attracts 3 out of 3 marks.

(e) Two good ideas, however not so good on the execution. For the first change, you haven't given much description of the change itself, for example, would there be multiple cameras per ward, who would analyse the footage? You need to give just a bit of extra detail here. Good discussion of impact upon results.

The second change is altogether too brief. You have identified the change and have given some hint about the likely impact upon the results. For full marks both parts (change and its effect) should be much more detailed. For example 'They could be asked about why they admitted the pseudopatient in the first place and why they said or did certain things, e.g. why they ignored patients, spent so much time in 'the cage' etc. This would have no impact upon original results – but it would help us understand why they did some of the things they did, e.g. why the doctors admitted them – did they 100% believe they were schizophrenic, or were they just being cautious?

(f) It is always more than handy to have some useful details up your sleeve such as some exact numbers for the main results and use them as you have done before. You also have some of the key themes (depersonalisation, stickiness) of the results and display both range and detail of understanding. Bit of a slip up on Type I and II though (they are the wrong way round – Type I is calling a sick person healthy) – easily done in an exam!

Chardonnay (2 + 4 + 4 + 5 + 5 + 7 marks = 27/36 marks)

REFERENCES

Adorno, T.W., Frenkel-Brunswick, E., Levinson, D. and Sanford, N. (1950) *The Authoritarian Personality*. New York: Harper. ▸page 182

Aitchison, J. (1983) *The articulate mammal: An introduction to psycholinguistics* (2nd edn.). New York: Universe Books. ▸page 52

Akelaitis, A.J. (1944) A study of gnosis, praxis and language following section of the corpus callosum and anterior commisure. *Journal of Neurosurgery*, 1, 94–102. ▸page 134

Allport, G.W. (1968) The historical background of modern psychology. In G. Lindzey and E. Aronson (eds) *Handbook of Social Psychology* (2nd edn, vol. 1. pp. 1-80). Reading, MA: Addison-Wesley. ▸page 150

APA (2005) http://www.apa.org/divisions/div30/define_hypnosis.html (accessed Jan 2006). ▸page 203

Arendt, H. (1963) *Eichmann in Jerusalem*. London: Penguin. ▸page 158

Asch, S.E. (1946) Forming impressions of personality. *Journal of Abnormal and Social Psychology*, 41, 258–290. ▸pages 19, 196

Asch, S.E. (1955) Opinions and social pressure. *Scientific American*, 193, 31–5. ▸page 152

Aserinsky, E. and Kleitman, N. (1955) Two types of ocular motility occurring in sleep. *Journal of Applied Physiology*, 8 (1), 1–10. ▸page 124

Baggaley J. (1991) Media health campaigns: not just what you say, but the way you say it. In: *AIDS Prevention through Health Promotion: Facing Sensitive Issues*. Geneva: World Health Organisation. ▸page 182

Bailey, A.A. and Hurd, P.L. (2005) Depression in men is associated with more feminine finger length ratios. *Personality and Individual Differences*, 39, 829–836. ▸page 21

Bandura, A. (1986) *Social Foundations of Thought and Action*. Englewood Cliffs, NJ: Prentice-Hall. ▸page 83

Bandura, A. (2004) Swimming against the mainstream: the early years from chilly tributary to transformative mainstream. *Behaviour Research and Therapy*, 42, 613–630. ▸page 83

Bandura, A., Ross, D. and Ross, S.A. (1961) Transmission of aggression through imitation of aggressive models. *Journal of Abnormal and Social Psychology*, 63(3), 575–582. ▸page 84

Banyard, P. and Kagan, G. (2002) Pre-degree Psychology: a Challenge to the Profession. Psychology Learning and Teaching Conference, York University. ▸page 98

Baron-Cohen, S., Burt, L., Smith-Laittan, F., Harrison, J. and Bolton, P. (1996) *Synaesthesia: Prevalence and familiality. Perception*, 25(9), 1073–1079. ▸page 63

Baron-Cohen, S., Joliffe, T., Mortimore, C. and Robertson, M. (1997) Another advanced test of theory of mind: evidence from very high functioning adults with autism or Asperger Syndrome. *Journal of Child Psychology and Psychiatry*, 38, 813–822. ▸page 44

Baron-Cohen, S., Leslie, A.M. and Frith, U. (1986) Mechanical, behavioural and intentional understanding of picture stories in autistic children. *British Journal of Developmental Psychology*, 4, 113–125. ▸page 48

Baron, R.A. and Byrne, D. (1991) *Social Psychology: Understanding Human Interaction* (6th edn). London: Allyn and Bacon. ▸page 200

Bartlett, F.C. (1932) *Remembering*. Cambridge: Cambridge University Press. ▸page 32

Bassett, K., Green, G. and Kazanjian, A. (2000) Autism and Lovaas Treatment: A systematic review of effectiveness evidence. Vancouver, BC: BC Office Of Health Technology Assessment. ▸page 48

Baumrind, D. (1964) Some thoughts on ethics of research: After reading Milgram's behavioural study of obedience. *American Psychologist*, 19, 421–423. ▸page 158

BBC (2000) Cherie Blair 'bad role model'. http://news.bbc.co.uk/1/hi/uk/660867.stm. ▸page 82

BBC (2003) Sesame Street breaks Iraqi POWs. http://news.bbc.co.uk/1/hi/world/middle_east/3042907.stm. ▸page 128

BBC (2004) Builder survives nailgun accident. http://news.bbc.co.uk/1/hi/health/3685791.stm (accessed October 2005). Bishop and Wahlsten, 1997). ▸page 110

BBC (2005) Reliving the London bombing horror. http://news.bbc.co.uk/1/hi/uk/4346812.stm; London explosions: Your accounts http://news.bbc.co.uk/1/hi/talking_point/4659237.stm (accessed December 2005). ▸page 178

Bègue, L. (2005) Self-esteem regulation in threatening social comparison: The role of belief in a just world and self-efficacy. Social Behaviour and Personality. See http://www.findarticles.com/p/articles/mi_qa3852/is_200501/ai_n9520808/pg_3 (accessed December 2005). ▸page 218

Bentall, R.P. (1992) A proposal to classify happiness as a psychiatric disorder. *Journal of Medical Ethics*, 18, 94–98. ▸page 190

Bishop, K.M. and Wahlsten, D. (1997) Sex differences in the human corpus callosum: myth or reality? *Neuroscience and Biobehavioural Reviews*, 21 (5), 581–601. ▸page 132

Blass, T. (2004) *The Man who Shocked the World: The Life and Legacy of Stanley Milgram*. New York: Basic Books. ▸pages 152–153, 158, 160

Boden, M.A. (1977) *Artificial Intelligence and Natural Man*. New York: Basic Books. ▸page 52

Bowlby, J. (1965). *Child Care and the Growth of Love* (2nd edn). London: Penguin Books. ▸page 70

Bowler, D.M. (1992) 'Theory of Mind' in Asperger Syndrome. *Journal of Child Psychology and Psychiatry*, 33, 877–895. ▸page 44

Brazelton, T.B. (1973) *Neonatal Behavioral Assessment Scale*. Philadelphia, PA: J.B. Lippincott. ▸page 71

Brazelton, T.B., Koslowski, B. and Tronick, E. (1976) Neonatal behavior among urban Zambians and Americans. *Journal Academy of Child Psychiatry*, 15, 97–108. ▸page 71

British Crime Survey (2004) http://www.homeoffice.gov.uk/rds/crimeew0304.html. ▸page 88

British Psychological Society (1993) *Code of conduct, ethical principles and guidelines*. Leicester: The British Psychological Society. ▸page 218

Broadcasting Standards Commission (BSC) (2002) Briefing Update: Depiction of Violence on Terrestrial Television. ▸page 88

Brosnan, M. (in press) Digit ratio as an indicator of numeracy relative to literacy in 7-year-old British school children. *British Journal of Psychology*. From his website http://staff.bath.ac.uk/pssmjb/blog/index_main.php?page=cv. ▸page 21

Bryan, J.H. and Test, M.A. (1967) Models and helping: naturalistic studies in helping behaviour, *Journal of Personality and Social Psychology*, 6, 400–407. ▸page 174

Bushman, B.J. and Anderson, C.A. (2001) Is it time to pull the plug on the hostile versus instrumental aggression dichotomy? *Psychological Review*, 108, 273–279. ▸page 83

Carmichael, L., Hogan, P. and Walter, A. (1932) An experimental study of the effect of language on the reproduction of visually perceived forms, *Journal of Experimental Psychology*, 15, 73–86. ▸page 37

Carson, B.S. (2002) Gifted hands that heal (interview by Academy of Achievement). http://www.achievement.org/auto doc/page/car1int-1 (accessed October 2005). ▸page 138

Charlton, T., Gunter, B. and Hannan, A. (eds.) (2000) *Broadcast television effects in a remote community*, Hillsdale, NJ: Lawrence Erlbaum. ▸pages 18–19

Clark, M. (2001) in O'Connell, A.N. and Russo, N.F. (ed.) (2001) *Models of Achievement: Reflections of Eminent Women in Psychology*. New York: Columbia University Press. ▸page 183

Colapinto, J. (2000) *As Nature Made Him: The Boy Who was Raised as a Girl*. New York: HarperCollins. ▸page 211

Comings, D.E. (1998) Why different rules are required for polygenic inheritance: lessons from studies of the DRD2 gene. *Alcohol*, 16, 61–70. ▸page 212

Coolican, H. (1996) *Introduction to Research Methods and Statistics in Psychology*. London: Hodder and Stoughton. ▸page 10

Cooley, C.H. (1902) *Human Nature and the Social Order*. New York: Scribner. ▸page 150

Corballis, M.C. (1999) Are we in our right minds? In S. Della Salla (ed.) *Mind Myths: Exploring Popular Assumptions about the Mind and Brain*. Chichester: John Wiley and Sons. ▸page 138

Coren, S. (1996) *Sleep Thieves*. New York: Free Press. ▸page 128

Corkin, S. (1984) Lasting consequences of bilateral medial temporal lobectomy: Clinical course and experimental findings in h. m. *Seminars in Neurology*, 4, 249–259. ▸page 113

Costa, P.T., Jr. and McCrae, R.R. (1992) Normal personality assessment in clinical practice: The NEO Personality Inventory. Psychological Assessment, 4, 5–13. ▸page 171

Criswell, J.H. (1937) Racial cleavage in Negro–white groups. *Sociometry*, 1, 81–89. ▸pages 190, 220

Daeg de Mott, D. K. (2001). Ethics. *Gale Encyclopedia of Psychology*. Available: www.findarticles.com. ▸page 180

Daly, M. and Wilson, M. (1998) *The Truth About Cinderella*. London: Weidenfeld & Nicolson. ▸page 103

Daniel, T.C. (1972) Nature of the effect of verbal labels on recognition memory for form. *Journal of Experimental Psychology*, 96, 152–157. ▸page 37

Darley, J.M. and Batson, C.D. (1973) 'From Jersualem to Jericho': A study of situational and dispositional variables in helping behavior. *Journal of Personality and Social Psychology*, 27, 100–108. ▸page 173

Darley, J.M. and Latané, B. (1968) Bystander intervention in emergencies: Diffusion of responsibility. *Journal of Personality and Social Psychology*, 8, 377–383. ▸page 174

Darwin, C. (1969) *The Autobiography of Charles Darwin: with original omissions restored*, edited with appendix and notes by his granddaughter, Nora Barlow. New York: W.W. Norton. ▸page 58

Darwin, C.A. (1871) *The Descent of Man and Selection in Relation to Sex*. London: John Murray. ▸page 58

Della Sala, S. (ed.) (1999) *Mind Myths: Exploring Popular Assumptions about the Mind and Brain*. Chichester: John Wiley & Sons. ▸page 40

Dement, W.C. (2001) *The Promise of Sleep*. London: Pan. ▸page 128

Dement, W. and Kleitman, N. (1957) The relation of eye movements during sleep to dream activity: An objective method for the study of dreaming. *Journal of Experimental Psychology*, 53 (5), 339–346. ▸page 124

DeVries, R. (1969) Constancy of generic identity in the years three to six. *Monographs of the Society for Research in Child Development*, 34 (3, Serial No. 127). ▸page 73

Diamond, M. (1997) Sexual identity and sexual orientation in children with traumatized or ambiguous genitalia. *Journal of Sex Research*, 34(2),199–211. ▸page 211

Dodds, P., Muhamad, R. and Watts, D. (2003) An experimental study of search in global social networks. *Science*, 301, 827–829. ▸page 153

DoH (Department of Health) (1992) The Health of the Nation: a strategy for health in England. London: HMSO. ▸page 218

DoH (Department of Health) (1993) One year on: a report on the progress of the health of the nation. London: HMSO. ▸page 218

Dollard, J., Doob, L.W., Miller, N.E., Mowrer, O.H. and Sears, R.R. (1939) *Frustration and Aggression*. New Haven, CT: Yale University Press. ▸page 83

Dovidio, J.F., Gaertner, S.L., Validzic, A., Matoka, A., Johnson, B. and Frazier, S. (1997) Extending the benefits of recategorization: Evaluations, self-disclosure, and helping. *Journal of Experimental Social Psychology*, 33, 401–420. ▸page 178

Dunn, J. and Deater-Deckard, K. (2001) *Children's Views of their Changing Families*. York: York Publishing Services/Joseph Rowntree Foundation. ▸page 103

Eagly, A.H. (1978) Sex differences in influenceability. *Psychological Bulletin*, 85, 86–116. ▸page 16

Eberhardt, J.L. (2005) Imaging race. *American Psychologist*, February–March, 181–190 (available online at http://www.apa.org/journals/features/amp602181.pdf). ▸page 118

Ekman, P. (1992) An argument for basic emotions. *Cognition and Emotion*, 6, 169–200. ▸page 45

Fancher, R.E. (1996). *Pioneers of Psychology* (3rd edn). New York: W.W. Norton. ▸pages 90, 222

Festinger, L., Riecken, H.W. and Schachter, S. (1956) *When Prophecy Fails*. Minneapolis: University of Minnesota Press. ▸page 5

Fisher, S. (1993) The pull of the fruit machine: A sociological typology of young players. *Sociological Review*, 41, 446–474. ▸page 217

Forer, B.R. (1949) The fallacy of personal validation: A classroom demonstration of gullibility. *Journal of Abnormal Psychology*, 44, 118–121. ▸page 221

Freud, A. (1946) *The Ego and the Mechanisms of Defense*. New York: International University Press. ▸page 87

Freud, S. (1900) The interpretation of dreams. In J. Strachey (ed. and trans.) *The complete psychological works: The standard edition* (vol. 4). New York: Norton, 1976. ▸page 93

Freud, S. (1905) *Three essays on the theory of sexuality*. Republished 1977. Harmondsworth, Middlesex: Penguin. ▸page 93

Freud, S. (1909) Analysis of a phobia in a five-year-old boy. In J. Strachey (ed. and trans.) *The Standard Edition of the Complete Psychological Works: Two Case Histories* (vol. X), pages 5–147. London: The Hogarth Press. ▸page 94

Freud, S. (1910) The origin and development of pschoanalysis. *American Journal of Psychology*, 21, 181–218. ▸page 101

Freud, S. (1933) *New Introductory Lectures on Psycho-Analysis*. London: Hogarth. ▸page **100**

Frith, U. (1989) Autism: *Explaining the Enigma*. Oxford: Basil Blackwell. ▸page **46**

Frith, U. and Happé, F. (1999) Theory of mind and self consciousness. What is it like to be autistic? *Mind and Language*, 14, 1–22 ▸page **43**

Gado, M. (2005) A cry in the night: the Kitty Genovese murder. http://www.crimelibrary.com/serial_killers/predators/kitty_ genovese/11.html (accessed December 2005). ▸page **172**

Gardner, B.T and Gardner, R.A. (1969) Teaching sign language to a chimpanzee. *Science*, 165, 664-72. ▸page **52**

Garth, T.R. (1925) A review of racial psychology. *Psychological Bulletin*, 22 (June), 343–364. ▸pages **182, 200**

Gladwin, T. (1970) *East is a Big Bird: Navigation and Logic on Puluwat Atoll*. Cambridge, MA: Harvard University Press. ▸page **223**

Goffman, E. (1961) *Asylums*. Garden City, NY: Doubleday. ▸page **197**

Golby, A.J., Gabrieli, J.D.E., Chiao, J.Y. and Eberhardt, J.L. (2001) Differential responses in the fusiform region to same-race and other-race faces. *Nature Neuroscience*, 4, 845–850. ▸page **118**

GP Notebook (2005) http://www.gpnotebook.co.uk/simplepage.cfm?ID=-1127219150 (accessed October 2005). ▸page **138**

Grossman, D. (1995) *On Killing: The Psychological Cost of Learning to Kill in War and Society*. Boston, MA: Little, Brown and Co. ▸page **88**

Griffiths, M.D. (1990a) The cognitive psychology of gambling. *Journal of Gambling Studies*, 6, 31–42. ▸page **214**

Griffiths, M.D. (1990b) Addiction to fruit machines: A preliminary study among males. *Journal of Gambling Studies*, 6, 113–126. ▸page **214**

Griffiths, M.D. (1990c) The acquisition, development and maintenance of fruit machine gambling in adolescents. *Journal of Gambling Studies*, 6, 193–204. ▸page **214**

Griffiths, M.D. (1995) *Adolescent Gambling*. London: Routledge. ▸page **212**

Guardian (2005) http://www.guardian.co.uk/attackonlondon/story/ 0,,1525460,00.html [accessed Sept 2007]. ▸page **202**

Guthrie, R.V. (1998) *Even the Rat was White: A Historical View of Psychology* (2nd edn). Boston: Allyn and Bacon. ▸page **201**

Happé, F. (1994) An advanced test of theory of mind: Understanding of story characters' thoughts and feelings by able autistic, mentally handicapped, and normal children and adults. *Journal of Autism and Developmental Disorders*, 24, 129–154. ▸page **44**

Harlow, J.M. (1868) Recovery from the passage of an iron bar through the head. *Publications of the Massachusetts Medical Society*, 2, 327–347. ▸page **110**

Haslam, S.A. and Reicher, S. (2008) Questioning the banality of evil. *The Psychologist*, 21(1), 16–19. ▸page **158**

Hayes, K.J. and Hayes, C. (1952) Imitation in a home-raised chimpanzee. *Journal of Comparative Physiological Psychology*, 4, 450–9. ▸page **52**

Hayes, K.J. and Nissen, C.H. (1971) Higher mental functions of a home-raised chimpanzee. In Schrier, A.M. and Stollnitz, F. (eds). *Behaviour of Non-human Primates*, 4, 50–115. New York, Academic Press. ▸page **52**

Hawthorne, J., Jessop, J., Pryor, J. and Richards, M. (2003) *Supporting Children through Family Change: A Review of Interventions and Services for Children of Divorcing and Separating Parents*. York: York Publishing Services/Joseph Rowntree Foundation. ▸page **103**

Herrnstein, R.J. (1973) I.Q. in the Meritocracy. Boston, MA: Little, Brown. ▸page **223**

Hewstone, M., Stroebe, W., Codol, J.-P. and Stephenson, G.M. (1988) *Introduction to Social Psychology: A European Perspective*. Oxford: Blackwell. ▸page **200**

Home Office (2003) World Prison Population List, http://homeoffice. gov.uk/rds/pdfs2/r188.pdf (accessed December 2005). ▸page **162**

Horne, J.A. and Reyner, L.A. (1995) Sleep-related vehicle accidents. *British Medical Journal*, 310, 565–567. ▸page **128**

Horsford, B. (1990) Cultural issues and psychiatric diagnosis. Paper delivered at Abnormal Psychology Study Day, Nottingham University, December 18th 1990. ▸page **201**

Hughes, H. (1992) Impact of spouse abuse on children of battered women. *Violence Update*, August 1, 9–11. ▸page **88**

Hussain, Z. and Griffiths, M. (2008) Gender swapping and socialising in cyberspace: An exploratory study. *Cyberpsychology and Behaviour*, 11 (1), 47–53. ▸page **191**

International Centre for Prison Studies (2008) http://www.kcl.ac.uk/ depsta/rel/icps/worldbrief/highest_to_lowest_rates.php [accessed Jan 2008]. ▸page **162**

James, I. (1988) Medicine and the performing arts, the Stage Fright Syndrome, *Trans Med Soc Lond*, 105, 5–9. ▸page **111**

James, W. (1890) *Principles of Psychology*. New York: Holt. ▸page **31**

Joliffe, T. (1997) Central *f* in adults with high-functioning autism or Asperger Syndrome. Unpublished PhD Thesis, University of Cambridge. ▸page **46**

Jones, R.L. (ed.) (1991) *Black Psychology* (3rd edn). Berkeley, CA: Cobb & Henry. ▸page **200**

Kamin, L.J. (1977) *The Science and Politics of IQ*. Harmondsworth, Middlesex: Penguin. ▸pages **91, 223**

Keller, K.L. (1987) Memory factors in advertising: The effect of advertising retrieval cues on brand evaluations. *Journal of Consumer Research*, 14, 316–333. ▸page **32**

Kellogg, W.N. and Kellogg, I.A. (1933) *The ape and the child*. New York: McGraw-Hill. ▸page **52**

Kline, P. (1993) *The Handbook of Psychological Testing*. London: Routledge. ▸page **221**

Kosslyn, S. (1975) Information representation in visual images. *Cognitive Psychology*, 7, 341–370. ▸page **3**

Kruger, J. and Dunning, D. (1999) Unskilled and unaware of it: How difficulties in recognizing one's own incompetence lead to inflated self-assessments. *Journal of Personality and Social Psychology*, 77, 1121–1134. ▸page **150**

Kunzig, R. (2004) Autism: what's sex got to do with it? *Psychology Today*, Jan/Feb [full text at http://cms.psychologytoday.com/articles/ pto-3207.html]. ▸pages **46, 48**

Kutchins, H. and S.A. Kirk. (1997) *Making us Crazy: DSM – the Psychiatric Bible and the Creation of Mental Disorder*. New York: Free Press. ▸page **198**

Ladouceur, R., Gaboury, A., Dumount, M. and Rochette, P. (1988) Gambling: Relationship between the frequency of wins and irrational thinking. *Journal of Psychology*, 122, 409–414. ▸page **217**

Laird, J.D. (1974) Self-attribution of emotion: The effects of facial expression on the quality of emotional experience. *Journal of Personality and Social Psychology*, 29, 475–86. ▸page **19**

Lashley, K.S. and Watson, J.B. (1921) A psychological study of motion pictures in relation to veneral disease campaigns. Typescript contained in the John Broadus Watson Papers, Manuscript Division, Library of Congress, Washington, D.C. ▸page **182**

Latané, B. and Darley, J.M. (1968) Group inhibition of bystander intervention in emergencies. *Journal of Personality and Social Psychology*, 10, 215–221. ▸page **173**

Latané, B. and Rodin, J. (1969) A lady in distress: inhibiting effects of friends and strangers on bystander intervention. *Journal of Experimental Social Psychology*, 5, 189–202. ▸page **174**

Le Bon, G. (1895) *The Crowd: A Study of the Popular Mind*. Translated 1898. London: Transaction. ▸pages **164, 182**

Lerner, M.J. (1980) *The Belief in a Just World: A Fundamental Delusion*. New York: Plenum. ▸page **218**

Lerner, M.J. and Simmons, C.H. (1966) Observer's reaction to the 'innocent victim': Compassion or rejection? *Journal of Personality and Social Psychology*, 4, 203–210. ▸page **176**

Levant, R. (2007) Visit to the U.S. Joint Task Force Station at Guantanamo Bay: A first-person account. *Military Psychology*, 19(1), 1–7. ▸page **168**

Levine, M., Cassidy, C., Brazier, G. and Reicher, S. (2002) Selfcategorisation and bystander non-intervention: two experimental studies. *Journal of Applied Social Psychology*, 7, 1452–1463. ▸page **178**

LeVine, R.A. and Campbell, D.T. (1972) *Ethnocentrism: Theories of Conflict, Ethnic Attitudes, and Group Behavior*. New York: Wiley. ▸page **200**

Levine, R.M. (1999) Rethinking bystander non-intervention: social categorisation and the evidence of witnesses at the James Bulger murder trial. *Human Relations*, 52, 1133–1155. ▸page **178**

Lewin, R. (1980) Is your brain really necessary? *Science*, 210, 1232–1234. ▸page **118**

Littlewood, R. and Lipsedge, M. (1989) *Aliens and Alienists* (2nd edn). London: Unwin Hyman. ▸page **201**

Lock, A.J. (1980) *The Guided Reinvention of Language*. New York: Academic Press. ▸page **54**

Loftus, E. (1979) *Eyewitness Testimony*. Cambridge, MA.: Harvard University Press. ▸page **38**

Loftus, E. (1997) Creating false memories. *Scientific American*, 277(3), 70–75. [full text at http://faculty.washington.edu/eloftus/Articles/sciam.htm]. ▸page **38**

Loftus, E. and Palmer, J.C. (1974) Reconstruction of automobile destruction. *Journal of Verbal Learning and Verbal Behaviour*, 13, 585–589. ▸page **34**

Loftus, E. and Pickrell, J. (1995) The formation of false memories. *Psychiatric Annals*, 25, 720–725. ▸page **38**

Lord, A.B. (1960) *The Singer of Tales*. Cambridge, MA: Harvard University Press. ▸page **223**

Lorenz, K.Z. (1966) *On Aggression*. New York: Harcourt, Brace & World. ▸page **82**

Lovibond, S.H., Mithiran, X. and Adams, W.G. (1979) The effects of three experimental prison environments on the behavior of non-convict volunteer subjects. *Australian Psychologist*, 14, 273–287. ▸page **164**

Luchins, A.S. (1957) Primacy-recency in impression formation. In C. Hovland (Ed.) *The Order of Presentation in Persuasion*. New Haven, CT: Yale University Press. ▸page **19**

Maddox, B. (1998) The Grimms got it right – renowned Grimm's Fairy Tales authors, Jakob and Wilhelm Grimm; stepfamily horror stories and step parents, *New Statesman*, October 16. ▸page **103**

Maguire, E.A., Gadian, D.G., Johnsrude, I.S., Good, C.D., Ashburner, J., Frackowiak, R.S.J. and Frith, C.D. (2000) Navigation-related structural changes in the hippocampi of taxi drivers. *Proceedings of the National Academy of Science, USA*, 97, 4398–4403. ▸page **114**

Manchester Evening News, www.manchesteronline.co.uk, 3 May 2005. ▸page **82**

Manstead, A.R. and McCulloch, C. (1981) Sex-role stereotyping in British television advertisements. *British Journal of Social Psychology*, 20, 171–80. ▸page **7**

Marcia, J. (1966) Development and validation of ego-identity status. *Journal of Personality and Social Psychology*, 3, 551–558. ▸page **13**

Matsumoto, D. (1994). *People: Psychology from a cultural perspective*. Pacific Grove, CA: Brooks/Cole. ▸page **78**

McGarrigle, J. and Donaldson, M. (1974) Conservation accidents. *Cognition*, 3, 341–50. ▸page **78**

McNemar, Q. (1946) Opinion-attitude methodology. *Psychological Bulletin*, 43, 289-374. ▸page **131**

Merrin, W. (2005) *Baudrillard and the Media: a Critical Introduction*. Cambridge: Polity. ▸page **162**

Milgram, S. (1960) Conformity in Norway and France: an experimental study of national characteristics. Dissertation: Harvard University. ▸page **152**

Milgram, S. (1963) Behavioural study of obedience. *Journal of Abnormal and Social Psychology*, 67, 371–378. ▸page **154**

Milgram, S. (1970) The experience of living in cities: a psychological analysis. *Science*, 167, 1461–1468. ▸page **173**

Milgram, S. (1974) *Obedience to Authority: An Experimental View*. New York: Harper & Row. ▸pages **157, 160**

Milgram, S. (1977) The familiar stranger: An aspect of urban anonymity. In S. Milgram, *The Individual in a Social World* (pp. 51–53). Reading, MA: Addison-Wesley. ▸page **153**

Milgram, S. (1992) (edited by J. Sabini and M. Silver). *The Individual in a Social World: Essays and Experiments* (2 edn). New York: McGraw-Hill. ▸page **153**

Miller, D.T., Downs, J.S. and Prentice, D.A. (1998) Minimal conditions for the creation of a unit relationship: The social bond between birthdaymates. *European Journal of Social Psychology*, 28, 475–481. ▸page **182**

Miller, G.A. (1969) Psychology as a means of promoting human welfare. *American Psychologist*, 24 (12), 1063–1075. ▸page **170**

Miller, N.E. and Dollard, J. (1941) *Social learning and Imitation*. New Haven, CT: Yale University Press. ▸page **82**

Miller, S.A. (1982). On the generalisability of conservation: A comparison of different kinds of transformation. *British Journal of Psychology*, 73, 221–230. ▸page **78**

Milner, P. (1970) *Physiological Psychology*. New York: Holt, Rinehart and Winston. ▸page **142**

Moore, C. and Frye, D. (1986) The effect of the experimenter's intention on the child's understanding of conservation. *Cognition*, 22, 283–298. ▸page **78**

Mowrer, O.H. (1947) On the dual nature of learning – A reinterpretation of 'conditioning' and 'problem-solving.' *Harvard Educational Review*, 17, 102–148. ▸page **98**

Muir, H. (2003) www.newscientist.com/article.ns?id=dn367. ▸page **43**

Myers, R.E. (1961) Corpus callosum and visual gnosis. In J.R. Delafresnaye (ed.), *Brain Mechanisms and Learning*. Oxford: Blackwell. ▸page **134**

Neimark, J. (1996) The diva of disclosure, memory researcher Elizabeth Loftus. *Psychology Today*, 29 (1), 48. ▸page **34**

Neisser, U. (1967) *Cognitive psychology*, Englewood Cliffs, NJ: Prentice-Hall. ▸page **62**

Neisser, U. (1982) *Memory Observed*. New York: Freeman. ▸page **32**

Neisser, U. and Harsch, N. (1992) Phantom flashbulbs: False recollections of hearing the news about the Challenger. In E. Winograd and U. Neisser (eds) *Affect and Accuracy in Recall: Studies of 'flashbulb' memories* (vol. 4, pp. 9–31). New York: Cambridge University Press. ▸page **33**

Nelson, L.D. and Norton, M.I. (2005) From student to superhero: situational primes shape future helping. *Journal of Experimental Social Psychology*, 41, 423–430. ▸page **83**

NOMS (2008) http://www.hmprisonservice.gov.uk/assets/documents/1000334D20080104SPSWEBREPORT.doc [accessed Jan 2008]. ▸page 162

Ogden, J.A. and Corkin, S. (1991) Memories of H.M. In W.C. Abraham, M.C. Corballis and K.G. White (eds) *Memory Mechanisms: A Tribute to G.V. Goddard*. Hillsdale, NJ: Erlbaum. ▸page 113

Orford, J. (1985) *Excessive Appetites: A Psychological View of Addictions*. Chichester: John Wiley. ▸pages 212, 218

Orford, J. (2001) *Excessive Appetites: A Psychological View of Addictions* (2nd edn). Chichester: John Wiley. ▸page 212

Orne, M.T. (1962) On the social psychology of the psychological experiment: with particular reference to demand characteristics and their implications. *American Psychologist*, 17, 776–783. ▸page 161

Orne, M.T. and Holland, C.C. (1968) On the ecological validity of laboratory deceptions. *International Journal of Psychiatry*, 6 (4), 282–293. ▸page 155

Orne, M.T. and Scheibe, K.E. (1964) The contribution of nondeprivation factors in the production of sensory deprivation effects: The psychology of the "panic button." *Journal of Abnormal and Social Psychology*, 68, 3–12. ▸page 161

Ornstein, R.E. (1972) *The Psychology of Consciousness*. San Franciso: Freeman. ▸page 138

Palinkas, L.A., Suedfeld, P. and Steel, G.D. (1995) Psychological functioning among members of a small polar expedition. *Aviation, Space and Environmental Medicine*, 66, 943–950. ▸page 128

Papert, S.A. (1999) *Mindstorms: Children, Computers and Powerful Ideas* (2nd edn). New York: Basic Books. ▸page 73

Papez, J.W. (1937) A proposed mechanism of emotion. *Journal of Neuropsychiatry and Clinical Neuroscience*, 7(1), 103–112. ▸page 111

Parkin, A. J. (1996) H.M.: The medial temporal lobes and memory. In C. Code, C.W. Wallesch, Y. Joanette, and A. B. Lecours (eds), *Classic Cases in Neuropsychology* . London: Psychology Press. ▸page 113

Pelham, B.W., Mirenberg, M.C. and Jones, J.T. (2002) Why Susie sells seashells by the seashore: Implicit egotism and major life decisions. *Journal of Personality and Social Psychology*, 82(4), 469–487. ▸page 182

Piaget, J. (1954) *The Construction of Reality in the Child*. New York: Basic Books. ▸page 72

Pinker, S. (2002) *The Blank Slate: The Modern Denial of Human Nature*. New York: Penguin. ▸page 71

Piliavin, I.M., Rodin, J. and Piliavin, J.A. (1969) Good samaritanism: an underground phenomenon? *Journal of Personality and Social Psychology*, 13 (4), 289–299. ▸page 174

Premack, D. and Premack, A.J. (1983) *The mind of an ape* (1st edn). New York: Norton. ▸page 52

Premack, D. and Woodruff, G. (1978) Does the chimpanzee have a theory of mind? *The Behavioral and Brain Sciences*, 4, 515–526. ▸page 42

Raine, A. (2000) Brain size linked to violence. http://news.bbc.co.uk/1/hi/health/630929.stm (accessed October 2005). ▸page 121

Raine, A. (2004) Unlocking Crime: The Biological Key, BBC News, December http://news.bbc.co.uk/1/hi/programmes/if/4102371.stm (accessed October 2005). ▸page 118

Rapoff, M.A., Altman, K. and Christophersen, E.R. (1980) Suppression of self-injurious behaviour: determining the least restrictive alternative. *Journal of Mental Deficiency Research*, 24(1), 37–46. ▸page 180

Reicher, S. and Haslam, S.A. (2006) Rethinking the psychology of tyranny: The BBC prison study. *British Journal of Social Psychology*, 45, 1–40. ▸page 164

Richeson, J.A., Baird, A.A., Gordon, H.L., Heatherton, T.F., Wyland, C.L., Trawalter, S. and Shelton, J.N. (2003). An fMRI investigation of the impact of interracial contact on executive function. *Nature Neuro-science*, 6, 1323–1328. ▸page 118

Riesen, A.H. (1950) Arrested vision. *Scientific American*, 408, 16–19. ▸page 112

Ronson, J. (2004) The road to Abu Ghraib – part two. *The Guardian*, October 30. page 138. ▸page 168

Rosenhan, D.L. (1973) On being sane in insane places. *Science*, 179, 250–258. ▸page 194

Rosenhan, D.L., and Seligman, M.E.P. (1989) *Abnormal psychology* (2nd edn). New York: Norton. ▸page 193

Rosenthal, A.M. (1964) *Thirty-Eight Witnesses: The Kitty Genovese Case*. Berkeley: University of California Press. ▸page 172

Rosenthal, R. (1966) *Experimenter Effects in Behaviour Research*. New York: Appleton. ▸page 16

Rosenthal, R. and Fode, K.L. (1963) The effect of experimenter bias on the performance of the albino rat. *Behavioural Science*, 8 (3), 183–189. ▸page 19

Rosenthal, R. and Jacobsen, L. (1966) Teacher expectations. *Psychological Reports*, 19, 115–118. ▸page 19

Rose, S.A. and Blank, M. (1974) The potency of context in childrens' cognition: An illustration through conservation. *Child Development*, 45, 499–502. ▸page 74

Ross, J.M. (1999) Once more onto the couch. *Journal of the American Psychoanalytic Association*, 47, 91–111. ▸page 92

Rutter, M. (2005) The adoption of children from Romania/The social and intellectual development of children adopted into England from Romania. The Research Findings Register, summary number 55. http://www.ReFeR.nhs.uk/ViewRecord.asp?ID=5 (accessed 18 April 2006). ▸page 71

Ryan, J. (2004) Army's war game recruits kids. *San Francisco Chronicle*, 23 September. ▸page 88

Rymer, R. (1993) *Genie: Escape from a Silent Childhood*. London: Michael Joseph. ▸page 211

Sacher, W. (1993). Jugendgefährdung durch Video- und Computerspiele? [Is there a danger to youth from video and computer games?] *Zeitschrift für Pädagogik*, 39, 313–333. ▸page 88

Samuel, J. and Bryant, P. (1983) Asking only one question in the conservation experiment. *Journal of Child Psychology*, 22 (2), 315–318. ▸page 74

Savage-Rumbaugh, S., McDonald, K., Sevcik, R.A., Hopkins, W.D. and Rupert, E. (1986) Spontaneous symbol acquisition and communicative use by Pygmy Chimpanzees (Pan paniscus). *Journal of Experimental Psychology*, 115(3), 211–235. ▸page 54

Sayal, A. (1990) Black Women and Mental Health. *The Psychologist*, 3, 24–27. ▸page 201

Schachter, S. (1964) The interaction of cognitive and physiological determinants of emotional state. In L. Berkowitz (ed.) *Advances in Experimental Social Psychology*, Vol. 1. New York: Academic Press. ▸page 176

Schopler, J. and Matthews, M.W. (1965) The influence of the perceived causal locus of partner's dependence on the use of interpersonal power. *Journal of Personality and Social Psychology*. 2 (4), 609–612. ▸page 174

Schreiber, F.R. (1973) *Sybil*. New York: Warner Books. ▸page 208

Shannahoff-Khalsa, D.S., Boyle, M.R. and Buebel, M.E. (1991) The effects of unilateral forced nostril breathing on cognition. *International Journal of Neuroscience*, 57, 239–249. ▸page 138

Shayer, M., Demetriou, A. and Perez, M. (1988) The structure and scaling of concrete operational thought: Three studies in four countries and only one story. *Genetic Psychology Monographs*, 114, 307–376. ▸page 78

References

Sidoli, M. (1996) Farting as a defence against unspeakable dread. *Journal of Analytical Psychology*, 41(2), 165–178. ▸page 98

Skinner, B.F. (1960) Pigeons in a pelican. *American Psychologist*, 15, 28–37. ▸page 61

Skinner, B.F. (1971) *Beyond Freedom and Dignity*. London: Pelican Books. ▸page 120

Skinner, B.F. (1974) *About Behaviourism*. New York: Alfred A. Knopf. ▸page 61

Slater, L. (2005) *Opening Skinner's Box: Great Psychological Experiments of the Twentieth Century*. London: Bloomsbury. ▸page 194

Slater, M., Antley, A., Davison, A., Swapp, D., Guger, C. Barker, C., Pistrang, N. and Sanchez-Vives, M.V. (2006) A virtual reprise of the Stanley Milgram Obedience Experiments. PLoS ONE,1(1), e39 doi:10.1371/journal.pone.0000039 [http://www.plosone.org/article/fetchArticle.action?articleURI=info%3Adoi%2F10.1371%2Fjournal.pone.0000039]. ▸page 158

Smith, P. and Bond, M.H. (1993) *Social Psychology across Cultures: Analysis and Perspectives*. New York: Harvester Wheatsheaf. ▸page 200

Sperry, R.W. (1964) from 'James Arthur Lecture on the Evolution of the Human Brain'. Quoted on http://faculty.washington.edu/chudler/quotes.html (accessed October 2005). ▸page 132

Sperry, R.W. (1968) Hemispheric disconnection and unity in conscious awareness. *American Psychologist*, 23, 723–733. ▸page 134

Spitzer, R.L. (1975) On pseudoscience in science, logic in remission, and psychiatric diagnosis: a critique of Rosenhan's 'On being sane in insane places.' *Journal of Abnormal Psychology*, 84, 442–452. ▸page 198

Szasz, T.S. (1960) *The Myth of Mental Illness*. London: Paladin. ▸page 198

Tajfel, H. and Turner J.C. (1979) An integrative theory of intergroup conflict. In: S. Worchel and W.G. Austin (eds) *The Social Psychology of Intergroup Relations* (S. 33–47). Monterey, CA: Brooks/Cole Publishers. ▸page 162

Terman, L. M. (1921) Intelligence and its measurement: A symposium (II.). *Journal of Educational Psychology*, 12, 127–133. ▸pages 91, 223

Terrace, H.S. (1979) *Nim*. New York: Alfred A. Knopf. ▸page 53

Terrace, H.S., Petitto, L.A., Sanders, R.J. and Bever, T.G. (1979) Can an ape create a sentence? *Science*, 206, 891–902.page 58

The Times (2004) Blair promises to end 'kitchen cabinet' government, www.timesonline.co.uk/article/0,,15629-1185343,00.html. ▸page 151

Thigpen, C.H. and Cleckley, H. (1954) A case of multiple personality. *Journal of Abnormal and Social Psychology*, 49, 135–151. ▸page 204

THINK (2004) www.thinkroadsafety.gov.uk. Tiredness kills – how to avoid driver tiredness. June 2004. ▸page 128

Tizard, B. (1986) *The Care of Young Children: Implications of Recent Research*. London: Thomas Coram Research Unit Working Paper No. 1. ▸page 70

Tizard, B. and Phoenix, A. (1993). *Black, White or Mixed Race?* London: Routledge. ▸page 103

Townsend, J, Roderick, P. and Cooper, J. (1994)Cigarette smoking by socioeconomic, sex, and age: effects of price, income, and health publicity. *BMJ*, 309, 923–927. ▸page 218

Trinkaus, J. (1990) Exiting a building: An informal look. *Perceptual and Motor Skills*, 71 (October), 446. ▸page 7

Trinkaus, J. (1993) Compliance with the item limit of the food supermarket express checkout lane: An informal look. *Psychological Reports*, 73 (1), 105–106. ▸page 7

Trinkaus, J. (2003) Snow on motor vehicle roofs: An informal look. *Psychological Reports*, 92 (3.2), 1227–1228. ▸page 7

Wagenaar, W. (1988) *Paradoxes of gambling behaviour*. London: Erlbaum. ▸page 214

Wagstaff, G.F. (1981) *Hypnosis, Compliance and Belief*. New York: St Martins Press. ▸page 203

Watson, J.B. (1924) *Behaviorism*. New York: Peoples Institute Publishing Company. ▸page 120

Webb, W.B. and Agnew, H.W. (1975) Are we chronically sleep deprived? *Bulletin of the Psychonomic Society*, 6, 47–48. ▸page 128

Wells, G.L. and Bradfield, A.L. (1998) 'Good, you identified the suspect': Feedback to eyewitnesses distorts their reports of the witnessing experience. *Journal of Applied Psychology*, 83, 360–376. ▸page 38

Wells, G.L. and Olson, E.A. (2003) Eyewitness testimony, *Annual Review of Psychology*, 54, 277–295. ▸page 38

WHO (2001) *Mental Health: New Understanding, New Hope*. ▸page 193

Women's Aid (2002) http://www.womensaid.org.uk/page.asp?section=0001000100050005&itemTitle=Effect+on+children. ▸page 88

Yagyu, T., Wackermann, J., Kinoshita, T., Hirota, T., Kochi, K., Kondakor, I., Koenig, T. and Lehmann, D. (1997) Chewing gum flavor affects measures of global complexity of multichannel EEG. *Neuropsychobiology*, 35 (1), 46–50. ▸page 110

Yahoo news, 2005) http://news.yahoo.com/fc/World/London_Bombings [accessed Jan 2005]. ▸page 178

Zimbardo, P.G. (1969) The human choice: individuation, reason and order versus deindividuation, impulse and chaos. Nebraska Symposium on Motivation, 17, 237–307. ▸page 164

Zimbardo, P.G. (1970). The human choice: individuation, reason, and order versus deindividuation, impulse, and chaos. In W.J. Arnold and D. Levine (eds), 1969 Nebraska Symposium on Motivation (pp. 237–307). Lincoln, NE: University of Nebraska Press. ▸page 183

Zimbardo, P. (2007) *The Lucifer Effect*. London: Rider. ▸page 168

INDEX